# Lonely Trail

*For Ann,*

# Lonely Trail

*The Life Journey of a Freethinker*

## Pat Duffy Hutcheon
AURORA HUMANIST BOOKS

Cover design by Rick Young from a watercolor
("Vanishing", 15¾ X 23½)
by Arlette Francière which is reproduced in full on the back cover.

ISBN:            Softcover            978-1-4363-7737-9

This book was printed in the United States of America.

*AURORA HUMANIST BOOKS* are published by
**Canadian Humanist Publications**
P.O. Box 3769, Station C
Ottawa, Ontario, K1Y 4J8
CANADA
*Manager@humanistperspectives.org*

**To order additional copies of this book, contact:**
Xlibris Corporation
1-888-795-4274
www.Xlibris.com
Orders@Xlibris.com
46619

# CONTENTS

To all my family, with apologies for any factual errors resulting from a too-active imagination at play upon an aging memory. My thoughts and hopes go especially to my great-grandchildren, and to the contributions I know they will make to a more enlightened and reason-guided culture of the future.

## Biographical Note

Pat Duffy Hutcheon is a writer, sociologist and educator with broad experience both in teaching at all levels of the public school and university system, and in policy-oriented research. She won the Governor General's medal and an IODE (International Order of the Daughters of the Empire") scholarship while at school, and received the Canada Council Master Teacher Award when teaching in Calgary. She was in the faculty of the new Regina university from 1965 to 1974, first as an Assistant Professor and then Associate Professor, when she headed up the then-new department of the Foundations of Education. She won a fellowship to Yale, but actually completed her doctoral work in sociology at the University of Queensland in Australia. Upon returning to Canada in the summer of 1976 she taught at the University of British Columbia, and also served as a research advisor to the Health Promotion Branch of the Canadian Department of Health and Welfare and as the BC director of the Vanier Institute of the Family.

Among her over eighty publications are *A Sociology of Canadian Education* (Toronto, ON.:Van Nostrand Reinhold—now Nelson of Canada ) published in 1975 as the first textbook, ever, on that subject. It was used in universities all across the country, and in some American ones as well. Her subsequent books are *Leaving the Cave: Evolutionary Naturalism in Social-Scientific* Thought (Waterloo, ON: Wilfrid Laurier University Press, 1996); *Building Character and Culture* (Westport, CT. and London, UK: Greenwood Press, 1999); and *The Road to Reason: Landmarks in the Evolution of Humanist Thought* (Ottawa, ON: Canadian Humanist Publications, 2001, 2003). The latter was subsequently translated and published in South Korea and Japan. It has also been used as a textbook in classes on the history of free thought. She was named 'Canadian Humanist of the Year 2000' by the Canadian Humanist Association and was also declared a recipient of the American Humanist Association's 'Distinguished Humanist Award' for 2001.

# Preface

I would like to express appreciation to all the family members and friends who have helped me in this recounting of my journey through life. First and foremost, even in death my husband Sandy made contributions to my story, in the form of a journal that the two of us kept in Australia, as well as the many 'seeds he planted' in my mind. The help of my brother Don and his wife Donna was invaluable as well, as they provided much of the information about the our early ancestry on the Duffy side—as did my cousins Thelma Dray and Betty Armitage in the case of the Armitage branch. I also depended on Don for helpful feedback, plus a few of his own enlightening memories. The same applies to my son Tom, whose memory proved to be a strong post upon which I could lean. Similarly, my sister Myrtle deserves considerable gratitude for keeping my early letters all through the years. Some of the other sources of valuable information—or confirmation—for me have been longtime friends and colleagues such as Anne (Gibson) Schedler, June Smith, Irving Rootman, Jim Struthers, Evelina Orteza, Joe Malikail, and Pam and Graham Humphreys. Also, without the quick response and care of family members such as Tom, Don and Vi, Carolyn, Jennie, Shane and Lisa during my recent health emergencies, I would not have been able to complete my book. Others upon whom I have depended throughout my years of working on this project have been those thoughtful, caring friends and neighbours who comprise the network of support which has allowed me to remain independent: notably Lorraine and Bryan Scowby, Joan Barnet, and Lorraine and Glenn Hardie. Bryan was an especially valuable aid throughout. The same applies to my ever-attentive and helpful niece, Mary Duffy.

Finally, I doubt that I would ever have completed the enterprise had it not been for the consistent encouragement and superb editing of my friend Margaret Wilkins, who brought to the task her background of unfamiliarity with the cultural and geographical context of my life journey as well as her artistic imagination, both of which contributed to her role in a vitally necessary, although often unexpected, way.

# Chapter 1

# THE TERROR OF TRUE BELIEF

My mother believed in Santa Claus. I was appalled when I learned the full significance of this in the summer of 1933, for I was still not quite seven years old, and too young for the awful responsibility of that knowledge. I had begun to suspect it in December of the previous year. My grade-one friends were all anticipating Christmas with boastful tales of the doll that each had ordered from old Santa.

"What kind of doll are you getting?" I was asked many times. Finally I responded, equally boastful, with a description of the baby doll in the Eatons catalogue which was to be mine. Why did I do it? I knew full well that my parents had no money for dolls. Indeed, I was all too aware of the fact that my father's struggling business—where we had lived in the small village of Acadia Valley, located near the Saskatchewan border in Southeastern Alberta's prairie country—had sunk in a sea of Depression-induced 'accounts receivable'. This, combined with unpaid insurance against the fire that had demolished his garage, was too much even for Lew Duffy. I knew that, since then, there had never been any money to cover even the barest necessities for our family. That autumn, my father Lew had been operating, and my mother cooking for, a traveling wheat-harvesting and combining operation. Meanwhile, we four children stayed with our grandmother in the neighbouring village of Oyen. Ever since 1931, for the remainder of each year after harvesting was over, all of us had been crowded into my grandmother's little two-bedroom house on the edge of town, while Lew sought work as a mechanic.

That approaching Christmas season had found me struggling with two worries. I was desperate to prevent my mother from hearing of my desire for a doll. Even then, I was beset by a vague suspicion that her faith in the powers of Santa—combined with her desire to satisfy the wishes of her children—might drive her to commit some inconceivable folly in his name. Equally stressful was my agony over what would happen when my friends discovered my doll-less state on Christmas morning.

All that I remember about that Christmas are the lies I told. To my mother I said I hated dolls and would never own one; that I much preferred the paper-doll cut-outs from the Eatons catalogue. She was obviously too relieved not to take my claims at face value. But my friends were a different matter. For weeks after the holidays they pestered to come home with me after school to play with the doll Santa had given me. They even brought their own new dolls to school to flaunt at recess time. Every day as classes ended there was another excuse to fabricate until finally, someone—perhaps the teacher—must have told them to drop the whole thing. The entire period cast a shadow over my childhood, and made me forever wary of the complications created by dishonesty.

The other experience seared into my memory reached its culmination on the first day of the following September, on my seventh birthday. All during my first year of school I had been invited to a number of birthday parties, and my mother must have yearned to do something equally special for me while, at the same time, repaying hospitality. Sometime during the closing week of August she told me that, if my friends could have a party, so could I.

"But how?" I asked. We had been eating fairly adequately from the garden my mother had planted in my grandmother's large yard, along with the eggs from our hens, but there was no possibility of decorated cake and fancy sandwiches for a dozen hungry little girls. My mother's response took the form of a blithe order to invite all my friends for the big day.

"Please, let's don't, Mama," I begged with a terrible foreboding.

"Nonsense!" came the assurance. "We'll get the money for the fixings somehow." But I knew, from daily struggles buried too deep to recall, that there was no money to be gotten. Not from my grandmother, with her meagre funds which, in those days, were un-enhanced by an old-age pension. And not from Lew, with his annual threshing arrangements which were yet to begin that autumn, and otherwise only his desperately sought-out and poorly paid machinery repair jobs.

It was easy enough to distribute the hand-made invitations but, try as I might, I could not hold back the dreaded day. It dawned all too soon and, as I had feared, while there was flour in the house, there was neither sugar nor candles for the cake. And there was nothing for the dainty sandwiches which had become the order of the day for birthday parties in my circle. Lew was to bring the rest of the requirements, Mama said. But he failed to come home for lunch. Desperate by then, she sent me to the garage where I found him beneath the tractor on which he was working. I carried in my hand a list of the crucial requirements: sugar, butter, ice cream, birthday candles and two cans of pink salmon. I remember his obvious sorrow and discomfort, then a long wait while he went off somewhere. Finally, the precious horde of money was in my hand. Heart beating wildly, I raced madly to the store and home, with scarcely a moment to spare before my guests began arriving.

"Keep them playing as long as you can," Mama urged me, as she rushed to mix the cake. And so I did. I was emotionally exhausted when finally, eyes agleam with the glory of true belief redeemed, she served her beautiful and bounteous fare.

The following spring, in 1934, we moved to the country, to a location about twenty-five miles south-east of Oyen, and back toward Acadia Valley country. As a last, desperate resort Lew had acquired one of the many abandoned prairie farms then available in return for the promise to assume responsibility for mortgage payments and unpaid taxes. He was obviously counting on a quick end to the severe drought which had reduced the prairie farm lands—especially in our area of South-eastern Alberta—virtually to desert. It was to prove a disastrous choice but, happily, we didn't know it then. Mama, with her typical unconscious cruelty, referred to the enterprise then and ever after as 'Duffy's last chance'.

In our little old model T with an open front seat and mini-truck back, Lew had to make two trips out to the abandoned farm in order to haul his wife and family—which now included five children with their few belongings—over a rock-strewn dirt track for what turned out to be almost a day-long journey. He had been 'camping out' on the farm by himself for several months, in order to get the seeding done. As a stove and kitchen cupboard had come with the house, Lew 'made do' with nothing more than his old couch from town. Now, on our first trip out with him for the actual family move, he was able to take much of our furniture in the back of the little Ford truck. He took us four older children along to help with the loading and unloading.

For me, that first trip to the farm seemed to last forever. My sister Myrtle sat in front with Lew, while I and my brothers Jack and Bobby crouched in the back with the furniture. I remember, as if it were yesterday, my hands clutching the worn wooden sideboards as we bumped and swerved along the rough, winding trail. I had discovered, long miles back, that if I leaned over the side and kept my face turned forward, I felt okay. No car sickness this trip, I'd promised myself, and 'so far so good'. The fresh summer wind, hitting directly into my face, pulled at my breath and I could feel it whipping my straw-coloured hair into a pattern of unaccustomed neatness. I was determined that nothing would spoil this day: the day of our long-awaited move to the farm.

"How fast are we going?" I shouted into the wind, realizing, but not caring, that no one could hear me. Just to call out, to feel my words as the wind snatched them and hurled them back at me, was sheer joy. Then, as if in response, something sharp hit my shoulder.

"Patty! The rocking chair!" came the voice of my brother Bobby, as the large wicker contraption bounced off the truck box on to the ground below.

'Lew! Lew! Stop! We lost something!" The medley of calls from the back of the truck chorused a rough accompaniment to the journey of the rocker as it rolled away from us toward a clump of what I later learned were Russian thistles. Already it was appearing more and more like one of those giant weeds as it receded into the distance. Our vehicle braked to a stop, and then I saw my father's head over the truck box. My sister Myrtle's voice broke through the clamor.

"We lost the rocking chair, Lew. We've got to get it back!"

My father took in the situation at a glance, then quickly maneuvered the truck around on the narrow rough dirt road. About a half mile back he stopped. "Alright! Everybody out! Let's see who finds it first," he called. Even Myrtle rose to the challenge, scrambling out with the rest of us and taking our dog, Sport, along with her. I was walking carefully, avoiding the clumps of cactus underfoot. My older brother Jack raced by me as I concentrated on trying to plant the soles of my worn running shoes onto the relatively even surface of dead grass. I could see poor Jack stumbling on the half-buried rocks and silvery-grey sagebrush, and slipping in the sandy areas. I always thought of him as 'poor' Jack as I was aware that he was somewhat 'slow' for his age, mentally as well as physically. My younger brother Bobby, as usual, won the contest. Jack had spotted the chair first, nestled in a clump of wolf-willow, but Bobby could move much faster.

'I won, but you two gotta help me carry it back to the truck," he declared, with the authority that had always come natural to him. Jack, with the truculence that seemed equally natural to him, turned away abruptly.

"I ain't gonna help," he declared. "You cheated!" So I ended up sharing the load with Bobby, as Myrtle said she had enough to do keeping track of Sport. We managed to wrestle the rocking chair back onto the truck, where Lew secured it once more to the top of the pile of furniture that threatened to overwhelm those of us settling in amongst it.

"It's awful rough back here. How come you're such a wild driver, Lew?" Jack was not in a very good mood after having lost the contest to Bobby. Lew's response was typical. "It takes a mighty good driver, son, to hit every stone on the trail," he said wryly. A short while later we turned onto an apparently more traveled road and passed a farmstead—the first in a very long time. I had begun to fear that the 'no-man's land' of untouched prairie surrounding us might go on forever. But at last there were fences—rusted barbed wire loosely fastened to leaning wooden posts, but fences nonetheless. I silently hoped we would turn in for a drink of water, but the farm buildings merely approached and then slipped away behind us. The truck laboured up a slope, only to rattle down on the other side. Then, beside the road, there suddenly appeared a string of giant poles, with a wire on top of them.

"What are those?" I called out. The response came quickly and authoritatively from Myrtle. "It's a telephone line, stupid. Like in town." So the countryside we'd been traveling through all day wasn't deserted after all, as I'd been fearing. The ideas of 'deserted' and 'desert' had been recurring in my mind for hours, to the tune of the chattering engine and the bouncing wheels. But now, as we rounded a curve in the road, I saw another farmstead in the distance; this one surrounded by trees. Suddenly, Lew stopped the truck, leaving the engine running.

'Look down there," he motioned. Off in the distance, just at the point where the wavering line of a trail joining ours met the sky, I made out the blur of a cluster of tiny objects rising from the grassland. He explained that it was our school: a school called 'Lonely Trail'. It looked lonely alright. I wondered how we could ever find it again. Then the truck's gears shifted and we moved on, all of us silent for once. The road rose and then fell behind us, and I noticed that the sun was setting. The wind in my face now carried a chill. Another farmstead, and this time someone was moving in the yard. There was a friendly voice from a man with a pail, and the bright flash of an apron in a doorway. And there was a sign at the gate. 'HAVEN' it read. Lew shouted something about our new post office being on this farm.

'What's a haven?' I called out in response. "Do you think they mean heaven?" Then I heard Bobby's laughter from behind. "This all looks more like hell to me!" he said.

At that moment the truck took a sharp turn to the left, and we were on a narrow, rough trail winding downhill into a ravine, then up the other side. Soon after that a large clump of trees appeared on our right, and we were turning off the road and through a gate. The truck stopped before a run-down-appearing, low, brown house.

"This is it. Your new home!" came Lew's voice. "Everybody out!

This initial glimpse of the farmyard was most unsettling to me, for it was surrounded by dead-looking trees that seemed to be struggling to peer out of a massive bank of grounded cloud. The cloud turned out to be more of the tumbled piles of giant round, brown, prickly weeds we had seen earlier, and which Lew had identified as dried Russian thistles, blown in by the dust storms of the previous year. I didn't know it then, but these weeds were host to the 'Say's grain bug' which attacked whatever wheat and barley managed to emerge from the dried-out soil. And there was a rickety windmill, with a nearby pump flanked by what looked like two rusty and jagged half-rounds of a giant barrel; and a leaning barn with a peaked roof and large, horizontally divided door. Beyond these I could make out an empty pig yard overgrown with surprisingly bright green weeds. I learned later that this was 'pigweed' and that it was good to eat. We discovered its taste was somewhat like that of spinach, and I believe the food value of the two is quite similar as well. In fact, pigweed was to prove essential to our survival at times, along with the mushrooms that grew wild on the prairie.

However, during those exciting early hours of our arrival it was the house that captured the attention of all of us. I realize now that it was a painfully small dwelling for a family of seven—just three rooms and a dirt cellar and tiny attic—but its size meant nothing to me then. What I remember most about our arrival is the wallpaper. Wallpaper was important to poor people in those days. It was one's way of demonstrating who and what you were, where taste was concerned. Mama seldom was able to afford to paper her walls, but nevertheless, the tastefulness and condition of whatever happened to cover them had always meant a lot to her. What amazed all four of us children as we rushed into what was to be our new home was the surface of the walls of the three rooms. From ceiling to floor they were covered with what we called 'the funnies': coloured comic strips from newspapers published before we were born. The wonder of it all was staggering to us. We raced about, shouting and laughing, as we recognized Orphan Annie, and Maggie and Jiggs and their cohorts in adventures from years long past.

We took time to eat a lunch which Myrtle prepared for us and then, under Lew's direction, went at the task of unloading the furniture and arranging it in the rooms. We were all more than ready to crawl into the beds once they had been put together, and I think everyone slept soundly through the night. The next day brought the long trip back to Oyen. And the day after that, Mama and baby Donny returned to the farm with us, over the now-familiar and less fearful—but still lengthy—road.

I'll never forget the moment my mother entered the door of her new home. I think that was the last moment of my childhood. Mama, who had been happily expectant during the long drive, walked into the house carrying the baby, and saw what we were all once more examining with such joy. I imagine the very idea of a house papered with garish, multicoloured 'funnies' had, until that moment, been beyond her wildest nightmares—even for the poorest of the poor. The play of sheer horror and desolation on her face is with me still.

I didn't know it at the time, but my mother was able to recover and set to work to make a home for us *only because* of her long-inculcated belief in the miracles wielded by the God of her Methodist childhood, and the Santa figure who (in her imaginings) did his earthly work for him. In the early days of their marriage, I think it must have been the same with my father except that, for him, it had nothing to do with the supernatural. As a 'Freethinker', he was atypical in that time and place. However, his all-too-typical American optimism about the future was probably the one thing they had in common. Something wonderful was bound to happen if they could just hang in there one more month, or one more year. Prosperity, for the Duffys, was always just around the corner.

It was during this last unfortunate farming adventure, however, that Lew's health began to deteriorate and, with it, his hopeful outlook. According to Mama's later account, it was then that he became seriously addicted to the habit of finding solace in the small, personal miracle of momentary forgetfulness offered by alcohol. She told me that had made things very lonely and difficult for her. It must have been hard for Lew as well, I would imagine, when he came back from town smelling slightly of beer and with only the bare necessities among the many groceries that Mama had ordered. For Mama had retained from her Methodist upbringing a horror of the use of alcohol in any form, and to any degree. To her, the minutest odour of it on anyone was a sure sign of drunkenness. It was from that time on, she later led me to believe, that my father developed a serious drinking problem. This has always been puzzling to my sister Myrtle and me, as neither of us can recall ever seeing him the slightest bit affected by alcohol, and we seldom even noticed it on his breath. I spent a lot of time with him, trailing in his wake and helping wherever I could with the chores, for I loved the outdoors. He encouraged us all to ride the horses, and I even learned the rudiments of milking the cow and manipulating the pump in order to water the livestock. Trips to town were few and far between due to the fact that our farm was located between Acadia Valley, twenty miles or so to the south-east, and

Benton, about eight miles almost directly north of us on the Goose Lake railway line. We were connected to both villages only by a narrow, rough dirt road. However, apparently this did not deter Mama from living in fear of Lew sinking into hopeless alcohol addiction.

As time passed, and the farming situation continued to worsen, I discovered that, more and more, I was being forced into the role of my mother's confidant. She and my older sister Myrtle were not very close, so every day she poured her troubles into my unwilling ears, in the minutest of detail. This probably served to keep her sane, but it was a heavy burden for a child to carry. As I quickly learned, there was simply no money from any source; no family allowance in those days. There was no prospect of welfare from a bankrupt farming district now designated as one of Alberta's 'Special Areas': the term given to a combination of regions which could no longer operate as separate municipalities because of a total absence of tax revenue. Saskatchewan at that time provided monthly 'relief' payments of up to $20.50 per farm family, but I don't think this applied in Alberta. However, Alberta farmers did have the option of mortgaging their holdings—or increasing already-existing mortgages—to the provincial government in order to obtain periodic relief in the form of some precious seed for the following year's crop. This was accompanied by a minimum amount of feed for the pigs and cattle.

Shipments of relief goods, including gifts of food from 'Back East', arrived periodically by rail, and all the local farmers would line up at the railroad station at Benton, with their 'Bennett buggies' ready for loading. These vehicles were the remains of their Model T mini-trucks, pulled by a team of horses. They were named, derisively, after the Prime Minister of the time—the Conservative Party leader, R.B. Bennett. What really transformed our daily lives were these occasional shipments of apples from Ontario and huge rounds of cheese from Quebec; along with salted or smoked cod fish from the Maritimes. Otherwise, (except for a few basics such as flour, yeast, oatmeal, sugar, salt, Rogers' Golden Syrup, peanut butter, canned sardines and soap) what my parents could not grow or raise on that drought-stricken stretch of no-man's-land, we did without.

Another life-saver was the sauerkraut made by Lew every autumn. We could usually count on cabbages surviving to maturity in our garden, unless they were destroyed early in the season by grasshoppers. Due to the fact that some of Lew's Duffy relatives back in Fairbank Iowa had married descendants of local German immigrant families, there was a tradition of sauerkraut-making in his family. I was always amazed at the process by which he would fill an entire wooden barrel with cut-up cabbage and vinegar, layer it with sprinkled salt, tamp it down with another heavy round barrel that fitted into the top of the first one, and then mix it regularly for about four months so that it would ferment. Then 'lo and behold!' it would end up as tasty sauerkraut which we happily ate away at until late the following summer. Mama must have become inured to this strange custom during a previous brief period of living in his home district of Iowa. Although she refused to taste it herself, she reluctantly allowed him to persist in making it.

She had accepted one other of his cooking practices, and we were forever thankful for that. It was the delicious American way of cooking roast beef—the long, slow baking of a previously browned roast. For part of the year, at least, we could usually count on a small but regular supply of beef, as the community had organized a 'beef ring'. This meant that, during the winter months, farmers would take turns butchering an animal and sharing the various cuts and 'innards' of these equally with their neighbours.

Lew had a couple of additional skills which came into good use in those years. He cut the hair of the entire family, Mama included. And he extracted our baby teeth by fastening one end of a string around the tooth and the other to the doorknob. My chief memory of this operation is of a certain amount of stress as the string was tied. The actual pulling seemed to happen like magic, as the door was suddenly closed with a bang and the tooth flew out as if by a miracle.

In the midst of these daily struggles, one experience in particular stands out in my memory. It was in the autumn following my ninth birthday when I began noticing a familiar recklessness in my mother. It happened that, in those cruel years of the Great Depression, the Eatons catalogue had become the symbol of all that we needed and could not have. One day Mama confided that she had made out an order to the catalogue, and requested that the parcel be mailed to her C.O.D. I was to take the order over to the Popes, who operated that Haven post office on their farm about two miles distant, along the road between Acadia Valley and Oyen. It was a road I loved because there was the telephone line alongside, with poles I would talk into, pretending that someone was responding at the other end. This was the extent of my contact with, and understanding of, that miraculous invention! I was not to let the rest of the family know about my trip to the Popes' farm, Mama said. She had ordered long underwear, sweaters, overalls, overshoes and socks for those of us whose heavily mended hand-me-downs had finally been reduced to rags. And, for herself, there was to be a *new house dress*.

"But how can we pay for the parcel when it comes?" I asked worriedly.

"The Good Lord will see that we get the money somehow." In her blithe reassurance, Mama had resorted, rather uncharacteristically, to the language of her mother, Viney Armitage. I remember being surprised, as I was well aware that she had rebelled, while still in her teens, against all the rituals, language and rules of my Methodist grandmother. It was then that I recalled the terror of my seventh birthday and realized that my mother still believed—not just in the harmless and possibly helpful promise of better days to come, as was typical of Lew—but in the actual existence of some supernatural and all-powerful Santa Claus. Even at my tender age I did not share this belief. I remember assuming that belief in such things was for innocents who didn't know, or wish to know, how the world really worked. I never told my friends this, however. Lew had warned me early on that it would hurt their feelings unnecessarily.

The following weeks were a nightmare to me. Finally there came the day when Mama called me in and told me that I was to go over to the post office and ask Mrs. Pope for the parcel from Eatons. I knew she had no money. She made no reference to how I was to manage the payment. I recognized the nature of my mission even though no words were spoken. Somehow I had to make it possible for her to continue to believe that miracles could happen. Somehow I had to persuade those kind decent people, the Popes, to let us have the parcel even though we could not pay for it. I trudged over in my worn out runners. I can't remember what my outer clothes were like, but I must have been a forlorn little sight. The details of the encounter that followed are mercifully blacked out in my memory. I only recall that I came home with the parcel. I think now that the Popes probably got in touch with Lew as soon as possible—and in considerable embarrassment—and that he somehow repaid them in labour. For he was an accomplished mechanic, and would work until he dropped.

My mother's beautiful cotton-print house dress was there, among the basic essentials for the rest of us. None of us had ever known her to own a new dress of any kind. Her usual costume was an old pair of men's pants—something seldom worn by women in those days. She had a younger working sister named Dot who would periodically send us her discarded clothes, and from these my mother would usually salvage a blouse for herself, and construct made-over dresses for my sister and me. Myrtle and I both hated these, for they were invariably of a sleazy fabric, darkly coloured. But we were accustomed to them. The idea of a new house dress was something else entirely. Periodically my mother removed it from the packaging to admire it. But she never wore it and, as the weeks passed, we children more or less forgot about it.

A week before Christmas, Mama again asked me to hike over to Popes' to pick up a parcel. And, once more, she warned me to get it into the house without anyone seeing it. I must have looked stricken, for she said hastily, "It's not C.O.D." I worried anyway, for I had learned my mother was not to be trusted when visions of Santa Claus danced in her head. But Mrs. Pope assured me that the parcel was mine to carry home. I sneaked it into the house and Mama took it from me quietly and disappeared with it.

I shall never forget that Christmas morning. Myrtle and I expected nothing, and it probably worried her, as it did me, to see the others all hanging up their stockings. But when morning came there was a filled stocking with a real orange in the toe, plus a tiny gift, for each of us! For a while I could almost join the innocents, and believe in Santa Claus. The whole thing seemed like magic. Later that day I asked Mama how she had managed it. She told me that she had ordered two 'Eatons Surprise Packages', one for girls and one for boys. From that pair of little boxes all our splendid treats and gifts had come!

"But . . . the money?" I asked. She changed the subject.

I might have known. The next day I glanced at the shelf where the house dress in its package had signalled its bright message of better days to come. The moment after my eyes noted the empty space they met those of Lew. There passed between us that flash of grief for past irrevocabilities and all-too-realistic future probabilities that only sceptics can experience. Happily oblivious, my sparkling-eyed, trouser-clad mother bustled from stove to table, between intervals of watching us play with our tiny perfect puzzles and games. It was then I knew for certain that Santa Claus and all his ilk could be cruel taskmasters—even when their other name is love.

# Chapter 2

# A SCHOOL CALLED LONELY TRAIL

One of the most significant thresholds of my early life was my first day at Lonely Trail School. In the early summer of 1934, we had moved to a farm in the parched prairie country of the Province of Alberta, Canada. It was about halfway between the small towns of Oyen and Acadia Valley, and about eight miles south of a tiny village called Benton, which no longer exists. The farm was one among many which had by then been taken over by the 'Special Areas' of south-eastern Alberta for non-payment of mortgage and taxes, and had become available at a bargain price. Or it would have been a bargain if the deadly drought and Great Depression of the 'dirty thirties' had indeed then been ending, as my father, Lew Duffy, hoped.

Lew had been living on the farm some time before the rest of his family followed during the Easter holidays. There were four of us who were old enough to attend school, beginning with the eldest, Myrtle, aged twelve. We were evenly spaced in age, approximately two years apart. Jack was approaching ten and I was then almost eight years old. Bobby, who would be six in early autumn, was to enter grade one in September. Lew had previously explored the school and its environs and had even accepted an invitation to become a member of the Board. Lonely Trail was about three miles from the farm, "as the crow flies" he said. But it was much further if one were forced to travel south, then west, and then back north again, in order to approach it by the narrow dirt road. At first I couldn't figure out why the crow's behaviour was relevant, but soon learned that he meant we would be crossing an unfenced, barren prairie countryside. Although the school could not be seen from our farmstead, Lew got us started off in the right direction that first morning, complete with a description of landmarks for guidance, and with over two hours to spare. However, both the journey and the arrival were to prove much more complicated than our parents could ever have imagined.

For one thing, we had no watches. What child did in those days? And, of course, we had no compass. And, having lived in small towns all our lives, we had never before been on our own upon the wide-open prairie. That first walk to Lonely Trail school began innocently enough. We were initially captivated by the apparent emptiness of the space, and then by what we began to find spread out before us in all directions. For, contrary to the negative expectations caused by our initial trip from town along the winding dirt road, at this particular time of year the grassland surrounding us was literally bursting with life. I fell in love with the wide-open prairie that day: with the sight and smell of the sagebrush and cactus and crocuses growing everywhere; with the endless expanse of clear blue, cloudless sky above and the unfailing breeze relieving the heat below. Because it was early in the season there were still small sloughs in the shallow coulees from the melting of the winter snow. These were surrounded by tired-looking poplar trees and somewhat scraggly caragana bushes, and on their surfaces we spotted a few ducks. Everywhere, we saw and heard crows. And little gophers, or 'ground squirrels', were running in all directions. We began to follow them to their holes, in amazement at the speed at which they disappeared down into these. But what intrigued us most of all were the meadow larks. Their song was the most delightful music I had ever heard. And, lo and behold! Myrtle discovered a nest in the grass with the eggs of one of these birds in it! After that we were all into a game of seeing who could find another nest.

Myrtle proved to be the most proficient here, as animal life of all kinds was her specialty. I often used to think that she displayed an empathy with cats and dogs—and even house flies—that she didn't appear to have for us kids. I believe now that her problems in relating to us all were rooted in our mother's lack of emotional bonding with her. The estrangement may have been initiated at Mama's first sight of the little dark-haired girl-child who appeared to resemble the Duffy clan and was subsequently named after Lew's older sister. Myrtle was doubly unfortunate in having been born only a year or so after the tragic still-birth of another daughter: a redhead like Mama herself and many of her Welsh ancestors.

Eventually, of course, our happy adventure had to end. But the rare joy of an utter absence of all the usual time-constraints—something we seemed to think was warranted by the rural setting—and the sense of blissful freedom induced by this, has remained with me always. We finally saw the school in the distance and I reluctantly followed the other two as they moved toward it. All too soon, we arrived at the school door, still filled with wonder and delight at what we had witnessed. It was only upon our tentative entry into the schoolroom that we realized something was dreadfully wrong. The students were in their seats, books and pencils out. The teacher, a rather bony stern-faced woman, looked up and glared at us.

"Well!" she exclaimed sarcastically. "So the Duffys are finally gracing us with their presence! Are any of you aware . . . ," at this she looked ostentatiously at the watch on her upraised arm, "that you are now a full hour late for the first day at your new school? Maybe you were allowed to do this sort of thing in town, but I'm warning you now that you won't get away with such behaviour out here!"

Thus began what turned out to be a rather strife-ridden relationship with our new teacher. I don't remember her name, likely because she made no positive impression upon me. My chief memories of her are of her railings against the "know-it-all Duffy kids." Another incident had to do with the drinking water available to the school's pupils. Apparently Lew, in his new role as school-board member, had insisted that the open water pail and common dipper be replaced by a container with a spout and a cup for each child; the latter to be brought from home in our lunch pails. The teacher seemed to take this order as a personal affront of some kind. She never tired of making remarks about how "the Duffys think they're too good to drink from the water pail and cup shared by all of us." I have thought since that, in their introductory conversation, Lew may have referred to the fact that he had been a schoolteacher in his younger days back in Iowa, and may have asked knowledgeable questions that she interpreted as being critical of her way of doing things.

My parents were more concerned about cleanliness than ordinary folks are today—and with good reason. We Duffy kids (all except Bobby, that is) had always been extraordinarily susceptible to illness. Bobby, on the other hand, seemed to have been born with a built-in resistance to disease and infection. Like most parents in those days, Mama and Lew were all alone in their battle against our germs and viruses. There were then no easy reparations, such as antibiotics, to make up for carelessness in this vital arena, and for the lack of access to doctors. It wasn't easy to keep a family of children clean, given our living and playing conditions, but our parents certainly tried. Sunday night was usually bath time. Our little round washtub was placed in a relatively secluded nook between the cookstove and the wall, and we took turns, beginning with the youngest, who would be handled by the capable hands of Mama. One by one we would climb into the soapy water and either be scrubbed down or wash ourselves 'all-over'. I think the bath water may have been changed about halfway through the process, but I'm not sure, as water was always in short supply. All this occurred in the light of a coal-oil lamp, and in the pleasant warmth of the wood-and-coal-burning cookstove.

In spite of our parents' concern about hygiene, our years at Lonely Trail were to be marked by a host of illnesses—not to mention accidents. In fact, long after we were grown, we discovered that we older kids had been exposed to tuberculosis although, fortunately, we had merely developed scars on our lungs. Colds were a constant every winter, and a vivid memory of my then-youngest brother Donny's early years involves his persistent attacks of bronchitis, and of my helping Mama arrange the boiling tea kettle and a tent formed from a sheet for the purpose of 'steaming' him. Another routine treatment for lung problems was the mustard plaster with which, I am sure, Mama saved our lives countless times. This treatment was especially critical during the winter in which we all fell prey to whooping cough. It failed to work for Myrtle one time, however. As she lay gasping for air during a severe attack of pleurisy, Lew bundled her up and raced the Model T over the long miles to the nearest doctor at a small town on the Goose Lake railway line called Cereal, where she had to undergo the draining of her lungs in a hospital bed with no anaesthetic of any kind.

I suffered from a succession of attacks of sore throat, so severe and persistent that Mama and Lew finally decided one day that there was no alternative but to drive me all the way to Cereal, for a tonsillectomy. We had to make the long return trip to the farm that same day, and during the night I almost choked to death from a blood clot. Fortunately for me, Mama was unusually vigilant where an ill child was concerned. That night she heard me gasping on the nearby bed and managed to get my breathing restored before it was too late. Strangely, however, Mama's attentiveness seemed not to apply to Myrtle, whose health problems tended to be ignored until they reached crisis proportions.

Mama was also a dedicated believer in preventive treatments, such as the use of sulphur and molasses, Epsom Salts or cascara for occasional constipation, and a generous dose of castor oil in the spring—for 'cleansing' purposes. She was constantly spending her nights by the bedside of one or the other of us—all except Bobby, who was scarcely ever sick. I think now that he may have come to feel somewhat rejected because of the lack of parental concern inevitably resulting from his good fortune at continuing to keep well while all around him the attention-requiring struggle with illness went on and on.

Recalling all this after so many years is a useful reminder of how totally dependent upon themselves for the care of their children were the prairie farm women in those days. This was driven home to me in a powerful way one time when we went over to visit our closest relatives, the Carry family. Only the day before, my mother's sister Mabel had given birth to what was to be their seventh and last child—a daughter, Rita. The midwife had just left and my aunt was still in bed, recovering. However, when we entered the room we found her bending over the side of the bed, scrubbing clothes on a washboard in a small tub. I was accustomed to heroic prairie farm women by then, but this was a sight that amazed me, and seemed to render my own complaints insignificant.

As always, these complaints involved the constant colds and sore throats. But those were not my only problems during that early period at Lonely Trail. One of the most potentially serious was self-induced. On a memorable day, at the beginning of our second summer at the farm, I kicked at Bobby in one of my many battles with him and hit, instead, the rusty old half-barrel used for watering our livestock. The gash in my foot was deep and painful. After Mama got the bleeding stopped, her major worry was, quite justifiably, the likelihood of infection. So I spent almost the entire summer holiday sitting in the house, soaking my crippled foot in warm, salted water. How I missed the bareback riding on our faithful horse, and the other outdoor activities with my brothers! I concluded that even the constant goading of Bobby and Jack was better than this enforced inaction. Their favourite pastime in those days was daring me to climb onto the top of the barn, knowing that I was petrified of heights. Invariably, this would result in my rising to the bait and struggling up to the very peak of the roof, where I would promptly freeze in fear until rescued by Lew.

Myrtle's worst health crises during our time at Lonely Trail were of a different order from mine altogether. She had developed a strange problem of almost total blindness in one of her eyes. This became so serious that our parents felt compelled to find a way to get professional help for her. It was sometime in 1935. Mama had heard about an offer by the then-Prime Minister, R. B. Bennett, to send $5.00 to any impoverished family facing a serious emergency. She wrote to him requesting this help, and received it forthwith. She and Lew then set off with Myrtle to the doctor in Cereal. After a few days of tests they learned that the only prospect for diagnosis would require an emergency trip to Calgary. They used the precious $5.00 to purchase a return ticket for Myrtle and managed to persuade Mama's reluctant youngest sister, Dot, who lived in the city, to meet the train.

This was ultimately to result in little in the way of satisfactory diagnosis of the problem, although drops were provided by the eye specialist which forced the closed-up pupil in the temporarily blinded eye to open slightly—at great pain to Myrtle. Her adventure as a guest of our aunt added another sad chapter to the story. On the evening of her arrival, this partially blinded and frightened thirteen-year-old was immediately left alone with her host family's young infant, Beverley, while the parents went out for one of their customary nights on the town. Exhausted from the trip, Myrtle managed to get the baby to sleep before collapsing on the couch which had been designated as her bed. This was located beside the gas stove in the kitchen. Knowing nothing about such sophisticated appliances, she apparently extinguished the pilot light. Dot and her husband, Bus, arrived home to find the house filled with gas, and both occupants unconscious. Poor Myrtle—now a doubly unwanted guest—awoke the next day to wild accusations from Dot about having almost killed their child.

Myrtle seems also to have been burdened with a sense of having brought her eye problems on herself. It was the custom in those days for both Mama and her mother, our grandmother in Oyen, to tell us that we would ruin our eyes if we read too much. Both Myrtle and I were avid readers. Not surprisingly, she became convinced of her own culpability not only in the near-death calamity at the house of our aunt and uncle, but where her own health problems were concerned.

Another of these problems, which also resulted in a trip to the city for medical care, was a leg injury which Myrtle incurred: an injury which seemed to have caused a perpetually swollen bone. However, on this particular trip they took all of us along in the old open-to-the-weather Model T Ford truck. My clearest memory is a terrifying one of the truck sputtering to a standstill on a railroad track as we approached the city. Lew, a skilled mechanic, had it going again very quickly, but the few minutes of panic involved seemed endless to me. Myrtle's problem had begun on the road to school when she was thrown from the moving buggy one morning during one of her recurring battles with Jack, and ridden over by the wheels. I don't think Jack was ever punished for this by our parents, probably because they suspected there was blame on both sides. At any rate, he was receiving more than enough punishment at Lonely Trail school then, as always.

In those days my brothers and I operated according to a code of honour which we had previously acquired in our play in the village of Oyen. We were happy to discover that this same code prevailed among the students at Lonely Trail School. Previously, in our after-school and weekend play in Oyen, we kids had been accustomed to roaming far and wide in groups throughout the town—even at night. Our typical games were skipping contests, 'hide and go seek', and 'run sheep run', and we had every reason to feel as safe playing them after dark as in the daylight. Another common pastime was playing 'jacks' on the floor of the village pump-house. Through all this play our unspoken code of honour ruled. What it meant was that no one tattled on anyone else and, if some misdemeanor were discovered by adults and an innocent person faced the threat of punishment, the guilty party was expected to confess. One result of this was that our parents knew very little of what we were up to on our own, but we did learn from our mistakes and didn't make trouble for one another. This worked well, so long as both parts of the code were adhered to by all parties. I remember how all three of us were incredibly shocked and disgusted by a cousin who made a practice of running into the house to 'tell on us' during the entire course of her (one-time-only) visit to our farm. This unwritten pact by which we had learned to live meant that, of course, I would never have thought of mentioning anything about the part my brothers played in my tendency toward reckless acts; nor about the provocation from Bobby which had led to my unfortunate kick at him.

I don't recall any specific cruelties administered to me by that first teacher whom we all feared and disliked so much, but she had a habit of twisting Jack's ear severely when his work failed to match her standards. Because he had suffered a burst mastoid in that same ear when younger, this behaviour of hers was a great worry to me. However, we soon discovered, somewhat to our relief, that we Duffy children were not the only ones who were 'picked on' by that teacher. She also had something against one of the other families, the Hannowiches. They were one of the many in that area of south-eastern Alberta who had immigrated from the Ukraine in the late nineteenth century. In fact, Ukrainians were by then the third largest ethnic group in Alberta, next to the Native Indians and British. In those days many prairie settlers of British background resented the Ukrainians, who were usually much superior to them in farming skills. They often referred to these neighbours as 'bohunks', a custom which Lew told us we were never to emulate. Our new teacher didn't resort to such name-calling but, during those first difficult months at the school, we noticed her ill treatment of the Hannowich family—the eldest, Eli, in particular. One day she ordered him to the front to be strapped, for some minor infraction of her rules. His response was one of the best lessons in moral integrity I have ever experienced. He stood up and, with quiet dignity, said simply, "No, you will not strap me ever again." Then he walked out of the classroom. He never returned.

I did see him numerous times in the years to follow, however, as I often 'slept over' at the Hannowich home, visiting with my best friend Caroline. I was always warmly welcomed—as was Myrtle, who was friendly with an older sister, Sophie. It was Mrs. Hannowich who introduced us to Ukrainian cooking, for which I've had a weakness ever since. Myrtle's closest friend was Mavis Simpson, and she also spent many a night with Mavis at the Simpson farm—no doubt discussing, as did Caroline and I, the vagaries of our teacher.

It was not only her obvious antagonism toward our family that made us wary of this new teacher. There was also her appearance. Her hair was cut short like a man's and she wore male-type clothes. In a social context where the concept of lesbianism was unheard of—even by most adults—we children found all this not only strange, but somewhat frightening. I wish now that I had understood the problem her frustrated sexual urges must have posed for the poor woman in that particular cultural context. I have wondered since if her loneliness—coupled with an obvious lack of the sense of moral responsibility for students required of a teacher—had fueled another kind of abuse of power. I had a shocking experience which at the time I did not associate with her in any way. Something which was then incomprehensible to me occurred when I went home for the night with one of my new schoolmates. Even on the tramp across the pasture on the way from school, discomfiting activities were proposed to me. As was expected, we were to sleep together in my friend's bed that night. We had no sooner got settled in than even stranger things began to happen. It was one of the most profoundly embarrassing episodes of my life. I was too horrified at the girl's weirdly intrusive activities to say anything, but spent most of the night in a chair a good safe distance from her. As was my habit as a child, I told no one about the experience. For the remainder of my years at Lonely Trail, I did my best to avoid that girl. Somehow I failed to make any connection between what she had done and the behaviour among the farm animals which I had already witnessed and puzzled over, other than that her attempts at intimacy were 'dirty' in the extreme.

My memory of the personally shocking nature of this incident brings home the fact that, in those innocent days, most of us never encountered anything remotely resembling sexual abuse, nor even sex play among children. It was just not a part of the culture. Sisters and brothers routinely slept together, and went to the outdoor toilet together. Often we would leave the toilet door open, as it would not have occurred to anyone to look for, or snicker at the sight of, bare bottoms. We 'wiped the bums' of younger siblings, in plain sight of passers-by, without a thought of anything untoward. One of my happiest memories is of our family going down to the Red Deer River each summer to camp out while picking our year's supply of 'saskatoons' which Mama would preserve in two-quart sealers. These berries, which are called 'saskatoons' by natives to the prairie like ourselves and 'Saskatoon berries' by others, are confined to the prairie Provinces where they grow wild along the rivers. They look like blueberries but have a wonderfully unique flavour. During our annual berry-picking excursion, I would routinely visit an eccentric old bachelor nearby, and would clean his messy abode for him. The possibility of his abusing me in any way would never have occurred to any of us.

Nor would it have occurred to any of our parents that a teacher might be guilty of such a thing. Fortunately, this teacher who appeared to dislike us all so much, left at the end of June—only a few months following our arrival. I suspect, however, that the negative effect of her influence on many of the students may have been irrevocable. Certainly, she had done a good deal of damage to our family's process of settling in and being accepted by the other children. The harm was especially acute and long-lasting in the case of Jack, who was inevitably easy prey for bullies.

The new teacher who arrived in September was Dorothy Tewksbury, from Calgary: a truly remarkable person. One of her first actions was to tackle the plagues of common-cold infections among her students by arranging with the school board for a regular supply of cod-liver oil, which she then administered to each of us on a daily basis. I believe that helped everybody a great deal. The extra Vitamin D was no doubt crucial for me, as I learned much later that I had suffered badly from rickets as a small child.

Looking back from all my subsequent years of experience within the field of education, I give Miss Tewksbury credit for much of what I was able to do with my life. I was at a crucial stage of development, and she proved to be an inspiration to me in many ways. For instance, she worked hard to build up the sparse library contained within two tiny book shelves. One way she did this was to encourage us to contribute spare books from our homes. I was already an avid reader, but was embarrassed about the fact that we didn't seem to own much in the way of books. Whatever library Lew had begun, his Canadian journey with must have fallen by the wayside in his many moves. He would sometimes discuss his most beloved authors, however—such as P. G. Wodehouse and Mark Twain.

Mama was probably too busy slaving over such things as the washboard and coal-fired stove to do much reading, other than her favourite womens's section of the prairie-farm newspaper, *The Western Producer*. In fact, my only vivid memory of her in a semi-relaxed state is of her rocking the baby and humming tunelessly, with that newspaper's "Mainly for Women" page in her left hand. The editor was a remarkable pioneering feminist named Violet McNaughton: someone whose contribution to this country's budding women's movement equals that of our great women's rights heroine, Nellie McClung, although it is seldom appropriately recognized. *The Western Producer* was of particular importance to Myrtle and me as well, as it contained a page for "Young Co-operators". Both of us contributed our early attempts at poetry to it. I had my first poem published there when I was ten years old. Also, it was through this newspaper that Myrtle was able to connect with 'pen pals' from all over the world.

A second publication which came to our home was *The Winnipeg Free Press*, edited by that famous prairie icon, John Dafoe. The third was that universally popular American magazine, *The Saturday Evening Post*. I have often wondered since, how we could have afforded the cost of subscribing to these, when it was clear that there was simply no money for anything. Even the peanut butter, which was the standard filler for our sandwiches during warm weather, often had to be purchased on credit in town. Many years later, Myrtle told me that Mama had paid for these publications with cash made by selling the surplus eggs from her chickens for three cents a dozen.

However, in my case there was, for a brief time, a fourth source of reading matter. It was a cache of books that I had found, almost immediately upon our arrival, packed away in the attic of the farmhouse. The former owner had obviously forgotten to take them with him. I was fascinated with this discovery and delighted in keeping it a secret from all the others. I don't really know whether I understood any of what I was reading in my private corner of the attic, being aware only that these were 'grown-up' books and no doubt, therefore, doubly precious.

One day Lew happened upon me up there. He picked up one of the books for a cursory examination, looked at me in a shocked manner, then read for a few more minutes. I watched silently and with increasing trepidation as he glanced through a couple of others, finally placing them all carefully in a pile in front of him. The expression of extreme distaste on his face frightened me, as did his prolonged silence.

"These books," he finally began, in a strange, measured fashion, "are written by members of something we call 'The Know-Nothing Movement'. It was popular among very ignorant people some years ago in the United States. Do you really want to grow up to be a 'Know-Nothing'? Because that's what will happen if you read garbage like this."

He went on to explain the meaning of 'bigotry' and 'racism' in simple language. These concepts were new to me, as I was still blissfully unaware of the Nazis and of what was to come in Germany. And then Lew told me a very scary story. It had happened, he said, only a short time before I was born. He was working late at his garage in Fairbank, Iowa. The Duffys were known as fervent Irish Catholics and, although Lew had himself left the church long before, it was the association of the Duffy name with Catholicism that had placed him in danger. Some members of Ku Klux Klan—a movement similar to the 'Know Nothings'—which had begun with the lynching of a Jew in the Deep South and then moved on to target Blacks and Catholics, suddenly appeared out of the darkness. These Klan members attacked him and he had to fight for his life. Fortunately, he was an excellent, well-trained boxer and managed to escape them, but they did set fire to the garage. He added that the Ku Klux Klan had emigrated to British Columbia in the early 1920s and to the prairies in 1925. And that their largest Canadian membership was in Saskatchewan.

Probably because of my habit of listening-in during Lew's winter-time conversations with visiting neighbours, and asking questions later if something had puzzled me, I had developed an extraordinarily close relationship with him where ideas were concerned. Even as a pre-schooler I would sit on his knee during such discussions. One of my strongest memories of him in those days on the farm was that he followed politics closely, and seemed extremely concerned about what was occurring in Germany at a time when few Canadians even thought about the matter. He also spoke of the role of both Protestantism and Catholicism in the undermining of German democracy. I realized much later that, from the moment of Hitler's disastrous key election victory in 1933, engineered with the collaboration of Franz von Papen who was the devoutly right-wing Catholic chancellor, people like Lew had good reason to worry. Even worse news for him must have been the Concordat of the same year, between Nazi Germany and the Vatican: an agreement of mutual cooperation similar to that reached by the Pope with Mussolini in 1929. But racism and its horrific consequences were far from my thoughts in those days.

I may not have understood bigotry and racism but I did know about bullies by that time. My brother Jack was somewhat below the norm in mental development. I'm not sure just when it was that I recognized the fact that he was a slow learner, for it was not something that was referred to in our home. I doubt that either of my parents ever fully acknowledged it in those days, even to themselves. Over the years at Lonely Trail, a few of our fellow students had a great deal of misguided fun at Jack's expense. There was a girl the same age as he (Kathleen Simpson) who suffered even more severe problems, in that her speech was badly affected. She was also the butt of much schoolyard cruelty. I tried my best to protect both of them, and it was my relative success in this endeavor that first led me to realize that the spoken word—not only the pen—could be mightier than the sword.

Much of my emerging talent at using 'the word' was due to the efforts of Miss Tewksbury. She had quite a crew to discipline and stimulate at Lonely Trail. In addition to the Duffy family, there were the Watrin boys (Lawrence and Melvin) and their older sister, Clara, as well as Jim Foster and Roy Hall. Others were Ruth and Margaret Diemert, the Hannowiches (Eli, Sophie, Pauline, Katie and Caroline), as well as Kathleen Simpson and her sisters Sheila and Mavis. There were a few more whose names I can no longer recall—possibly because they were not particular friends of mine.

I believe that most of us were greatly inspired by Miss Tewksbury. Although apparently oblivious of the schoolyard bullying, she always tried her best to discover and encourage the hidden talents of us all. She was particularly gifted at teaching singing, dancing and acting, and at organizing Christmas concerts. The tap-dancing steps she taught me still return automatically, after all these years, as do the words and tunes of some of the songs. The chance to act in plays, and to attempt general public speaking at that early age, was no doubt critical to any success I may have achieved in my subsequent professional life. It was something few of my generation were then fortunate enough to experience—at least not poor country children.

The musical opportunities provided by Miss Tewksbury were especially meaningful to me. We had little experience of music in our home. We did own a small radio at the time, but my strongest memory of it concerns what seemed to be a perpetual need for the re-charging of its 'A' battery (the kind then used for cars). When the radio was working, it provided almost the only music we were ever exposed to—other than a few can-shaped old records we had played earlier on my grandmother's crank-up gramophone in Oyen. There were tunes such as "Here Comes Tootsie!" which we liked to turn on whenever my mother's sister Jessie—known as Tootsie to all the family in those days—was within hearing distance. The one other exception to this music-less situation in our home was the occasional visit to our farm by Lew's fellow-Irish friend, Jack Shields, the butcher from Oyen. When he came out to see us, the two men would sing all the old Irish ballads, such as "Danny Boy", "An Irish Lullaby", and "When Irish Eyes are Smiling". How I loved those sessions! For some strange reason Mama did not. And afterwards, whenever Lew would begin to sing these songs to us, she would say, disparagingly, "You can't even carry a tune!" At the time, I found this puzzling in the extreme, because he had a pleasant baritone voice, and the songs sounded beautiful to me. And poor Mama merely uttered strange sounds when she sang to the baby as she rocked him. Later I decided that she had likely been tone-deaf all her life. Family members or acquaintances must have made similar hurtful—and incomprehensible—comments to her when she was young and she used them, in turn, merely as a way of putting someone down.

Another incident which is seared into my memory occurred in 1935. It was related indirectly to education, but more directly to my parents. The educational aspect had to do with Lew's concern about the Provincial election that year. He was very much opposed to the political party which had recently emerged in Alberta. He was one of the few people in the entire Province in those days who had not bought into the new right-wing Social Credit theory. It was my first real introduction to politics. There was a great deal of fevered discussion of the issues and the candidates in our home, and much questioning and information-sharing at the supper table. Things grew even more interesting in the days leading up to the election, as Lew had taken on the duty of visiting as many of the neighbours as possible, in order to explain the issues and ask them to join him in voting against 'Bible Bill' Aberhart. The fact that the district polling station happened to be at our place was to make the entire affair even more memorable for me.

Election day passed in a blur of people coming and going. Lew was busy from morning until closing time, driving voters from their homes and back. But at the end of the day, when the votes were counted, we discovered that only one vote had been registered against the Social Credit Party! Obviously, even my mother had voted for Aberhart, tempted by his empty promise of a monthly $25.00 dividend for each family. I think the humour in all this, not to mention the lesson about populist politics, made it one of the high points of my time at Lonely Trail.

In the autumn of 1937, when I was beginning grade six, we discovered that Miss Tewksbury had resigned in order to marry George Pope, the son of the couple who operated the local post office from their farm home, and with whom she had been boarding. She was replaced by a new teacher, Frank Sickoff. Again, we had struck it lucky! Mr. Sickoff, newly graduated from Calgary's Normal School, tackled the bullying problem head-on. The atmosphere in the schoolyard altered drastically, as he spent every moment of the recesses and the noon play-periods out there with us. At first there was an organized resistance to the new order: a resistance in which, to my everlasting shame, I was persuaded to participate. One day during recess, when he was out patrolling the schoolyard, I allowed myself to be pressured into drawing an insulting picture of our new teacher on the blackboard. He had exhibited a strange habit of slapping his own face when frustrated or angry and, because my picture showed him doing this, the students found it extremely amusing. Mr. Sickoff's response was a command that we all remain silently in our desks after school until the culprit confessed. It did not take me long to obey. I will never forget the expression of shocked surprise on his face. I apologized abjectly and he forgave me with a firm reprimand, then dismissed us all with no further comment. That incident marked the end of much of the behaviour that had previously made of each school day a 'lonely trail' for misfits such as Kathleen Simpson and Jack Duffy.

Another pastime to which Mr. Sickoff put a stop was our custom of skiing behind galloping horses at recess and during the noon hour on winter days. One or two of us would each hold onto a rope which was then tied around the horn of the rider's saddle, and the race would be on! A student was badly injured in the midst of one of these races soon after our new teacher arrived, and that was the end of that! I guess I had a streak of recklessness rather uncommon among girls at that time, for I loved joining the boys in this sport. The only thing I didn't wish to join them in was their daily task during the spring and summer of 'drowning out' gophers and killing them in order to cut off their tails. The term 'drowning out' came from the process of pouring water down the hole to force the victims from the safety of their holes. There was some kind of a cooperative plan among teachers, school boards and provincial governments in those days whereby it was arranged that schoolchildren would be paid the sum of two cents for each gopher tail, as the plentiful little creatures posed such a serious threat to the crops.

However, an adventure I did get involved in that year raises questions about just what kind of kid I was. One of my greatest fears was of the weather, especially in the winter when a blinding blizzard made the journey home across the open expanse of prairie highly dangerous, if not impossible. Our typical winter transportation was a horse and 'cutter', or small sleigh, which Jack drove across the open prairie. I remember my constant worry about Jack when, on bitterly cold mornings, he would have to remain outside to get the horse settled in the barn before joining the rest of us around the school's pot-bellied heater. Although the consequences of becoming lost in an all-engulfing dust-storm in the late spring and autumn were not as life-threatening as were the winter blizzards, we had good reason to fear them as well. A typical dust-storm (or 'black blizzard') would approach like a giant, dark wheel rolling toward us, filling the entire horizon. When it reached us we were immobilized in heavy, impenetrable dust—in one frightening instant rendered incapable of seeing more than a few inches in any direction—and able to breathe only with difficulty. At home, our custom was to cower together for safety down in the dirt cellar beneath the house.

One day in late September, just such a storm struck in the early afternoon while we were still in class. When it finally subsided we were all covered with a heavy, dark-grey, chalk-like material, as were our desks and books as well as the floor. Mr. Sickoff set us to work cleaning up the place. Before we had quite finished he departed for the Pope's farm, where he boarded, but gave us strict orders as to how to complete the task.

For some strange reason the storm had made me crave even more adventure. I was curious about how it would feel to be trapped in the school after dark. Once free of our teacher, I suggested that we all stay there for the night, pretending that the dust storm was still raging. The plan was that, sometime before bedding down on the floor, we would go and beg food from the old bachelor who lived across the road. We had plenty of water in our large container with its mandatory spout. And, of course, we had the two outdoor toilets, or 'outhouses' with their wealth of wiping paper from the Eatons catalogue. The kindest way to explain this action of mine is that I was ahead of my time with the romantic 'survivor' theme. Everybody loved the idea and apparently not one of us gave a thought to what we would be putting our parents through. If Myrtle had still been going to school, she would no doubt have put a stop to it. Only the Popes—who lived on the main road—had a phone, so none of the families with children in attendance had any way of knowing what had happened at the school during the storm, or that their children were not the only ones who had failed to return home.

We had a wonderful, totally carefree experience for several hours that evening. Then the first of the parents arrived, anxious and utterly uncomprehending. When Lew came in, worn out from searching the slopes and lowlands of the rolling prairie between our farm and the school, he seemed to have a hard time accepting the fact that I was the instigator of the entire fiasco. I didn't understand it myself. But I did learn an important moral lesson that night. The sight of my father's stricken face drove home to me, as no punishment could have, the fact that I had heedlessly brought pain to others. No matter what had caused me to do what I did, my capacity for empathy got a major boost at that moment. Mr. Sickoff reinforced this. Rather than punishing me afterwards, he ordered me to write a story about a child who had become lost in just such a 'black blizzard' as had struck that day, and been killed by a car driven by someone who could not see the road because of the heavy dust. I had to write it from the perspective of the mother of the child who began to worry when her daughter did not arrive home after the storm.

The explanation which our far-flung neighbours ultimately reached, for my having led the group into our mischievous caper, was that I was too imaginative and read far too many books. Mr. Sickoff must not have agreed with this, for he continued to encourage that imagination, along with my curiosity about everything and my love of reading. It's no wonder that I sensed the loss of a precious teacher-learner connection when I had to accompany my pregnant mother and little brother Donny back to Oyen in the spring of 1938, and when we were all subsequently forced to move there late that summer, in the midst of yet another total crop failure. Mama took us children back to the house of my grandmother in Oyen, until Lew was able to follow after a few months and rent a place for us to live in. Eventually he found work as a mechanic in the town garage.

I didn't know it then, but Mr. Sickoff was also never to return to Lonely Trail. However, by one of those marvelous coincidences of life I did meet him again. It was nine years later when I was a young country schoolteacher, attending summer school at the University of Alberta, in Edmonton. At a social gathering one evening I noticed a man staring at me from across the room. I suddenly realized who it was, and approached him.

"Thank goodness!" he exclaimed, when I introduced myself. "I thought none of you would ever escape that god-forsaken place."

However, that was not to be my last connection with him. By an even more unlikely series of contingencies, a strangely worn-looking letter arrived at our Vancouver home in 1982. It was addressed simply to Pat Duffy at Oyen, Alberta. Nothing else in the handwriting of the sender, although a number of notations were added in various places on the envelope. Amazingly, none of these contained my current address or surname. How I would love to know the trail that envelope took, from its mailing to the moment it was finally slipped through the slot in our door by the local mailman! In the letter, Mr. Sickoff had written that he intended to record the story of his first year of teaching, and was trying to track down the pupils from Lonely Trail School. He implied that he had cancer. I responded immediately and received one more brief note and never any other.

I have wished ever since that I had begun my reply with "To Sir, with love." (Even though he had taken me—not "from crayons to lipstick"—but from crayons to Shakespeare.) His second and last letter ended with the following: "Patty, you always had a special place in my heart. I was so happy to hear that you are fulfilling the potential I saw in you. Especially when I think how desperately your parents wanted a better life for you kids than they themselves had."

Somehow that comment gave me a jolt, and brought back a flood of memories. Had Mama and Lew been together on that one thing at least? I had never thought of them as agreeing on anything. For me the lives of the two of them, so different in every way yet trapped in an unhappy marriage, were forever epitomized by the name of that 'Lonely Trail' of my childhood. Just as my own life was to be, for a long, long time.

# Chapter 3

# AND THE RIPPLES SPREAD

*Our every act is like a pebble*
*Tossed into a moving stream.*
*The ripples spread beyond our knowing,*
*As the river of life keeps on a-flowing,*
*And consequences reign supreme.*

A young woman sat on her horse, profiled against the evening prairie sky. To my Aunt Jessie, who told me this story on her deathbed, the auburn-haired rider was sight to behold. On hearing about it, so many years later, I felt that the image represented the very essence of the free-spirited Nellie Armitage Duffy I had known most of my life. Apparently, even in her advanced stage of pregnancy, my twenty-one-year-old mother was beautiful.

It was the summer of 1920. The 'Great War' and devastating Spanish Flu following in its wake which, together, had slaughtered well over ten million people, were now behind them. However, in addition to these calamities, and unbeknownst to almost everyone, a 'silent enemy' had been carried home and spread throughout Canada by returning soldiers. And it was now beginning what was to become a long-term devastation of the lives of thousands—of the yet-unborn as well as the living. What was never publicly acknowledged in this country was the fact that the incidence of venereal disease among Canadian veterans was the highest of any army in the world—possibly because so many were innocent young boys from small towns and farms. Fortunately, Nellie's two brothers who had been in the army were safely returned, and appeared to have escaped all these scourges. Fred Armitage, like Nellie, an impetuous and spunky young person not given to accepting authority, had deserted in Ontario and fled to the United States. Then he had managed to avoid apprehension and serious punishment by re-joining later under an assumed name. He was shipped to England and missed all the action. However, he was in considerable danger of being sent to Russia with the unfortunate Imperial Force which spent a year or so in Murmansk following the Revolution. After the war, Fred somehow ended up in Spokane, where he spent the rest of his life running the Crown and Anchor and various gambling games on Midways. I always loved having this fascinating uncle come back to visit.

The older of the two brothers who enlisted, Les Armitage, had racked up a very different war record. A letter to his mother from the Lieutenant Colonel of his regiment records his citation for "conspicuous gallantry and unflinching boldness during the advance of the First Canadian Battalion in the battle of Caix on August eighth, 1918." He was awarded several medals for bravery as a machine gunner, and returned to the family homestead in the Benton-Oyen district a decorated war hero. But he was one of the many who had been 'gassed': something which affected his health for the rest of his life. Upon release from the military, Les decided to go back to Manitoba, whence the family had come. He left the Armitage farm in the hands of the eldest brother, Ed, who had escaped the fighting altogether. In order to avoid conscription when war was declared, Ed had chosen to join his mother in this south-eastern Alberta countryside and assume management of the family farm by the lake which was later named after them.

Now, almost two years after all this, my mother's second-youngest sister, Jessie, had ridden her horse over to the Duffy homestead which—although also in the Benton area—was located some miles to the southeast of Armitage Lake, in the direction of the village of Acadia Valley. Upon finding no one at the little two-room house, Jessie set off to search for her sister Nellie Duffy in the garden and beyond. She told me that, in spite of being only fourteen at the time, she always felt that the anguishing period in which they lived had rendered her mature beyond her years. She was therefore well aware of her sister's condition, and horrified to discover her, also on horseback, in the pasture bordering the yard. Profoundly shocked by the very idea that even her impulsive sister Nellie would be riding a horse at this stage of her pregnancy, she called out. Nellie, startled, twisted backward. At the same instant the horse neighed and reared violently. The rider was almost thrown as she struggled to control her mount.

Jessie was thankful that Nellie did not appear harmed by the severe jolting. After all, their mother had sent her expressly to care for her pregnant sister in the period preceding and following her confinement, and she felt doubly responsible for what had just occurred. Sometime in the night, however, she woke to the sound of Nellie moaning in pain. Not long after that, Lew (my father) called out, directing her to saddle the horse and ride at full speed to the home of Mrs. Fitzpatrick, the local midwife, to inform her of the emergency. It was several agonizing hours after Mrs. Fitzpatrick had arrived by horse and buggy that they were shown the still-born baby. According to Jessie, it was a red-haired girl; and it was badly deformed. Nellie, lying exhausted on the bed, took one look, touching the red hair as she did so. Then she made a strange, keening sound, and pulled the bedcovers over her face. Lew sat as if turned to stone. A little later, he told both women that Nellie wanted the entire episode to remain a secret. Jessie could not tell me anything about a burial, or about how Lew and Nellie Duffy managed to recover. Apparently Lew had advised her that it would be best if she were to return at once to the Armitage homestead, where she lived with her mother, brother Ed, and youngest sister Dot. The remaining girls in the Armitage family of nine—now officially Mabel Carry, Laura Cutlan and Essie Mack—were, like Nellie, married by that time and no longer living at home.

This tragic incident could well have been the beginning and root of it all: of the unhappy, mutually destructive road taken in this marriage of two very different people. Nellie and Lew were a couple with radically different ways of being in the world, and with incompatible dreams and goals. Lew was thoughtful and invariably reasonable and focused on ideas, while at the same time extremely sociable, and with a typically Irish, ironic sense of humour. Nellie, on the other hand, always struck me as someone given to spur-of-the-moment reactions with little thought of consequences. She seemed primarily focused on her children and home, and revealed little interest in other people or events. I have always marveled at the improbability of the disparate pathways of these two people happening to collide at that critical moment when each was ready to take on a life partner. What were the unpredictable contingencies of life that had brought two such conflicting personalities and life experiences together? With the passage of the years this question has continued to intrigue and challenge me. How was it, I wondered, that they had met and been attracted to one another in the first place? What were the wandering pathways of their life histories that had happened to intersect at that decisive instant? The more I learned about the variety of channels flowing into our ancestral past, the more fascinating it became to think about how the consequences-driven stream of life had brought these two together.

Who could have predicted at the time, away back in the mid-nineteenth century, that the coincidental but totally unconnected decisions of an eighteen-year-old boy in Ireland's county of Armagh and of a member of the landed gentry in England should have functioned as key 'pebbles' contributing to the two particular streams which intersected on that fateful day in late 1918 when my parents met? The Irish boy took a job on a cattle boat headed for the United States. The English gentleman shipped his 'problem son' off to Canada with the bribe of a generous annual 'remittance', so long as he never again showed his face in the country of his birth.

When my parents—the grandchildren of these immigrant families—happened to meet, Lew Duffy was then already thirty-eight years old and, as my grandmother (Nellie's mother) recounted it years later, a widely respected and successful businessman, mechanical expert and farmer. He had been traveling up to Canada from Iowa annually since 1907, as he and his younger brother Tom operated a threshing and plowing business which took them through Montana and North Dakota, moving northward as the crops ripened. For several years—during periods in the spring and after harvest—they worked at 'breaking the sod' for many of the early homesteads as far north as the relatively fertile Rosetown region of Saskatchewan.

Lew was a twenty-seven-year-old country schoolteacher when the two brothers first decided to launch this adventure. It is possible that their original tractor was manufactured by Aultman-Taylor, as that was the company for which Lew was later to work in the Acadia Valley and Benton area, after a railway branch-line had been built to Empress—about twenty miles to the south of 'the Valley'. In those later days he operated as both a service representative and maintenance man for the farm equipment he sold. There was no dealer network at the time, so the machinery was shipped by flatcar directly to him. However, I believe it to be more likely that the first tractor with which the Duffy brothers had earlier done the sod-breaking in Saskatchewan was, instead, what was known as a 'Stanley Steamer'. Being steam-driven, it would have pre-dated the gasoline-powered 'Aultman-Taylors' that Lew was subsequently to sell and repair. The reason I think this was the case is an event that occurred not long after I began my teaching career in a remote little country school between Acadia Valley and Empress, a village located just across the Red Deer River to the south. One Saturday, a local farmer told me he had something to show me. He took me to a ditch by the side of the road a few miles north of the school, where I saw the rusted remains of a large vehicle. He referred to this as a Stanley Steamer, and informed me it had been my father's first tractor. Lew may have brought it with him when he moved westward from Saskatchewan to file for a homestead in Alberta in 1913, after his brother decided to give up on their joint business venture and return permanently to the United States.

As luck would have it, however, Lew's timing was bad. By the time his application for Canadian citizenship had ground through the bureaucracy, the war was underway; and the United States had passed a statute prohibiting its citizens from becoming naturalized in any foreign country. So it was not until late June of 1919 that he was actually able to become a Canadian citizen, and thus the legal owner of the first quarter section of his homestead. Official ownership of the second quarter was not finalized until February of 1921.

More than three decades after his arrival in the district, when I was introduced to that giant machine, the sight of its complex inner workings brought home to me for the first time just how mechanically gifted my father was. He had to have been an extremely scientifically oriented, self-taught engineer, working at the leading edge of an agricultural revolution, rather than merely the simple mechanic I had always assumed him to be. The farmer who was showing me the rusted relic reinforced this insight, as he recounted tales of how Lew Duffy had routinely resolved any and all of the puzzling situations arising from the operation of the new machinery in this pioneering community. I was told that the farmers were all in awe of him, as there was never a problem he could not resolve. This neighbour thought it likely that the reason the remains of the Stanley Steamer had not been removed in all the intervening years was that, for the older generation, it represented a sort of unofficial memorial to that breakthrough in farming represented by the replacement of horses with machinery—as well as to my father's role in the process. When I saw it, however, I was too young to recognize the full significance of what struck me then merely as a rather pathetic wreckage. And, by that time, the marriage of my parents had long appeared to me as a similarly pathetic wreckage: one which Lew had not, however, been able to repair.

According to my grandmother, Nellie was rather difficult to control in her adolescent years. This was assumed to be related to the fact that, at the age of twelve, she had suddenly lost the father who doted on her. Sometime during the autumn of 1910, my maternal grandparents, Charles and Lavina ('Viney') Armitage, had decided to give up their lease on the farm they were operating near Pilot Mound, Manitoba. There was finally a way by which ordinary working people could fulfil their dream of owning land. For a ten-dollar fee, would-be settlers could register for a quarter section in one of the new grassland areas that had been opened to homesteading; while at the same time receiving interim entry to an adjoining quarter. Official ownership of the entire homestead was obtained after three years, subject to certain prescribed development and improvements to the first quarter section. This arrangement no doubt contributed to the fact that the period from 1909 to 1912 was to see the greatest-ever sustained establishment of homesteads in the Canadian West: about 40,000 per year on average.

Because of this railway-induced boom in the southern area of the western Provinces, most of the good farming land had been claimed by the time Charles and Viney considered homesteading. Charles therefore decided to take advantage of the recent opening of the Peace River country, located along the northern border of British Columbia and Alberta. The plan was that he and the two oldest sons (Ed and Les) would make the trip and spend a couple of years getting established before sending for the rest of the family. The following winter, after giving up their farm lease, they arranged to rent a house on Pembina Street in Pilot Mound. While waiting for this to become available, Viney decided to take their four younger daughters with her to Gainsborough, a village on the border of Saskatchewan and Alberta. She intended to visit for a week or so with her brother George, who published and edited the local newspaper there. She particularly wanted to go through the belongings of their mother, who had died in George's care two years previously. Charles remained behind on the farm with the three boys, in order to organize the selling of the livestock and equipment and to make plans for the long trek to the northwest. He was suffering from a bad flu at the time. On the day of the auction sale the weather turned extraordinarily cold and windy. Charles came down with pneumonia that night and died a few days later, all alone in a hotel room in town.

The shock of hearing this news must have been horrific for the entire family, but especially so for Nellie. I happen to know she was her father's favourite because he had left word that, of the nine children, it was she who was to inherit his mother's portrait. And my grandmother (Viney) always said that, for some reason, 'Charl' had persisted in 'spoiling' this third daughter.

Viney rushed back to Pilot Mound and oversaw the removal of the family belongings to their new dwelling. She then arranged for a simple home-memorial service for Charles, and managed to complete all the other unfinished business as well. Sometime during the tumultuous period following the tragedy, Viney made a brave, but possibly too precipitous, decision. I suspect that her brother George influenced her greatly in this. She and two of her sons decided to proceed with the homesteading plan, but to settle on the short-grass plains of southeastern Alberta, rather than on Charles' previous choice of the fertile—although much-more-distant and difficult to access—Peace River country. As a newspaperman with no knowledge of farming, George may have had a somewhat romantic view of the vast empty prairie stretching invitingly to the immediate northwest of Gainsborough. The 'Great Plains' from Brandon in southern Manitoba to Alberta—from Lethbridge up to Edmonton—had been avoided prior to, and during, most of the first decade of the century. However, by the time Viney made her decision, the concept of Palliser's 'desert triangle' was long forgotten, along with the warning implied by the term; and the times were optimistic.

The expedition led by John Palliser had set out in May of 1857 with the official mandate to explore the prairie country of what was then known as British North America. This area was then a wild, unpopulated wasteland, long isolated from the rest of the 'new world' by the barriers of the tenuous river-approach to the icy waters of the Hudson Bay to the north and east; the impenetrable mountain barriers to the west; and the unsettled Indian lands of the United States to the south. Palliser's final report contained the conclusion that the entire south-western part of these prairie lands was so limited in terms of rainfall, with the resulting lack of timber and water, that it was utterly unsuitable for farming. This area was subsequently referred to as 'the Palliser Triangle'.

However, history is soon forgotten, and few could have guessed in the early nineteenth century that the favourable moisture conditions of those years were abnormal, and were providing a false stimulus to settlement from which terrible consequences would flow less than a decade later. Or that an even more tragic and persistent drought would strike a decade after that, returning much of the settled land to desert—referred to by those who lived in it as 'the dust bowl'.

Because Viney was a widow, she was allowed to make a homesteading claim in her own name. She was probably unaware at the time that this was a privilege granted only to that one category within the female gender. This unjust law applied in Canada, but not in the United States. It had the consequence of forcing a number of our most able prairie women to move south into Montana during the period in which the West was being settled. It was not until the 1930s, when there was virtually no free land remaining—and no one wanted it anyway—that Canadian women, as a general class, finally gained the right to homestead.

The Canadian Pacific Railway was by then in the process of being extended westward from Winnipeg, but the area to which my grandmother headed in 1911 had not yet been reached by the new branch of the railroad called the Goose Lake Line. This meant that she and her family could travel by train only as far as Kindersley, Saskatchewan. From there they, along with all their worldly goods, proceeded westward in a covered wagon, or 'prairie schooner', as they were called. Viney's chosen destination was a section of land beside a lake, one-half of it registered in her name and the remaining half in that of Les. Fred was not yet of legal age, and Ed had previously decided to settle near Gypsumville, in Northern Manitoba. My grandmother's homestead was located on the edge of what came to be known as Armitage Lake. This was in an area bordered by the small, fairly recently established villages of Benton to the north, Oyen to the west, and Acadia Valley to the southeast. Obviously, Viney and her son were attracted by the scattering of trees surrounding their virgin land, while remaining innocently ignorant of the significance of the large rocks among the trees and of the sandy soil beneath. They were also quite unaware that there would be no school for the children to attend. And that the only religious organizations in the entire area, except for a small Jewish community near Sibbald—a village to the east of Benton—were the Mormon church and a settlement of Mennonites.

Nine years later, in 1920, my grandmother's brother, George Flewelling, began to show symptoms of lead poisoning. This was an occupational hazard in his line of work. He then decided to retire from the newspaper business. He moved to Oyen in order to be near Viney and her family, hauling with him all the antique household furniture brought to Canada by their forebears a century before. He purchased a large lot on the outskirts of the village, and arranged for the construction of a house and barn and other out-buildings. He lived there until one day in 1929, when a neighbour discovered him on his bed, dead from a lung hemorrhage. George had bequeathed his entire estate to his sister Viney. After his death she moved into the house at Oyen, leaving her son Ed to operate the farm. By that time, her second son, Les, had met and married Anna Matilda Hopper, and they had decided to remain, for the time being, in her home district of Mather, Manitoba.

Viney appears always to have been extraordinarily courageous and independent, for a female of her time and place. Except for religion, that is. She never swayed from her strict Wesleyan Methodist upbringing, nor questioned its tenets, in spite of the fact that her husband, Charles, did not share these. She was the only daughter in a family of five children—one of whom, a brother Edward, had died as a child. Her family withdrew her from school at the age of thirteen, as was then customary in the case of girls, in order to have her help with the daily housework. They would also have wished to prepare her properly for the kind of marriage and role in life that was expected for women of their social station. Her grade-eight teacher was angry about this, and called on her parents, Edward and Mary Flewelling. He informed them that Viney was a more gifted scholar than any of her brothers. Yet the three of them, Henry, John and George, were all receiving some form of higher education or training. This visit brought no results, but it was something that my grandmother recalled with pride to the end of her life.

The Flewellings did believe in education—but only for males. They were what was known as United Empire Loyalists, although Edward's parents (Abraham and Martha Flewelling) had not actually emigrated from Detroit, Michigan until sometime between 1815 and 1819. Loyalists were those Americans who remained on the British side at the time of the American Revolution. No doubt United Empire Loyalists would have found life in the new United States increasingly difficult during and after the war of 1812. When they arrived in Canada their name was spelled 'Flewwelling', and long before that, when their ancestors left Wales for America, it had been written as Llewellyn. Interestingly, the name was still evolving as late as 1887. On Viney's certificate of marriage, her surname is spelled with two 'f's while her brother's witnessing signature has only one.

Abraham and Martha brought with them four sons and four daughters. The boys were Abraham, Edward, James and William, and the names of the girls were Martha, Hannah, Edna and an earlier Lavina. The Bensons, Martha's birth family, also from Detroit, emigrated at the same time. Viney's mother, Mary Metcalf, whom Edward Flewelling married in 1854, had also come to Canada as a child—although she was from Yorkshire, England. By the time her aunts had all wed, Viney's immediate relatives included the Boys, Atkinson, McQuire, Elmslie and Fice families, as well as the Bensons and Metcalfs. They were among the solid upper-middle class of the Salem/Guelph/Walkerton/Kitchener/Waterloo area of Ontario, and Viney was made to understand early on that her parents expected their only daughter to achieve at least an equal status when the time came for her to marry.

But this was not what happened. In the autumn of 1886, just after her nineteenth birthday, Viney was allowed to make an extended visit to relatives in a region near London, Ontario. On the route from town to their home, she noticed a handsome, curly-haired young male tending the tollgate on the covered bridge over which they were driving. She was told that he was the son of the man who owned the land on both sides of the river, and that his name was Charles Armitage. She also learned that Charles' father was a 'Remittance Man' from England. This was a nomenclature which carried a whiff of both mystery and romance in those days. It was generally known that such men were the sons of members of England's landed gentry who had disgraced their families in some way. They were paid quite generous annual or monthly sums for their entire lives, so long as they promised never to return home. According to my grandmother Viney, the story was that the Armitage clan, from which this supposed wastrel (or worse) had descended, were aristocrats who had originally come to England from Normandy with William the Conqueror. And there was more. This particular Remittance Man had committed another grave sin after his arrival in Canada. He had taken as a wife someone whose father—a Scottish fur trader—had broken the rules of polite society to the extent that he had dared to wed a Mohawk woman. In the crude racist parlance of the times, the family was out of bounds for decent young ladies like Viney because it had 'an Indian in the woodpile'.

In her old age my grandmother Viney liked to recall how she had met my grandfather Charles and how, not long after they began passing the time of day at the bridge, they fell in love. He was her first and only boyfriend. Her parents were most unhappy about the affair and refused to welcome Charles into the family. A small wedding was arranged in Guelph, and the couple abruptly moved down to Vermont, where Charles had found work. Viney never again lived anywhere near her large extended clan—except for her bachelor brother George, who eventually moved west to Gainsborough, Saskatchewan, on the southern part of Alberta's eastern border. However, she and Charles did return to Canada a few years later. Charles worked in Brandon until they settled on some rented land near Pilot Mound, Manitoba, where they remained until the tragedy of his premature death. I have a letter written by George Flewelling during these years, in which he expressed regret because Viney was never able to attend any of the family reunions back in Ontario. "You must not feel," he wrote, "that life is passing you by."

There is one more intriguing aspect to the mystery surrounding the origin of the Armitage clan. My grandmother once showed me a picture of Charles' sisters: four (or possibly five) extraordinarily beautiful young women all with long straight dark hair and brown eyes. She identified one who had been hired as a nanny by a family which was moving back to England. This particular sister accepted the job expressly for the opportunity to go there, with the intention of looking up the Armitage relatives and reporting back home as soon as possible. She was never heard of again! Charles' mother died not long after this, in her mid-forties, from an untreated burst appendix. There appears to be no record of when his father died or what happened to his remaining sisters. Many years later, when Viney had been a widow for some ten years, the moment arrived when her third daughter would be making a decision as crucial as her own had been. It was a decision which was to initiate a chain of consequences as life-altering as those flowing from Nellie's parents' first glimpse of one another at that tollgate. In spite of having had no schooling since the age of eleven, Nellie Armitage was actually very literate, and reasonably competent with numbers. An older widow named Mrs. Ford, who operated the post office in Benton, evidently befriended her and took her in. She was given low-paying work serving customers there, whenever she failed to find anything more lucrative. In the haying and harvesting seasons she was usually employed as a cook's helper by one of the more prosperous farmers in the district. According to my grandmother's account many years later, it was during these years of 'working away from home' that Nellie 'ran wild'. Apparently, she committed the unpardonable sin of dating a number of boyfriends. Even worse, she wore men's pants at a time when no female did this, and rode one of the 'new-fangled' bicycles whenever she got the chance.

By the way, it has been said, and with good reason, that the invention of the bicycle was the most revolutionary breakthrough of the period from the standpoint of women's equality. I think now that my mother was actually an early feminist. She was certainly never in awe of men—in fact, I sometimes felt that she had no use for them whatsoever. And yet . . . and yet . . . as Nellie's life unfolded from that early youthful independence and critical stance concerning males, an ironic contradiction came to characterize her attitude toward her own sons. It always appeared to me that, in her eyes, these precious boys could 'do no wrong'!

Now, in light of my subsequent experience of both parents, I can understand why my grandmother Viney was so relieved when this wandering daughter met Lew Duffy. He had brought his threshing outfit to the farm where she was working, in order to do the autumn harvesting. His own homestead happened to be somewhat to the west of that of Joe Carry, who was a returned soldier originally from Carstairs: a village located north of Calgary on the edge of the Alberta foothills. My grandmother wasn't sure of this, but she thought that her daughter Mabel, two years younger than Nellie, met this young Joe Carry at about the same time that Nellie became acquainted with Lew. Before long, Mabel was being courted in a dignified fashion by the handsome and musically gifted young war veteran. It soon became evident that Nellie was being courted as well, by a successful and widely respected older businessman. My grandmother thought that both girls had hit the jackpot! The fact that Lew was raised as a Catholic did not seem to worry her, since he had left his family religion. However, she no doubt had something to do with the fact that, after they were married in Calgary on the fourth of March in 1919, the marriage was officially registered by the Methodist minister in Oyen. The United Church of Canada, which subsequently amalgamated most of the country's Methodist and Presbyterian congregations, was yet to be created. Mabel and Joe were married three days before Christmas of that same year, also in Calgary. In their case, this location was probably selected so that the Carry family of nearby Carstairs could meet the new bride. My grandmother Viney appears to have attended neither wedding.

Nellie seems to have known very little about the man she married, or even to have considered the possible impact of their almost-twenty-year gap in age and radically different backgrounds. However, one can easily imagine what might have attracted each to the other. My younger brother has no trouble understanding why Lew fell for our mother, and vice versa.

"From Nellie's perspective," said Don, when we discussed the matter, "Lew was a handsome, articulate Irishman, a successful businessman who owned a car and was much better educated than the neighbouring farmers' sons. His reputation as an unbeatable bare-knuckle boxer would have added a touch of excitement, as well as a feeling of security in a time when women really did have to fear for their physical safety. Our mother was always a courageous risk-taker, even when I knew her, so his being a stranger from a somewhat different culture would not have caused her to hesitate. For Lew, the tall, slim, spunky redhead—brighter and a lot more refined than most of the women he would have met on the frontier—would have appeared to be someone he could take home and introduce to his mother and sisters without embarrassment."

Don's 'bare-knuckled boxer' reference reminded me of a story an Acadia Valley farmer once told me about Lew. Apparently he was standing with a group of men when one of them called a passing girl a whore. Lew whirled and struck him a resounding blow in the jaw. Then he spoke to the cowering fellow in a slow, measured fashion, emphasizing every word.

"Nobody . . . , he said, "nobody . . . ever refers to any lady like that in my presence!"

This comment was absolutely consistent with my own experience of my father. He was a 'gentleman of the old school' and unfailingly respectful of the female sex. In fact, I never heard him use a foul word, or even slang. Nor did he ever raise his voice, no matter what provocation Nellie might offer. And I witnessed a good deal of provocation through the years, as her difficult life meant that my mother's temper was invariably on a short fuse. I hated the quarrels, during which Nellie shouted and sometimes even threw things, and Lew became increasingly silent. I remember her throwing her mirror at him once, when she was unhappy with the haircut he had just given her. In the years to come, whenever I inquired about what it was that went so wrong between them, Nellie would reply merely with one or the other of her two favourite maxims: "Marry in haste and repent at leisure" and "When poverty comes in the door, love flies out the window."

Unfortunately, the poverty problem became a factor soon after their marriage. The Canadian prairie-farming situation had taken a downturn in 1917. By 1921, after five crop failures in a row, no one could even consider investing in machinery. In fact, there was soon little need for any of the services offered by Lew Duffy. Land-breaking had become a thing of the past, to be followed into temporary oblivion, ultimately, by commercial harvesting and the purchasing of farming equipment. Over half the farms in the short-grass area of Western Canada were abandoned during the years between 1921 and 1926. Sometime in early 1923, Lew made the decision to cut his losses and join the exodus—in his case, back to the United States. At the time, Nellie was excited and happy about the prospect of living in her husband's hometown of Fairbank, Iowa. By then, their little family included a baby daughter, named after Lew's older sister, Myrtle. With his father's help, he was quickly able to establish a garage business in Fairbank. According to what I was told almost fifty years later by his sister-in-law, my aunt Kate, the business was reasonably successful, but Lew and his father did not work well together. For one thing, the issue of religion was a continuing and pressing factor, as Lew had long since renounced Catholicism. Another problem may simply have been Lew's way of conducting business. My mother always maintained that he was not noted for firmness with his employees, nor for persistence in collecting the money owed by customers. Added to this, according to Aunt Kate, was Nellie's obvious discomfort among the large extended family of the Duffys, who were all uncompromisingly Catholic.

In the autumn of 1924 Nellie gave birth to their first son, whom they named John Charles. Nellie was overjoyed to discover that he had the red hair and hazel eyes of the Flewellings. Aunt Kate told me that Jack was a difficult child from the time of his birth. She noted that the little daughter, Myrtle, seemed to grow ever more demanding as well, possibly in response to the fact that so much of her mother's attention had to be focused on the baby. Most of the time, Nellie was left on her own to deal with the children. She must have felt very lost and lonely, as Lew was forced to work long hours getting the business established.

I can imagine how overwhelming Lew's family must have seemed to this unsophisticated young woman from the Canadian prairies. The town and surrounding countryside were literally brimming with Duffys and their relatives, which by then included a number of the descendants of immigrant families from Germany, with whom the Duffys had intermarried. Lew's grandfather, Patrick, had been one of those immigrants who left Ireland during the bitter years following the famine. This had begun in the 1840s when blight struck the potato crop, and over a million Irish farm people—about twelve percent of the population—died of starvation as a result. The leases which Patrick and his older sons eventually abandoned were near the Parish of Newtownhamilton, in the county of Armagh. However, the family appears to have actually lived in or near the 'townland' of Tulleyvallon, which was located about five kilometers to the south.

Lew's family name is one of the most prevalent and ancient in Ireland. In fact, there is a town in Ireland called Lissyduffy. 'Duffy' is said to have evolved from the Gaelic name of 'O Dubthaigh'. The fact that 'Dubh' means 'black' provides an intriguing clue as to its origins. In the early Christian era there was a great deal of traffic back and forth between members of Spanish monasteries and those in Ireland. I can remember Lew telling us that his own particular blend of physical characteristics—dark hair and blue eyes—was typical within the Duffy family, and a common manifestation of the melded Spanish and Celtic origins of many of Ireland's people. Many years later I was reminded of this when hiking in Cornwall. We were told by our guide that the trail we were following had been the major thoroughfare in the early Christian era for Irish monks traveling from monastery to monastery, through Wales and then down to the Cornish coast, where they would set sail for Spain.

No doubt there had been many of my ancestors on that trail long before I encountered it. It seems that, in the seventh century, Duffys were prominent in the church in Monaghan, the County bordering Armagh. By the twelfth century they were widely known to be exceptionally gifted craftsmen who built and decorated monasteries and churches throughout Ireland. More than a few Duffys were notable historical figures, in Australia as well as Ireland, and a number were editors and journalists.

By the early 1800s, life had become extremely difficult for the Irish people, even for the Duffys in Armagh, which was a relatively prosperous county. Of the eight million people in all of Ireland at that time, approximately three million owned no land and had no jobs. The majority of those who had the opportunity to farm were leasing their land from British landlords. Britain's Penal Laws had forbidden Catholics to own land in 'fee simple' since the days of Queen Elizabeth. Even though these had been revoked in the late eighteenth century, almost all the land in Armagh over fifty years later was still held by English landlords who spent most of their time in London. The land was divided into 'townlands' of two-to-three-hundred acres in size. These were leased in small parcels to local farmers for annual cash rents. Poverty was prevalent everywhere. Although 'corn' (or what we call wheat) was grown in larger commercial acreages for export, potatoes provided the major sustenance for the local people. In fact, for most, the small potato farm was the sole means of survival. Until, that is, the catastrophe of 1845 when a blight struck the crops, causing all the potatoes to rot soon after harvest.

It was probably due to the economic stagnation in the period immediately following the widespread 'potato famine' resulting from this fatal blight that, in 1853, my great-grandfather Patrick Duffy's eighteen-year-old son Michael Bernard Duffy bravely took off on what was to prove a fundamentally life-altering adventure for the entire family. He obtained a job as a steerage worker in a cattle boat headed for the United States, and appears to have traveled with a family by the name of Shannon. After three years as a farm labourer in the state of New York, Michael set off once more, again in the company of the Shannons, to the forested country of Iowa: a state which was undergoing frenzied pioneering settlement at the time. What they found was largely untamed wilderness, with few roads and no railways. On July 4, 1856, Michael Duffy filed his 'Intent for Citizenship' in Buchanon County, Independence, Iowa.

Then, on a spring day in 1857, Michael hitched a team of oxen to a wagon for the trip to Dubuque to meet his family, who were now following along the trail he had blazed for them. His parents (Patrick and Alice Byrnes Duffy) had set off for America with their three daughters (Catherine, Mary and Bridget), eleven sons (two born since Michael had left) and a fourteen-year-old niece (another Alice Byrnes). The boys were John, Patrick, James, Frances, Owen, Hugh, Peter, Matthias, Edward, Thomas and Joseph. They had boarded the ship 'Calhoun' at Liverpool and arrived at the Port of New York on May 18, 1857. Three weeks after their arrival in Iowa, the eldest Duffy daughter Catherine married James Shannon. Mary died the following year at the age of twenty four, presumably from the after-effects of the harrowing trip.

Patrick filed for citizenship in November of 1857. In 1860, he moved his family to Black Hawk County, Lester Township, some five miles southwest of Fairbank, Iowa. It was there that he carved out his farm, which had reached 200 acres in size by 1870. When Alice Duffy died in 1883, Patrick took Margaret Minnihan (Monahan/Moynahan?) as his second wife. Some of the other Irish families who had emigrated by then—and into which his offspring subsequently married—were the Wades, McLaughlins, Malloys, McCloskys, Murphys and McDonoughs. Lew's father was Patrick's eleventh son, Thomas, and his mother was Johanna, one of the Minnihans. The Duffy holdings increased considerably over subsequent years, as the sons grew up and eight of them established farms of their own in the area. Not surprisingly, there is a 'Duffy Road' near Fairbank.

The original farmstead was inherited by the youngest son Joseph, who eventually bequeathed it to his son Aloysius. I met the latter when I went to see the farm in 1970, on my one and only visit to my father's birthplace. By that time, the Duffy clan had spread far and wide across North America. Interestingly, there were even two connections to Waterloo, Ontario: the very area in which the Flewellings had settled. Lew's uncle, Hugh Duffy, died there in 1938 at the age of ninety four—no doubt leaving a number of Duffys in his wake, to help populate Ontario. And Lew's sister, Vera Kane, appears to have moved to Waterloo as well; as did Lucy, although she was later to return to Iowa.

Lew was the fourth of Thomas' eight children. He had five sisters, Ethel, Lucy, Susan, Myrtle and Vera. His two younger brothers were Stephen and another Thomas. The Aunt Kate with whom my husband and I stayed when we visited the family was the widow of Stephen. She was all alone at the time, as their only son had died of what was termed 'a massive heart failure' while on a hunting trip to Canada. It was then I learned that such unexpected, sudden deaths were common among what she referred to as the 'Monaghan' branch of the family. It was to be many years before I fully understood what that was all about.

Aunt Kate described her efforts to befriend Nellie, including a visit with her one day when she was about six months into yet another pregnancy. To her concern and amazement, Kate discovered her pregnant sister-in-law busily papering the walls of their rented house. Then, about two months later, something occurred that was even more perplexing to Kate, and to Lew as well. Nellie apparently made the sudden decision to leave Fairbank and return to Canada. Knowing that Lew would never permit her to travel alone in her precarious condition, especially with two small children in tow, she told him nothing about her plans—departing while he was at work. He came home that day to find a note on the table telling him of her intention to go home to Armitage Lake, in order to give birth to the baby under the care of her mother. She also asked that he ship the trunk with all her treasured belongings to the Benton post office as soon as possible. This forced him to conclude that she had no intention of returning to Iowa.

So it was that I came into existence on the Armitage homestead, only one short month later—the first non-Aboriginal child ever born there, according to my grandmother. I was given Lavina as my middle name, after her, along with the first name of Patricia. The birth was a difficult one, and the local midwife soon realized that Nellie would need professional help. Someone (probably Ed) left in a rush for Cereal, over thirty miles away, where the nearest doctor was located. My mother suffered for a long time before I was born, and when I did finally emerge it was with the cord fastened tightly around my throat. Fortunately, the doctor arrived just in time to save my life.

Lew returned to Canada later that autumn, after having hurriedly arranged to leave the business in the hands of other family members. He managed to find temporary work as a mechanic in the small border village of Alsask. Our family remained there for a brief period, then moved down to Acadia Valley, where Lew began the struggle to establish another garage business. The farming situation had recovered considerably by then—especially in the clay-soil or 'gumbo' area south of town—and he was able to make a satisfactory living there for the next few years. A second son, Robert Lewis, was born to them in October of 1928.

I have only jumbled childhood impressions of that period in Acadia Valley. One was probably induced somewhat later by one of our rare family snapshots. It shows a table, laden with largely emptied plates, the chairs bare of inhabitants except for the one which held me—at the table's head. I am sitting there all alone, totally absorbed in eating. I was told that the occasion was my third birthday, and that I had demonstrated more of an interest in finishing the left-overs than in joining my guests at play. Another flash of memory is of a mischievous playmate called Andy McGhee, who lived close by.

My sister Myrtle supplied me with one of her most memorable experiences of that particular period. She recalls a day when she was about seven years old. She and my brother Jack were playing at the hand pump of the well from which our family depended for drinking water. Jack jumped forward unexpectedly and was accidentally hit on the head by the pump handle. As he fell to the ground, appearing stunned, Mama came flying from the house screaming, "You've killed Jack! You've killed him!" Myrtle says she ran to the home of neighbours, and cowered there in a terrified state until Lew came looking for her after work. He assured her that Jack was quite okay, and escorted her home. But it was obvious to me, as I listened to the story many years later, that the experience had served to fray even further the already fragile bond between mother and daughter, casting a dark shadow over Myrtle's childhood. Mama—focused on caring for the little one-year son, Bobby, as well as on

Jack's many needs—was probably quite oblivious to the consequences of the words she had uttered in the heat of the moment. I seem not to have figured in the picture at all. No doubt I was, as usual, bent on making myself invisible. The 'peacekeeping' role which I assumed early on may have been the result of a number of such explosions of dynamite within the strange dynamics of our family relationships.

Life took another dark turn for Lew at the beginning of 1930, with the news that his beloved mother, Johanna Minnihan Duffy, had died suddenly of what appeared to be a massive heart attack. He had always told me that I 'took after' her, so it seemed a loss for me as well, even though I had never met her. Accompanying this sorrow for Lew would have been the dawning recognition that a second, and much more prolonged, drought was settling over the prairies by then; and with it the Great Depression of the 'Dirty Thirties'. Suddenly, none of the clients whose machinery he was servicing had any money for their debts. Years later, when I was teaching in the district, I grew quite accustomed to being approached by then-successful farmers with the story of how much they appreciated the fact that Lew Duffy had never refused to do their work, even though they were seldom able to pay him.

By 1931, Lew and Nellie were destitute because of the weight of these unpaid accounts. The final straw for them was a tragic accident. One night their garage burned to the ground, taking many valuable tools with it. Like most people in those dark days, Lew had no insurance. Once more, a hard-fought-for business had to be abandoned. And, once more, they returned to the security of my grandmother Viney's home—this time to the house in Oyen. In a desperate effort to raise some money, Nellie attempted to sell her diamond engagement ring. She discovered that the diamond had been exchanged some time before for a worthless piece of glass by an itinerant jeweller who had 'kindly'—she thought at the time—offered to clean her ring. So they were totally without funds.

During the following three years Lew worked as a part-time mechanic in the local garage, while organizing a threshing crew to handle whatever work could be found for his harvesting machinery. They were unable to afford a home of their own during that dreadful period, but seem always to have been made welcome by my grandmother. Nellie assumed responsibility for the garden and the chickens, and took over most of the cooking, at which she excelled. She also cooked for Lew's threshing crew at harvest time. It was a particularly difficult period for their marriage. Nellie told us later that she resented the fact that, for much of the time she was feeding these men, they were not actually working. And she was made unhappier still by the fact that they were spending their spare time making moonshine. But, for Lew, the set of consequences engendered by the ripples of the stream in which they were immersed was clearly 'the only game in town'. Like Nellie in her role of mother and homemaker, he did his level best to stay afloat—and even, where remotely possible, to swim against the overwhelming current of the times.

# Chapter 4

# A ROCK ON THE WINDSWEPT PRAIRIE

We called Lavina Armitage, our maternal grandmother, 'Ma', just as we addressed our father only as 'Lew'. Well, after all, those were my mother's names for them, and it was simply not in Mama's nature to assume the perspective of her children—or of her husband, for that matter—even where such traditional matters were concerned. None of her siblings were known as 'Aunt' or 'Uncle' to us either, even though we learned to call her own uncle 'Uncle George'. Because she was on a first-name basis with her brothers and sisters, so we must be the same. The fact that we had never been similarly encouraged to call her 'Nellie' was always a bit of a puzzle to me. It's possible that she thought of herself exclusively as a mother from the time of her first, tragic experience of childbirth. Perhaps she insisted that Lew refer to her that way as well, for he always used the term 'Mama' not only in reference to her, but when he addressed her directly. But apparently the special status conferred by parenthood was not one she was about to share, not even with the husband who had impregnated her and who, to the best of his ability in those precarious times, 'brought home the bacon'. Thinking about my mother's ways all these years later, I am confident that none of this was consciously thought out by her; nor was it done with any malicious intent; or even ever considered in terms of the consequences for all of us.

For, of course, there were consequences. In so many ways, Lew must have suffered from the isolation imposed by the ambiguous role assigned to him within the family. But that's another story. I'm thinking now of my grandmother, and of how I would love to have referred to her as 'Grandma' or 'Nana', as was the custom in the families of my friends; and of how impossible it was for me to do so. And of how like an imposter I always felt in addressing her as 'Ma', as if I were pretending to be her daughter. For, as it happened, circumstances transpired to make our relationship a particularly close one. Yet, all through the years until her death, it had been rendered virtually impossible for me to address her by any intimate name at all.

One of my earliest memories of Ma was in early April of my seventh year, when my second-youngest brother, Donny, was born. We were all living with her at the time. How she found room to bed the lot of us in her small abode with its two tiny bedrooms is a wonder to me now. One day I overheard my parents and Ma discussing something mysterious. Lew was being sent out for a woman who, apparently, was urgently needed. Her name was Mrs. Fitzpatrick. My curiosity was aroused by the secretive nature of the proceedings. That night I was awakened frequently from my sleep on the cot beside the kitchen stove by Ma and Mrs. Fitzpatrick moving about, accompanied by a profusion of strange sounds and movements. But no one would answer my worried questions. Then I heard a baby crying. It was only later that we all learned about how Mrs. Fitzpatrick had gone to fetch the doctor sometime during the night as Mama was having a difficult time giving birth; and of how he had refused to come because we owed him money. Apparently, Lew had made himself scarce, as husbands were wont to do in those days at the first sign of an impending childbirth. The morning's news of the arrival of a new baby brother, Donald Armitage, was exciting, but somehow did nothing to resolve my problem. I was convinced that Mrs. Fitzpatrick—whom I had heard referred to by the adults as a 'hard' woman—was somehow responsible for my mother's night of suffering. I wondered, also, about the absence of Lew from the goings-on in the back bedroom. Had the strange woman chased him out as well? He did appear at the breakfast table, however, and that increased my confidence. As soon as Mrs. Fitzpatrick joined us I decided to challenge her.

"Why are you such a hard woman?" I demanded.

There was a moment of dead silence during which my sister Myrtle kicked me under the table, in her usual, embarrassed signal for me to keep my mouth shut. Meanwhile Mrs. Fitzpatrick was glaring angrily at me. Lew seemed to be more puzzled than anything. Suddenly, Ma burst out laughing.

"She must have heard us say we'd have to send for the 'hired' woman. And didn't understand the meaning of 'hired'," she explained hastily.

I was grateful to Ma for the timely rescue, and began to appreciate her in a new way. As a child, I had always treasured her unique appearance: the calm, even-featured face with the large knot of hair at the back of the head. I used to love watching her brush that enormous length of hair. It had never, ever, been cut, she once told me. However, it was actually later, in the early springtime of the year I was eleven years old, and long after we had moved to a farm near Lonely Trail, when our special relationship really began. I did not at first understand what was happening to my mother and, consequently, to all of us during that terrible winter of 1937-8. Mama was sick almost all the time. Myrtle, who was then fifteen, had dropped out of school the previous year after having suffered an injury to her leg. She was also having serious, undiagnosed eye problems which had almost blinded one eye. As soon as she was well enough, however, she began to earn a little money by going over to the school periodically to clean the place and empty the ashes from the pot-bellied heater. During the same period she was also riding a horse around to the neighbours, selling buttons and other small items. And now, more than ever, Myrtle was being called upon to do the cooking and cleaning at home.

Then, during seeding time, there was a sudden change in our situation. Literally out of the blue at the supper table one evening, we were all informed by Mama that she was moving back to Oyen, to Ma's house. There had been no previous warning; nor was any explanation offered. I have often wondered whether even Lew had been told before that moment. Mama was never one for dithering around after being forced to make one of those difficult life choices with which she was too-often faced by the circumstances of the times. We learned that she intended to take with her only the youngest child, Donny, who was then almost four years old—and me. I'll never forget the look of utter loss and rejection that crossed the face of my brother, Bobby, who was two years younger than I. Myrtle quite typically revealed none of her feelings, and my other brother Jack—two years my senior in actual age but, sadly, far below in mental development—appeared not to have registered the actual significance of what was happening.

The following morning, after Lew had packed our meagre necessities into the old Model T Ford, we all attempted an awkward farewell. Except for Bobby. He was nowhere to be seen. So we never said goodbye to him. His mother's unexplained desertion of him when he was a mere eight-year-old, and her apparent favouring of the sister whom he had always viewed as his arch competitor, may well have had something to do with the separateness which he manifested ever afterwards. In fact, he appeared bent on maintaining that aloofness from the rest of the family—especially me—for all of his adult life. I always thought it was no accident that he spent most of that life in either the Ottawa area or in Halifax, while the rest of us settled in the West. I think now that the enduring personal resentment which I always sensed in him began at that moment. How could he have been expected to understand at the time, when it was never explained to any of us, that the sole reason it was I who was taken along was my critical role in caring for Donny? By then Mama must have known she would no longer be able to do it. And, at his tender age, Donny could not have been left behind as Bobby was. Mama would never have considered trusting him to Myrtle, who was not known for dealing empathetically with her younger siblings.

There was ample reason for this, from a psychological perspective. One of my earliest memories is of Mama responding to any attempts on Myrtle's part to intervene or discipline any of us by telling her "You leave my kids alone!" It's therefore not surprising that my older sister grew up feeling excluded from all family members except our father Lew. Anyway, Myrtle's forte seemed to be housework, although she was also skilled at drawing and writing poems. I had always been the child-minder and story-teller, as well as the would-be peacemaker between Myrtle and Jack. I lived in perpetual fear that they might kill one another. In fact, as we left that day, I remember my concern being more for the welfare of Jack than for Bobby, who had always struck me as extremely able and independent. But he was only eight years old!

Upon our arrival in Oyen it was obvious that we were not expected. Nevertheless, Ma welcomed us in her usual brusque manner, taking it all in stride as if we had merely popped in from next door. Had she ever failed to extend a welcome to any of her family of six daughters and three sons when they came home for help? As it turned out, Mama's visit was to be brief. I had scarcely gotten started back to the local school, where I had been welcomed by my special pals from primary-school days, Lucille Willison, Josie Kruski, Colleen Trewin and Pat Ford—the granddaughter of Mama's old friend and benefactor, Mrs. Ford of the Benton post office—when my mother became extremely ill. I can't recall the details, but somehow it was arranged for her to be rushed to the closest hospital, at Cereal, a neighbouring town some miles to the northwest on the Goose Lake railway line.

It was only in the days following this crisis in late May that I learned what was wrong with Mama. Lucille approached me excitedly after school one day.

"When's your mother going to have her new baby?" she asked. "My Mom says she's 'expecting'."

Now, from the distance of over seventy years, I find it hard to imagine why I did not receive the news with relief that Mama had not been afflicted with some fatal disease. I guess, in my childish innocence, I had never really entertained that possibility. But the fact is, I was more angry than anything. Angry that no one had told me. Angrier still that my parents had been so foolish and irresponsible.

For I had just that previous year learned the 'facts of life' from my cousin, Murray Carry. He had accomplished this in the most direct way possible. We were visiting Mama's sister Mabel Carry and her family on their farm, about ten miles to the southeast of ours. Murray, a year older than I, was sitting on a rock in the field chatting with me as we rested from some game the group of us were playing. Some yards away, two dogs were apparently wrestling. Then their behaviour altered abruptly. I had previously witnessed similar actions among cattle and was decidedly curious. So I ventured to ask about it. Murray seemed happy to enlighten me, extending the explanation to sexual relations among adults and then to the entire matter of human childbearing. I was horrified to learn all this, and unutterably thankful that my parents had obviously stopped indulging in the disgusting practice after the birth of Donny. If there was anything I was certain of in those precarious times, it was that Mama and Lew had produced more children than they could afford to feed and clothe! Once I learned it was due to their own actions, I felt somewhat reassured about the entire matter, as I knew they did not sleep together. Murray had told me that it was in bed that people 'did it'.

From the time we first moved to the farm, Mama had shared one of the beds in the larger of the two bedrooms with little Donny. The other bed had been intended for, and at first occupied solely by, Bobby and Jack. Lew had the couch in the kitchen. Myrtle and I were assigned the tiny second bedroom. However, I had problems with Myrtle as a room-mate, due to her habit of ejecting me from the bed with both feet at the first call from Mama for her, as the elder daughter and four years my senior, to get up to help with the preparing of breakfast and making of school lunches. So I moved to the larger bedroom and into the bed with my two brothers. The three of us, then aged ten, eight and six, took turns as to which one would sleep at the foot. We seemed to manage just fine. Their willingness to accept me as an extra bedfellow was largely, I think, due to the fact that I regaled the entire crew with a story before we went to sleep each evening—usually a long, rambling, continuing tale.

Not long after Murray's shocking revelation, however, I was awakened one night by the sound of Mama leaving her bed and slipping into the main part of the house that doubled as a kitchen and front room. When she hadn't returned after some time, I got up and followed, struck by a suspicion instilled by my new-found knowledge. To my utter horror and dismay I saw that she was on the couch with Lew, encased in his arms. This was rendered doubly shocking by the fact that I had never ever witnessed the slightest exchange of affection between them. I remember exclaiming, "Please don't make any more babies!" but don't recall what must have been their thoroughly startled response.

So now we would all have to suffer the consequences, I thought bitterly, on the day Lucille told me the news. This initial surge of anger was almost immediately accompanied by a sensation of extreme embarrassment that my ignorance of such intimate and important family news would now likely be revealed to all my classmates. The up side, however, was that at least I would be able to talk to Ma about it all. When I broached the subject, she said she was glad that I knew, and had been uncomfortable about the fact that Mama had made her promise not to mention it. We then decided together that Donny was too young to understand, although I began to try to prepare him. I enhanced my previous attempts at reassuring him about why our mother had left us so suddenly, by making up stories about people going to the hospital not only for a good long rest, but sometimes to get a new baby.

Donny's welfare was uppermost in my thoughts during those stress-filled days of late May and early June. Because I had to be in school on weekdays, he was forced to spend far too much time with only Ma for company. She was as solid as a rock as far as basic care went, but not exactly adept at entertaining a four-year-old. She was then seventy-three years of age, already quite deaf and partially crippled by a cyst-filled knee and a foot with a large, protruding bunion and twisted toes. I now have an intimate understanding of the problems with her knee and foot, as I inherited them!

I was not at all sure that Donny was old enough to be literally on his own all day. However, I reminded myself that it had been a considerable time since he had to be watched carefully. In fact, I couldn't remember any problems in that regard after the day, about a year before, when we children had all been picking raspberries in the garden. Some time after returning to the house, I noted that Donny was missing, and went back out to look for him. I found him happily picking and eating what he clearly thought were berries. To my horror, I saw that they were, instead, little red potato bugs.

Now he was obviously much more mature, and he and I were very quickly able to develop a routine that seemed to satisfy and comfort him. Ma's home was located about a half-mile from the southern edge of town, on the far side of a stretch of open prairie. It was on a large acreage which her brother, George Flewelling, had purchased when he came to Oyen to be near to her after his retirement from work as a newspaper editor and publisher in Gainsborough, Saskatchewan. Upon George's death, Ma had rented her share of the original homestead to her son Ed, and moved into the place in town. Her 'lot' also housed a barn, hen house and small wooden toilet, or 'outhouse'. There was a vegetable plot as well, although by then Ma was physically unable to do much gardening.

About halfway across the stretch of plain separating us from the school was an enormous rock. Donny would walk with me as I left for school in the mornings, until we arrived at the rock. He would then climb up onto it and wave goodbye. My last sighting of him when I was about to move into the border of trees surrounding the school was the shape of that rock against the horizon, with the tiny figure outlined on top. As I returned in a rush for lunch each day, and again after school, that sight was what I looked for. And he was always there. I worried about how he filled his long days, alone by the rock, and asked Ma about it.

"I see him running around the rock and climbing up and down on it. He seems to do lots of playing there by himself," she assured me. "And sometimes he comes back here for something to dig with, and sometimes he stays here a while to help when I'm trying to work in the garden. He's a very independent little boy."

And so he was. And dependable as well! For he was invariably on his perch, waiting patiently, whenever I came home from school; and ready to accompany me as far as the rock when I left. How sad to consider what we have done to our culture and society in the long years since, in undermining the safety of our commons! Where are the rocks for today's lonely little children?

Ma was the rock in my life. She had been there for my parents throughout the Great Depression—every time they found themselves in financial trouble and needed a refuge. She was there for us now, a few weeks later, after the difficult and dangerous birth of the little boy who was to be the last child of Nellie and Lew Duffy. My memory of the actual course of events is unclear, but it seems that Lew appeared suddenly, late one afternoon in the old Model T, and picked me up on his way to Cereal. He had been visited that morning by our only neighbour with a telephone, Mr. Pope, whose wife operated the local branch of the post office which had the official name of 'Haven'. It was from the Popes Lew learned the appalling news that Jack was badly hurt. My poor, much-bullied brother had only just emerged from the door of the school when a couple of boys rode their galloping horses over him—no doubt deliberately, I suspected. After bandaging Jack to the best of his ability, our teacher, Frank Sickoff, had acted with his usual competence. He first sent a student off to the Popes to ask them to inform Lew, and then managed to contact the bachelor farmer who lived not far from the school and persuade him to set off immediately for Cereal with the patient. Lew and I were now following in their wake.

The next couple of days are a blur. Apparently Jack had suffered yet another head injury, and one arm was badly broken. Mama was seriously ill as well. Whether the news about Jack had anything to do with it wasn't clear. She went into labour soon after we arrived at the hospital, but the birth was long and difficult. And that was not the end of it. We learned some hours afterwards that she had hemorrhaged very badly following childbirth, and almost died. We returned to Oyen as soon as she was out of danger. A few days later we were able to bring Mama and the baby back to Ma's place, where Lew left us. The new arrival, Gerald Alan Duffy, subsequently known as Jerry, was the only one in the family other than Jack—whose birthplace was Fairbank, Iowa—to have been born in a hospital, and thus to have had his birth duly registered.

I am unclear about exactly how long an interval then passed before Jack was able to join us and we all four returned to the farm. I know I completed grade six at Oyen, so it could not have been before the end of June. Through it all, Ma was there for us, and the rock in the field remained Donny's refuge. But I find myself wondering, now that it's much too late to ask, how eight-year-old Bobby managed the solitary trek across the barren prairie to Lonely Trail School during those two long months. And if he ever found a rock of his own.

Ma remained a steadfast support for me. Three years later, when Bobby and I needed a place to stay, she took us in and kept us for about four months. Then, after I dropped out of high school at the end of grade eleven, and had been working for a year, she persuaded me to return to Oyen to complete my grade twelve. She needed help, she said, but I suspect that she was thinking chiefly of my welfare. That experience was one of the best of my life, and proved to be a critical turning point for me.

And, then, a few tumultuous years after that, following the birth of my son Tommy, she spent part of the summer with us at our farm south of Acadia Valley. When we collected her she insisted on bringing her antique sewing machine along, as a gift for me as a new mother. It was one of the very first Singer Sewing Machines ever produced, she told me. I used it for years, pumping away with the foot treadle as I sewed. Ma also wanted us to load up the old ancestral family organ. She had decided I was to have that as well, as I was the only grandchild who had ever spent any time playing it. But my husband objected, insisting that we had no room for it in our small truck—nor in our house.

I'll never forget the way Ma limped and staggered about during her stay with us, proudly and lovingly caring for her little great-grandson. With the approach of harvest in early September, we took her back to Oyen, the plan being that she would remain there for only a brief time before leaving to spend the winter on the farm in the Alberta foothills where Mama then lived. But she later changed her mind, saying she did not want to be a burden to anyone; she was still in her own home when December arrived. I remember being very worried about her as I had noticed, when we picked her up the preceding summer, that she had been eating semi-spoiled food without realizing its condition. My concern was to prove well-warranted for, on the tenth of December, she apparently fell while lifting a boiling tea kettle from the stove. She lay there helpless for about five days until my uncle Ed happened to come in from the farm. I never saw her again, for she died in a hospital in Calgary not long after. After a lifetime of supporting others, there had been no rock for Ma in her time of need.

# Chapter 5

## HARD TIMES

In the end, my father died as he had lived, struggling with physically challenging labour, beholden to no one, and isolated from the family he had loved and tried his best to support. It was in late March of 1943. The years between that tragic occasion and the summer day in 1938 when Mama and I and little Donny returned to the farm with baby Jerry had been extremely difficult for all of us. I remember our first week back home with more clarity than I would wish. I was almost twelve years old, and my sister Myrtle had just celebrated her sixteenth birthday. It was immediately obvious that she had done an excellent job of being in charge of the household. When we arrived that day, driven by my father Lew in the old Model T, we found the place tidier than usual, with a wholesome meal of fried chicken and garden vegetables awaiting us all. My brother Jack, by then almost fourteen, was clearly relieved and overjoyed to see us. He was also immediately fascinated with the baby whose red hair was similar to his own—so different from the dark locks of Myrtle and my younger brother Bob; and the blonde ones of Donny and myself. However, we did not see even a hair of Bobby's head for several hours, as he had disappeared just before our arrival. And the otherwise-happy atmosphere of our homecoming lasted only until we were served dessert.

Myrtle proudly brought out a jar of her prize preserves. She had 'canned' (preserved by sealing hot in jars) a large supply of applesauce from our family's share of the remains of the previous season's crop which those faithful Eastern Canadians had shipped to the prairie farmers. Upon tasting this treat I discovered a new and pleasant flavour, and exclaimed loudly that I had never before eaten such wonderful applesauce! I should have known better. My comment proved to be a mistake: one with much worse consequences than the only time I had ever experienced a spanking. That day, almost two years before, I had just returned from a two-week summer visit in Oyen at the home of my friend, Lucille Willeson. I mentioned to Mama that Lucille's mother, who was of German background, cooked chicken differently from the way we had it at home. And, I added, it was really special! Before I had a chance to assure her that her chicken was also special, Mama had dragged me into the bedroom, shoved me onto the bed, and begun to strike at my behind with her open palm.

"That'll teach you not to come home with a lot of 'high mucky-muck' ideas and insult me about my cooking!" she kept exclaiming as she whacked away. At the time her actions made no sense whatsoever to me. But I came to realize, as I matured a bit, that she must have been tortured by feelings of insecurity and inferiority in her relationship with Lew. It's possible that she was ashamed of her lack of schooling, and saw her only claim to expertise as resting in her cooking skills which were, indeed, quite remarkable.

Now I was recognizing the same warning signals once again flashing in Mama's eyes, as she abruptly pushed her dish of applesauce away.

"What in heaven's name did you put in this?" she asked Myrtle. "It tastes absolutely disgusting! You've gone and spoiled it all and wasted our whole winter's supply of apples."

"But I only did what Mrs. Pope told me to do. I used her exact recipe. It said to add a little ginger along with the sugar and water."

"Well, this stuff tastes weird. It's not fit to eat. We're just going to have to empty all the jars and throw every bit of it out. Anyway, I'm going to need those jars for the summer crop of saskatoons. We'll be going down to the river for them soon."

Myrtle, who seldom showed her feelings, looked completely stricken. Lew attempted to intervene on her behalf, saying he loved the flavour of mild ginger, and it would be good for his digestion. But that comment made Mama even angrier. Somehow I knew in that instant that some irredeemable line had been crossed which marked, for her older daughter, the final destruction of any meaningful relationship between them. In recalling this incident long afterwards, Myrtle informed me that, before leaving home following this incident, she had told Mama she hated her; that she always had and always would. The expression of cold loathing in my sister's eyes as she repeated the words all those years later sent a shiver of sorrow and regret through me—at the lost opportunities for both mother and daughter—and I found myself propelled back in time to that long-ago moment when I had first witnessed the expression stiffening her features.

We didn't know it then, but another total crop failure was to force the rest of us to abandon the farm by the end of harvest. Our particular situation had not been helped by Lew's unsettling discovery, at the approach of seeding time the previous spring, that Mama had surreptitiously used much of his precious supply of 'relief' seed for feeding the chickens over the winter. "A bird in the hand is worth two in the bush," was her defence, as she indignantly explained that the chickens would have starved to death otherwise and, this way, at least we had chicken meat and eggs to eat. At the time Lew appeared utterly nonplused but, as usual, he kept his calm. I think he must have recognized, at that grim moment, that 'Duffy's last chance' was rapidly petering out. In fact, Mama was proven tragically correct later that summer, when not only our family, but many of the other surviving dry-land farmers were forced to give up the struggle. Mama's sister Jessie and her husband, Carl Stevenson, had settled on a farm along the main road between Benton and Sibbald some years before. They pulled up stakes that year as well, and somehow managed the long, difficult route to the more fertile north country, eventually getting their large family settled—temporarily, as it turned out—in the Peace River area. As for us, once more my parents threw themselves upon the mercies of my grandmother, Ma. And once again we were all welcomed into to her house in Oyen. Before too long, however, Lew had obtained a temporary part-time job as a mechanic in the local garage, and was able to rent a house for us near the village centre, almost next door to the Catholic church.

It is that location which reminds me of some of my most unpleasant experiences during those first few months in our new home. In previous winters Lew had made a small area of ice on the farm and taught us to maneuver with old hand-me-down skates which he invariably managed to obtain. So Jack and Bob and I had no hesitation in happily joining the other children at the neighbouring skating rink. However, we soon learned that this particular rink was on Catholic church property, while the only other one in town—the United Church rink—was considerably further from us. Quite naturally, given our unchurched background, we never gave such matters a moment's thought. Until, that is, we found ourselves being chased off the rink. We stubbornly persisted in using it our newfound opportunity and developing skill in the sport was a joy to all three of us in spite of the old, second-hand skates we had to wear. Increasingly, however, the other skaters were making us feel unwelcome, as more and more of them learned that we did not belong to their church. The situation got so bad that, several times before we finally gave up, I found myself joining my two brothers in fierce hand-to-hand combat with our Catholic neighbours and 'landowners' as they literally threw us out the gate. It was my first experience of the 'Us versus Them' tribal syndrome. This entire issue was obviously most upsetting for Lew, because of his own Catholic background, but he could do little other than assure us that what those children were doing was very, very wrong.

What further contributed to the dark underbelly of all our subsequent Oyen school days was the fact that we were made to feel like interlopers at the Protestant rink as well. As a result, I never did become a very strong skater, nor did Jack. But Bob did, in spite of the odds. Years later, in response to a query of mine concerning the presumed difficulty of his early months in the Canadian Air Force he wrote, "Anyone who survived my experiences in Oyen can survive anything!"

In fact, my strongest memories of that first year back in Oyen have to do with incidents of bullying. It was not that I was myself actually the object of attack, other than from some of the more undercover nastiness practised in those days by girls. For example, a few of the members of my class—jealous of the long-standing friendship between Lucille Willeson and myself—tried to undermine it by manufacturing stories about how each of us had secretly maligned the other. But this type of thing was of minor concern, compared to the suffering of Jack. It was his brutalization by the teacher as well as fellow students, both within class and outside, that made the year miserable for me and unbearable for him. By this time he had been failed a couple of times and was in grade seven along with me. I have always thought that the cruel treatment meted out to him by our female teacher during class time served to legitimize and reinforce the bullying carried out by the boys in the schoolyard. One day Jack simply refused to go back to school, and I didn't blame him. It was not long after his fourteenth birthday. Our parents did not force him to return. I think that Lew, at least, may finally have been ready to admit that the child who had been slow and awkward since birth; who had suffered two head injuries by then, plus a burst mastoid in his ear as a toddler, was to some extent mentally and emotionally handicapped.

By this time Myrtle had left home for good. Due to Ma's connections to the United Church, the minister there had been happy to give her granddaughter a lead on a job as kitchen helper for a family in the town of Cereal. The lives of all of us were to prove so hectic from then on that we saw very little of her.

My own most frightening experience during that grade-seven year was a private matter. It involved the somewhat premature onset of menstruation—something that had not yet occurred for my close friends. I was in class when the pains began, and then the flow of blood. I was terrified and, having never even heard of the phenomenon, was convinced that I must be dying. Upon rushing home in quiet desperation I was both puzzled and hurt to note that, when I shared the grisly news with Mama, she responded with what appeared to me as surprising aplomb and unconcern. After she explained this particular fact of life to me and showed me how to use safety pins to fasten the required fragment of worn-out towel in the appropriate place, I faced her in considerable anger.

"Why didn't somebody tell me about this before?" I asked accusingly.

"Well, I naturally thought you'd have heard all about it; that Myrtle would have told you. And, anyway, I figured you always read so much you seem to know everything there is to know," she said. For a few minutes I couldn't decide whether to be flattered or insulted by that response, but at least my anger and sense of betrayal were somewhat diminished by the amused exasperation that her words aroused in me.

Overshadowing even this bolt from the blue during those adolescent years, however, was the beginning of the Second World War in 1939. It happened just as I was entering grade eight. Germany invaded Poland in the early morning of the first day in September. Britain declared war two days later, with Canada following closely in its wake. From the start, I think that my perspective on the war was very different from that of most of my classmates. For one thing, I had read Erich Maria Remarque's great works, "All Quiet on the Western Front", and "The Road Back", and been profoundly moved by what I learned in those books about the utter madness and futility of the First World War. Also, my best friend's mother was from Germany, and still had close family ties there. She agonized incessantly about her fears for the future; in fact, she was convinced that Armageddon beckoned. So I was saddened and terrified by what was happening, in spite of being forced, finally, to recognize that the Allies had no other choice. Still, I could never quite join in the joyous patriotism that the war provoked.

As usual, I was greatly influenced by my father. Lew was not a pacifist, but he had been very much opposed to the 'Great War' of 1914-18. I recall that he was always an admirer of Mackenzie King. But no one then knew about the latter's fascination with the occult. King was a hero to many moderates as it was he who, in 1926, had built the modern federal Liberal Party by forging an alliance with the Progressives of the time. Lew had applauded King's comment the previous winter that "war would settle nothing, prove nothing, help nothing". In the early days leading up to it, Lew would sometimes express the opinion that perhaps we should back off and allow the Nazi-Fascist coalition and the Communists to destroy one another. He suggested that Britain and her allies might then be able to help the people in those countries build democracy upon the ashes. However, after Stalin and Hitler reached their infamous Soviet-German Pact of August 29, 1939, he changed his mind abruptly and began to speak out strongly in favour of Winston Churchill's position. I imagine this was the route taken by many liberal thinkers at the time. Of course, had they known then about what Hitler was doing to the Jews, and to gypsies and homosexuals as well, they would probably have been supportive of going to war much earlier.

Lew used to say that all fanaticism is dangerous, but that religious fanatics are the most dangerous of all, because they believe they have a 'hot line' to some all-powerful, all-knowing, other-worldly being. He called both Hitler and Mussolini 'religious fanatics', and Stalin a secular one. For a many years I was puzzled over this. How, I wondered, could Hitler have been religious, when Christians and other religionists the world over habitually referred to Nazism as an atheistic doctrine? This was clarified for me only long after the war, when I learned that Hitler had been educated in a monastery school, and had actually imagined that he was creating a new religion of Volkism, with himself in the role of God's interpreter, and the Aryan Volk as the authentic 'Chosen People'. He believed Jesus to have been an Aryan who was murdered by the Jews. Upon reading all this I recalled Lew once telling me of Hitler bragging about how his anti-Semitism had been inspired by the Christian Social Movement, and of how he always claimed he was "fighting for the work of the Lord" when attacking the Jews. No doubt Lew had found all this, and much more of the same type of thing, in "Mein Kampf", which I was to encounter only much later.

In the autumn of 1940, we moved into a house belonging to Mama's sister, Laura Cutlan. Laura and her family had resettled further north in the relatively prosperous district of Sylvan Lake and, as they could find no buyer or renter for their Oyen abode, she allowed us to use it rent-free. Mama was relieved not to have to wash everything down with vinegar in order to kill off the bedbugs so that we could sleep in peace at night; as she had been forced to do when we moved to the farm and most of her previous dwellings.

By that time I was enjoying life a great deal. The new teacher of my junior-high classroom was Mr. Harold Hall, who was to prove a great inspiration to me. He liked to tease all of us—especially me. When I began to insist on being called Pat, rather than 'Patty' or 'Paddy', he pretended to get confused about the name of 'Pat Duffy' and would, instead, refer to me as 'Dat Puffy'. I enjoyed his teasing, although I did object to the term 'Dufflebag' by which we Duffys were scornfully addressed by many fellow students. Our cousin,

Phil Carry, who was attending high school in Oyen at the time and—like Bob and me—earning top marks in his courses, had to suffer the consequences of his academic success in a similar fashion by being derisively labeled 'Carry Me Home'. Phil's brother, Murray, would have been in my grade, but he had quit school early. Ever an independent spirit, he was now planning to work on his own as a cowboy in the foothills country, rounding up wild horses and sending them to war-torn Britain, where they were in great demand for butchering. I was critical of Murray's idea of an attractive business enterprise, but realized that he had never been as interested in studying as were his brothers Phil and Wendell or, for that matter, as I was.

It was doubly fortunate for me that Mr. Hall took over our classroom the year I was beginning grade nine. In those days, the decisive Departmental Exams were administered upon graduation from junior high. It was then actually a more critical threshold—and affected far more students—than the end of grade twelve. This was simply because only a relatively few of the more privileged youth had the chance to complete high school. Of course I had no idea of it at the time. It was only after the exams were marked the following summer that the school superintendent, Mr. Laverty, told me I had won the Governor General's Medal. It seemed that I had received the highest marks in the entire Acadia School Division, which had been formed in 1937 in a desperate attempt at re-organizing the impoverished schools of the drought-affected area extending south to the Red Deer River, east to Alberta's border with Saskatchewan, and west to Hanna. I felt that much of the credit for my success in the dreaded 'Departmentals' was due to Mr. Hall's instruction. Two years later, my brother Bob, who was never one to be outdone by his sister, received the same distinction—albeit in a different location within the Province.

One of Mr. Hall's routines operated greatly to Bob's advantage when he entered the junior-high classroom as a grade-seven student, at the beginning of my grade-nine year. Before the first class of the day, all three grades were subjected to a joint test of rapid mental arithmetic. Bob invariably emerged as the winner here, even though he was one of the youngest in the entire room. He was similarly able to beat me at any and every card game that I could ever be persuaded to play with him. Manipulating numbers was simply not my forte. I decided, after I had studied child development many years later, that my lifelong problem in this arena had probably stemmed from a deficiency in the development of 'spatial relations' as a baby and toddler. Mama often mentioned that I was an extremely placid child who could be left for hours playing by myself in a wooden crib fashioned by Lew. It was likely due to this propensity that I—unlike my brothers—was assigned to the crib for my first couple of years of life, rather than sleeping with Mama at night and demanding most of her attention during the day. My evident satisfaction with this state of affairs no doubt contributed to making life bearable for her because of all the attention required by Jack; and then, just over a month after my second birthday, by the new baby, Robert Alan.

All these years later my strange affliction was noticed by Mr. Hall. He was always amused by the way that I could evidently understand the most difficult concepts in mathematics and explain them clearly to my friend, Lucille, then invariably end up making a number of simple errors in addition or subtraction that would render my mark on an exam lower than hers. He didn't realize how hard I had to work at relating those concepts to my surroundings; nor how deficient I was even in knowing what direction to turn when I went out a familiar door.

I also recall particularly appreciating Mr. Hall's head-on tackling of the problem of body odour, which was all-too-common among adolescents in those days. Rain barrels were consistently empty, and water from the town well in the pump house had to be carefully doled out. He told us a joke about a student whom he had scolded because of his revolting smell. The student replied, "I don't know why I smell bad. Every morning I wash up as far as possible and down as far as possible." Mr. Hall claimed that he had responded by telling the boy to try washing 'possible'. He then told us he realized water was scarce but all each of us required every morning was merely one cup of it. That would do the trick, he said, so long as we remembered to use it not only for the face and hands, but for under the arms and—even more important—for washing 'possible'.

Another tale of Mr. Hall's, which apparently became a favourite long after I had left his classroom, was one he told about me. It had to do with my little brother Donny. I heard it—and had to admit to its truth—when Mr. Hall was introducing me prior to my first professional presentation at a conference of the teachers of Acadia School Division about five years later. After informing my new colleagues that I had been a profound nuisance as a student because of my tendency to complete his sentences for him when he was teaching, he launched into the story of how I had once abruptly leapt out of the window during class and raced to the rescue of my kid brother, who was being attacked in the schoolyard by a group of older boys.

Donny was always my special concern. I had taught him to read quite proficiently when he was only four years old, so that by the time he started school he was far ahead of the other children. Unfortunately, this turned out to be a handicap rather than a help to him at school, as the primary-room teacher seemed to resent his skills. In fact, rather than placing him in grade two where he obviously belonged, she appeared to do her best to make his life miserable.

As for me, school just seemed to get better and better during that period. One of the classes I was able to take was music. That subject, along with art, was taught by a Mr. Goddard. I found this a very an exciting experience. We learned singing, music appreciation and music theory. Although the theory was boring for most of my classmates, it provided an entirely new and abundantly practical opportunity for me. I discovered how to play Ma's organ. I began spending most of my free time at her place, hunting up all the worn sheet music from days long past. I taught myself all her old Civil War songs—such as "The Faded Coat of Blue"—by reading the music for the right hand while playing chords with the left. I sometimes amused myself, as well, with her ancient record player which used cannister-shaped records and required continuous cranking.

How I longed to take piano lessons! But, of course I knew this was totally impossible for someone like me, so I never even mentioned it to anyone. We were also all expected to try our hand at singing in that music class at school; and those who had passed muster according to the teacher's minimal standards had to compete at the annual School District music festival. To my utter horror I was one of those selected to represent our school. I can still remember the exact phrasing for the song, "The Minstrel Boy", which I had to sing at the festival. Needless to say, I didn't win.

The principal of the school in those years was a rather strange man. My memories of him are in a vastly different league from the happy experiences associated with his colleagues. Many years later I learned that he was found guilty of murdering his wife and two children only a few years after having left Oyen.

Although my class time in those days was happy, by autumn of 1940 things were steadily deteriorating on the home front. Lew's part-time repair jobs at the garage had become few and far between, and the economic situation in our household was reaching crisis point. Ma was being increasingly approached by Mama for grocery money, and was more and more reluctant to oblige. At one of those times Mama told me of how she had learned, over the years, that it was always better to ask Ma for larger than for smaller sums. It seems that our grandmother could be counted on to come across in generous terms for serious calamities; but a request for smaller amounts on a regular basis tended to elicit nothing but a scolding. According to Mama, this would invariably end with the maxim: "It's time you learned that, if you look after the pennies, the dollars will take care of themselves."

I began to notice that Lew was suffering more and more from digestive problems. He was now experimenting with eating garlic in an effort to decrease his abdominal pain. Predictably, Mama had little patience with this, and we heard a great deal about his insufferable breath. Actually, none of us paid as much attention as we should have to his symptoms at the time, for he was never one to complain. Also, my life was in high gear just then. It was during this period that I saw my first 'moving picture'. The excitement of that evening is with me yet, colouring every visit to the theatre even today. I have three powerful memories of those early movie-going experiences.

The first of these was the general sense of admiring wonder that I felt for the man on the ledge above us who produced those fascinating moving pictures simply by turning some kind of a crank on the machine beside him. Lew later removed the mystery of it for me by explaining that the pictures were on a celluloid tape which was threaded from the front to the back of the machine. Another memory involved the embarrassment of arriving home weeping uncontrollably after attending a sad movie with my friends. The family had all gone to bed, but everyone teased me the next morning about having been awakened by the sound of wild sobbing in the kitchen. The third memory is of my leaving the other kids and walking out of a gratuitously violent movie. At least it was violent according to standards then, but would not even cause a moment's recoil in viewers today. I felt strongly at the moment the portrayal turned unnecessarily nasty that I could afford neither to expose myself to such behaviours nor imply consent to them by continuing sitting there. I could not have known it then, but this decisive moment when I departed from my friends at the movie house was the beginning of my lifelong effort to educate people about the harmful effects of media violence on the human capacity for empathy—and, consequently, for morality.

It soon became clear, however, that we could not afford to continue going to movies, nor to do anything else that required money. Our financial problems became so serious that Lew was finally forced to the decision that, if he were to feed his family, he must look elsewhere for work. He packed up his precious tools and left in the tiny old Ford truck one day in early November, promising to send funds home as soon as he could. He intended to try Calgary first, possibly because Myrtle was then working there. He wrote to us just after his arrival, telling about meeting Myrtle for lunch. Apparently she had brought out a cigarette after the meal, but he assured us that he wasn't too worried, "I think she was just trying to shock me," he wrote. He had gauged that right, as Myrtle never did become a smoker, even though it was rapidly becoming the 'in-thing' for young people to do in those days.

From that time on our situation spiralled downhill rapidly. Jack and I had to walk over to Ma's place after dark to fetch and carry home a couple of pails of coal each night. We didn't want the town kids to know that we couldn't afford to buy it. Mama was now selling off the furniture, piece by piece, for grocery money. Jack began to steal small amounts of money whenever he could, although we were not then aware of it. One day he came home proudly flourishing treats of candy for us all. We learned later that he had been caught robbing the post office. After that, we Duffy kids were blamed for every minor crime in town. In the midst of all this stress and heartbreak, we gave little thought to the war. Were we even aware of the fact that the 'Blitz of London' had begun in late December? I had no way of knowing that what was happening in Britain would have an effect on my own future life: an effect more personal and tragic than I could ever have imagined. What concerned me at the end of December of 1940 was, instead, a letter from Lew which I discovered in the trash one day. I placed it in my private cardboard box of treasures, along with a picture I found of him as a young man. The letter ended with the words, "I'm sorry that I have so little money for you this time. But I promise to find steady work so I can send more soon, or I'll die in the attempt."

Not long after this, Lew surprised us by arriving back home, dejected and discouraged, still with no reliable job prospects in sight. By then, Mama had decided—with her typical independence and courage—that she would have to strike out on her own. Without telling anyone, she answered an advertisement in the *Western Producer* (the major Saskatchewan newspaper) for a housekeeping job in the farming country near the village of Veteran, over seventy miles to the northeast of Oyen. Then, one evening in February after we had gone to bed, she disappeared with the two younger boys. Donny was then in grade one and Jerry was two years old. Mrs. Fitzpatrick, the village mid-wife and long-time family friend, came over the next morning to inform us that Nellie and the kids had stayed with her for the night in order to catch the train early in the morning at the station near where she lived. Not long after this, Lew arranged for Bob and me to be taken in by our grandmother while he closed up the Cutlan house. I have an especially poignant memory of discovering him having a bath in the little round tub in the kitchen when I walked in the door one day just after having moved out. He had a bloated-looking, sagging stomach, and the arms that had always been so muscular were now wrinkled and thin. Somehow he struck me at that moment as touchingly vulnerable. The kitchen was almost bare by then, except for a coal stove and kitchen table belonging to the Cutlans. Mama had previously sold most of our small supply of furniture, other than the old kitchen couch and the badly worn washboard and little round tub and old rocking chair from the farm. Lew departed a few days after this for Saskatchewan, taking Jack with him, obviously hoping for better luck there in his increasingly desperate hunt for steady work.

I learned from Don many years later that Mama and the boys had arrived in Veteran in the midst of a snowstorm which rendered the road impassable for motor vehicles. However, Mr. McCurdy, the farmer whose advertisement Mama had answered, picked them up at the station in an enclosed sleigh. This vehicle had a window in the front and a slot for the reins controlling the horses. Mr. McCurdy had thoughtfully provided heated bricks and blankets to keep them warm during the journey to his farm.

By the time the summer was over, it had been arranged for me to go to Saskatoon to live with Mama's youngest sister Dot, whose husband Bus Richards, a member of the Royal Canadian Air Force, was stationed there at the time. I was to 'earn my keep' by helping with the housework and tending their small daughter, Beverly, after school and on weekends. Bob was being taken in by Mama's brother, Les Armitage and his wife Annie, at their farm near Caroline, Alberta. They had a daughter, Thelma, who was Bob's age, and a son, Harold, about a year older than I.

There was a singer to whom I loved listening during this sad time, whenever I had access to a radio. It was Woody Guthrie, who was actually pioneering folk music, but of course we were not aware of it at the time. Our penniless and home-less state was acutely exemplified for me by Woody singing his own lines to the tune of a popular religious song called 'This World is Not My Home". His version began with: "A rich man took my house and he pushed me out the door. And I ain't got no home in this world any more."

Sometime that summer, Lew finally managed to land a regular job as a mechanic. It was in a garage at Biggar, Saskatchewan, a town on the railway line to the west of Saskatoon. Mama and the two little boys returned briefly to Ma's place at Oyen after the harvest was finished at Veteran. Mr. McCurdy had driven them back home in his Model T which, like ours, was open to the wind and clouds of attacking grasshoppers. A short time later, Lew managed to make the trip back to collect the remnants of his family, along with the few belongings still remaining at the Cutlan house. I recall being told about how the precious old rocking chair rode perched on the top of the jumble in the back of the old Model T—just as it had years before when we moved to the farm.

Jack was waiting for them at the new home in Biggar, as was Bob. I remained in Saskatoon until the beginning of the Easter holidays. When I finally got to Biggar, Myrtle was there as well. She had married an airman who was stationed on the Queen Charlotte Islands, assigned to the building of runways at Nasset. She was about eight months pregnant when she joined the family.

On looking back on the following four months of my life, it almost seems that time must have speeded up somehow. From my perspective, at least, so much was happening. My first memory of it all is not of my arrival, however, other than my first sight of the sign, "New York is big, but this is BIGGAR!". I recall most clearly being in the hospital visiting Myrtle, who had just given birth to a tiny, four-pound, premature baby daughter, whom she named Linda. They were discharged after only a couple of days, in spite of the baby's precarious condition. Another vivid memory is of the baby sleeping all the time, and refusing to suck or swallow; along with one of Myrtle and me bedded down on the floor of the front room at night with the little baby basket between us. Another is of the basket's tiny inhabitant suddenly beginning to turn blue. Then there were the two of us with tiny Linda in a taxi, frantically speeding to the hospital in Saskatoon; all the while desperately hoping that the struggling little creature would survive. I had to return at once with the taxi, but later learned that Myrtle had a dreadful time persuading the hospital to accept the baby, simply because she couldn't pay for the service—all this in spite of the obvious fact that the child was on the verge of death. After finally being taken in by the hospital, Linda did survive in spite of the odds, and remained hospitalized for a month or so. During that month, Lew traveled to the city as well, for a medical examination, the results of which he did not discuss when he returned.

Myrtle did not come back to Biggar from Saskatoon. There was really no room for a mother and new baby in the small house we were renting. Her husband's parents, who lived up in Clinton, invited her to move in with them temporarily. She eventually settled in Calgary, as she was accustomed to being on her own by then, and was receiving the minimum monthly allowance provided by the government for the wives of the men who had signed up for the war. It was the custom for these airmen, sailors and soldiers to sign over additional funds as well, from their pay. However, Myrtle's husband Bill never did.

I attended the Biggar high school for only about four months, but I learned a lot. For one thing, I witnessed a teacher being virtually 'run out' of her classroom. Observing her ineffective attempts at teaching, and the mob behaviour of that roomful of out-of-control students, was the best lesson in what not to do that any prospective teacher could have had. Not that I had the slightest idea, then, that I would end up being a teacher. Another extremely fruitful experience was having a future Provincial Premier, Woodrow S. Lloyd, as my school principal and history teacher. I think he was then already a member of the Co-operative Commonwealth Confederation or CCF—formed out of the Ginger Group within the former Progressive Party in 1933—which was eventually to become the NDP, or New Democratic Party of Saskatchewan. It was Lloyd who, two decades after I knew him, inherited the difficult task of implementing Tommy Douglas' pioneering universal medicare system in that Province. Certainly his influence in my 1942 grade ten classroom helped to further the longtime interest in history and politics which my father had implanted in me, as well as to add fuel to the flame of my already deeply ingrained concern for equality and justice.

I made many good friends in those grade-ten classes. I also had my first actual date that spring. It was a disaster, but a valuable eye-opener as well. Almost immediately following my arrival, a boy named Elmer began to signal that he found me attractive. One day he asked me to go out with him on the coming Friday evening. I obliged, but soon after he picked me up at home, I began to feel uncomfortable. I had assumed that we would be attending a movie. However, he merely said he wanted to go for a walk. I was then led into a nearby field where, with no warning, my date grabbed me and began to attempt to fondle and kiss me. At the same time he was groping beneath my skirt. Fortunately, I was strong and athletic, and quickly managed to escape him.

Not long after this, another boy asked for a date. Due to my recent experience, I agreed only reluctantly, and insisted that he be specific about what we would do. Before the arranged evening had arrived, however, one of my classmates told me that she had overheard Elmer and this second boy making a bet on who would be the first to 'lay' the new girl from the city. I took great pleasure on the night of the supposed date, in watching through the upstairs window as my brother Jack—at my request, and repeating my exact words—told the young would-be date-rapist that I was not at home, and would not ever be, as far as he and his pals were concerned.

Although I had been totally turned off dating, I did establish a close friendship with a male fellow-student. He was a boy of Chinese background who worked in his family's restaurant, which happened to be across the street from the garage where my father worked and where he had obtained a job for me as service attendant and book keeper that spring and summer. After school each day, we two youngsters developed the habit of walking to and from work together. We soon discovered that we had a great deal in common. Typically for those times, none of the other young people at school had much to do with my Chinese-Canadian friend.

That interlude in which I had the opportunity to work so close to Lew was one of the highlights of my entire life. Once the school holidays began, we ate our bag-lunches together at noon. It was then, for the first time, that he shared some of his trials and tribulations with me.

During this period I was able to consolidate what I had not fully recognized until then as the world view of non-supernaturalism which Lew had shared with me from early childhood on. He explained in simple terms what it meant to be a Freethinker in a world populated mainly by believers in gods. I came to recognize clearly why I was always so out-of-step with my friends and even with my mother and her entire family in so many ways concerning basic ideas about how the world worked. Lew remarked one day that the life journey of people like us was a "lonely trail", but he had always found it a non-contradictory and satisfying one.

One day I learned that he had been diagnosed with bowel cancer in the hospital in Saskatoon and, contrary to what he had told Myrtle at the time to lull her fears, had been informed that emergency surgery was required immediately. But, of course, there was no money for it. However, he said there was a good chance the necessary funds would arrive at any time, so we mustn't give up hope.

Meanwhile, I was experiencing a problem that I did not share with him, given my knowledge of his own load of worries. The man who was the boss of both of us was harassing me at work, although I would not then have known what to call it. Whenever I had to be alone with him in the office to work on the bookkeeping he would pat my hips or breasts and make other suggestive moves. I was trapped, as I didn't dare risk losing the precious job; or, what would have been much worse, causing Lew to be fired as a result of his predictable reaction to my telling him about what was going on while he slaved away under the trucks and other machinery in the back of the garage. So I made a game of it, laughingly brushing away the man's overtures, and continually moving to the opposite side of the desk when he was around. My maneuvers worked, and I managed to keep him perpetually at bay, while at the same time not offending him. In fact, the pattern I established, by means of the training unintentionally provided by this horny lout, was to stand me in good stead through all my future work as a waitress. I developed a way of dealing jokingly and politely with men—dodging advances without provoking their anger—no matter what they said or tried to do.

One day the mailman delivered an envelope addressed to Lew in care of the garage office. I could see it was from his favourite sister Lucy. In a flash I realized what he had meant when he referred to the money for his surgery which was soon to arrive. I rushed into the work area and gave it to him. He opened it expectantly. I will never . . . ever . . . forget the look on his face when he glanced at the enclosure. After an uncomfortable moment or two he sighed and then, without a word, handed it to me. It contained only a card, with the message 'Get Well Soon! Love from Lucy'. There was nothing else—not even a letter.

Lew's health situation was never discussed at home, but Mama must have known about it. Apparently she had decided that he would not be able to continue working for much longer. In spite of his long hours, the pay would have been quite minimal. I remember, with a sensation of the same wry humour that I felt at the time, a comment of his to Mama one day. She had complained that she had to have a new washboard. His thoroughly untypical and—given the basic nature of the object of her request—ridiculously inappropriate response to this plea was: "You always seem to think I'm made of money."

So my mother once more bravely took the initiative and answered an advertisement for a housekeeper. This time it was from a farmer located far to the west of us, on the edge of the Alberta foothills, near a village called Cremona. And, once more, none of us knew about it until immediately before she was to leave, around the beginning of August. Bob returned to the Les Armitage farm near Caroline soon after my mother, along with Don and Jerry, departed for Cremona.

I stayed behind with Lew and Jack, wanting to continue earning money at the garage for as long as possible. When Lew had to close up the house, I set off for Cremona as well. I arrived at the farm west of town where my mother was working for fifteen dollars a month plus room and board for herself and two sons. From there I was soon able to find a job for myself for the harvest season. I was extremely fortunate in landing at a fairly prosperous farm between Cremona and Carstairs, where they allowed me to work outdoors as well as in the house. I was taught much there that was to prove valuable to me in later life. One of my responsibilities was caring for the pigs. I mixed their feed and fed them regularly, carrying a large, heavy pail of mush in each hand. Someone took a picture of me doing that, and Mama submitted it to *The Western Producer*, where it was subsequently published.

While living in Saskatoon with my aunt Dot the previous year I had learned to be a meticulous ironer. It was a good thing, for this particular farmer's wife had almost a fetish about the task. She insisted that I iron even the sheets and the men's socks. All in all, however, the family members were most helpful to me. Their daughter came home for a visit once, and while there, she encouraged me to clean my teeth regularly—something I had never been taught to do. Neither dental hygiene nor dental services of any kind, other than Lew's last resort of pulling our teeth, had been a part of our lives. This older girl also gave me some pointers about men. For example, I was advised never to allow one to walk arm-in-arm with me unless I was serious about him, as this move on his part was 'a declaration of possession'. And the farmer's wife located a place in the town of Carstairs where I could earn my room and board while attending the local high school. By working at the farm until the end of the harvest season and starting school two months late, I was able to build up a small fund for some necessary clothes and books.

Lew left Biggar that autumn as well, and moved to Calgary, in order to be closer to the rest of us. Finally, he had choices, as economic conditions were improving rapidly by then because of the war. He was hired as a mechanic by a large garage: Union Tractor, the Southern Alberta distributor for Caterpillar. Jack, just turned eighteen, had recently joined the army. Mama and I visited Lew once, traveling by train from Carstairs. He met us and took us to his single, tiny room with a bath and toilet down the hall. In discussing Jack's enlistment in the army, he said wistfully that he hoped the experience would make a man of him. We spent one uncomfortable night together, with Mama and me managing to squeeze onto the couch while Lew sat all night in the only comfortable chair. When I expressed concern about taking his bed, he assured me that he could no longer get any sleep lying down anyway; that his abdominal pain and back problems were more bearable in a sitting position.

That visit was the last time I was to see him alive. Not long after, on a cold, wet day in early April, Mama called my school with appalling news. Lew had suffered a massive, fatal heart attack, underneath a tractor he was repairing. Apparently, the company for whom he worked phoned her immediately, offering to provide a funeral because her husband had died on the job. One of the sons of Mr. Graham, her employer, drove her to Carstairs, where I joined her. We boarded the train late that afternoon for Calgary, and settled in a hotel room for the night. I did not discover until the following morning that, when asked about a venue, she had suggested the Catholic Church. This was no doubt simply because Lew had been raised a Catholic. It revealed a lot about how little she had understood him.

I shall never forget the torments of that ghastly night. There was not a moment's sleep for either of us. Mama spent eight long hours complaining to me, over and over, about Lew's abject failure as a husband and father; about how he had been a hopeless alcoholic all his life; about how he had invariably found money for pipe tobacco even though there was none for groceries; about how he had never . . . ever . . . been fit to operate a business of any kind, yet had insisted on attempting to do it; and about how he had never even remotely managed to support his family. During the early part of it, I lay in utter agony—not recognizing the father I had loved in the caricature she was maligning. I wondered desperately why she could not, even for a moment, view the situation from the perspective of this daughter at her side who had just lost her treasured parent. Why could she not think of how I must be feeling?

As the night wore on, however, something extremely strange began to happen to me. Gradually, I found myself buying into her version of Lew, and of their life together. I began to empathize with her! Could I have been mistaken about him all these years, I asked myself? Had he, in fact, been nothing but a wastrel and drunkard all along? Was that why everything he tried to do had ended so badly? Was that the real reason his family had disowned him, and refused his plea for help in the end? This outcome was doubly ironic in that, as I realized many years later, it had been herself that she was attempting to persuade. My poor, childlike, confused mother, crippled by her lifetime lack of empathy for others, had to somehow justify her own actions and to make it possible to live with their consequences. But if the night had been a nightmare, the morning was even worse. For me, the entire experience of the funeral at that Catholic church was tantamount to being thrust suddenly into some strange 'never-never' land of blackest magic and superstition. The figure of the dead Jesus on the cross at the front added to this impression, as did the priest in his weird garb waving his wand as he sprayed strange-smelling incense along the aisle. Compounding the nightmare was the fact that the entire ceremony was in Latin. However, the worst moment of the day was when we were herded to the coffin. Before I realized what was occurring I found myself being forced to view the body of my father: a sight and event so foreign to all that he had been, or would have wished to happen, that it haunts me still.

There had been scarcely anyone at the service. Afterwards, the tiny group of mourners gathered at the home of Myrtle's old friends, the Simpson family, from our Lonely Trail days. Myrtle and Jack were both there, although there was no sign of Bob. I discovered only many years later that he was not informed of his father's death until several weeks after the funeral, when he received a letter from Mama. I was told that, typically, he disappeared for a long time upon learning the news, and subsequently made no reference to it. I recall only a couple of Mama's sisters accompanying us that bleak day, so I have to assume that the majority of her family did not know about it either. However, the gathering did provide a degree of emotional comfort, for the moment at least, in that those few who had come expressed a fond respect for Lew and admiration of his honesty and intellect. In stark opposition to the dark picture in which I had been smothered during the long hours of the previous night, I heard some extremely positive stories about him. However, all this left me in a state of utter confusion—torn by contradiction whenever I allowed myself to think about my father. How I managed to complete my grade-eleven classes and daily household chores during the ensuing months is inconceivable to me now. But the consequences of it all for my own life choices were to be more far-reaching than I ever could have guessed. It is just as well that we cannot read the future.

# Chapter 6

## LOST YESTERDAYS

I have always found reminders of the loss of life during the Second World War overwhelmingly difficult to bear. This may be partly due to the fact that the most poignant of my wartime memories concerns a young man named Max McCurdy—one of the many who 'never returned'.

I met Max in the summer of 1941. I was not quite fifteen years old at the time. My father had been desperately seeking work for several months and we were on the brink of starvation when my mother obtained a housekeeping job at the McCurdy farm near Veteran, Alberta, in February of that year. She took my two youngest brothers, Don and Jerry, with her. My twelve-year-old brother, Bob, remained behind with me at our grandmother's place in Oyen. When school closed for the summer holidays, Mama sent for the two of us to join her. However, she warned us not to let the McCurdys know that she was our mother, or even that she had a husband who was off job-hunting. Apparently, she had told Mr. McCurdy (a widower) that we were her niece and nephew. I assumed that, when answering the advertisement for the job, she had been afraid to acknowledge her married state and 'raft' of children. I was old enough to understand the situation, but I sensed at the time that Bob was experiencing all this as a rejection, in a personal sense. During the almost two months of our visit at the farm, we both settled on addressing our mother only directly so that no naming was necessary, and never referring to her in her absence. Characteristically, we didn't discuss our feelings, but it was obvious to me that Bob shared my discomfort about the charade.

In spite of my being forced to live under a cloud of pretense, that summer turned out to be one of the happiest of my entire life. Max, the son of Mr. McCurdy, took me under his wing from the very first day. With remarkable patience he taught me how to help him with the haying—including 'stooking'—and numerous other outdoor tasks. He had just celebrated his eighteenth birthday at the time, and had graduated from high school. Under his tutelage I discovered that I loved outdoor farm work, and I think I must have been reasonably good at it. I even managed to handle a lively four-horse team. In our spare time the two of us wandered the meadows, with Max explaining everything we encountered. I recall receiving a lesson, one day, on how to make dandelion wine. We discussed our opinions and knowledge about everything, and discovered that we were looking at the world through the very same 'free-thinking' window. Max reminded me of my father in that he was one of those classy country gentlemen of the old school whom a young girl could trust completely. There was a concern and even tenderness toward the fourteen-year-old in his care, and at times a suggestion of commitment. But, looking back now at that blissful, dream-like summer, I realize that he never so much as touched my hand in any way suggestive of a sexual overture. Would that my teen-age world had produced more Max McCurdys!

In the final week of August, Bob and I had to return to Oyen, in order to leave as soon as possible for what were to be our new temporary abodes. Our departure from the McCurdy farm had come without warning. Just after Max left on an errand one morning, a neighbour dropped by. He mentioned that he was traveling down through Oyen country. Mama grasped at the chance to obtain a ride for us, thereby saving us from the long and costly route south through Hanna and then east by train. I considered asking that we wait a half-hour or so, as Max was expected to return any minute. But I was afraid that might appear presumptuous. So I never said goodbye to Max.

Almost immediately following our arrival at Oyen, Bob set off for the farm of our kind and caring uncle and aunt, Les and Annie Armitage, near Caroline, Alberta. A few days later, I was sent to join my mother's youngest sister and her husband, Dot and Bus Richards. At that time they lived in Saskatoon, where Bus was stationed as a member of the Royal Canadian Air Force, or RCAF. Although I was not then familiar with the term, I think the best way to describe what I experienced during those first few weeks in Saskatoon is 'culture shock'. I found myself thrust into a context that was, in every way, the direct opposite of what had existed on the McCurdy farm. In the first place, the city environment was then totally unknown to me. And the lifestyle of my aunt and uncle struck me as utterly foreign as well.

It was not that the entire situation was unpleasant. Bus was a kind, easy-going man, and let me know that he enjoyed having me with them. And the little toddler, Beverley, was a pleasure to care for. But Dot proved to be something else entirely. She was certainly not an unattractive woman. Indeed, she reminded me of Judy Garland in appearance and in many of her mannerisms. The problem was that, from the very first day, she seemed to resent me on a number of counts. She and Bus were deeply into the partying lifestyle then prevalent among many of the young families involved in the military. I had never before seen women smoking and drinking alcohol, and made it clear at once that I would not participate. I also tried to avoid contact with the airmen who came to the house regularly for these drinking bouts, although Dot did her utmost to draw me into their partying. I soon learned that, at the first sign of uniformed visitors, it would be in my best interests to beat a hasty retreat to my room to study or read. My attitude offended Dot, and she fell into the habit of accusing me of thinking I was too good for her friends, who were all offering to die for their country.

She also appeared to resent my academic success as the school term wore on, telling me once that her Beverley would far surpass my accomplishments when she was old enough for school. As time passed, she began to pile on more and more housekeeping duties, including all of the family laundry and ironing. My performance at these tasks was never up to her standards. For example, the concept of an electric washing machine was totally new to me. In fact, one of my major memories of my mother is of her bent over the washboard, scrubbing away. I remember one day at Dot's place when, in doing the laundry, I mistakenly put one of my cheap blouses—of a bright pink shade—into a load of light-colored clothing. Everything came out pink! Dot happened to be in the room when I unloaded the machine. In a fury, she grabbed the soaking wet blouse and threw it in my face. Bus always did his best to smooth things over when his wife was out of earshot, and to attempt to make me feel less unwelcome. She often vented her anger on him as well, and I guess we tried, as fellow victims, to help one another.

A good part of the problem was my utter ineptitude. I had never been trained to do housework of any kind. I was always the child-minder at home—in the days when we had a home. My older sister, Myrtle, had been the ever-efficient cook's helper and cleaner. In fact, I was so little inclined to the typical female pursuits that, when the time came for me to study home economics in grade eight, I had opted instead to be the first and only female in the Oyen junior-high school to insist on signing up for industrial arts. So I was quite unprepared, in both skills and motivation, for the tasks required of me by Dot—other than the babysitting, which I enjoyed.

Three very specific and vivid memories of my seven-month stay with the Richards family in Saskatoon come to mind. One concerns a bout of dreadful illness, which was finally diagnosed as 'yellow jaundice', or what is now known as hepatitis. This eventually proved to have caused long-term damage to my liver and, for most of my life, I suffered from an inability to digest animal fats. The upside has been that, even in old age, I have not had to worry about high cholesterol—nor have I ever been bothered by weight problems. The second memory is very different, but not much more comfortable. My best pal from school lived directly across the street from us. Without telling me, she hatched a plan to get back at my aunt for her treatment of me. At Christmas time this friend slipped a greeting card for 'Mrs. Dorothy Richards' into their mail slot, with a comically insulting message on it—supposedly from her 'henpecked' husband. The plan backfired, however, as Dot was convinced from the moment she laid eyes on it that I was the culprit, and I was made to suffer the full force of her explosive temper.

The third memory concerns Max McCurdy. Very soon after my departure from Veteran I had received a warm letter from him, and our correspondence continued during the months to come. He joined the RCAF shortly after we parted company and, because he was already trained as a pilot, was almost immediately shipped overseas. Our letters were actually journals in which we described everything in our daily lives. The result was that, throughout the following year, we became even closer than before.

By Easter of 1942 I was only too happy for the chance to join up once more with the rest of my family. They had been reunited in Biggar, Saskatchewan, where my father, Lew, had finally managed to locate a full-time job as a mechanic in the local garage. So the last few months of my grade-ten year were spent in the Biggar high school. I worked at the garage during the late spring and ensuing summer. Then, as it became obvious that Lew's health problems were increasingly threatening his ability to continue with the strenuous labour demanded of him at the garage, my mother decided to re-locate once more. In early August she took the two youngest boys and left Biggar for a housekeeping job on a farm a short distance from the Alberta foothills, to the west of the village of Cremona, which is located near Carstairs. At the end of the month I joined them and managed to find work for the harvest season in the same district.

It was in the midst of this action-packed period that devastating news came about Max. One day in late-August I was notified that the Lancaster bomber in which he operated as a tail gunner had been shot down over Germany. A week after that, I received a birthday present from him with his final letter. The gift was a beautiful silver pen-and-pencil set. And, only a few days later, another package arrived: this one containing my letters to him. The sense of extreme loss is with me still. During all the years to follow, with any and every reference to young lives snuffed out in battle, I think of Max—and I feel the tears well up from somewhere deep inside. For me, the untimely death of this fine young human being serves as the very epitome of the tragedy and senselessness of war.

It was not until the beginning of November of 1942 that my harvest job finished and I was able to begin grade-eleven classes in the town of Carstairs, Alberta. Once more, I was working for my board and room. Unfortunately, the family with whom I lived provided a climate even more uncomfortable than had my aunt. Again, the man of the house was most helpful and sympathetic. This time there was nothing personal about the wife's attitude toward me. It was just that she made it very plain that I was in their home in the role of a servant, and should behave accordingly. She would often meet me immediately outside the school door with the two small children in tow, letting me know I was responsible for them during the remainder of the day and evening. That would not have been so bad had I not also been expected to help cook the dinner and do any of the daily housework she had failed to complete. But at least she always provided me with explicit orders, which I was all-too-happy to follow, given my general ignorance about such matters.

I learned at once that I was not allowed to eat with the rest of the family in the dining room. For some reason this struck me as the most insulting of all the treatment meted out to me in any of my work situations. My weekends were devoted to general tasks such as doing the laundry and giving the entire house a thorough cleaning. I developed the habit of taking advantage of the family's record collection when I was alone in the house with the children—or when only the husband was at home—and was absolutely thrilled with the classical music. I had never before had the opportunity to get acquainted with Beethoven and Mozart, for instance. However, my lady boss came in unexpectedly one day and discovered me listening to her music as I scrubbed the floor. I was informed, in no uncertain terms, that the record player was out of bounds for me.

Sometime early in the year of 1943 I came to the realization that there was simply no way I could make top marks in my courses if I remained in that house. Luckily, by this time I had a good friend at school who was able to persuade her parents to take me in. In exchange for room and board with them, I did whatever chores I could, and we all got along just fine. For some reason what I remember most clearly about my stay there is the big bowl of oatmeal porridge with which we began each day, and the wonderful apricots preserved in jars with almonds and dates added. I used the same recipe for many years to come. It was fortunate for me that I had made the move when I did, for this family proved to be most supportive when the disaster of my father's death occurred in April.

My mother and I had visited him on a Saturday in his small apartment room in Calgary only about a month before he died. I was forced to leave for Carstairs the following day, so as not to miss school on Monday morning, and he took me to the station on his way to work. How I have wished ever since that I had realized what he was attempting to communicate: that he was telling me a final goodbye! As the train approached he gave me some money, and then drew me to him. He hugged me closely—something that was just not done in our family—and then he spoke slowly and softly.

"Tell the boys to be sure to go into science," were the words I heard. "That's where the future lies."

Sadly, in my teen-aged self-absorption, I was overwhelmed with puzzlement and anger because of his apparent assumption that I, as a girl, could not also contemplate studying science. It surprised me as well, for he had always been far ahead of his time in treating me exactly like the boys, as far as intellectual—and even physical—expectations went, and in encouraging me to feel equal to males in every way. Thus, in that moment of parting, his comment had inadvertently taken my attention away from the impending tragedy implied by what I was to realize, in retrospect, were intended to be his final words of farewell. Offended by his apparent favouring of the boys, I turned and rushed off to board the train. I was to be haunted for many years by the deep sense of loss at my father's death. It was a loss made more bitter by the fact that I hadn't said a proper goodbye to him; that I had, instead, merely struck off blithely with a casual wave of the hand, not realizing that the chance for a meaningful farewell would never come again.

One of my friends at the school in Carstairs during this trying period was Vern Wishart, the son of the local United Church minister. Vern was later to become the head of the United Church in Canada. However, the chief reason I have remembered him all these years is not due to his subsequent accomplishments, nor to any particularly close relationship between us that year at school. Rather, it is the fact that Vern unknowingly took the summer job which I had managed to arrange for earlier. By this time I was well-experienced in planning ahead, and had sought out one of the local storekeepers early in the spring to ask if I could work for him during July and August. He had promised me the job was mine. The sense of security this provided no doubt helped me navigate the extremely difficult months following my father's death.

Somehow I managed to persevere and to complete all my class work. When the final exams were marked I was probably more surprised than anyone to learn that I had made honours in almost everything. However, an unexpected shock awaited me when the report cards were handed out on the last day of school. I discovered that I had not received credit for one of the key grade-eleven courses. Assuming this was an accident, I rushed into the principal's office to inform him of the obvious error. This principal was an Aboriginal man—one of the very few to have made it to a successful position in any organization in those days. It had never entered my head for a moment that the omission had been intentional. But if the bizarre thought had occurred, I would have expected that someone with his background of experienced injustice would have been the very last to be responsible for such a thing. But I would have been wrong! He ushered me to a seat in a rather officious manner.

I was then informed that, because I had begun the year's work so late in the autumn, I was not present the number of days required for any student carrying a full load of courses. Therefore, he said, the rule about attendance dictated that I could not be given credit for all of them. It was as simple as that! After all, he said, that rule was very important and necessary, as its purpose was to prevent students from taking on more work than they were able to handle.

"But . . . but I made either honours or 'A's in all my courses! Doesn't that indicate that I was able to handle the full load of courses in spite of having to start school over two months late?" I asked, bewildered by his logic.

"That has nothing whatsoever to do with it. My first duty is to see that rules are not overlooked or disobeyed."

This was a body blow to me at the time, coming as it did so soon after my father's sudden death. And it was not that the man didn't know about the tragedy. My mother had contacted the school before she came into Carstairs to pick me up on her way to Calgary on that terrible day, and I had been called to the principal's office to hear the news from this very person. What his current decision meant was that I would be one crucial course short—and thus unable to graduate—at the end of my grade-twelve year. If I was even allowed to enter grade twelve without that required course! However, there was to be an upside to this disaster. I didn't realize it until many years later, but the insight provided by this experience was one of the best gifts a future educator could possibly have gained. I have used it countless times in classes as an example of the typical bureaucratic mind-set: of the way administrators all-too-often tend to substitute the mere slavish following of a rule for the objective that the rule was originally intended to achieve.

It was only a few days after this that I received another piece of devastating news. I had gone to see the storekeeper who had promised me the summer job, to check on when I should begin. With considerable embarrassment he told me that he had given the job, instead, to my friend Vern. He explained why he had felt unable to refuse Reverend Wishart's request that the job be assigned to his son rather than to me.

"After all," he said, "I'm a member of that church, and you just don't turn down your minister when he asks for a special favour." The following day, I received a visit from the minister's wife. Somewhat shamefacedly, she handed me a large bag and then rushed off. In it were a bunch of worn-looking second-hand clothes which had been donated to the church. So much for Christian benevolence!

This last blow proved to be one too many. I felt as if life had literally beaten me into the ground. I was forced to the devastating conclusion that higher education, and the opportunities to which it led, was simply not an option. The message had come through loud and clear by then. The finer things of life were available to people such as Vern Wishart, but they were not for the likes of me. From that moment on, without having made any conscious decision, I gave up on the idea of ever finishing high school.

Needless to say, I did not remain in Carstairs very long after this incident. I took the train into Calgary and, in my desperation, decided to risk asking my aunt Dot if I could stay with her and little Beverley, while hunting for a job. Bus had been shipped overseas by then, after having been moved temporarily to the Air Force base near Calgary. This base was part of the Commonwealth Air Training Plan which resulted in young men from all over the world being located near certain Western Canadian cities. Dot and Beverley were now alone in their small, rented house in the city. Her greeting, when I appeared without warning, was all-too-typical, and would have caused an abrupt about-turn on my part had I any other place to go.

"I was saying only yesterday," she exclaimed upon sighting me, "that if any more relatives arrived on my doorstep with a suitcase in hand, I'd just bang the door in their faces!"

But she didn't, and instead I was allowed to come inside. I had come to realize, by then, that Dot's bark was usually worse than her bite. She had a tiny spare room in the basement which was reluctantly assigned to me, on the understanding that I would pay her $7.00 a week for my bed and board. I immediately began my search for a job that would provide at least that much. Myrtle was then living in Calgary, so I asked her for advice. In order to supplement her meager allowance from the RCAF, she had obtained a housekeeping job with a relatively wealthy family. They allowed her to keep her baby with her in her room within their home. She gave me some leads in locating work. My first job was cleaning bathrooms in a hotel, which I discovered was not the most desirable task in the world, but at least it allowed me to pay Dot her weekly board money.

A few weeks later I managed to obtain a position in a drugstore where Myrtle had previously worked. This drugstore, like many in those days, operated a short-order restaurant along one side. I was to receive $8.00 a week, and have one day off. These sums now seem pitifully small, but in the summer of 1943 the dollar bought a lot more than it does today. I was relieved to learn that my pay would cover the cost of my room and board at Dot's, with a little change left over. I actually enjoyed my various tasks at the restaurant. I quickly mastered the preparation of the 'fast-food' snacks in which the bar specialized, and became quite proud of my newfound cooking skills. However, the endless dishwashing by hand, to which I was assigned, left much to be desired. One day I became so exhausted I fainted into the sink, and recovered consciousness flat on the floor in front of it. I learned many years later that my blood pressure tended to be lower than normal, and this caused fainting spells whenever my system became overly stressed.

An incident occurred that summer for which I have never been able to forgive myself and for which, I suspect, my brother Bob never forgave me either. Another bitter memory of lost opportunities! Bob dropped into the drugstore one day. He was spending his school holiday visiting our mother and younger brothers on the Graham farm and helping with the chores. Overwhelmed with the usual busyness of the job, I could afford to spend little time talking to him. However, I told him to order whatever he wished for his lunch and I would look after the cost. Some time later, in the midst of preparing a rush order, I looked up in response to a flurry of activity by the outside door. Bob was being grabbed by the manager, and accused of trying to sneak out without paying his bill. By the time I could leave the frying pan and rush out to explain, he had paid and disappeared. My negligence in the matter had caused a result so egregiously embarrassing for someone with Bob's sensitivities that I decided perhaps the best thing I could do then was not ever to let him know what I had witnessed. I think now that I was wrong. I should have phoned out to the farm that night and apologized.

On the brighter side, the job offered many advantages and memorable experiences. An example was the opportunity it provided for me to meet and converse with airmen from other countries of the Commonwealth, and to become adept at deciphering—and recognizing—their various accents. I also learned a lot about those countries: in particular, New Zealand and Australia.

Life was becoming increasingly difficult at the Richards home, however. I think what bothered me most was Dot's habit of complaining about the amount of food I ate. As harvest time approached in mid-August, I began to consider the possibility of escape. If I could find work on a farm for a couple of months it would be possible for me to earn a considerably increased wage. Dot told me she had friends who farmed between Calgary and Drumheller, on some of the most fertile land in Alberta. She contacted them and arranged that I meet them one day at the hotel at which they had spent the previous night. On the strength of their promise to hire me, I quit my drugstore job. The day I was to join them I discovered that, after paying Dot her weekly board money, I had only one twenty-five cent piece left in my purse. My pride wouldn't allow me to ask her for anything. The quarter would pay for the bus ride downtown, but if things didn't work out, I would have no safe way to return at night to the shelter—such as it was—of Dot's basement. I decided I simply could not bear to remain there without paying my way, so would take the gamble. After packing my small store of precious possessions in my one and only small cardboard suitcase, I set off.

The couple whom I met at the hotel that evening struck me at once as somewhat strange. I think now that, had I possessed the return bus fare, I would probably have beaten a hasty retreat. They were ready to leave the hotel by the time I arrived, so we went immediately to their car. They instructed me to place my suitcase on the floor in front of the back seat and to get in beside it. So I did, trying to relax and anticipate a reasonably pleasant journey to the country. But the car headed, not to the highway leading east, but downtown to the squalid area of the city centre which I had always strictly avoided. It was soon parked near one of the tougher hotels. I was given no option but to accompany the couple inside for 'one for the road'.

At the beginning, I wasn't too worried because I was thirsty and really appreciated the bottle of 'pop' which they bought for me at my insistence, after their failed attempt to press beer upon me. But I became increasingly uncomfortable as my companions continued drinking. It must have been at least an hour before they finally got up to go. Then, when we arrived at the car, we discovered that they had neglected to lock it. At my stunned exclamation, they said they weren't concerned because nothing of value had been left in it. Only the little suitcase, with all of my worldly possessions! And it was gone!

I don't remember anything about the trip to the farm, other than some rather scary driving and a deathly silence filled with my private grief at this terrible, and terrifying, loss. Much more difficult to bear than the fact that I was heading into unknown territory in the company of a couple of weird strangers—utterly broke with nothing except the clothes on my back—was the realization that my treasured keepsakes were gone forever. Among these was my father's last letter home, with the final words, "I'll find steady work and send you more money or I'll die in the attempt". And there was the only surviving copy of a particular photo of him which I had loved. And my Governor General's Medal. And there was the packet of letters from Max, and mine to him. And his birthday gift of the exquisite silver pen-and-pencil set.

We finally arrived at the farm and disembarked. Upon entry to the house, the woman showed me into the bathroom first. I noticed only one rather dingy towel and washcloth, and asked if I could have a set for myself, to keep in my room. She replied gruffly that one towel was all they ever used at a time in that house, and I'd better get used to it. Then she took me into the bedroom which was to be mine. With a mumbled goodnight, she handed me a key and told me in an urgent tone to be sure to lock my door. As I lay sleepless an hour or so later, I realized there was good reason for this advice. Someone tried several times to get into the room.

The following month or so of harvest proved to be an exciting and even, at times, somewhat perilous experience. I had to watch the farm owner like a hawk, as he was continuously making sexual overtures when his wife wasn't around, and attempting to enter my bedroom at night. A couple of his harvest workers were no better. One of my routine tasks was to take the noon meal out to the field for the men. I didn't fully realize how dangerous this was until one day when I set out in the truck with one of these farmhands. I could see the combine working some distance to the northwest. However, to my growing discomfort, I began to notice that our truck was heading in the opposite direction, toward a vast, unoccupied field of summer fallow. By the time the driver stopped the vehicle I was prepared, and tried to leap out the door before we ground to a halt. But he was ready as well, and was soon upon me. Fortunately I was athletic and stronger than most girls my age, and put up a fierce battle. I was gradually losing, however, and he was at the point of tearing off my clothes when I heard the roar of another truck. It was the most welcome sound imaginable, as was the shout of the man who emerged from it on the run.

"Get off her, you dirty bastard!" This fierce shout came from the runner, whom I recognized as one of the other workers, as he leapt toward us and began to wrestle with the would-be rapist. I was so thankful I could scarcely speak, but did manage to ask my rescuer how he had known what was going on. He said he'd just happened to glance over toward the farmstead, anticipating dinner, when he saw the truck heading in the wrong direction. Fortunately for me, he guessed at once what was occurring. My attacker apparently had been bragging about what he intended to do to me whenever he got the chance. I found it difficult to serve this despicable fellow that night at the supper table, and during the following weeks; but realized that reporting him to the boss would be worse than useless. I was relieved to note that, from that day on, my young hero appointed himself the one and only person who would drive the truck back to the house for me and the hot food which I helped the farmer's wife prepare each mid-day for the threshing crew.

Another source of excitement and grave concern was the outbreak of a prairie fire only a few miles from the farm where I worked. One day we looked out window and saw that the entire horizon appeared to be ablaze. Every crew from the farms for miles around immediately stopped harvesting and rushed to fight the fire. Fortunately, it was extinguished before it reached us, but the event was a disaster for some of the neighbouring farmers who lost their entire year's production of ripe wheat. Not too long after this, the last of my employers' crop was in the bin and I was paid and taken back to Calgary. To my relief, the farmer's wife made sure that she came along on the trip. They deposited me at Dot's house. There they were welcomed much more warmly by Dot than was I, and all three promptly proceeded to head downtown for a drinking bout in celebration of the end of harvest. I was thankful to settle down with little Beverley.

I made Dot happy by almost immediately locating another job. It was at a butcher shop. From the very first day, the butcher was so kind to me I could scarcely believe my good fortune. He viewed me as being far too thin and obviously undernourished. I had never dared ask Dot if I could make a lunch and take it to work but, anyway, this new boss informed me that would not be necessary. He encouraged me to help myself to the pre-cooked snacks sold over the counter; and even more enticing was his open invitation to cook myself hot meals of fresh sausages and steak. All the while he'd be exclaiming, "Somebody's got to feed you up!"

I learned a great deal at this job. For example, I handled the turkeys and chickens from the moment they arrived. I would remove the feathers and 'draw' the interior parts, then hang the birds in the exactly right temperature for exactly the required time. In addition to serving customers, I learned how to prepare all the various cuts of meat and to arrange them on the shelves for sale. I was also taught to make the sausages, in huge quantities and more varieties than I had ever known existed. In order to accomplish all this I had to hustle large quarters of beef and pork from one location to another. I managed that as well, disregarding a number of warning signals from my lower back. Through it all, I came to see that butcher as more of a friend and mentor than the sort of boss I had been accustomed to in the world of work. I wish now that I had told him how much his kindness and concern meant to me, but it was not my way.

Throughout the fall and winter of 1943-44, the lives of the remainder of my family were fully as hectic as my own. That autumn Bob started high school, along with our cousin Thelma. As no secondary education was available in Caroline, their nearest village, the two of them were sent to an all-girl's boarding school some distance away. The arrangement was that Bob, as the lone male student in the institution, was to do the chores in order to earn his board and room. In his spare time he made some spending money by shooting crows and being paid a few cents for each pair of claws. Apparently this, along with remuneration for gopher tails, was arranged by the provincial government through the school system.

My mother had taken the two younger boys and abruptly left the Graham farm in the Cremona area sometime late that previous summer. She never discussed the reason, but I suspect that she found herself in the position of being forced to consider marriage to Tom Graham, the elder of the two sons of the old man, if she were to remain. Tom was a very decent person, somewhat younger than she, but sadly lacking in general knowledge and quite limited intellectually. No doubt seeking to escape the developing situation, Mama responded to a newspaper advertisement for a housekeeping job on the farm of a Mr. Parrish, near Vulcan, to the south of Calgary. Don, who had been attending Big Prairie School a few miles from the Cremona farm, was once again uprooted. Still an independent little loner, he had successfully completed both grade three and four in the one year. Unfortunately, however, he was not able to attend school in September at their new location. He was required to look after four-year-old Jerry, for one thing, and the only school was some distance away.

Altogether, the position at the farm near Vulcan proved most unsatisfactory, so my poor, brave mother was forced to pull up stakes once more. Yet again, by means of answering an advertisement in *The Western Producer*, she managed to locate a job—this one on the Ullry farm in the Olds district between Calgary and Edmonton. They arrived there just after Christmas. Don was at least able to continue with his schooling at the new location. However, his travels to and fro, as well as his experience in the Hainstock country school, were to prove utterly terrifying for him. The bullying of unprotected little boys who were intellectually inclined was the norm in country schools in those days. He just didn't fit in and was made to suffer for it. As seeding time approached, Mama must have come to the conclusion that she had no choice but to return to the Graham farm. Mr. McCurdy had kept in touch with her ever since her sojourn with him, and I suspect that he would like to have married her. I've always felt it would have been a wonderful thing for all of us if she had gone to him instead. But the fib she had told when she worked for him, about having been a widow at that time with only the two children, was probably an insurmountable obstacle for her. My mother was never one to admit to her minor dishonesties once she had thoughtlessly committed them. So she headed back to Cremona and to the future awaiting her there: to another loveless marriage (at least, on her side) from which she now believed there was no escape, if she were to provide an acceptable home and livelihood for her children.

For my sister Myrtle and older brother Jack, the winter and spring of that year was a difficult period as well. The only means available for Myrtle to ensure security for her baby and herself was to work as a housekeeper. Her lady boss was of the same mold as the one I had known in Carstairs, with even greater illusions of superiority to the working class. And I had grave concerns for the future of her marriage after witnessing something which I kept a secret for many years. On his one and only visit back to see her and his baby, her husband Bill told her he had to leave the very next day, mentioning a time of departure when she happened to be tied up with her housekeeping duties. On hearing about this, I quietly decided that I would surprise him by seeing him off, as it was on a Sunday when I had some free time. An old Oyen friend of mine, Colleen Trewin, was in town, so the two of us went to the railroad station at the appointed time. Upon sighting Bill just as he departed the crowded waiting room, we began to fight our way through it and toward the platform. Then I noticed that, rather than preparing to board the train as we had expected, he was meeting someone—a young woman. They grasped one another lovingly and then headed back toward the waiting room. Colleen and I followed silently until we saw them leave the station, still hugging one another.

The entire episode was rendered doubly difficult to forget by something else that happened. As we tried to navigate the almost immovable shoulder-to-shoulder crowd of people on our way out of the station, I reached into my pocket, searching frantically for a handkerchief to wipe away the tears brought on by what I had just witnessed; and by what I felt it boded for the future of Myrtle and little Linda. Suddenly the woman next to me began to shout, "Help! Pickpocket!" Apparently it was in her pocket rather than my own that my fingers had been groping. Exactly as a guilty person would have done, I made a rapid escape, with my friend Colleen—utterly confounded by now—running in my wake.

My brother Jack's experiences, and my own part in them, were an even more immediate source of worry. Late one afternoon when I came home from work I discovered him hovering in the bushes near the back door leading directly into my little room in the basement of Dot's house. His uniform was bedraggled and dirty, and he was obviously in desperate need of food and shelter. He begged me to allow him to stay. "But don't tell anyone I'm here," he warned.

So began what was probably the most desperate of my many efforts to protect Jack. Apparently things had gone badly for him in the army. He told me that the other men were always beating on him and the officers were always shouting at him and punishing him and he didn't understand why. I learned that he had gone absent without leave from the base, and could not face returning.

The following few weeks were a nightmare, as I had to smuggle food and drink into my room for him and share my couch with him at night. I was forced to sneak him in after dark every evening and then out again before daylight in the morning; as well as cover for him when he had to go to the one and only bathroom in the house. I would typically go up and engage Dot in conversation some place as far as possible away from the bathroom, then go to it myself for the requisite flushing operations as soon as Jack had time to finish and quietly descend once more to the basement. As always, he was like a helpless child, driven to act recklessly with no thought of consequences for others, or even for himself.

This impossible state of affairs continued until a few days after I had finally decided to discuss it on the phone with Mama, who was by then back in Cremona country and married to Tom. She and the two little boys were living with him in their still-unfinished house on one of the quarter-sections of land which he owned. Then one night I waited in vain for the usual tentative tapping at my door signaling Jack's evening arrival. I lay awake, expecting him any moment, through the long hours of darkness. But he failed to appear that night, or on any of the nights thereafter. Finally I received a phone call from him. Our mother had 'turned him in' he told me bitterly. I was initially appalled at the possibility, but came to realize that she must have felt there was simply no alternative. She was aware, as I was not, that he was still merely 'AWL' but would soon be in quite another category: the criminal one of 'deserter'. Especially when the country was engaged in war, this would result in serious jail time—if not worse. Apparently, the military police had been waiting for Jack at Dot's back door on the evening he disappeared from my world. He was being shipped overseas the following day, he said. And so he was, just in time to join the Canadian forces for the invasion of Europe in early June.

All these experiences were taking their toll on me, I guess, but no doubt what finally did me in was the physical stress placed on my slight body by the heavy lifting at work. One day I felt an unbearable stab of pain in my lower back, followed by an inability to stand upright or even sit or move my legs. My boss drove me back to Dot's where, after a few days flat in bed, I came to the realization that I would have to quit the job at the butcher shop and find refuge somewhere until it was possible to move without severe pain. Mama informed me that Tom said I was welcome to stay with them.

The trip out to Tom Graham's newly established house and yard was agonizing. Dot helped me to the station and on to the train. At the Carstairs end, I had arranged to be met by my best friend from my school days there. She persuaded her father to drive me the rest of the way. During the seemingly interminable journey out to the village of Cremona, and then over the bridge on the Little Red Deer River and to the farmstead with its small house and barnyard a couple of miles beyond, I writhed in excruciating pain at every bump and twist in the rough dirt road. And all the while, my friend filled the car with a glowing account of the happy event she had attended the previous afternoon and evening. It had been the day of the grade-twelve graduation in Carstairs.

# Chapter 7

# A TIME OF HOPE

I began the summer holiday period of 1944 in a partially crippled condition, due to a back injury sustained while working at a Calgary butcher shop. However, generally healthy teenagers tend to recover fast, and I was no exception. I enjoyed the chance to spend some time with my mother and younger brothers at their brand-new farm home, and to get acquainted with their neighbours. Don was then ten years old, and had been happy to return to Big Prairie School to complete his grade five year, after their difficult wanderings in search of an alternative home. Jerry had just turned six, and would begin school in September. Bob, the brother two years younger than I, had come down for one of his holiday visits from our aunt and uncle's place near Caroline as well. My mother, clearly happy to have finally provided a secure home for her children, seemed more settled and relaxed than I had ever known her. So we were able to enjoy what amounted to a brief reunion for the majority of our usually scattered family. Looking back now on this relatively serene time, I am amazed that we—along with other Canadians—were utterly unaware of the grisly fact that millions of Jews were being shipped by railway to death camps during that very summer. It was a world away: a world which we could not have imagined in our darkest nightmares.

The closest thing to a nightmare for me during that period was an experience with an angry bull. I had found a summer job at a neighbouring farm, where I lived with the family who owned it. I helped with the chores indoors and out, including the daily milking of three cows. My adventure occurred one morning as I was sitting on the milk stool, relaxing to the rhythm of the pulling of teats and the rewarding accompaniment of duly spurting milk. Suddenly my cow jumped and mooed, and I looked up just as a bull, with head lowered threateningly, entered the barn door and began to advance upon us. I leapt to my feet and ran out the opposite door, closing it behind me a bare instant before the by-now raging bull reached it. Then I raced around and secured the other door, again just in time to trap him inside. The farmer appeared soon and was able to quiet the animal and get him safely closeted, but I lived in fear of that creature for the remainder of my time there. This man assured me it was the cow that the bull was interested in, but I was unconvinced. However, I was able to join him in a good laugh about it all. Once more I had a very kind employer. During the brief time I worked for this farmer he also taught me to drive—both his truck and car—a skill that was to prove most beneficial for me in the years ahead.

I enjoyed all of the friends I made in the Big Prairie and Cremona community that summer. My employers also encouraged me to ride one of their horses in my spare time—bareback, of course. I greatly appreciated that, as I hadn't had a chance to do much riding since leaving Lonely Trail for the small village of Oyen several years earlier. They also took me to a number of barn dances. These occurred in a community hall that had actually been an old barn. It was in bush country in the foothills to the west of us, which everybody referred to as 'back west'. The folks living there had remained relatively isolated and seldom traveled even as far east as Cremona. They were the nearest approximation to hillbillies I have ever known. I discovered that I loved square dancing: something at which the 'back-westers' excelled. One evening an acquaintance, who was a good singer, was invited to perform during a break from dancing and—to my embarrassment, as I was definitely not a good singer—she insisted that I join her. We sang Danny Boy, with me having to slip into the alto on the high notes. To my relief, it went over well with the apparently undiscriminating audience.

Another friend whom I met at these dances was a young man from a farm to the northwest of town. He indicated rather quickly that he would like to go 'steady' with me, but I was not ready for anything like that. On our first date he took me along to what turned out to be a meeting of his family church. It was fascinating to me from a disinterested observer viewpoint, but rather horrifying in its implications. It made me realize anew how charismatic leaders can so easily incite a crowd of gullible believers to follow in whatever bizarre direction they might wish to lead them. The experience shed light for me on the process by which most of the German people had come to support Hitler and his Nazi regime Those attending this affair were gathered in a large circle holding hands and, while I was puzzling over this and feeling decidedly embarrassed at being a part of it, I was startled to hear everyone around me suddenly begin wailing and 'speaking in tongues'. The experience confirmed me strongly in my distaste for myths concerning the supernatural, and in my uneasy feelings about this particular suitor.

Sometime during August I received a letter from my grandmother, urging me to join her in Oyen in order to resume my high-school studies there. She told me she needed my help. However, I guessed that what had motivated the request was mainly concern for me, as the family had all been told that her eldest son, Ed, came in from the farm every week to do her heavy chores. By then I was only too happy to accept the kind offer for, as I approached my eighteenth birthday after a year as a high-school drop-out, an indefinite future as a either a waitress or a farmhand and kitchen chore-girl was rapidly losing whatever appeal it may have had.

From the moment I arrived by train in Oyen and walked through town to the furthermost outskirts where I reached the Armitage house, my world seemed to take a turn for the better. My grandmother, Ma, was clearly happy to have me with her, and I could see at once that I was actually needed. It was no doubt an indication of increased maturity that I found myself chuckling at those of her characteristic habits and mannerisms which had sometimes annoyed me during previous visits. The old organ was a welcome sight, in spite of Ma's stipulation that I must never play anything but hymns on a Sunday. She informed me at once of another rule that must be obeyed. I would not be allowed to go out in the evening, except for school-based affairs. "You just don't know the pitfalls," she muttered darkly. Rather than becoming annoyed and rebellious at this point, as I might have done a few years earlier, I merely found myself amused.

"I'm afraid," I told her, "that I know much more about those pitfalls than you could ever imagine. And I'm quite happy to have an excuse for avoiding them now."

I missed a number of my closest acquaintances from primary-school and junior high days. Both Lucille Willeson and Josie Kruski were now in training for their future occupations: Lucille as a nurse and Josie as a secretary. However, I connected immediately with a couple of my former friends who had been a grade behind me throughout my childhood, but who would now be in the same class. One was a jolly, short and plump, red-haired girl named Connie Munroe. The other was Anne Gibson, who became my closest pal and a life-long friend. It was Anne's family who put me in touch with the man who was to prove the most helpful and loyal of supporters throughout that momentous year. He was Jimmie Wong, the proprietor of the town's only Chinese restaurant. Every prairie village had one Chinese restaurant in those days. Anne's brother Gordon had worked for Jimmie during his high-school years, and was now off to the University of Alberta where he was eventually to graduate as a medical doctor. Anne and I applied for Gordon's job at the restaurant and were immediately hired to help out after school and on weekends. I was overjoyed at this opportunity, not only to earn some money for necessary clothes and books, but also for sharing with Anne the honour of being the first non-Asian females in the entire vicinity ever to work in a Chinese restaurant.

School was wonderful from the very first day. I was happy to learn that a favourite teacher from my junior-high years, Harold Hall, was still at Oyen. He was now teaching science and math in the high school. Mr. Hall welcomed me back literally with open arms. My second discovery was that we had the most remarkable school principal imaginable. His name was Maurice Freehill. After discussing my academic record with Mr. Hall, this principal made the decision to allow me to carry one extra math course to make up for that which had been so unfairly taken from me at my previous school in Carstairs. In addition to his administrative duties, Mr. Freehill taught the required grade-twelve English language course as well as a 'Survey of English Literature'. He also offered two other optional courses: drama and acrobatics! In addition to geometry, algebra, biology, history and typing, I chose to take all four of his courses. And what an experience that proved to be!

What was it about these two teachers that made them so special? And how did it come about that both happened to be working in this mediocre little school in the tiny prairie village of Oyen: a village without even a dentist or doctor? It's possible that the very fact that few opportunities existed for gifted people in that place and time meant that a large proportion of them fell into teaching as a career. For me, the sheer luck of the draw played a large part in it for, by the end of the term, Maurice Freehill had left Canada for better opportunities elsewhere. Mr. Hall, on the other hand, was to continue as a leading light and mentor for younger teachers throughout the entire Acadia School Division for many years to come. Both men were multi-talented and student-oriented, while at the same time demanding a high standard of accomplishment from those they taught. Both possessed that essential ingredient of good teaching: the ability to stand in the shoes of the learner and to begin the teaching process from 'where the learner's at'. They certainly did that for me.

There was something else that made the year especially memorable for me. One of my closest cousins, Wendell Carry from Acadia Valley, was attending high school in Oyen as well. Although a year younger than I, he was now in the same grade, and was taking many of the same classes. Furthermore, he lived in a boarding house only a few blocks from us. This meant that he spent a lot of time at Ma's place, and we fell into the habit of studying together in the evenings. One of the traits I had always appreciated about Wendell was his mischievous sense of humour. And, as well as being highly intelligent, he was extremely gifted musically. In fact, he had been playing the saxophone from a very young age. One of his favourite ploys in class was to produce a tune with his tongue by manipulating a thin wire in his teeth—all the while giving the impression of being innocently absorbed in his work. The teacher would look around the room with a puzzled expression, and we fellow students would pretend not to hear the sound.

Wendell also liked to make naughtily hilarious comments to me under his breath when the two of us were home with Ma because he knew that, due to her increasing deafness, she could not hear him. He invariably had me in stitches, while poor Ma could only look on with a puzzled, and decidedly suspicious, expression. Because his remarks were often aimed at Ma and her cooking, I always felt guilty about laughing. But I simply could not resist his humour. For example, she had a habit of cooking prunes for almost every meal—an imperative that any older person will understand but which we, in our youthful ignorance and arrogance, viewed as merely one of her comically puzzling quirks. She even baked prune pies, which seemed to us to be approaching the limit of the totally bizarre.

I now realize that Ma was far ahead of her time where healthful eating was concerned. She was opposed to the pan-frying of food, and the very concept of deep-fat frying almost reduced her to shock. Her sole method of cooking anything and everything was slow steaming on top of the stove. Her typical meal was this appropriately 'boiled' beef or chicken with onions, mashed potatoes and cabbage, accompanied by prune pie with an inordinately tough—probably almost lard-less—crust. We also had lots of rhubarb and other local fruit in season for desserts. Although I would not have admitted it to Wendell, I genuinely looked forward to her suppers, as I was always starving by then. For lunch she usually made herself meat-and-vegetable soup from leftovers, while I rushed downtown to Jimmie's where I grabbed a bite during work. And every Sunday at noon Jimmie sent me home to collect her and bring her back to his restaurant. There he would serve us a free meal of whatever we selected from his menu.

That year I learned much from Jimmie that was to prove helpful in later life. Among the many valuable lessons he taught me during my tenure with him was that coffee should always be made fresh with each order, and that it must be brought to a full boil in a small saucepan and then served at once. There were no electric coffee-making machines in those days. He also inspired me to acquire some ability at manipulating chopsticks, and at eating soupy food from a bowl held close to the mouth. Those wonderful, nourishing meals of his are probably the reason why one of my favourite foods to this day is Chinese—especially Mandarin. This is the official language of China today, but because most immigrants to Canada in the years since my youth have been from Hong Kong and southern China, where the language and cooking are Cantonese, Mandarin restaurants became increasingly rare in Canada. In one of our quiet times, Jimmie told me about how he had been forced to pay a burdensome Head Tax when he immigrated, and of how the Chinese Exclusion Act of the time had prevented him from bringing his wife with him to his new country. It was a sad story, and I was fighting back the tears by the end of it.

Because of Ma's curfew I was not able to take part in much of the town's evening social life. I didn't mind this, as there was the most remarkable organization formed that year—our Canada Club—centred around our high school activities. Much of the leadership for this group was provided by our wonderful school principal and teacher, Maurice Freehill.

We had only three male students in grade twelve, including Wendell and a pleasant, athletic farm boy called Bud Thygeson. The other candidates were either already in the war or had dropped out to work at home on the surrounding farms. Years later, my friend Anne asked me if I recalled the third boy: the one who was "so crazy about you", as she put it. His name was Wesley Johnson. He was a scholarly type, and we actually had many interests in common—except that I considered him a bit too doctrinaire in his socialist views. I did my best to discourage him, as I had no intention at that time, with Max still so deeply entrenched in my memory, of getting romantically involved. At any rate, I had more than enough men to handle at the restaurant every day. My previous on-the-job training in dealing with sexually aggressive moves in a joking manner—while at the same time avoiding offence—once more stood me in good stead. In those days a waitress was almost universally considered 'fair game' for the working man in search of a little 'no-strings' sexual relief and entertainment.

School was pure joy, although I really had to work at the math. I found the typing course difficult as well, chiefly because we all had to share the one and only typewriter, and I was seldom able to take a turn at it due to my busy schedule. Wendell, on the other hand, excelled at typing. I also sat in on a class in Latin, although I didn't take it for credit. I wanted to get the feel of the language but, unfortunately, didn't succeed in learning very much. It was Mr. Freehill's classes that came to mean the most to me. English seemed to be my natural forte, and my goal in life at that time was to become a journalist. "Someday," this beloved teacher once told me, "you will be a writer." This was in spite of his previous horrified discovery that I had totally missed out on grammar on my spotty journey through a succession of high schools. He gave me a small book on the subject and would grill me once in a while after class about what appeared to me to be a profusion of unutterably boring and unnecessary details concerning verbs and nouns and predicates. After all, I just 'knew' what was correct by the feel of the sentences! I didn't need to be able to explain 'why' this was so!

'You may think not," was his reply to my complaint, "but the examiners marking the grade twelve Departmental finals might very well disagree."

One day Mr. Freehill gave us a poetry assignment. We were to write an original poem. He gave Wendell's and mine top marks, and read them aloud to the entire class. A good sign of how the very concept of poetry has changed since that time is the fact that what was evaluated highly then would not even be considered poetry today, due to the fact that it possessed all four of the then-recognized defining characteristics of that unique form of literature: rhyme, rhythm, a concise and meaningful message, and powerful imagery.

I managed to keep that particular poem all through the years to follow. It comes across now as a bit melancholy for an eighteen-year-old, but it was inspired by my experience of witnessing closely, and empathizing with, my grandmother's aging process. In addition, I suspect there is within it a reflection of the horrors of the war we were all then living through—and specifically, for me, a lingering sorrow concerning the death of my dear friend, Max McCurdy, a scant two years before. It probably reveals, as well, daily fears for my brother Jack who was, at that very time, somewhere at the front—participating in the ongoing invasion of Europe.

*EARLY FROST*

*The snow is on the grass again;*
*With grim finality the night*
*Has o'er the land a cover lain,*
*A cover cold and deathly white.*

*Was it not just a moment since*
*We felt the warmth of early morn—*

*When life was surging in our veins*
*And all our hopes and dreams were born?*

*Time was when time was limitless,*
*And bottomless the future's store;*
*When chances squandered recklessly*
*We dreamed that life would soon restore.*

*But all too soon the autumn winds*
*Blow cold and twilight follows day;*
*As, twisting in the webs we've spun,*
*We watch our future pass away.*

*Regret creeps in like early frost*
*Confirming what can never be,*
*And on the frozen pane we weave*
*For those to come a parting plea.*

*Live every moment to the full*
*Tho' it be drear and dark with pain,*
*For all too soon the days grow short*
*And snow is on the grass again.*

Actually, 'the snow was on the grass' even more directly for me at times that year. Perhaps it was the long hours I was putting in that had made my body vulnerable to certain infections somehow missed during my childhood. I was often short of sleep as well, as I loved to read books from the school library late into the night, in my bed and by the light of the 'coal-oil' (kerosene) lamp. So it was probably not surprising that I came down with a succession of illnesses, beginning with the red measles, which we had somehow missed at Lonely Trail School. Then came an intensely sore throat. Anne's parents, the Gibsons, kindly rushed me off to Cereal for treatment. I discovered that the doctor who had removed my tonsils many years previously had bungled the operation. As the current doctor painted my throat with iodine, he informed me that the inflamed roots of the tonsils remained, and would likely render me highly subject to such infections for the rest of my life. And he was right.

The third plague to down me was chicken pox: another one missed in childhood because of our farm-community's isolation. At Christmas time I had traveled by train back to Carstairs, in order to spend the holiday out at

Cremona with my mother and the boys. It happened that Mr. Freehill was heading for Calgary on the very same train. We had a glorious trip, filled with inspiring conversation which I have never forgotten. However, he began to feel unwell toward the end of the journey. Then, during my return trip a similar experience befell me. The morning after arriving back at Ma's I became extremely ill, and the nature of the disease soon made itself evident. Upon recovering, I discovered that Mr. Freehill had been down with the same affliction all during his Christmas vacation. I was so smitten with my teacher by then I almost felt it had been a privilege to have shared the chicken pox with him.

In the midst of all this I began to suffer from toothache. I shall never forget that visit to the dentist—the first ever in my life. The best thing I can say about it was that it was brief. By the time I had a chance to ask what could be done for my aching molar, the dentist had already extracted it. I was horrified, as it had been located immediately to the right of the front teeth—with the now-gaping hole in plain view whenever I might smile. I suspect that, all in all, my experience with dental care both at home and in the professional sense—or rather, with the utter absence of dental care—was all-too-typical for working-class and farming people in those days.

In fact, my friend Anne had lost all of her teeth by then. None of her classmates knew this until one day in class when we experienced one of those incredibly hilarious episodes that cause people to burst into uncontrollable laughter—even when it's at someone else's expense. We had all been standing at attention beside our desks waiting to be asked by our teacher, Mr. Hall, to take our seats. At the very moment that Connie Munroe's plump behind landed on her chair, the thing collapsed beneath her. In that first instant, as the wave of laughter swept the room, Anne's lips opened wide in a whoop of merriment, and her entire mouthful of false teeth burst forth—striking the top of the desk. The laughter following this second embarrassing accident was so extreme that it propelled a number of my neighbours to the floor, where they lay writhing and screaming with glee. At the moment that I, too, almost lost my balance, I felt myself being propelled back to reality with a jolt. It was a reality both warm in its strangely familiar moistness and ice-cold in the message it communicated. I had wet my pants!

With all this fun at school it's no wonder that my sense of hope for the future was restored that year. No doubt part of the reason was that—in spite of the seemingly endless string of illnesses—so many good things were happening in my life. Not only was I finding immense fulfilment in my classes, I quite enjoyed all my out-of-school activities as well. I remember wanting very much to fit in. As was then the fashion, I would take great pains to twist my hair up in little rags at night to produce Shirley-Temple-like curls. And it was during this period that I decided to refer to my mother as "Mom', a term used by all my friends, rather than 'Mama' which I was told was a bit childish.

The restaurant work continued to be a joy, with Jimmie invariably in the background, supporting and protecting me at every move. He paid me so generously that I could, for the first time, afford to purchase a few decent clothes. Anne and her parents were always available when I needed them, and Ma offered unfailing encouragement at home. Her demands upon me were few, actually, as she loved doing her own unique type of cooking and cleaning. One of her main problems had been that she was no longer able to manipulate her washing machine, or 'clothes mangle': a strange, wooden, cradle-like affair with an attachment which had to be rocked back and forth as it whipped away at the clothes. I was happy to work the thing for her. I even learned how to clean her un-washables, by employing—at her meticulous directions—the highly dangerous practice of heating a large container of gasoline on the top of the stove, and using that. I also did the grocery shopping, in order to save her the tortuous, limping-and-swaying journey on foot to the downtown area. I noticed, with some concern, that even the morning trip to the outdoor toilet appeared to be getting increasingly difficult for her, and especially so in the cold weather. Another way I was able to help was by hauling in our water supply and the daily coal and wood, and by filling the lamps with 'coal-oil' when required. We both had our 'sponge bath' each evening before bed, in the small wash basin in the kitchen. And, in the mornings, part of my routine was to empty the pots filled with urine from beneath our beds.

I think the only attitude and behaviour of Ma's that I recall having no patience for was her slavish subservience to her son Ed. Contrary to what we had all assumed, I discovered that he actually did very little for her. But whenever he came in from the farm she would rush to meet him at the door with a cup of coffee in hand, and cluck over him like an old hen with a chicken. She asked little of him in return, and expressed almost no interest in his wife, Leila, who was usually left alone at home.

Meanwhile, at school we seemed to be running at least on time-and-a-half. Under Mr. Freehill's inspiring leadership, our Canada Club with its choir and musical accompaniment, along with its drama and acrobatics classes, was preparing a concert. If successful, it was intended to be presented at a number of the villages along the Goose Lake Line. Wendell, Anne, Bud and I and a few others were active in acrobatics, which would provide part of the entertainment. I was never as skillful at that as they, however, so it was not included in the team that would be part of the concert. That team was eventually made up of Anne, Wendell, Bud Thygesen and another girl. Nevertheless, I was loving the exercise, and my back problems had not returned. The same situation applied to my participation in the choir. I was among those members who failed to qualify for the stage presentation, while Anne and a small group of other students were selected. None of this mattered to me, however, for my chief focus was on the play which was being prepared as the main feature of the concert. It was "Arsenic and Old Lace". I had been given the leading part, and was soon deep into the role of the old maiden aunt with murderous proclivities. Wendell had the lead in the musical section of the concert, and Anne sang in the choir. Unlike the rest of us, Wendell was already quite an old hand at the entertainment business. His parents, Mabel and Joe Carry, had a family orchestra which played for all the dances in the Acadia Valley district.

Our concert succeeded beyond our wildest dreams and, by the time all the excitement of our travel and various stage performances waned, we were well into the final term of school. The feeling of dread concerning the safety of my brother Jack was easing for me by then, as the news from the front was improving steadily. Then, suddenly on the eighth of May, came VE Day, marking the end of the European phase of the war! I shall never forget the wave of relief and sheer joy that swept through me when we heard the news at school. Almost immediately, it seemed, Oyen's officials began to plan a celebration. There was to be a parade and a town meeting at which people would make speeches. The mayor asked me to be one of the speakers. I was to represent the 'future leaders': that new generation which was fired with confidence that we would never, ever, have to face the kind of nightmare with which our older siblings and parents had been forced to deal. We were all so very hopeful concerning humanity's potential for civilization, and convinced that the savagery and futility of the mass killing of innocents would never again occur.

To say I was nervous at the prospect of my first public speech in such an important forum is to put it mildly. But I managed it, and experienced for the first time that indescribable rush which accompanies the awareness that one has been reasonably successful in connecting with the listening crowd. I recall that I made an effort to dwell on the tragedy of the sacrifice required by war, as well as on the innocent confidence shared by all of us that day about a future in which there would be no more need for it.

It seemed that the final exams were almost immediately upon us. And then we graduated. Our celebration was a far cry from what high school graduates came to expect in subsequent years. The brief ceremony at the end of classes consisted chiefly of an inspiring address by Maurice Freehill. It was subsequently printed in "Fallen Leaves", a small publication describing the goals and activities of our Canada Club during that momentous school year of 1944-5.

"Out of the depths of avarice and ruin," he began, "will come a wave of hope and idealism—its crest full of purpose and enthusiasm tempered with sympathy and steeled with faith in the worth of man." His presentation ended with the following words: "When red leaves fall and twilight closes down and we are dimmed in the mist of time, I trust that what we tried to do this year will serve as clear signposts planted with vision. I hope, too, that you will all be stronger, keener, kinder and happier, and our mutual experiences will have counted in your destiny. That is success! With a strong mind and a warm heart, come then to your task, filled with daring, hope and pleasant memories."

Our beloved teacher also presented both Anne and me with one of his paintings, as well as a farewell note to the two of us. On reading the note once more, after all these years, I find it surprisingly sad. I wonder now if he was then leading a very lonely private life. And if we had a far more important part in it than we could have ever known.

Other than Mr. Freehill's talk to the class, our only graduation celebration was a small picnic which we students organized at a slough to the north of town. There was still water in the slough from the spring run-off, so it was decided that the entire class would go swimming. I couldn't swim a stroke, never having had a chance to learn, but apparently didn't consider that worth mentioning to anyone. I joined in, wearing my borrowed swim suit. I planned only to wade in the shallow end, but had scarcely entered the water when, all of a sudden, the slippery sand gave way beneath me. It all happened in an instant, and I was deep in the water before I could even attempt a cry for help. Three times I struggled to the surface, but each time, just as I tried to rear up my head in order to utter a scream, I sank once more like a stone. I remember vividly my last conscious thought. "All that work and study . . . all for nothing!" That was what resounded in my panicked mind—no noble regrets concerning the love and grief of family and friends, nor fear about what death would bring. No 'out of body' mystical experience. Only the sense of waste—the appalling waste! It was an ironic end to my time of hope!

When I came to I found myself lying on the sand, gasping and choking, with my athletic schoolmate, Bud, pumping at my chest and holding me up so that I could expel the water. Apparently, a chance look had caused him to notice my predicament just as the back of my head sank below the surface for the third time. He had saved my life. Talk about good luck! Later that afternoon I was sufficiently recovered to join in the softball game. As I ran around the make-shift bases all I could hear was the sound of the slough-water plopping about somewhere inside me. And all I could feel was an overwhelming sense of gratitude for being alive, and an inexpressible optimism and fully restored hope for the future!

# Chapter 8

# OVER-REACHING MY 'STATION IN LIFE'

Long before my grade-twelve graduation, I had begun to think about plans for the coming year. My ever-supportive school principal, Maurice Freehill, was, of course, urging me to go on to university. But it always struck me as an impossible dream for someone in my circumstances. I would have loved to have been in a position to take his advice, but didn't dare express that desire even to him. However, I did venture to share my ambitions with Jimmie Wong, my boss at the restaurant where I worked as a waitress during the day whenever I wasn't in class. His immediate reaction was to offer to pay the entire cost of a university program in the field of my choice. I was absolutely dumfounded by the generosity of this fine human being. But something in me wouldn't allow me to accept his offer. I think I felt that it was far too much to be owing to anyone who had known me for such a brief period. I didn't understand then what it would probably have meant to this lonely man, who had never been allowed the privilege of bringing his wife with him to Canada, to have been thus virtually able to 'adopt' a daughter. I have wished many times in the years since that I had responded differently.

For some reason I was burdened with the misguided notion that one could ask a favour of such magnitude only of family members to whom one had been closely connected for years. So I went to my aunt, Mabel Carry, who had always been my mother's closest sister. Because the Carrys had survived the Depression and become successful farmers in the relatively fertile black clay-soil area immediately surrounding Acadia Valley, I thought that perhaps they might be able to lend me the funds to allow for a year of teacher-training at the Calgary Normal School. By then I had concluded that teaching was the only career requiring a brief and not-too-costly preparation period for which I might be suited. Neither nursing nor secretarial work, the other two job-options for girls in those days, seemed a possibility. My best friend, Anne, was already committed to a nursing career; and another friend, Josie Kruski, who had completed her high-school education in a Catholic boarding school in the city, had chosen to be a secretary. But for me, even teaching was a sort of fall-back position—never my first choice. Journalism was what I really wanted to do. However, I had been asked to help various teachers with their classes too often during my own school years not to be aware that I was reasonably capable of the task. So it was only after much soul-searching that I decided to approach my aunt Mabel about helping me achieve this relatively modest aim. I shall never forget her response, when I broached the issue upon her arrival at Ma's one afternoon during a trip to Oyen to pick up her son Wendell, who had been attending school there with me. Wendell was considering a military future by then, and had just joined the Air Force.

"Don't try to get above your station in life," my aunt advised, obviously with the kindest of intentions. "You're a darn good waitress. I think you'd better stick with what you know how to do! And anyway, you'll probably be getting married before too much time has passed."

That threw me for a while, and I almost gave up the struggle—just as I had two years previously when I dropped out of high school. Then came what folks less sceptically inclined than I would call a miracle! Maurice Freehill, my beloved teacher and principal of Oyen school, sent me a message one day just as he was himself preparing to leave for a better future in the United States. He had news for me. Apparently my marks on the Departmental finals had been so high that they came to the notice of Mr. Goresky, the School Inspector for the Acadia School Division, who promptly applied in my name for one of the rare scholarships then available. It was from the I.O.D.E., or 'International Order of Daughters of the Empire'. He included in the application my previous record of having been a recipient of the Governor General's Medal. No doubt due to Mr. Goresky's influence, the scholarship had come through posthaste. Mr. Freehill now had the gratifying task of informing me that my university tuition and cost of board and room would be financed for one year. This happy news reinforced my previous inclination not to attempt the university-degree route but to study something which would provide a means of livelihood after a single year of college. So that is how—in spite of my aunt's advice to the contrary—I presumed to apply for teacher training!

I learned that two classmates from my grade twelve-class were also planning to sign up for what we learned was the 'War Emergency Teaching

Certificate' program at the Calgary Normal School. One was Marie Norris, a farm girl from north of Sibbald—a small village along the Goose Lake railroad line between Benton and Alsask. The other girl was Stella Cwikelewich, a friend who came from a farm not far from Oyen. The three of us quickly made plans to travel together to the city to register in the program, and to search for a cheap dwelling place which we could all share. We settled on a basement room in a house not too far from the Normal School location on the corner of Fourteenth Street and Sixteenth Avenue, immediately to the northwest of the downtown area. We would each have a small couch of our own to sleep on, and would share one hot meal a day with the family upstairs. There was a large sink for the family laundry just outside our room, which was made available to us for the washing of our clothing and ourselves. We were also told that we would each be allowed one bath per week in the main-floor bathroom. It looked and sounded like sheer luxury to me, and the price was right!

I made time for a brief visit in late August to the farm at Cremona to see the family. My mother and her husband, Tom Graham, were well-settled by then into the cozy little house on the part of the family farm which he owned. The 'Little Red Deer' river flowed through their land, and my brothers Bob, Don and Jerry were discovering that the hunting and fishing in that area were just great. Tom not only made me most welcome, but he offered to lend me a small sum for buying books and a few necessary clothes—something not provided by the scholarship. However, he struck me as rather resentful and possibly jealous of Bob and even, to a slightly lesser extent, of Don. However, Jerry, the youngest of Mom's sons, apparently posed no threat to Tom's shaky self concept and was obviously a favourite with him. In spite of these worrying undercurrents, it was a relief to see that Mom and my three younger brothers had a secure home at last.

It was during this happy time that the news came about the dropping of the first atomic bomb on Japan. We had become so accustomed to hearing more hopeful news from the war front by then that the implications of what had been done by the Allies failed to fully register. The immediate results should have been shocking enough. Five square miles of the city of Hiroshima were obliterated on the sixth of August when the bomb fell, and the final count in lost lives, including those of many American prisoners, was over two hundred thousand. Then, three days later, the second bomb fell on Nagasaki, killing about seventy-five thousand more. We also scarcely noticed when Russia somewhat opportunistically declared war on Japan and invaded that same day. But even Alberta farmers celebrated when Japan surrendered the following week.

In the midst of all this I also touched base with a few friends from whom I had been hearing during the previous year. Then it was off to Calgary, to join my roommates and prepare for classes. And what marvelous classes they were!

The old Normal School was just that year being re-organized as the new Calgary branch of the University of Alberta's Faculty of Education. This meant that those students fortunate enough to be aiming for a degree in Education would be studying with us more lowly creatures for some of their courses: those not concerned with the immediate requirements of teaching. It also meant that we in the War Emergency Program would have access to a much wider range of studies than would have been the case previously.

From the very first day in class I felt as if I had discovered a wonderfully appropriate intellectual home. I found myself in an ordered context where everything seemed to make sense. In those days, the professors who were responsible for presenting the content of what we were to teach, and the procedures for teaching it, were knowledgeable and experienced in the actual business of the school classroom. And those who taught the theoretical classes came across as highly competent in their fields as well. What an adventure it was to encounter for the first time the great theories and theorists of education, such as John Dewey! And to learn about child development, based on the work of revolutionary thinkers like Jean Piaget! Altogether, in that relatively brief passage of time, I was introduced to some of the most remarkable ideas ever produced by humans throughout history. For I was given the opportunity to study not only the leaders in educational philosophy and psychology but also Bertrand Russell and other great contributors to the world of ideas: a world in which I immediately felt at home.

Even so, for the first couple of months I didn't have the nerve to enter the class discussions dealing with theory. I was probably deterred by the fact that the conversation was being totally monopolized by the males in the class. I found this unsurprising however, as one of my first strong impressions concerning my fellow students was that the females, especially those with the privilege of being in the three-year university-degree program, seemed to be more interested in locating an upwardly mobile husband than in serious scholarship.

My most memorable experience in our psychology course was the day the professor decided to demonstrate the effectiveness of hypnosis. He asked two students to come to the front of the class and proceeded to hypnotize them. A little leery of the process, I had deliberately seated myself in the back row. But that didn't work. I found myself floating away in a strange fashion, and was so disturbed by the possibility of losing control that I quietly left the room. I remember being struck by the fear that I would be hypnotized and left behind unnoticed. Another incident which has remained with me was the negative reaction of the art teacher to a realistic drawing of mine over which I had laboured and taken great pride, as I had always had some skill at a strictly photographical type of rendering. Apparently, realism in art was then rapidly going out of style as the new 'abstract' type of painting became popular.

One of my favourite courses was on the Philosophy of Education. I read like mad, late into the night—often removing myself to the outer area of the basement so that my room-mates could sleep. When the time came for us to submit our first written assignment I was confident that I had a product of some worth. I shall never forget the day that our essays were returned to us in class. The professor began by saying that the one to which he had assigned the top mark had been written by 'Mr. Pat Duffy', and that he would like that young gentleman to come forward. There was a moment of dead silence, while the full import of his words struck home to me. Of course! Any student who did well in philosophy had to be male! Then I stood up. And there was the sound of collective indrawn breath followed by an even deeper silence. It took the stunned professor several minutes to recover and offer a lame apology.

I think it was at that precise instant that I began to acknowledge the existence of an anger deep inside me: a sensation spurred by a profusion of memories of various injustices experienced over the years. I realized at the same time that I would have to keep the feeling buried, and not allow it to embitter me, even as I recognized that it would always be there to motivate and possibly inspire me. Without any conscious decision on my part, I began to view my mission in life as a battle against any and all instances of the kind of social injustice which had come so close to stifling my own life chances.

Something else was building in me as well: something which I failed to recognize until, at one fateful moment in the future, it impelled me to make a tragic life choice. It was a kind of hubris. I was becoming over-confident in my ability to take on anything that life could throw in my direction, and to beat the odds no matter what. I was the strong one who could attend to anyone in need of help. I was becoming the 'rescuer of the weak' par excellence—in my deluded imagination, that is.

It was during this exciting time that I first became aware of how pervasive the smoking of cigarettes had become, even among young girls. I soon realized that we three room-mates were the only non-smokers of our acquaintance. Smoking held no attraction for me—then or ever after. I think there were three reasons for this. For one thing, I could never have considered spending my precious, hard-earned money on anything so useless. Another deterrent was the smell, and the way it lingered on people's clothing. I had always rather liked the odour of my father's pipe, but that was quite different and, at any rate, he had not been a heavy smoker. A third reason why I was never even remotely tempted to indulge was that I had become sufficiently mature by then to enjoy being different from the crowd. I wish I could pretend to having been influenced by a suspicion about the addictive qualities of cigarettes, or by a clever prescience concerning the terrible toll that the habit would impose on society—in particular, the six-hundred-percent rise in lung cancer among females in the coming half century. But I'm afraid I was as ignorant as everyone else at that time concerning the longtime dangers of smoking.

My brief period of precious study at Calgary's new Faculty of Education passed all too quickly. I have only fleeting memories of events outside of class time. I soon learned that sleeping in on Saturday and Sunday mornings was mandatory. It was a good thing I went along with the wishes of my roommates in this. I had never before had the opportunity for such dalliance and, although I had no way of knowing it then, it was never again to be a part of my life. The daily supper with the family upstairs was another experience in unaccustomed luxury. For the first time ever I watched, with appalled disapproval, as children were allowed to eat second servings of dessert, even though they had previously only toyed with their vegetables and meat or fish servings. Also, during that exciting period, I had the experience of having two male classmates vying for my affections, and of having to share visiting space, when one of them called in the evening, with two and sometimes three or four other people in one crowded basement room.

Meanwhile, back at the university, I was particularly enjoying the class devoted to teaching beginners to read. This happened to be just before the advent of 'Dick and Jane' and the 'look-and-say' method of memorizing words. We were still being taught, instead, the use of phonics, involving old grade-one 'readers' with worn-looking brown covers: readers containing meaningful and morally insightful little fables. The latter part of the course was devoted to a series of practice-teaching sessions in the public schools, during which I discovered that I felt most at home with grade-two students. I remember more than any other experience of that eventful eight-month term the sheer joy of teaching these enthusiastic little people who were already well on the way to mastering basic reading skills—and of feeling that this was exactly where I could do my best work.

Another satisfying experience that year was being selected for the new university women's basketball team. This was a great surprise, as I had never before had the opportunity to play the game. But as soon as I had tried-out in a couple of class practices, I realized that all my previous experience of playing softball, running, horseback-riding and doing gymnastics seemed to come together in the movements and skills required for basketball. Of course, my slightly taller-than-average height also helped in the catching of the ball as it flew over the net, and in aiming for the basket. I didn't know it then, but it was to be the last time I would ever have the opportunity to participate in this wonderful game.

Our training program finished just before Easter. Sometime earlier, Mr. Goresky had been in the city 'head-hunting' for teachers and I felt I simply couldn't refuse him when he asked me to take on one of his many teacher-less country schools. So I already had a job to go to for the spring term, as did my two room mates.

The graduation exercises were great fun except that, when the time actually arrived, my favourite suitor failed to ask me to be his partner. He had been growing increasingly attentive throughout the year and, as a result, I had refused his competitor when he invited me for the event. Consequently, I found the sudden withdrawal of my chosen one, practically on the eve of our big day, extremely puzzling and upsetting. However, I decided some time later that he was a very ambitious, bright young man and had realized, almost too late for both of us, that he did not want to become seriously involved with anyone at that particular stage in his career. So I was left without a date for my graduation exercises.

There was a graduation dance as well, for which I borrowed a fussy blue balloon-skirted evening dress from my aunt Dot. It wasn't a very good fit, but it served the purpose. I think it was just at that time that long, full skirts and frilly dresses were making a re-appearance. In spite of my partner-less state, I danced with joyful abandon all evening. All in all, and in spite of a few imperfections and disappointments, the experience of this wonderful year confirmed for me that I had indeed managed to climb aboard that fateful train which would, at some future time, deliver me to an exciting new 'station in life'.

# Chapter 9

## WATER

Mr. Goresky, the school inspector, looked distinctly uncomfortable. He wants to get away but is concerned about leaving me here, I thought, with a flash of empathy.

"You've done all you could," I assured him. And he had. All during the drive from the town of Oyen—all twenty-five miles of it along the rough dirt road—he had carried on a lively conversation, pointing out from among the surroundings those things he endeavored gamely to make into points of interest. Partly because I had learned to be rather restrained around authority, I deemed it unnecessary to tell him that he needn't have bothered. Back in the bleak years of the Great Depression this area had been all-too-familiar to me. I was far too intent on assessing the changes in the land itself to mention this, however. It was now early spring of 1946, and much of the remembered desert-like bleakness had disappeared. Fields of stubble interspersed with freshly turned earth were encroaching on what, in my childhood, had been vast stretches of unfenced, rock-strewn pasture-land with wild rose bushes climbing its crevices; and with sage and cactus peppering its undulating plains. Grain-storage bins had now sprouted where none had been before. One in particular caught my eye, a little over halfway into the day's journey. Suddenly, by the side of the road—windows boarded up and a small pile of wheat by the door—appeared the schoolhouse of my childhood. Lonely Trail, an alien building alongside the other more traditional granaries, was now relocated in an alien place, removed from its old home in the middle of unused land in the old 'school quarter' a couple of miles from this main road to town. Transplanted! Like me, I thought, but now I've come back.

124

Nonetheless, I was feeling increasing dismay and regret at my decision as the drive progressed. It had been over eight years since my family had walked hopelessly away from the drought-stricken farm which was now merely one among the many cheerless, uninhabited places on the trails near which the road to my new school wandered wearily past. Why had I come back here, with the War Emergency Teaching Certificate clutched in my hand? Why had I allowed this pleasant, chatty man to talk me into it when I encountered him during recruiting week at Calgary's new Faculty of Education, which had recently evolved from the old Normal School into a branch of the Edmonton-based University of Alberta? Had it been merely the promise of a secure seventy dollars a month for the remainder of the school term and the year to come? Why had I succumbed so easily to the fear of joblessness? After all, the war was now over and the Depression far behind. Surely I could have done better! Or was it possible that I was driven by a sense of responsibility to some little child such as I, myself, had been: someone trapped in a lonely, isolated place, with no hope of a teacher capable of opening doors to a brighter future? Who knows what motivates our choices, especially when we're young?

The drive over the rough road, in the intense heat and dust of an early spring, was tiring. But the arrival proved much worse. Only after the car was parked in the treeless yard did the terrible isolation and desolation of the school and the teacherage really hit home. Not a single farmstead to be seen, in any direction! And the schoolyard—so strangely bare of grass!

"Horses," said Mr. Goresky, in answer to my unspoken question.

"Horses?" I asked, picturing wild herds stampeding by the door.

"Your pupils all have to ride or drive horses to school," he explained patiently. "They live too far away to walk. And they've been attending school here at Empress View all through the war, doing correspondence courses under the care of one of the farm women. Their horses eat the grass in the yard all day."

Mr. Goresky must have sensed my dismay at this news of the long-term teacher-less state of my future charges, for he bustled about even more enthusiastically from that point on—helping with the unpacking of my few belongings, opening the teacherage and school, and showing me the barn and two outdoor toilets. Disgusting smells greeted us at each location: the sickly sweet odour of dead mice in the teacherage; that familiar mixture of stale sweat and chalk in the schoolhouse; horse manure in the barn; and the unspeakable fumes issuing from the dirty, open holes in the wooden seats of the two outdoor toilets.

As if to make up for it all, Mr. Goresky was more than helpful. He carefully engineered the pumping-up and lighting of the 'liquid gas' lamp, making sure that I could repeat the process. As I had been raised with only what we called 'coal-oil' lamps—except for my experiences of electricity during brief stays in urban areas—this strange form of lighting was utterly new to me. He tackled the pile of uncut wood, splitting a week's supply for my cooking, he said, and he showed me how to light the fire in the school's pot—bellied heater, in case the weather changed.

"As for the smell in the teacherage," he told me, with an air of reassurance, "at least you can be sure it's not rats. Even though you're only a few miles from the Saskatchewan border, this district is rat free. Alberta hires a 'rat man' who does nothing but patrol the entire border area, poisoning all the rats that wander in." Somehow this information did little for my peace of mind.

"What if some of the poisoned rats wandered into these buildings to die?" I asked, expecting no answer. For it was now clear that the time had come for the kindly school inspector to leave. He took a few steps toward the car, then suddenly stopped. Retracing his steps, he reached out to pat my head; then chucked me under the chin.

"Keep smiling," he said, and rushed away without looking back.

In an attempt to dispel the sudden flood of loneliness, I decided that a careful reconnoitre was needed. The situation seemed precarious, to say the least. There had been no mention of a telephone, and I saw at once that no poles or wires of any kind lined the narrow dirt road passing the school. And, of course, I had no means of transportation. Only now, in the absence of any sighting of a neighbouring farmstead, did a recognition of my car-less state as a possibly serious problem begin to strike home. I had several weeks' supply of non-perishable groceries and canned goods, but Mr. Goresky had told me that the village of Empress was more than ten miles southward down that lonely road. Walking for provisions would simply not be feasible.

Some other vague worry had been nagging at me ever since our arrival, something important that I should have asked about. Suddenly it struck me. Where was the water? I began to run, scrutinizing every corner of the large enclosure. No sign of a pump anywhere. Not even an open well with a pail on a rope. Exhausted from the surge of fear that had almost overwhelmed me, I returned to the teacherage. Only then did I notice the small, covered barrel at one corner. It was empty, but there were signs of moisture. Surely it had contained water fairly recently—probably until the school had closed for Easter! There was hope, then.

Going inside, I chided myself. Why the unaccustomed panic? Tomorrow was Monday, the first day of school after the Easter holiday. The children would know about a water source. Three families there were, according to Mr. Goresky, all immigrants from Europe in the decades before the war. Two of them had come from Germany. They provided seven of the eight pupils, each of whom was in a different grade. Only grade six was not represented. And there was a grade-nine student who would enter the high school at either Acadia Valley or Empress next year, if he passed his Provincial Departmental exams. His parents were from Romania. All spoke English, the school inspector had said, but with heavy accents. Thinking of them and memorizing their names cheered me considerably, and I decided to get busy cleaning the place before night fell.

On closer perusal I found the teacherage still foul-smelling but adequate, if one could manage to ignore the mice scurrying around. I examined the two small rooms with their walls bare of plasterboard and furnished sparsely with bed, dresser, clothes closet, tiny kitchen cupboard, table and chairs and a wood-and-coal cooking stove. Next came the schoolhouse. It was patterned upon a thousand others. There was the outside door leading into the cloakroom with its shelves for the syrup pails that served as lunch containers, and the pegs on the wall for coats. There was the large classroom with a pot-bellied, wood-and-coal heater in the centre, which Mr.Goresky had identified as a Waterman-Waterbury. And there was the usual blackboard covering the front wall, the desks lined up in four neat rows, and the windows along one side.

By dark I had accomplished everything that could possibly be done without water. I had shovelled fresh earth into the toilet holes, and swept the school and teacherage after having brushed them clean of mouse droppings and what looked like an entire winter's tracking of dust and mud. The first day's teaching plan was ready. I locked my door with two knives inserted into the jamb, then I made up my bed and slept. Fortunately, I was still at the age when one can sleep through almost anything, so I was not unduly disturbed by the mice.

The first week of school was a mixture of wild contrasts: moments of blissful gratification interspersed with endless hours of sheer terror. The larger of the two German immigrant families arrived early Monday morning in a horse-drawn buggy, with a cream-can of fresh water with which to refill the little barrel. Oh, the relief of it all! They were absolute gems—the entire five of them. None could read with any facility, not even the boy in grade five. However, what was that but a worthwhile challenge to my newly minted teaching skills? And my one grade-nine student, like the other two older boys comprising the second German family, rode horseback. He was intelligent, ambitious, and boundlessly appreciative of my efforts. What more could a beginning teacher ask?

Well, for one thing, I decided after the first day, one could ask not to be burdened with the two older German-Canadian students. Nothing in my all-too-brief period of teacher-training had prepared me for anything remotely as daunting as these fellows. During the first recess I realized that they had been operating a reign of terror in the little school for years. The other children informed me that the 'sitter' who supervised their correspondence courses had been so afraid of the two large, teenage brothers that she always closeted herself in the school during recess and noon-hour breaks, refusing to intercede no matter what happened. I knew full well that I must do the opposite, and pounce like a hawk at the slightest sign of bullying. This meant not a moment of relaxation away from the pupils—not even for lunch—and numerous head-to-head clashes in which I was forced to assume a forbiddingly strict persona which clearly proved more frightening to myself than to the problem students.

By the time classes were over on Friday I could scarcely wait for the children to leave. I waved them off, as usual, watching until they were out of sight in case the bullying warriors doubled back and attacked the family of younger children from some hidden foxhole along the road. Each family lived in a different direction from the other two: the younger children to the south of the school, and Mike, the grade nine student, to the north. The two difficult boys lived—fittingly, I couldn't help but think—five miles to the east, toward what I now pictured as rat-infested Saskatchewan.

I had learned by then that the two families from Germany were long-time enemies. This seemed to have something to do with the fact that the one living to the East spoke 'high' German, had left their country of birth only a few years before the war, and were committed Communists. The native tongue of the other family was 'low' German; they were longer-established immigrants, and somehow had come to associate Communism with Nazism. To them, the 'high' Germans—obviously totalitarian—were supporters of the madman who had destroyed their homeland and the reputation of all Germans.

I never did know for sure how this mistake had occurred, but guessed it was related to the fact that 'NAZI' was the German-language acronym for 'National Socialist Workers' Party'. So it is distinctly possible that ordinary Germans had experienced the two movements as having grown from similar left-wing roots. And very soon I decided the confusion about it at this particular school also likely had something to do with the propensity of the 'high' German boys to draw swastikas on all available spaces. They had begun flaunting these on that first Monday morning, covering every page of work assigned, obviously waiting with hopeful anticipation for the expected outburst of shock and horror from the new teacher. My intuition, gained through long experience with four brothers, told me to ignore the decorations, which I had already noted on the walls and doors. The two would-be Nazis kept up their game but, as that first week wore on with no response from me, the swastikas gradually appeared to become a shade less prevalent.

Now, at last, I was alone, with a blessed weekend ahead for rest and preparation. 'A nice cup of tea', I decided, resorting to my grandmother's terminology, and a gripping book that has nothing whatsoever to do with teaching! With my usual awkwardness at the unfamiliar task, I eventually managed to light the stove and get the wooden kindling—if not the chunks of coal—burning fairly steadily. Dipper and tea kettle in hand, I rounded the teacherage, toward the water barrel. And stopped. Something was decidedly different. A long moment passed before I realized what was wrong. The lid was on the ground, and the barrel had been flung onto its side. The marks of horse's hooves dented the surrounding ground. Horrified, I realized that not a drop of water remained, and a long, dry, utterly isolated weekend loomed ahead!

My head felt dull and heavy, as heavy as the kettle in my hand. Heavy? I saw that there was a cup or two of water at the bottom of the kettle. Thank goodness! If worst came to worst I could survive on that. But why hadn't I thought to check that precious water supply before the family who brought it had left? And why hadn't I stored a few jars of water in the teacherage each day, as insurance against just such a calamity?

Jars of water! A memory from long ago suddenly resurfaced. There was a farm, some thirty miles to the northwest, where I had come into the world—the first non-Aboriginal child to have done so, in that forsaken area. Three years before that, in 1923, my parents had abandoned their homestead and machinery-and-harvesting business in Acadia Valley in the midst of a prolonged drought, and moved back to the Duffy home base at Fairbank, Iowa. With financial help from his family, my father had established a garage business there. But in the summer of 1926, my mother, almost eight months pregnant, suddenly decided to chuck it all and had taken their two children and returned to Canada.

There was only one other baby ever born on what had been, since 1911, the Armitage homestead. That baby came about nine years after my arrival, and it had died. It was the child of my uncle Ed and his wife who had, by then, taken over the original family farm. Few members of the Armitage family ever returned to visit, for Aunt Leila had 'gone queer' they said. It was then still some years before she was to be 'put away' in an institution in Ponoka—that town whose very name evoked a vision of madness in the minds of most Alberta residents in those days. The interminable drought, and the death of her only child, had taken a terrible toll on poor Leila.

Only once had I ever visited my birthplace. That memory was now upon me, and with it, the precise form the poor woman's 'queerness' had taken. The little house had been jammed with bottles and jars: all filled to the brim with water. All through those dark years of the 'Dirty Thirties', Leila had saved water! It was one of the saddest sights of my childhood: a sight so hurtful that I suspect I had never dared face the memory of it. Until now.

"She's saving for a rainless day," quipped my father, long since returned from his hastily and disastrously disposed-of business in Iowa.

"But every day is rainless now," I admonished him. "Maybe it's just that she was once very, very thirsty for a long, long time." And the strange woman had indeed looked as if she yearned for water. The pale eyes, perpetually searching the cloudless sky, had seemed as distant and barren as the vast expanse above. "It's enough to give you the shivers," my mother sighed.

Our Duffy household had never been thirsty. It was true that, during the dry summers when there was no snow for melting, we had been forced to skimp on water for cleaning ourselves and washing clothes. But for drinking we had used the pump in the yard. Because it was forever on the verge of going dry, we always doled out the well's precious output frugally—sharing it with the school horses and milk cows. We were sometimes hungry in those terrible years of the Great Depression, but not thirsty. Who knows . . . I had wondered at the time of that visit to the old Armitage farm, while immersed in my sorrow for Leila, who knows what being thirsty might do to you?

Now, by late Saturday afternoon, my own tiny store of water was long gone. I sat by the roadside much of the day, hoping to flag down a passing farmer, but the road remained eerily empty. Seeding time, I reminded myself. No one goes to town on Saturday in the midst of seeding. One other option finally occurred to me. The 'low' German-speaking children had identified a reclusive bachelor, living several miles down the road, as my closest neighbour.

"But he's afraid of women!" volunteered Jimmy, the oldest boy. "He don't mind kids though. He fixed our buggy wheel once, when we broke down near his place."

After a supper of a can of peas in their precious juice, I set out—a covered Roger's syrup pail from the school cloakroom in either hand. At the end of an hour's walk, I was thankful to find a light showing through the window of the small shack in the ramshackle yard. I approached the door as noisily as possible, so the old bachelor would get a chance to see me coming, and then knocked at the door. And knocked and knocked. Occasionally I heard movements within, and once I saw a shadow near the curtained window. I tried to explain loudly what had happened. No response. Finally, I resorted to begging pitifully for a drink of water. All to no avail. "That man really is afraid of women," I complained into the darkening night, as I trudged drearily school-ward.

By Sunday evening, in the midst of slurping down my last can of tomatoes, I was finally able to laugh at the situation, and to marvel at the exaggerated dimensions of my fears. On Monday morning the children who supplied the water were aghast and apologetic when they arrived with their brimming cream can and were told what had happened. Mike was full of sympathy while the two problem students were clearly disappointed to see me still capable of wielding chalk and yardstick. I ushered them all into the school and began to follow. Then I stopped. For ten minutes, I decided, the bullies could wreak whatever havoc they desired. I returned to the teacherage, and began to gather empty containers from the cupboard. Rounding the corner several times, I filled my jars and bottles from the little water barrel, and lined them up along the wall.

"There's room," I murmured confidently, "for plenty more."

# Chapter 10

# A CHOICE TOO SOON

Young people tend to make the most critical of life choices with a terrifying lack of attention to evidence and, consequently, with little or no application of reason and values to available facts; or assessment of these in the light of lifetime goals. In the absence of such crucial components of wise judgement, what tends to rule are unrecognized emotions derived subconsciously from previous experience. This is the source of our much vaunted human 'intuition' which, unfortunately, is only as sound as our original processing of that previous experience: a process which was to prove, during the winter and spring of 1947, to have been sadly deficient in my case. For I had no inkling, in that far-off winter at Acadia Valley, that I was stepping into a tragic trap which would darken my life, and that of others, for many years to come.

I had begun my first experience as a country schoolteacher at the end of the Easter week of 1946, upon graduating from the eight-month 'War Emergency' program at the new Calgary branch of the University of Alberta. By the time the summer holidays arrived I was enjoying every day of my new job, and I think the students were as well. Even the two bullies, who had been terrorizing their fellows all during the wartime period when the school had merely been supervised by one of the neighbouring farm women, appeared to have been at least partially tamed. So I left the isolated teacherage and my little group of students at the end of June feeling quite sanguine about returning in September.

My destination was Edmonton, where I had enrolled at the Faculty of Education for their summer session. However, as I had to travel by way of Calgary, I decided to stop there for a night with my aunt Dot. She had come to my aid in earlier, desperate times—albeit reluctantly and always gracelessly.

I wanted to repay her and show off a bit as well, by taking her out to dinner. As I was feeling quite wealthy, due to having saved a fair amount of my salary of $70 a month, I even found myself including a visiting cousin, Audrey Stevenson, in the invitation. Dot was, as usual, over-dressed for the occasion in a flowered and frilled satin dress which, happily, I no longer had to worry about inheriting. We ate in a simple place within my means, but probably no restaurant bill was ever handled with more pride and flourish. Then it was on to Edmonton.

Both of my former roommates from Calgary were there as well, and we once more shared a minimal residence. We discovered that it was located near the marvelous North Saskatchewan River which flows through the city, and we soon came to enjoy wandering the river banks. We also spent considerable time tramping about, exploring the parks and other wonders of what was to me a big-city environment. Meanwhile, the three of us were becoming acquainted with a larger group of Education students, many of whom shared stories of fearsome introductory teaching experiences rivaling mine. We all felt generally hopeful about our chosen careers, however, and were full of plans for gradually working our way toward a degree by attending 'summer classes' which would be supplemented by correspondence courses from Queens University in Ontario. That entire summer passed in a haze of happy adventures, both within-class and out, with Marie Norris, one of my former university room-mates, becoming even closer as a support and confidant.

I had earlier decided to major in history and minor in drama. For my first course in the latter I selected an introduction to stage design. Everything went swimmingly in class, right to the last week when we had to present a model of an original design for a previously designated play. I recall that session clearly because of something that happened the day that all the individual projects were being assessed. I had worked most of the previous night on mine, which was decidedly experimental for me as I was trying for the spare and modern, rather than the traditional style. It was therefore with considerable trepidation that I watched the professor approaching, then scrutinizing my work with what looked like increasing interest. Suddenly he sat down, apparently to get a different angle on it. This move was accompanied by piercing scream from one of my fellow students. He had sat on the desk which held her design, squashing it flat! I received a top mark on mine, but never learned what he gave the poor girl whose un-assessed design he had accidentally ruined.

It was on another exciting day some weeks previously, when we were all at a Faculty party, that I met once more an inspiring teacher from my childhood at Lonely Trail School: Frank Sickoff. I was to discover many years later that it was an encounter as memorable for him as it was for me. Obviously he had not expected ever to meet a survivor from that drought-stricken south-eastern prairie environment, and certainly not at university.

When the dream-like summer session ended I was able to spend a week or so at the farm in Cremona country, where my widowed mother had married for the second time in order to provide a home for her children. A would-be suitor from my previous visits was still around and continued to be persistent. And I continued to feel uncomfortable with him, mainly because of his evangelism. But I didn't want to hurt his feelings, so merely put him off by insisting that I had to spend all of this too-brief visit with my family. Mom and the boys seemed as happy to see me as I was to be with them, although I was surprised to discover that my brother Jack was no longer there. Even my stepfather, Tom Graham, was quite welcoming. However, I had learned from previous visits that he seemed somewhat intimidated by his new family. My worries about the marriage relationship and his attitude toward the older boys were not eased by what I saw and heard during my stay. I became convinced of something I had only guessed before. There was little or no sexual intimacy involved in the marriage, and not much emotional commitment on Mom's part. Tom was obviously puzzled and hurt by the nature of the relationship. This may have been at the root of his complaints about 'those lazy Duffy boys' who were simply no help around the farm. As Don quite often supplied Mom with fresh fish for their meals and was already demonstrating extraordinary expertise and persistence at farm work, I found these complaints most unfair.

As for Bob, he had returned to the farm at the end of the previous school year, and taken his grade twelve at Cremona high school, riding a bicycle back and forth over the considerable distance every day. His previous years of high school had been at a girls' boarding school near Caroline that he, as the sole male student, had attended with our cousin Thelma. There, he earned his board and tuition by serving as chore boy and by shooting crows. Now he was back with the family, but I saw little sign of bonding where he and Don were concerned. Don obviously admired his older brother, and was trying his best to please him, and to support him when he was under fire from Tom. But Bob's response was invariably an attitude of contemptuous superiority. At times it was even worse. He seemed to derive amusement from demonstrating his physical superiority as well, with some unnecessary punching and shoving. Mom would intervene, telling him (foolishly, I thought) that Don would get even by giving him a good beating up by the time he was twenty-one. Of course, for Bob, it was all about getting back at Mom for favouring Don and Jerry over him. The jealousy and the continued experience of rejection by his family must have been a terrible weight to bear.

I saw that this was still going on. Once, at mealtime, Tom claimed Bob had his long legs stretched too far under the kitchen table. He then stood up and kicked the boy repeatedly, simply because Bob hadn't withdrawn his legs when told to do so. I felt that it was no wonder this brother of mine was looking desperately for a chance to get away. He was currently on the wait-list for the RCMP. He had rejected an offer from the marine division of the Air Force—now long since ceased to exist, having been replaced by the Coast Guard. The old St. Roche, famous for having made the first two-way crossing of the Northwest Passage, was actually an RCMP Marine Division ship.

For the coming term Bob had decided to accept a job supervising a country school. It was the 'Water Valley' school, named for its surrounding district, which was eight or nine miles to the southwest of 'Big Prairie' where Tom's farm was located. Meanwhile, it seemed to me that Bob was more than earning his keep on the farm. When I was there, he even brought home a freshly shot deer. I found it to be the most delicious meat I had ever tasted.

Jerry had apparently remained in a category of his own: a specially favoured little fellow who, by definition, required absolutely no controlling or guidance from anyone. This worried me terribly, for he was obviously getting little discipline at the local school. They had been without a teacher during 1946-47, while Don took his grade seven, although the veteran who was currently supervising their correspondence courses did a satisfactory job, according to Don. As had one of his previous teachers, a Mrs. Frizzell, who had recognized his unique ability and allowed him to proceed at his own pace. So, all in all, the Big Prairie school experience had proven of considerable benefit for Don, who was now already entering grade eight. But the entire home-and-school socialization process was very different for seven-year-old Jerry. Tom seemed to be even out-doing Mom in his catering to this one of the Duffy boys who was sufficiently young to pose no threat to his self esteem. And the problem was not helped by Mom's habit of allowing Jerry to stay home from school whenever he complained of feeling slightly unwell. Mom considered him a sickly child, and he may well have been adversely affected by the after-effects of numerous illnesses, most notably rheumatic fever, which I was told had left him with a heart murmur.

When we sat down soon after my arrival to a sumptuous dinner of roast chicken, fresh garden vegetables and Mom's famous lemon-angel-food cake, I queried her concerning the whereabouts of Jack. There followed a dead silence, during which the other boys looked uncomfortable and Tom mumbled angrily about "that thief" never darkening their door again. I waited until Mom and I were alone before raising the issue once more. She required no further urging. One of the saddest stories I had yet heard about my wayward brother poured out. Through it all, she looked past me, into the distance, as if gauging the sort of life that lay in wait for her eldest son.

Not long before I was due to visit, Jack had driven their car for her and taken her into Carstairs, a town to the east of the tiny village of Cremona and situated on the main highway between Calgary and Edmonton. She had planned a special shopping spree and gone off on her own, arranging to meet him at a certain time and place. When she arrived, no doubt laden with bags, there was no sign of either Jack or the car. She waited several hours until, as darkness set in, she was forced to phone home and reveal to Tom what had happened. He came for her in the farm truck and drove her home. He conceded to her wishes that they not call the police, but declared that the "no-good scoundrel" would never again be allowed in their home. Nothing whatsoever had been heard from Jack since. Mom's sorrow, as she recounted the tale, was so great that I felt she was aware, somewhere deep in her being, that her much-loved first son had finally launched himself upon a road from which there could be no turning back.

I continued my lengthy train journey to Empress and was met and taken out to Empress View by a couple in town with whom I had become friendly. My arrival at the school was a bit dismaying, as the mice had once more over-run the place. However, this time I had made sure that I was well-supplied with drinking water, fuel for the stove and gas lamp, and a surplus of canned goods along with other essential household items. I discovered that my grade-nine student from the previous term had departed for one of the larger neighbouring towns where high school was available. The remaining pupils arrived in a more unruly state than when they had left in late June, but I soon got them back to order. I resumed two routines established in the spring which had seemed to work well. One was, in place of the established Lord's Prayer first thing in the morning, I substituted a simple, popular song chosen each week by a student who would then lead the singing. That seemed to aid in group bonding and the arousing of enthusiasm for the day's work.

When the school superintendent introduced me to the school the previous spring he had told me about the traveling library in the form of a small 'bookmobile' which visited isolated country schools on a regular basis in those days. This had proven to be a lifesaver for me, as it allowed me to obtain numerous books for various ages of young readers. In an effort to get them all involved in reading, at the end of the noon-hour break I chose as a 'gathering in' ceremony, the reading aloud of a few pages from a classic, such as David Copperfield. I would purposely never finish the book before beginning a new one, in order to leave their interest unrequited. I think I always felt most rewarded by witnessing the progress in reading that was evident in all of them, although the grade-five member of the larger of the two families continued to struggle almost in vain. I began to suspect that he had been left too long in a state of semi-literacy which he had learned to mask by pretending to read while the school 'sitter', in a misguided attempt to help, did his correspondence lessons for him.

The two families were clearly happy to have me back, and soon I was invited to both homes. The visit with the 'Low-German'-speakers was very pleasant but the one at the residence of the 'High-Germans' turned out to be quite the reverse. Their young teen-age boys (the school's two longtime bullies) had been sent to convey me by horse and buggy on a Sunday morning. As usual, I found it difficult to make conversation with them, so the ride was mostly silent. Upon arrival, I discovered that the parents were even stranger than their sons. They were obviously well-educated people, but extremely dogmatic Communists. While the food on the dinner table was definitely 'different', it proved to be very good—especially the red cabbage which was new to me. However, the conversation consisted of nothing but endless preaching of their ideology, accompanied by a stubborn refusal to hear any opposing argument. Finally, I broke in by asking them if I could go to out to visit the toilet. I was told there was no such thing on their homestead; that they merely used the barn or went into the bushes when necessary. They didn't mention the-then customary 'chamber pot' under the bed, but of course I wouldn't have used that anyway. As I knew the two boys were roaming about outdoors, my by-then pressingly necessary foray in search of privacy was a memorable experience! Needless to say, I avoided any future visits to that farm.

The first neighbours with whom I had become acquainted during the preceding spring term were two bachelors: the Smith brothers. I had met them one day early on in my residence at the teacherage when I became sufficiently desperate for a supply of groceries to try sitting out on the road that wound past the school, and flagging down any passerby for a ride to town. Fortunately for me, the first to come driving along were Bill and Don Smith, who lived several miles to the west of the school. Bill had recently used his Veteran's Settlement to purchase land adjoining their father's homestead and the two sons were now farming their parents' land as well. The Smith brothers had quickly become my most reliable friends, picking me up almost every weekend for a trip to Empress for provisions.

Not long after my return to Empress View, I discovered that something very exciting had been happening during my absence, where Bill Smith was concerned. His girlfriend, whom he met and became engaged to while serving in England during the war, had now immigrated. They were married in mid-September. June Smith proved to be a wonderful person, and we soon became close friends—friends for life, as it turned out! Both her intelligence and sense of humour were immediately captivating. For example, at our first meeting she told two great stories that had everybody laughing. One concerned her supposed reason for packing up in a hurry and sailing for Canada. According to her, Bill's letters were becoming increasingly laden with references to "the new blonde schoolteacher". Another tale was about her arrival at the station where Bill and his parents met her train. She attempted to explain her exhaustion by telling them that the porter had 'knocked her up' very early that morning. The shocked expression on Mrs. Smith's face told her that her words must have conveyed a vastly different message in Canada than in England.

It had been Bill Smith who warned me about being careful around certain men in the district who had a bad reputation where single women were concerned. In fact, I soon discovered that it was foolhardy to trust any male I didn't know, given my isolated and unprotected living circumstances. I had a scary experience one day when a young man who said he lived some distance past the school, offered to give me a lift from town with my shopping. When we arrived he got out of the car with me, although I had refused his help with the carrying of my purchases. As we approached the door I thanked him and began to say goodbye, but he abruptly began to push his way in. I managed to get the door closed in his face, while the groceries flew to the ground all about me. What a relief it was to get my knives into the door jamb! He pounded for a few minutes, swearing at me, then gave up and left.

I made the mistake of recounting this adventure to the would-be suitor near Cremona, in one of my infrequent responses to his all-too-frequent letters. A couple of weeks later, I received a small revolver in the mail from him. Needless to say, the very sight and thought of using it was almost as frightening to me as was the prospect of being attacked by a rapist. I don't remember what happened to the gun. I had already been shocked to the core by the careless use and prevalence of shotguns in rural Alberta. I had no intention of joining the 'gun culture'.

A second pair of brothers in the community became good friends as well. They were a pair of twins who were always referred to as 'the Burke boys'. I soon learned that they were enthusiastic dancers, especially gifted at square-dancing, and very dependable in every sense. They developed the custom of giving me a safe ride to and from the community dances, something that made my out-of-school life much less lonely. While school was on, however, I felt I lacked for nothing, for I was able to watch my youngsters learning more successfully with every passing day.

I was continuously plagued by one serious concern during this entire period, however. I was being struck by spells of severe pain in the area of my appendix, sometimes even while school was in session. Twice I managed to get to the doctor in Empress to ask for help, but both times he merely dismissed my complaints. "Country schoolteachers invariably suffer from constipation," he would say nonchalantly, "And I imagine you know full well why!" I had to concede that getting to the outdoor toilet was well-nigh impossible during the school day, so decided there was no choice for me but to suffer in silence. This went on until one Saturday morning the pain became so extreme after a number of hours that I passed out. By the time I regained consciousness the condition was beginning to ease. After that nightmare experience the attacks ceased completely. Many years later I discovered that my appendix had, in fact, burst, but instead of this resulting in death—as is usually the case, and had happened to my great-grandmother Armitage—I was told that my ruptured appendix had somehow become attached to the wall of my upper bowel.

Not long after this misadventure, in early November, I received a visit from Mr. Goresky, the superintendent for the Acadia School Division who had hired me in the spring. He informed me that I was about to be moved northwest into the village of Acadia Valley, to teach the middle classroom which comprised grades four, five and six. Apparently the young male beginning teacher currently in charge was unable to handle them, and the children were totally out of control. With my already-established record of imposing discipline, he said he was confident that I would soon have them in shape. I hated the thought of the educational future of my little handful of charges at Empress View once again being placed in jeopardy, but it was made clear to me that I had no choice in the matter. An awareness of the approaching prairie winter probably operated as a spur to settle in a less isolated place. I think now that the school superintendent had that in mind as well. Also, the fact that my relatives, the Carry family, had been farming for many years five miles to the north-west of 'the Valley', may have influenced my acquiescence to Mr. Goresky's suggestion. My aunt Mabel would have been known to him as the driver of a school bus. He wanted an immediate switch-over, with the young male teacher—whose place I was assuming—moving out to my teacherage at once. So by mid-November I was already packed up and ready to take on my new duties.

My move up to Acadia Valley was so rapid and unplanned that I had no choice but to take a room in the town's only hotel until I could locate a boarding place. That turned out to be more of an adventure than either Mr. Goresky or I had expected. It happened that the only available room was located immediately above the beer parlour. Acadia Valley had a well-deserved reputation as the drinking capital of the entire countryside. The place was boisterous late into the night and, I felt, highly dangerous for me. Or at least it would have been but for the almost immediate appearance of a heroic protector in the person of the man with the worst reputation in the area. He was from the community's most notorious 'family of losers' and his name was Andy McGhee. The name and general appearance rang a distant bell for me the moment I opened my door to his knock on the second evening of my residence at the hotel.

"Paddy Duffy", he exclaimed, "Don't yu even know it ain't safe t'be open-nen' yur door without askin' who's there?" My father, Lew, had often talked about how the mischievous little Andy had been my best pal in those happy early-childhood days at 'the Valley' when we had owned the town garage. Sadly, however, since my arrival at Empress View I had been hearing about how badly my childhood friend had 'turned out', and how his entire family were blacklisted by the community. In spite of all this, I had no qualms about inviting him into my room for a visit, probably because, even as he entered, he continued to drill me on rules of safety that I should be following—given my precarious location. From then on, Andy became my self-appointed guardian, although I suspect that few of the townspeople knew our history or understood the nature of our current friendship.

I found the middle-classroom at the Valley school quite a challenge for the first few weeks. The pupils had obviously been running wild all fall. I came down very hard at the beginning and even resorted to using the strap once—something I had always sworn I would never do, and never did again. But it worked! Gradually everything settled down and the learning began. I discovered that grades four, five and six presented an exciting and rewarding level at which to teach. Not only were they a lively bunch in a physical sense, but eager to learn as well. My colleagues were Gert Niwa, the primary teacher who taught grades one, two and three, and Ellen Krempien, who was responsible for junior high, or grades seven, eight and nine. They were remarkable people who remained good friends of mine for many years to come—especially Ellen.

Sadly, I lost touch with the Empress View students from then on, as their community revolved around Empress rather than Acadia Valley. In those days people didn't tend to travel anywhere beyond their own handiest village, which depended more on access road than distance. The Burke brothers did maintain contact, however. I discovered this was because their cousin and his wife lived in Acadia Valley. Tom and Joyce Burke were leading lights in the town. He operated a successful garage business and was the local dealer for Cockshut machinery. She had a reputation for being active in community projects. At this particular time, she was well into the last stage of her second pregnancy, a prior one having ended in the newborn's death. In spite of her condition and the tiny size of their house, Joyce agreed to provide me with a temporary bed and board. I was more than thankful to accept the kind offer. The 'Burke boys' told me they were concerned about my reputation as a teacher in the community if I continued to have Andy McGhee hovering about me, so I decided the move would take care of that possible problem as well.

Almost immediately I was introduced to Joyce's brother, a large, handsome man named Jack Westcott. He was a war veteran, only recently returned from overseas. As in the case of Bill Smith and many others, his Veteran's Settlement had allowed him to purchase land adjoining his father's farm south of town. I soon learned that Jack had served in the Military Police in London throughout the blitz. Unlike other soldiers and civilians, the Military Police had to remain out on the hazardous streets throughout the terrifying bouts of bombing. This explained for me a few things about him that had at first struck me as strange. I realized that he was one of the 'walking wounded': psychologically wounded, that is. He was living in town for the winter in a house near the Burkes, one of two that were owned by his and Joyce's father, Harry Westcott. But Jack appeared to have no interest in winter employment of any kind. He spent most of his time sitting around watching Joyce as she did her housework. He didn't seem to read or have any hobbies either, and I saw no sign of friends. I was told that he had been engaged to my older cousin, Jean Carry, before the war, but that she had 'ditched him' when he returned in such an obvious emotional and psychological mess. It was all-too-apparent that he was still suffering the after-effects of numerous horrendous experiences in the London streets throughout the episodes of bombing, and was not getting any help with his problems. There was no recognition of such a thing as 'post-traumatic stress disorder' in those days.

Ever the confident 'helper of the needy', I immediately took Jack Westcott under my wing as my special project without even considering what the consequences might be for either of us. It's also possible that I was so grateful to my kind and pleasant hosts, Joyce and Tom, that I felt I owed a measure of care and companionship to the troubled brother. And here, I may well have thought, was a chance for me to pay homage to the memory of a dear lost friend, Max McCurdy, by helping one who, in spite of having lived to return—as Max did not—had been deeply injured in some hidden way. In addition, I'll never know to what extent my worries about my own brother Jack, and my inability to help him, may have figured in the picture.

So it was that most of my out-of-school time came to be spent with Jack Westcott. Before I realized what was happening, the entire family, Jack included, were viewing me as his girlfriend. It was as if a prairie dust storm had swept me in a direction that had not occurred to me, much less been foreseen, and before I recognized what was happening I was discovering myself blown into a place where I had never sought to go. This was brought home to me in a shocking moment one day when I was visiting my aunt, Mabel Carry, who had come out to the farm from the new home to which they had recently moved in Calgary. Suddenly she turned to me and said, "I hope you haven't just been leading Jack Westcott on. He's been in such a bad state ever since Jean threw him over I'm afraid if you did the same thing it'd finish him off for good."

All these factors were no doubt entangled in a vague longing, somewhere deep within my subconscious, for a romanticized sense of security and happiness which I had projected into my childhood years on our farm at Lonely Trail—combined with a more common-sense awareness of how critical to security on a farm was the nature of the land involved. I was probably being driven by the vision of a secure life on a farm in what I then viewed as the heart of the fertile black-soil country surrounding Acadia Valley. I think also the fact that Jack seemed to avoid drinking alcohol was a major factor in my unreasoned rush to commitment, in spite of the total lack on my part of any feelings of sexual attraction or love. At that time I had fully bought into my mother's version of the cause of my father's financial problems, and both feared and abhorred the widespread custom of heavy drinking within the community.

Sometime in early January I had my first real date with Jack. We arranged to attend a dance with another man whose girlfriend taught in a country school south-west of town. We had to go by way of the winding dirt road toward Empress, past Empress View school, in order to pick her up. Then we wended our way westward to the site of the dance: a small community centre near the school where my cousin Jean Carry had taught for some time. The Carry orchestra was no longer available, although it had provided the music for these dances since 1927. My uncle Joe was an expert on the violin and trumpet, and my aunt Mabel accompanied him on the piano. Their daughters Jean and Rita had played the drums, and Wendell the saxophone.

We were now in the dead of a prairie winter so, not surprisingly, the drive to the dance was a bit slow-going. The event was fun for me, although I was disappointed with Jack's lack of interest in dancing and obvious absence of skill. Then, about mid-way through the evening it began to snow, and by the time we set off for home a blizzard had engulfed us. We were okay until we had dropped off the other girl, but not far from Empress View school, catastrophe struck! The road was completely engulfed in a large snow drift, and when we tried to drive through it the car became hopelessly stuck. We knew that we had no hope of rescue, so our only chance for survival in that temperature was to somehow walk the considerable distance over the open field to the Smith farmstead. To make matters worse, I had, with the typical recklessness of the young, worn only high-heeled shoes and silk stockings to the dance.

The blizzard conditions were so bad and the snow-banks so high that it was almost impossible for me to struggle along. Because we were never quite sure that we were still headed in the right direction, we called for help almost continuously as we went. I think I managed to remain upright for about half-way, then my legs and feet became useless and the two men had to drag me along. Fortunately for us, Bill Smith happened to be outside, seeing to some livestock, when he heard us. He and June were by then living alone on the farm. He came toward the sound, to investigate, and found us just in time to rescue me. Now there were three to carry me, and we managed to make it to the house, where I was immediately tucked into a warm bed. I was soon doubly concerned to discover that June was in a much worse condition. That very afternoon her foot had been driven over when she and Bill were attempting to move some machinery. This news, along with my shock and frostbite, caused me to shake so much that the entire bed was bouncing up and down. I eventually became aware of June staggering in to sit at my bedside. She told me that the three men, equipped with shovels, had headed off in the Smith truck to try to clear the road to Empress so that they could return and get her to the hospital for treatment.

Then, as I was beginning to recover, June apparently decided to make us some hot tea. Almost immediately I heard a scream of pain. I stumbled to the kitchen and found her sprawled on the floor, moaning and holding an arm which had obviously been badly burned. She had fallen on the surface of the hot coal stove while attempting, in her crippled condition, to lift the teakettle of boiling water. Fortunately I remembered the first-aid lessons taught to all teachers-in-training in those days. I immediately immersed her arm in warm water and kept it there, as I sat beside her on the floor. We were in a terrifying situation, all alone and with no idea of when the men would be back. At that time there were still no phone lines in the vicinity. Meanwhile, I didn't dare try to move June.

After what seemed an unbearably long time, we finally heard the welcome sound of a vehicle in the yard. The men had succeeded in opening the road leading to Empress! I removed June's arm from the water which I had kept at a consistently warm temperature and gently sponged and covered it with a warm damp cloth for the trip to the hospital. Then, almost immediately, they were off, leaving me all alone in the house. However, I later learned that Jack had been able to phone his dad upon their arrival in Empress. Sometime in the early morning of the following day, Tom Burke managed, with a few helpers, to clear the road from Acadia Valley and arrive to take me back. Jack and our male dance companion made it home soon after, with the news that the doctor in Empress said I had done the right thing in my treatment of June's badly burnt arm.

Our sharing of this appalling incident had the effect of making Jack cling to me even more. And it made me sense, ever more strongly, that I could not extricate myself at this point in the relationship without doing irreparable damage to him. On the evening of Valentine's Day, with an awkward attempt at romantic flare, he asked me to marry him. I felt that I had no choice but to accept, in spite of vague feelings of unease. I attempted to placate those feelings by telling him that if things didn't work out between us I reserved the right to divorce him, for I didn't want, ever, to suffer the kind of unhappy marriage I had witnessed in my own home during my childhood. What a way to begin a relationship with a man burdened by serious emotional problems and a precarious self concept!

Not long after this, Tom and Joyce decided that she should be moved down to Empress to await the baby's birth. I was uncomfortable about remaining after she left, and expressed my concerns to my fellow teacher, Ellen Krempien. Ellen responded by inviting me to board with them, on their farmstead a few miles to the south-west of town. She already had her hands more than full, having two school-age boys and a husband with the all-too-typical 'Valley' drinking problem. As Ellen expressed it to me once, he had been raised on the small Mennonite community north of town, and when he broke away from that he seemed to think that he was free of all moral constraints as well—especially those associated with alcohol abuse. Apparently he and Ellen had met when she came to the country school located two miles east of the Carry farm which his religious group attended and used as their church as well.

Ellen and I shared the housework at their place and became even closer friends in the process. I also enjoyed helping with her little boys, Doug and Brian. Both were in the primary room at school. Then, sometime in the early spring, Joyce Burke gave birth to a boy named Wayne. Although the Westcotts were Anglican, Joyce had converted to Catholicism when she married Tom. For their sake I joined Jack in attending the christening at the Catholic church which was located in the country a few miles to the south of the Smith farm. I felt my usual embarrassed discomfort at entering such a place. This was heightened even more in light of the sad story of how, because Joyce and Tom's first child had died before being christened, she was not allowed to be buried on church property but had been relegated to the field on the far side of the church fence. Added to this was the memory of how I had hitched a ride down to Empress one day while at Empress View school and, when passing this place, had witnessed a crowd of worshipers marching in circles around the church and praying in unison for rain. I remember feeling that I must be having a nightmare in which I'd taken a fall about a thousand years back through history.

Around the time I went to live with the Krempiens, Jack had caused me considerable dismay by voicing the expectation that I would quit teaching once we were married. Life as a farmer's wife was a full-time occupation, he said. In light of this, I decided to apply for a teaching position back at the Big Prairie school in Cremona country for the coming term, in order to help Jerry before it was too late to save him. I explained my decision to Jack, telling him that I wished to spend my last year of teaching where I could do the most good for my family. He argued about it at first. Then he settled on a move to Calgary for the winter where he would try for a job working as a prison guard, in order for it to be possible to visit me on weekends. However, he made me promise that we would plan our wedding for the following summer, in July of 1948.

The Big Prairie school board was very happy to be able to hire a trained teacher. I felt that my choice had been the right one. I even managed not to allow myself to be deterred when I received word from Bob a few days later, concerning an adventure at his school not far from where I would be teaching—in the heart of the 'back west' foothills country. One of the parents had been unhappy with punishment meted out to his son, who was caught spraying Bob's only pair of good pants with ink from behind. The father had charged in during classes one day flourishing a shotgun and threatening to 'shoot the teacher'! Bob managed to face him down, but told me he decided at that moment to give up on waiting for a suitable job with the RCMP and apply for the Canadian Air Force, in the hope of landing in a less dangerous occupation than teaching.

One day Bob made a trip to the city and dropped in for a brief visit with the Carrys. Mabel later recounted how she had looked out the window and seen a young man approaching on the sidewalk. She noticed him particularly because he was totally immersed in reading a book while walking along. She said she knew at once that it had to be one of the Duffy kids!

When the school year ended in late June I was more than ready to head back to Cremona. For one thing, there was the promise of a teacherage, with a phone. I intended to persuade Mom to allow Jerry to live with me there during the week, in the hope of imposing some discipline on his life. I had purchased a guitar and lessons for it which I thought might provide him with a project that he could handle and enjoy. I had learned enough of the basics that I believed I could teach him to play. I also arranged for a set of 'World Books' to be shipped to Don, to help with the coming years of high school—all of which he would be doing by correspondence from home, while helping with the farm work.

That summer I once again headed off for Edmonton to summer school. And, once again, I loved almost every minute of the experience. Again, I was part of a wonderful group of friends. I became somewhat upset, however, by their negative reception of the news of my impending marriage, and what it would mean for my future. Their astounded comments and questions made me realize fully for the first time, just what was involved in my choice to marry Jack. They all found it difficult to understand how I could possibly be contemplating vacating my career at that stage in order to settle on a farm in the midst of the prairie without what they considered the most basic amenities of life—such as a telephone, running water and electricity.

"Do you really want to spend the rest of your days ironing a man's shirts with an iron that has to be heated on a coal stove?" one of them asked derisively. I recall replying that I liked ironing and was quite proud of my skills in that department. I think now that, in a rather desperate attempt to justify my reckless decision, I was mustering all the good memories of my work on various farms and burying all my negative ones. The girls were also appalled when I informed them that I had succumbed to Jack's plea (or was it an order?) for me to quit teaching for the present. I attempted to ease my own discomfort with that decision, as well as to satisfy their concerns about it, by assuring them that I intended to continue my studies by means of correspondence courses from Queen's University, and definitely would not give up my career in the long term.

I found my family on the farm west of Cremona much the same, except that Jerry's self-absorption had worsened while Don's work responsibilities appeared to be considerably increased. Bob had left before my arrival, to begin what would become a lifetime career in the Air Force. He headed to Nova Scotia, where he entered what turned out to be a lengthy period of very rigorous training. Once in a while when a need arose, Mom was looking after Myrtle's youngster, Linda, and in recounting various stories about this, she demonstrated a warm, and apparently loving, attachment to her little granddaughter. I recall thinking how sadly ironic it was that she had never bonded in this way with Myrtle herself.

I immediately moved into the teacherage, and was happy to discover it was large enough to crowd a couch for Jerry into the cooking area. He and Mom had agreed reluctantly to the plan that he stay with me during the school week, which Don thought was a good idea. Don was, of course, all-too-aware of the extent of the problem, and probably knew that Jerry and Mom had to be separated if at all possible, while there was yet time to undo the results of all the years of 'spoiling'.

I soon discovered that Big Prairie school was quite an undertaking. With the recent arrival of a new family from Calgary in the district, there were almost forty students, in grades one to eight. Because they hadn't had the benefit of a qualified teacher for some time, most of them were not reading at their grade level. There was a piano, however, and I discovered I was still able to play well enough to accompany them in singing. So that was a help in getting them on board the learning train. I immediately instituted the routine I had used at Empress View—opening classes in the morning with a sing-along and in the afternoon with a continuing story.

I also decided to test them all to determine their skill-levels in reading, writing and numbers, so that I could begin from where each was currently able to work successfully. I gave them an intelligence test as well. The results amazed me where Jerry was concerned. He tested so high he was almost off the chart, with his total of correct answers exceeding those of the grade-eight students. As a result of the information gained from all the testing, combined with a couple of weeks of careful observing, I was able to have each student begin lessons at their actual level of ability. I was also in a position to assign a 'helping partner' for each, so that while I was busy with the class at large and the needs of the problem students, more routine help could be attended to quietly by my group of little partnering 'teaching aides'. All this seemed to work well, once I managed to get the system into place.

One of my most memorable experiences that autumn was a visit from the school inspector. This man couldn't have been more different from Mr. Goresky, the supervisor who had been such a help to me in the Acadia School Division. It was just as school was beginning in the morning. I was at the piano, manipulating the keys in my unprofessional fashion while the pupils were happily singing one of the country songs then popular, when the door opened suddenly. I turned and discovered a middle-aged man dressed in a suit and tie. He seemed shocked, but whether it was at my ineptitude as a pianist or at what he discovered we were doing in place of the Lord's Prayer, I wasn't sure. When he had introduced himself I decided to brave it out and ask him to take a seat while we finished the song. He remained for most of the morning, observing from the back. Then suddenly, during a reading lesson, he interrupted a grade-four child who was reading aloud from a grade-one reader, proudly showing off his new-found skill. He was one of those who had been passed along the grades even though never taught to read, but was making excellent progress since I began working with him. The inspector took the book from the boy and examined it, then asked him what grade he was in. Upon receiving an answer from the stricken child, he said to him, in a challenging manner, "Then why are you reading only at a grade-one level?"

A little later, when the inspector rose to leave, I followed him outside and closed the door. In no uncertain terms, I proceeded to tell him what I thought of his behaviour. I also took the opportunity to explain to him about the problems faced by all these educationally neglected children—problems of which it was past time that he made himself aware if he were to do his job. I have often chuckled to myself about what he must have written in his report about me. I may well not have been so brave had I intended to continue teaching in that district.

Another memorable moment at Big Prairie school was my personal version of Bob's experience with the shot-gun-toting parent. One day I was forced to discipline a boy who was misbehaving. I had relegated him to a desk which I placed in the corner of the porch—where he couldn't continue to disrupt the class in order to get attention—and I'd given him a special assignment to do. It happened that he lived fairly close to the school and had, instead, run home. I hadn't noticed this and was totally stunned when he suddenly burst into the classroom shouting and aiming a shotgun at me. I don't recall how I did it, but somehow I managed to advance on him slowly, talking soothingly all the while, until I was able to reach for the gun. I visited the family afterwards and we had a serious talk about how they should be storing their shotguns.

For the first few weeks the experiment with Jerry seemed to be working. I had taught him to tidy his bed and belongings each morning and to help with the dishwashing. He was no trouble in class, as he was naturally shy and learning came so easily to him. However, he tried his best to avoid the role of 'helping partner' which I was gradually instituting. It was during recess and noon-hour that I began to recognize a more worrying pattern. In those days the game that everyone played, when there was no snow on the ground, was softball. Because I was continuing in my custom of remaining outside whenever class was out and watching everything from the sidelines, I soon realized that Jerry was as extraordinarily gifted at sports as he was academically. But this was presenting a problem.

The group's simplified version of softball, known as 'scrub', did not involve teams competing against one another. Instead, individuals took turns at bat while a pitcher and catcher were assigned and the rest played the three bases and the field. The batter continued in the starring role so long as he, or she, continued getting home runs. Jerry was so skilled at the game that I noticed he was almost constantly the one doing all the batting. After watching this for several days I spoke to him about it one afternoon, suggesting he make a habit of insisting on moving to a fielding position after making ten home runs in a row, so that others could have a turn. He was enraged at the idea, so much so that he immediately grabbed his clothes and headed off at a run toward home. As he only had about a mile-and-a-half to cover along an old wagon trail through the bush, I wasn't worried about his making it before dark. I was really concerned, however, by this reaction to my first attempt at persuading him to think of others rather than putting his own desires first. But what really saddened me was the fact that he didn't return to school for about a week, and he never again stayed with me in the teacherage—clearly preferring his daily walk from home to having to endure my attempts at discipline.

Meanwhile, Jack Westcott's efforts to be hired as a prison guard in Calgary had not succeeded. He came out to the farm for a brief visit one Saturday in late autumn, with the news that he was returning to the Valley. In the hope of raising his spirits I asked him to make arrangements before he left the city for our wedding there in July, as he wanted it to be in an Anglican church. I told him my only requirement was that it be small and as informal as possible. I told him I planned to ask my good friend from high school, Anne Gibson, to be bridesmaid, as she was then studying nursing in Calgary. When he confessed that he hadn't any friend who might serve as best man, I suggested my cousin Phil Carry, who was working in the city at the time. We arranged that, with his father's help, he would pay for the wedding and honeymoon while I devoted my minimal savings to the purchase of a sofa and bedroom suite for the farm house we were to share, during the summer and harvest season, with his father, Harry Westcott. Jack had only then informed me that Harry was planning on removing everything except for the kitchen furniture and the bedroom pieces in his own room at the farmhouse, to one of his houses in town.

The Christmas season was upon us very soon after that. During the brief times that I had worked or visited in the district in previous years I became acquainted with a girl who lived in the Water Valley district, near a community centre which housed barn dances and was used for Christmas concerts as well. She was a great help to me in planning and rehearsing the first school concert for which I was solely responsible. It turned out well as I had lots of talented youngsters to choose from for the leading parts. I even taught some of them to tap-dance. Sadly, Jerry was too shy to participate much. My idea about his learning the guitar had not worked.

The busy months of teaching rushed by all-too-quickly, and almost before I knew what was happening, I had handed out the final report cards and said farewell to my students. The summer, with the wedding in its wake, was upon us. I don't recall much about the actual service at the church in Calgary, but I have a photo which proves that it happened! For the first time I met Jack's young half-brother Bill, who hadn't lived with his father since he was small, as Harry's second marriage to the live-in housekeeper who replaced Jack's dead mother, hadn't lasted long. I was to become very close to Bill in the following years, as we established the custom of having him spend his summers with us in order to provide some much-needed stability in his life. Of course my mother and Don and Jerry were at the wedding as well.

For our honeymoon we decided to drive all the way to Campbell River in the northern reaches of Vancouver Island, British Columbia, to visit with my sister Myrtle and her second husband, Mike Pridie, along with their baby, Michael, and little Linda. Mike, also a war veteran, was a kind and responsible man who worked as a carpenter at the town's new pulp mill. The plan was that our wedding night would be celebrated in Banff. It was a disaster! I realize now that all the years I had spent fending off men who were seeking sex, along with my utter ignorance about such matters, was the poorest possible preparation for an intimate relationship; for actually loving a man—any man. That, combined with Jack's previous experience of sex having been limited to encounters with prostitutes on the streets of war-torn London, made for a truly tragic beginning for our marriage. I think the seeds of all our problems through the years to follow were planted on that night.

# Chapter 11

# ONE LAST DANCE

Dancing! After all these years, whenever I attempt to pull together my early experiences as a country schoolteacher, there is one recurring theme calling out to me. Dancing was an activity which, like teaching itself, seems to have been an expression of the innermost being of the innocent, overly confident and joyful self of the young Pat Duffy. I had loved it ever since first being taught tap-dancing at Lonely Trail School and performing on-stage at our annual Christmas concerts. One of my happiest discoveries about the Acadia Valley-Empress area was the importance of 'the dance' to the community at large, and especially of their commitment to square-dancing. It was therefore not surprising when, at the age of twenty one, I became a farmer's wife and moved to the area south of Acadia Valley to live with my husband Jack and his father, Harry Westcott, I was expecting to continue experiencing 'the dance'—whether in the form of the two-step, fox-trot, waltz, square dance or tango—as a regular and supremely important social ritual.

Equally unsurprising, however, was the fact that, until that first harvest period was over, I scarcely had time to spare a thought to anything but sheer survival. This was due chiefly to the fact that I had never really learned how to cook. While growing up on the Alberta prairies in our poverty-stricken Depression-era family, I was the designated care-giver for the Duffy boys, while my only sister Myrtle had been assigned the role of kitchen helper. Working as a waitress and general 'dogsbody' on farms during my teenage years had taught me more about getting along with people, washing dishes and cleaning tables, as well as doing outdoor chores, than with the preparation of food. During my time as a teacher previous to my marriage I had either boarded with someone or managed to exist on canned food and other essential non-perishables such as oatmeal, fruit, nuts, raw carrots, lettuce and 'bought' bread. I saw nothing wrong with that nor, indeed, did I recognize it as socially unacceptable, until one day I heard a story that the Valley grocer was circulating. It was apparently generating considerable amusement throughout the community.

It appeared that our grocer was fond of recounting how he asked me when I came into the store one day how I was progressing with learning to cook for my new husband and father-in-law. According to him, I assured him that I was doing just fine. "Then," he said, "that schoolteacher proceeded to buy nothing but a stack of canned and baked goods." I was forced to accept that he wasn't exaggerating when, many years later, my good friend and neighbour, June Smith, said she couldn't recall their ever being offered anything other than cinnamon toast when they dropped in for tea during my early days on the farm. Her story brought to mind another memory. It happened on Thanksgiving and was my first experience of a 'Valley' community potluck for the celebration of special events. I had proudly contributed my very first attempt at home-baked pumpkin pie. As the meal progressed I noticed that those who had taken a piece of the pie were leaving it, unfinished, on their plates. With gathering foreboding I tried some of it myself, only to discover that I had forgotten to put any sugar in it!

All this reminds me of the most shattering experience of all—at least of those having to do with cooking. Soon after I settled in, my new father-in-law let me know, in no uncertain terms, that 'bought' bread just would not do. He offered to teach me to bake my own, and proceeded to tell me exactly how he liked it done. I decided to try following his directions one day when the men were in the fields. It was an utter disaster! The loaves had the texture and weight of rocks. I was so embarrassed by yet another failure that I rushed outside frantically and buried the tell-tale evidence deep in the soil of the pig-yard. I decided I would purchase a good recipe book and, from then on, get my cooking advice from that, and wouldn't mention my failed attempt to the men. However, by the very next day the pigs had dug up all of my hidden loaves. What made the issue doubly unfortunate for me, and the topic of increasing merriment for Jack and Harry, and eventually the neighbours, was the fact that the pigs were unsuccessful in their attempts to eat the cement-like objects. I decided that the next time I got into town I'd send a C.O.D. order off to Eatons catalogue for "The Joy of Cooking", which I understood to be the standby of every young farmer's wife.

Still, I was determined to try my best, in spite of extremely difficult circumstances and continued failures. Harry Westcott was an intimidating man, addicted to having his own way even in the running of the household.

His older daughter, Grace, had left home after the death of her mother, while still at a very young age. I soon came to understand why. I think he resented me from the start. One of the first intimations of what was to come was a bit of gossip repeated to me about a comment by my new father-in-law. When asked to describe me he was said to have responded, "Well, she calls herself a blonde." I realized that he was referring to the fact that, as I matured, my hair was darkening somewhat and turning into what was then referred to as a 'dirty blonde' shade. During this period I quickly learned that my husband Jack was accustomed, no doubt from early childhood, to being somewhat scorned and told what to do by his father. It was only when it became clear to me that I was expected to obey unquestioningly as well that I began to realize the appalling extent of the worrisome consequences issuing from my choice in marriage.

There was no electricity in that particular countryside in those days, and no phone line ran past the Westcott land. However, the road to Empress, near where the Smiths lived, was then in the process of having a line built alongside it that would connect with the bordering farms. The Smith farm was over five miles east of us, across open prairie—even further if one traveled on the connecting trail to the north. And we were a couple of miles from the winding dirt road further west of us that eventually wandered northward to Acadia Valley. At that time there were no plans for a phone line in our direction. What made our situation even more precarious was a problem with the water supply. The water available from the barnyard well was minimal and not safe to drink, although it was used for the farm animals. I soon began to understand why Harry was happy to continue living in town during the winters. One of the many outdoor tasks assigned to me was to manipulate a small horse-driven dray—a platform-like vehicle operating on tiny wheels in the summer and sled runners in winter—to the community well a few miles away. Once there I had to fill several cream cans with our weekly supply of drinking water.

I was also expected to take charge of the garden, which was then at the stage where its season's produce was ready for harvesting and preserving. Harry introduced me to the hole which had been dug in one corner of the basement and filled with dry sand. This was called a 'root cellar'. It was where the root vegetables would be stored for the winter, by being buried as deep as possible. I learned I would have to arrange them carefully and remember exactly where the potatoes, carrots, turnips, beets, etc. could be found. Other vegetables such as green beans and peas, as well as any fruit that had been successfully grown, would have to be preserved in jars by means of a boiling and sealing process.

Other tasks were feeding the chickens and collecting the eggs, as well as milking and caring for the cows. In fact, I discovered that, during the time when the men were busy with seeding and harvesting the grain crops, even the pigs were my responsibility—as was the weekly cleaning-out of the barn. In the house there was a 'milk separator' which allowed the cream to rise to the top and be skimmed off, and a hand-operated churn for making butter; both of which I already knew how to use because of my previous employment on farms. There was also a giant rectangular barrel of water in the cellar, known as a cistern. I learned this was replenished by water from the rain and/or melted snow from the roof, by means of the eaves troughs and roof drains. It was necessary to shovel ice and snow into the cistern in late winter in order to keep its water cold for as long into the summer as possible. A small pump in the kitchen provided access to the water from it, for non-drinking purposes. It was placed as far as possible from the furnace, beside which was space for a small store of coal and wood. It was in this cistern that I was told I would have to learn to hang the items of food and drink requiring what passed for refrigeration in those days.

The house had three bedrooms as well as a small couch in the attic, a living room, and a good-sized kitchen with a few open shelves on one wall, alongside the coal stove. It also contained an awkward chest-high cupboard for washing hands, etc., and a wooden table large enough for a few visitors, along with sufficient chairs. And there was a low bench on which a round tub and washboard were placed. My savings from teaching had all been used for the purchase of a bedroom suite for our room, as well as a sofa and corner-cupboard for the living area. I was neither surprised nor disturbed by the filthy condition of the outdoor toilet, which was easily remedied. It was the general setting of the place that most discouraged me. The view from the door, which opened onto the back yard rather than the front, was one of the dreariest imaginable. Jack and his father shared a long-entrenched habit of emptying the slop-pail from the kitchen, and the contents of the chamber-pots as well, merely by slinging them out the door onto our only entrance-way.

Of course there were compensations. A good friend and colleague from the Acadia Valley school, Ellen Krempien, was helpful as always. For the first month of my 'settling in' process she was still enjoying summer holidays, so was able to take the time to teach me many of the skills necessary for my new life. One of these was totally new to me, and it stood me in good stead for years. It was the old Mennonite method of curing sausages, ground from the meat of butchered livestock. I had been accustomed to making sausages at the butcher shop where I once worked as a teenager, but this primitive curing and smoking process was much more complicated. However, it was an excellent way to preserve meat products in those days without electricity and before I was able to afford a stove-top steamer which allowed me to 'can' it easily and safely in jars.

Altogether, it proved to be a complex and difficult time, although replete with learning. Through it all I often thought of the reaction of my aunt Leila to the news of my impending marriage. Leila had 'gone queer' as a Depression-era farmer's wife on what had been the original family homestead of my grandmother Armitage—located some thirty miles or so to the north-west. The last time I ever saw her was at Ma's house in the village of Oyen, during one of her rare visits there. I had made a special trip from Acadia Valley to announce my engagement. At the news Leila appeared to freeze, staring at me with an expression of horror in her usually empty blue eyes.

"Please . . . ," she begged in a strangled voice, "please don't do it!" I didn't know it then, but a few years later she would be committed to a mental institution in Ponoka, Alberta. I never saw her again, but her face and words came back to haunt me many times in the following years.

Somehow that memory of Leila was connected with an uncomfortable sense of losing control which I was experiencing increasingly during my early settling-in period. This may have been reinforced by the fact that, almost immediately after the wedding, Jack had queried me about life insurance. Did I have any, and who was it made out to? I told him I had taken out a minimal policy when I began teaching; and that it was in the name of my mother. He then asked me to change it immediately in order to make him the beneficiary. I was so shocked by the fact that he would raise this issue at such a time, and then proceed to make such a demand, that I refused. My excuse was that I intended to wait until the financial security of my mother and younger brothers was more firmly guaranteed. The subject then became a sore point between us and was to remain so.

It may have been this event that caused me to tell Jack that, due to the financial insecurity of my early life, I was very uneasy about having nothing whatsoever in my own name. I came up with the idea that he and his dad assign me one of the female calves in the small herd, and I would henceforth own her descendants. I explained to him that it would be in his interest as well, as it would give me an incentive to do all the chores that were apparently expected of me. He may have read it as a threat to go on strike for, after talking it over with Harry, he acquiesced.

By the time this agreement was threshed out, and the grain threshed as well and safely stored in the granaries, I began to breathe a little easier. However,

I learned that selling the crop was a problem in those days, so there was little financial return for us to count on. I also soon learned that there was one final task which Harry was determined I must be taught before he left us on our own for the winter. It was the butchering of the young roosters, and of any hens that were past their prime, preparatory to preserving a year's supply of their meat. Apparently, his custom before my arrival was to take any of the excess meat into Acadia Valley for sale. He proceeded to teach me how to do the required task by going through the 'wringing necks' routine, along with the removal of feathers and innards. This wasn't as shocking to me as it would have been if I hadn't had previous experience in a butcher shop. Nevertheless, I quietly decided that, when I took over the task the following year, I would wield an axe for decapitating purposes and, in each case, beyond sight of the waiting victims. That seemed a mite less cruel.

Around the time Harry moved back to town for the winter, social life was beginning to revive in our country community. Jack and I were invited to a dinner party at the home of our nearest neighbours, Lillian (his brother-in-law Tom Burke's sister) and her husband Bert Elliott. They lived at the corner where the trail from our place met the narrow dirt road which accessed Acadia Valley to the north and meandered south-eastward to connect eventually with the Empress road as it approached the bridge across the river a considerable distance to the south of us. That evening I had a chance to mix with most of the people living in the general vicinity. I was already acquainted with a quite a few of them, including a young man who had wanted to date me when I was teaching at the Valley school, before hearing that I was already 'spoken for'. Upon learning of my intentions at a dance we were both attending, he had actually gone so far as to warn me against getting further involved with Jack Westcott, maintaining that I had picked the one man in the entire community who was least suitable for me. To my subsequent regret I reacted in anger, abruptly leaving him on the dance floor. My chief memories of this particular dinner party are therefore some sense of embarrassment at meeting this young man again and discovering he was a neighbour, coupled with Jack's reaction to my behaviour during the course of the evening. Fairly early on, I had drifted over to where the men were discussing politics and become enthusiastically involved in the conversation. This was after having grown bored by the housekeeping chatter of the women. On the way home a little later, I was amazed when Jack began to rage at me concerning this.

'That was *man's* talk," he shouted, above the roar of the old half-ton truck. "You had no business to be sitting with us!"

My new husband's attitude about 'the place of married women' was further driven home to me soon after this. At the dinner I had heard about a dance to be held in the near future. In the expectation that we would be attending, I consulted with Jack about what he would like me to wear. I was told, in no uncertain terms, that married people did not go to such events; they were intended only for singles. So much for the joy of dancing! Somehow, I suspected that *The Joy of Cooking* wouldn't quite compensate for what I now seemed fated to be missing.

However, something happened a few weeks later that began to resurrect my hopes for the future. On a visit to town, Ellen told me about a project in which they wanted me to become involved. It was a play to be presented in the town community hall for Christmas. The group planning it were apparently counting on me to take the leading female part. I decided my only hope was to announce my intentions of accepting this request to Jack in no uncertain terms, rather than to ask for his permission. Ellen said she would arrange transportation so that I could attend practices as well as the actual performance. Once we got underway I discovered that the young neighbour who had warned me not to marry Jack was also in the play and had offered to give me a ride whenever I needed it. Jack got rather moody about it all and retreated into silence. To my relief, he didn't cause any trouble—not until the night we were about to present the play, that is. Because I had been taught to apply stage make-up in a drama course I was made responsible for that task, in addition to acting. On the evening of the performance, Jack had driven me in, and I expected him to be seated in the audience. Instead, he appeared suddenly backstage, happening upon us just as I was in the process of applying this particular young neighbour's make-up. It was the first time I had seen Jack almost literally explode in a fit of temper. All my fellow actors, as well as some members of the audience, witnessed his being dragged and pushed out the back door, shouting to all and sundry that he had caught us in the very act of having an affair. Somehow it had never occurred to me that anyone would consider the professional application of stage make-up as a form of sexual intimacy.

In the midst of that horrifying incident, I had noticed an unfamiliar odor surrounding Jack. As the awareness that it was alcohol struck home, I realized why he was so opposed to the custom of drinking, which was then powerfully embedded in the Valley culture. It was because alcohol led to an utter loss of control where he was concerned!

For the time, however, I knew I had to put what had just happened—and any possible explanations of it—completely out of my thoughts. The director was signaling that the curtain was about to go up. Fortunately, the magnitude of what was required of me in the leading role served to propel me into what was virtually a different world. The play came together like magic and, for several hours, the present moment was so fulfilling it was all there was for me. Acting had always functioned similarly to dancing where I was concerned. Ever since my wonderful experiences as a child performing both activities in Christmas concerts, they were associated with one another, and with utter happiness within the self that defined me. As with the dance, I was now in a situation where a perfection of control prevailed. But it was a control which, in the heart of the activity—the actual stage performance—seemed to require nothing more of me than an intuitive response. It was as if I had soared away to a totally different world from that into which my marriage had so recently plummeted me.

But after all the happy celebrations had ended, I had to go back to the farm. Because I was worried about how Jack would receive me, I asked the Krempiens merely to drop me off in the yard. I could see that they weren't comfortable doing it, but I persuaded them that it would be for the best, as Jack was least likely to get further upset that way. The house was dark, and when I went around to the door at the back I discovered it was locked. After knocking in vain for a while, I found my way over to the barn and decided that sleeping in the straw with the cows was my best option. I had scarcely settled in, however, when Jack appeared. He stood there staring at me for some time, silent and surly, then indicated that he wanted to lie down with me in the straw. I thought some comforting might be in order, but after a few minutes of intimacy he stood abruptly.

"Now I know you'd be willing to do it anywhere—and with anybody!" I heard him snarling this while turning and rushing out the barn door.

His attitude all evening had been so weird and extreme that I found myself utterly bereft of words. I was reduced to following him, desolate and despairing, into the house. I realized at once, however, that Jack's current behaviour, on the heels of the earlier accusation which had been so public and so serious, meant that I could no longer avoid recognition of the full extent of his problems. And of the form they were beginning to take. I now knew that, for some time at least, I would have to give up any thought of mixing with my friends in the community, and focus instead on my husband's alarming condition. I was even forced to face up to the dismaying possibility that I had not done him a favour by marrying him in the hope of providing much needed emotional help; but that I may well be the worst possible person for him. All that I represented—my appearance, professional abilities and social interests—were a threat to him. What he had needed was a farm wife with no ambition other than being just that. He should have married a simple, obedient, plain-looking country woman of the old school with no interests outside the home. My desolating suspicion was reinforced a few days later, when the young male neighbour came over for a hurried consultation after he had seen Jack driving into town. He assured me he would avoid any encounter with me in the future, for my sake, but said he wanted me to know that he would always be there if I needed him. Our mutual fear of Jack's early return resulted in his remaining for only a moment or so. Ironically, we were being forced by circumstances to act and feel as if we were guilty of some misdeed.

From then on I was much more fully aware not only of the extent of Jack's war-induced problems, but of my own current ones as well. I would have to make myself into the kind of wife his condition required, and try my best not to be the cause of any further increase in his insecurity. Nevertheless, there was one last event which, when the time came, I simply could not miss. Near the end of the subsequent solitary winter devoted to focusing on Jack's needs, I was gratified out of all proportion when invited to the end-of-season Acadia School Division curling bon-spiel, held by the curlers among all the teachers in that widespread area. I had learned the sport of curling a couple of years previously while teaching at Acadia Valley school, and loved it. Of course I had not been able to participate during the current season, but was invited to the bon-spiel and follow-up party anyway. I decided it would be my 'one last hurrah'. I informed Jack of it and told him he was also invited to watch the bon-spiel and attend the party along with me. But at winter's end when the time came, he refused to go. His excuse was that he had never been interested in curling. Ellen Krempien came to pick me up, and Jack seemed to feel reassured by the fact that her husband Howard was also not attending the event. He may even have had the impression that the game was an all-female affair, although I had not said that. But I admit I did nothing to disabuse him of the assumption.

After the difficult months of attempting to build up Jack's self-esteem, what a pleasure it was to relax and be myself once more, touching base with old teaching acquaintances from schools all the way from Hanna to Alsask and down to Empress! I even managed to become totally absorbed in watching this typically Canadian country game from the sidelines, although my real interest, where sports were concerned, had always been in playing rather than being a spectator. By the time the annual 'season's end' party got underway I was, for one of the few times since my marriage, able to relax totally and lose myself in the joy of the moment. Through all the happy visiting and reminiscing, the music was playing softly in the background. Then the dancing began, and I was in my element once more! Later, near the evening's close, the orchestra shifted to waltz music. A colleague from Hanna—one of the Polish airmen who had escaped the Nazi occupation by taking a plane and flying it to Britain—had remained seated until then. Suddenly he rose and came over to ask me to dance. Other couples began to move onto the floor as well. I sensed at once that a unique experience was beginning for me. My partner was one of those exquisite ballroom dancers that only Europe seemed to produce in those days. As we whirled and dipped, all my troubles and tensions seemed to fade away. It was as if the music formed a cloud of light and we were floating on it, a world removed from the dark and terrifying bog in which I had so recklessly buried myself. Gradually, it dawned on me that all the other dancers had moved to the edge of the room and were watching us. Then, all too soon, the music came to an end. My partner bowed to me and I curtsied to him, and the audience clapped. The feeling of blissful relaxation remained with me throughout the night and for days to follow. I had no way of knowing that this would be my "one last dance".

# Chapter 12

# THE POWER OF THE PULSE OF LIFE

I learned a great deal during my first two stressful years as a prairie farmer's wife. And, even more important, I survived to tell the tale. First and foremost among those lessons was the power of the pulse of life, not only as I witnessed it in the rapidly growing crops and garden, the newly born calves and chickens but, one day in the autumn of 1949, within my own body as well. In fact, it was that first actual experience of a pulsing sensation which confirmed for me a growing awareness of the fact of my pregnancy. And a growing sense of wonder and awe at being a contributing part of that marvelous life process sparked countless ages ago by the collision of asteroids in space: a collision that produced the dust which then spread over the earth for further millions of years.

My sense of being part of the network and cycle of life was heightened in a very different way one evening by a phone call from the family of my long-time friend, Marie Norris. What they had to convey was horrifying in the extreme. Marie, like me an avid horseback rider, had been trying out a new pony at her country school, with her students looking on. The pony reared unexpectedly and Marie was thrown from her saddle. The same thing had happened to me a few years previously but, having intuitively hit the ground in one of the rolls taught in acrobatics, I had emerged unscathed. However, in Marie's case the luck of the draw was against her, and she landed in an awkward position, breaking her neck. She was already dead when the first onlooker reached her. She had dropped in for a quick visit to check up on me that previous summer. Upon hearing the dreadful news, I was thankful for the brief interval we had been able to spend together, and glad that we had not known it would be our last. How hideous it would be if, as some spiritualists would have us believe, we were able to experience premonitions of 'last times' as they occur increasingly in our journey through life!

In spite of all the turmoil, I was able to manage all my tasks during this second harvesting season. In fact, I found the work not nearly as difficult as it had been the previous year. Fortunately for me, my father-in-law, Harry, now had a woman friend in Empress, so he left for the winter about the time I began to experience morning sickness. Not so fortunate, however, was the fact that my morning sickness soon turned into an almost continuous state of overwhelming illness. With this there suddenly developed a great deal of severe pain in both my back and frontal area, as well as a strange swelling—not of the lower stomach which I had expected—but at the waist and mid-to-upper parts of my body. However, isolated as I was, and with no means of communicating with friends, I had no way of knowing that all this was not the normal state of affairs with a pregnancy. My friend, June Smith, had given birth to her first child the previous year, and had now taken him to England for an extended stay with her family there. My other best friend, Ellen Krempien, was having increasing problems with her husband Howard's drinking, so I didn't wish to brave the trip to town on a weekend in order to bother her. And my sister-in-law, Joyce Burke, was very occupied with her little boy, Wayne, who was proving to be a difficult child with what appeared to me to be learning problems. I wrote fairly regularly to Mom and my sister Myrtle in those days, but didn't want to cause them concern by offering other than a somewhat whitewashed record of events after they had occurred. Most of all, I didn't want to worry my husband Jack, whose 'nervous state' (as I referred to it in letters to Myrtle) had appeared to be improving somewhat that summer.

I was unable to ignore my condition for long, however. By mid-November the pain was rapidly becoming unbearable. Then, one day, bleeding began, and I had to beg Jack to get me to the hospital as quickly as possible. I was afraid to chance the ride all the way down to Empress in our old half-ton truck, so I suggested that he rush over to the nearest neighbours, the Elliots, and ask them to drive us in. He eventually returned with transportation, but the neighbour driving the car following him was not, as I had expected, one of those Burke relatives who lived at the nearby crossroads. It was, instead, the young man who had so aroused Jack's jealousy the previous winter. I was in a hideous state, and in spite of being barely conscious throughout the drive, experienced a continuous sense of mortification at the mess I was making in the back seat. Jack had apparently felt compelled to remain on the farm to care for the livestock, so it was that helpful neighbour who delivered me to the hospital.

My stay there was extremely unpleasant. But at least Dr. McNeill, the sole doctor in the entire community, was able to prevent a miscarriage. For me, this was all that mattered. 'Doc' told me, however, that my kidneys were in a precarious condition. As soon as I was able, I asked a friend in Empress, who visited me daily, to phone my mother. This girl was part of a couple who had befriended me in my days as a teacher at Empress View school, and we three had remained close ever since. As soon as Mom heard the news, she invited me home to the farm in Cremona country, where she would care for me. But there was simply no way I could travel across almost the entire Province, much as I longed to go. So when Jack finally made it in to see how I was doing, after I had spent a couple of weeks in hospital, I had no option but to return to the farm.

Once the uncomfortable drive was over, I was pleasantly surprised to discover that Jack had attempted to compensate for his continuous indoor smoking by washing down the walls and ceilings of the entire house. There was even a meal ready to heat up. I had scarcely settled in, however, when the first really bad blizzard of the season struck. That proved to be the beginning of the worst winter the district had experienced in years, with a long run of temperatures of minus fifty or below. After awakening one morning in late December to a condition of rapidly increasing pain and nausea, I realized that it was no longer possible for me to remain in that isolated place. As I was utterly unable to do anything, I asked Jack to pack up my necessities, then hitch a team of horses to an old, broken-down 'cutter' that hadn't been used for fifteen years. He managed to get me into it, wrapped to the neck in blankets, and we began the long trip through the snow-blocked trails into Acadia Valley. When we finally arrived, Jack deposited me at his sister Joyce's home and left at once, while returning safely to the farm was still an option. As I wrote in a letter to my sister Myrtle soon thereafter, "This is a terrible country! Now I understand why Leila went crazy! Only the strong survive." At the time, I didn't expect to be one of those survivors.

I had just received word from Mom that Leila's husband, my uncle Ed, was now temporarily in Oyen with Ma, my grandmother. He hadn't shown up for so long that she became concerned and called the police, who went out to his farm to investigate. Upon finding Ed ill in bed and Leila crouched in a corner, screaming for food, they phoned my cousin, Jack Carry, who lived on his parents' farm. When he finally succeeded in navigating the snow-blocked road my cousin discovered both Ed and Leila in a precarious condition. Leila was taken into government care and subsequently committed to an asylum, while Ed was to spend the remainder of the winter in town with Ma. It greatly relieved me to hear this news. I had been worrying about my grandmother since the winter weather struck, in light of the fact that she had written about being confined to her yard—or 'lot', as she referred to it.

Meanwhile, my husband Jack had not returned to town, nor did we hear from him at all during my stay with Tom and Joyce. I was profoundly uncomfortable throughout the following weeks—not only physically, but emotionally as well. At that time their little abode was merely a three-room building, and Joyce was forced to share the only bed with me while Tom crowded in with little Wayne on the couch in the kitchen. I was all too aware of how difficult that was for them, as I had slept on the same couch when I boarded at their place briefly while teaching at the Acadia Valley school two years previously. Now, the long month of my forced visit seemed like an eternity.

All I was able to do, in my crippled and pain-ridden condition, was to knit baby clothes and endeavour to keep some food down each day, for the sake of that struggling little pulse of life within me. Nevertheless, when Jack finally made his way into town, I decided to return to the farm with him, as I couldn't bear to continue being such a burden on Joyce and Tom. We had scarcely made it home, however, when I was struck by the most hideous pain experienced thus far. I realized then that my baby and I would not survive without medical care. Yet another blizzard was raging, but as soon as it became daylight Jack set off cross-country on horseback for help. He chose the farm of Joe Matz, a neighbour located some miles to the south of us on the Empress road. They eventually returned: Joe with a team of horses and 'cutter' and Jack on his horse behind. Joe and I set out immediately for Empress, with Jack remaining at home—once more—to look after the livestock. What followed was the worst trip of my life. We headed directly overland toward the bridge crossing the river near Empress, as Joe said that the road to town was totally impassable. During the seemingly endless journey, the horses would rear up and plunge into the banks of ice and snow, time and again, until they had worked their way through a particularly stubborn blockage. That bridge, when it finally came into view, was a welcome sight!

It was an indescribable relief to get checked into the hospital, but I could tell at once that, in Dr. McNeill's opinion, time was running out for me. The pain kept getting worse, with only a brief half-hour of relief following each morphine shot. Doc came in the next morning with the news that my kidneys had stopped working completely. Soberly, he informed me of his decision. Only by aborting the pregnancy, he said, could my life be saved. And that had to be done at once, even though there was no possibility of the child's survival at this stage of its development, and in the condition it was bound to be.

"But it must be almost six months along!" I remember gasping." What if I could manage to survive for another month? Could you save it then?"

His response was not hopeful. "I advise strongly against that course of action," he said. "Your kidneys have failed." He then asked where my husband was, and said he would send someone out to inform him of the emergency. "I can only give you this morning to decide," he warned. "I'll need to operate later today."

It didn't require the remainder of the morning for me to realize that, for good or ill, I and this stubborn little pulse of life within me were irrevocably connected. We had been fighting the battle for survival on these stormy seas of pain far too long for me to throw the helpless little creature overboard at this juncture. When I told Doc my decision he was obviously disapproving, but lost not a moment in trying to persuade me. First, he asked if I had any close family for him to notify of my impending death, so I gave him my mother's phone number. He said he had already asked the friendly couple who visited me each day to try to get out to the farm to let my husband know what was happening. By that time I was vomiting all of the water they tried to force into me, and apparently they couldn't get a drop of urine from my bladder. So Doc began to improvise.

I was put on intravenous feedings, and a stomach pump was inserted. For the following couple of weeks my daily treatment consisted of six needles of streptomycin, twelve pills for pain, three doses of Epsom salts and two enemas—along with several blood transfusions. I was buried in heating pads so that the sweat would pour from my body profusely and continuously. A tube down my throat was used every two hours to wash out my stomach. The pain was excruciating, but I had a half-hour respite from it every four hours, after my shot of morphine. Mom arrived as soon as was possible, given the tedious and round-about train route between Empress and Carstairs. She remained at my side almost constantly throughout the ensuing ordeal, just as she had done during the health crises of my childhood. I don't think I could have survived without her presence. There was no sign of Jack, but the couple who had been sent to inform him about my condition told the doctor he was tied up with a sick cow and couldn't leave the farm. I hadn't really expected him as I understood, by that time, that Jack simply could not bear to face up to any such crisis.

One afternoon, when Doc calculated that I had passed the crucial seven-month point, the birth was instigated. Labour proved to be extremely difficult for me, in spite of the fact that the pain involved did not begin to compare with that which the kidney failure had caused. I remember very little of it, however, as I lost consciousness early in the process.

When I came to, I was back in my hospital bed. My nurse told me that Doc had been forced to extract the baby by means of instruments. The problem was I had no strength whatsoever by that time. As Doc informed me afterwards, "You weren't much help, you know. You passed out just when we needed you." He then added that he had never seen a female with such strong and hard stomach muscles, and their reluctance to expand to make room for my baby may well have contributed to my problems throughout the pregnancy. He also told me that I must never again attempt to bear a child.

I waited through most of the day for news of my baby's condition. I was told only that it was a boy. Almost immediately I began to think of him in terms of the name which Jack and I had settled on some months earlier. We had chosen Tommy, after his Uncle Tom Burke, and his step-grandfather Tom Graham. Also, my paternal grandfather had been named Thomas, as was my father's favourite brother. Jack wanted his son's official first name to be the same as his, however, so as soon as he arrived a day later he arranged the birth registration in the name of John Thomas Westcott. Tommy weighed in at a little less than five pounds. My nurse told me they had improvised a make-shift incubator, and hinted at where it was located. I was so worried that I struggled from my bed the afternoon following the birth—before Mom arrived with Jack—and managed a tortuous trip down the hall to where the babies were kept. My tenacious little Tommy, in his strange box, was a sight to behold. His pitifully tiny, skeleton-like body was worrying enough, but the fact that there was a lump on the side of his head almost as large as the little head itself—from the instruments used for the difficult birth—made me agonize with fear. Clearly this was why they had not brought him in to me.

I shall never forget the nurse who was always there for me and, subsequently, for my baby, in spite of the fact that she had not been in attendance for the actual birth. Her name was Loreen. Her devoted nursing of both of us went so far beyond the requirements of duty that it is difficult even to imagine in this day and age. During the entire period when I was hovering on the brink of death, she spent countless 'off-duty' night-time hours sitting by my bedside. Later Doc was to tell me that she did the same in the case of Tommy, once I had been forced to leave and return to the farm. In his opinion, the tiny long-starved infant would not have survived without Loreen's rigorous and attentive care.

My health began to recover immediately; so rapidly, in fact, that I was discharged less than a week after the birth. My only problems were chronic back pain and a miserable bout of what Dr. McNeill told me was 'milk fever' due to not having been able to nurse my child. I figured that I could deal with that. I was familiar with the problem in cows, but hadn't been aware that it could occur for humans as well. Doc guessed that the baby would have to remain in hospital for at least a month. Mom already had completed the sewing of a supply of cloth diapers for him. (In those days we laundered our diapers, making one set do until the baby was 'potty-trained'.) She presented these to me, just before Jack and I left for the farm, then set off on her own back to Cremona on the roundabout train-and-bus trip which included a brief stopover with Ma in Oyen.

Jack's spirits seemed to revive considerably at his first sight of the baby. Little Tommy had my legs and hands, and his eyes were like mine as well. Also, I saw an expression on his face that reminded me of Lew, my father. But, in general, everyone noted and remarked upon the strong Westcott resemblance. This obviously pleased Jack, and the two of us left for the farm in a state of euphoria and general relief that the long ordeal was over. The roads were now good enough for me drive back into Empress at least twice a week during the following month, until we were finally able to bring Tommy home. By that time he had progressed amazingly. Although still incredibly thin, he then weighed all of six-and-a-half pounds and had a round, happy little face. In looks, he struck me as a mixture of his dad and my brother Bob. We brought him home just in time for Easter. Joyce and little Wayne came out for a few days so she could help me get the baby settled in and establish a routine of care. She brought with her a 'bathinette' which a group of my women friends in Acadia Valley had gotten together to purchase for us. I had been given a basket for the baby by then as well, and Myrtle had sent several lovely hand-knitted outfits for him which were vastly superior to the one I had managed to complete.

In early July, as soon as seeding and other early summer tasks were done, I left for Cremona with little Tommy. It was wonderful to be home once more, and to see my two young brothers and step-father Tom as well as Mom! The visit was much too brief, however, as Tommy and I had to return to the farm at the 'Valley' by late July, in time for the arrival of my aunt Dot's only child. Beverley was slated to spend a month of her holiday on the farm with us. This became a regular occurrence from then until she finished school.

My return to the Valley was nothing if not stressful. Not only did I discover a dirty house waiting for me, but our critical milk-and-cream separator and hand-operated churn for making butter were in a dangerously filthy condition as well. This had potentially serious ramifications, and a great deal of scrubbing and soaking with bleach was required to render these appliances safe to use. For the following weeks I was immersed in housework and baby-tending, and was very thankful for the help of young Beverley. Then, soon after Beverley left in mid-August, Jack Carry brought Ma out from Oyen. Two weeks later we drove her back home. Our visit had passed all too quickly, and it was with considerable misgivings that I left Ma on her own that day. My concern was eased only by the understanding that she would accept Mom's invitation to spend the coming winter with them.

Tommy was getting more cute all the time. He had proven to be a very easy child to handle. By the beginning of August he was already using his high chair, apparently very aware of his surroundings. He was sitting up and paddling the water in the little tub when I bathed him; and sleeping all through the night from 6:30 p.m. until 6:00 a.m. He began thumb-sucking in the first week of August and I discovered him sucking a toe five days later. It was around this time that I received one of my brother Bob's typically ironic letters. In the midst of offering me a cursory view of his busy training experience in the Air Force training school in Nova Scotia he asked, "And how is Tommy? Is he walking and talking yet? Does he take after you or is he intelligent?"

When I responded I told him about how Tommy had decided one day, at the age of seven months, he no longer wanted to drink from the bottle. When I gave it to him he would fling it over his shoulder. After losing several of our glass bottles this way I realized that he was communicating his desire to drink from a cup as we did. From that time on he refused to suck on a nipple.

In spite of the pleasure and sense of pride provided by Tommy, I had little chance to relax during the harvest season. Supper wasn't until 7:30 p.m., when the men came in from the fields, so I always settled Tommy down for the night before they arrived. By the time I had the kitchen cleaned up in the evening I was fit for nothing but bed. How I managed all the washing and drying of diapers—with my washing board and make-shift, outdoor clotheslines; along with the endless cooking and baking for the men and preserving of garden produce and the year's crop of chickens—I simply cannot imagine. And always there was the weather and the worsening of the crop situation resulting from it. The overwhelming problem was that, although the spring and early summer of 1950 had been fairly dry, the rain began in mid-July and continued to come down in torrents throughout the next two months. Now, all during what should have been harvest time, our fields were a crowded mixture of fresh green and over-ripe wheat along with 'Russian Thistles' growing higher than the crops. The outlook for our supply of marketable wheat was not good.

In fact we eventually discovered that, although we had a plentiful store of feed for the livestock, there was absolutely no income from the crop. We had failed to sell enough even to pay expenses for the year. The only financial help available was a 'dry bonus' from the government, which gave us a bare living. However, the one upside was that, as in the case of the previous year, there was no income tax to pay. My cousin, Jack Carry, who was renting part of the family farm by then, was in even worse financial straits. Later that winter he was forced to leave his wife, Pat, at home to manage with their children, while he went off to find a job. He was also a war veteran like the other two Jacks in my family and, like them, suffered from the effects of the war. One of the results was his all-too-typical Valley drinking problem which didn't help the situation.

Meanwhile, Ma had never gone out to Cremona, as planned. In early December I received a momentous message from my uncle Ed, informing me that he had come in from the farm and discovered her on the kitchen floor, almost dead. She had fallen and lain there on her own for about five days. They had then shipped her to the hospital at Calgary, where my aunt Mabel could be with her, but she had refused all sustenance and lived only for a brief period. I wasn't surprised at Ma's hastening of her own death, as I knew she had never wanted to end her life as a burden to her family. I was able to take Tommy and drive to Oyen to attend the small funeral for her. The only others who managed to get there were my cousin Jack and his wife Pat, his mother Mabel, and my aunt Annie from Caroline. While we were together, Annie was kind enough to take a snapshot of me holding little Tommy on my lap. As we didn't own a Kodak in those days, it was only the second picture I was ever to have of my son at that early stage of babyhood. The first was of him in his baby carriage taken by my Empress friends on the day we brought him home from the hospital.

The year to follow was somewhat better for the Valley farmers, although it began badly. In what should have been autumn, winter set in with a vengeance, bringing with it almost continuous blizzard conditions. However, a fortunate lull in the weather during the holiday season allowed me to drive and myself into Oyen for a brief visit with my school friend Anne Gibson. I think it was then that I had the chance to get a proper photo of Tommy. And we did manage to get into Acadia Valley for Christmas dinner at Joyce and Tom's.

But from Christmas on, I had no opportunity to speak to anyone but Jack and Tommy for over four months. My chief source of enjoyment in those difficult days was watching Tommy's development. For example, he first sat up on his own on January tenth, and by early February was traveling around the house in his walker and pulled himself up to a standing position near the end of that month. He also had most of his front teeth by then.

Once in a while Jack managed the treacherous roads to town in order to purchase bare necessities, but it was never safe for us to accompany him. Then, just after Tommy's first birthday, as we were hopefully contemplating the end of winter, another blizzard struck. Never, in my wildest dreams, had I imagined anything remotely like that storm. All we could see was a cloud of whirling snow until, eventually, all the windows in the house were as solidly blocked as if a dense white sheet had been drawn over them. We were able to open the door for only the first few hours. But even then, if we had ventured a mere step or two outside, we would have been totally lost. The storm lasted two days and nights. All during that time we were trapped indoors, cuddled together under blankets around the coal stove in the kitchen. We had developed the habit of storing the coal supply out in the garage, so were forced to resort to burning coal-dust from the cellar, along with cardboard storage boxes and anything else we could find in the house.

It wasn't until the storm eased up that the radio began to work again. The first news we heard came as a nasty shock for me. It was about the death of Mrs. Fitzpatrick, the midwife who had helped with my brother Don's birth in Oyen. Some years previously, her family had moved to a farm in the Acadia Valley country. The newscaster announced that she was discovered dead in her yard. Apparently, she had attempted to cross it to the shed with food for her dog.

Another item of the news that day concerned the trains on the Goose Lake Line to the north of us. For the entire storm they had all literally been stopped in their tracks: a historic first, it was said. One of these was trapped for two days near the crossroad leading down to Oyen, until snow plows managed to reach it. Other frightening news included that fact that the blizzard death toll had by then reached ten. Among these was a baby found dead in the wreckage of a small cabin; a teen-age boy smothered in a snowbank; and a woman struggling to get to her neighbour's house. Another pair of young victims had gone out in the storm to get a toboggan-load of coal.

Other news of interest now available to us by radio had to do with talk of a possible settlement of the Korean war, as well as with how the new Shah of Iran had launched a program by which peasants were, for the first time ever, to become owners of designated tracts of vast areas of royal land. A more negative item dealt with the further spread of atomic bomb facilities, with Britain announcing their pending production of them—quite isolated from the American undertakings, they claimed. And another concerned the condition of the slave labourers in the Soviet Union's camps. They were being treated much worse than the dogs inhabiting the same camps, according to the reporter.

As we gradually dug ourselves out, we began to discover casualties of our own among the livestock. The insistent barking of our dog led us to investigate one of the many snowdrifts in the yard. Deep down into it we discovered our pregnant sow. She had left her pigpen, which was to remain under a fifteen-foot pile of snow for a month or more. We managed to rescue her, but her piglets were subsequently all born dead.

The scariest thing, however, was a snowdrift as high as the barn across the only gate exiting our farmstead. It wasn't until the middle of May that we were able to get our old truck out of the yard and as far as our nearest neighbours' place. We had a wonderful surprise a few weeks prior to that, however. My old friends from teaching days, the Burke brothers, arrived on horseback. I had always enjoyed their visits, but that time I think I must have chattered non-stop for several hours. By then Tommy was crawling freely among us and pushing a chair around the house in order to walk, and a week later he stood alone. Then, a week after that, he was walking freely. His vocabulary, in those days, consisted of words such as "bath", "more", "mine", and "cap", and his first two words spoken together were "more water". When asked, he could even tell us what the chickens, cows and kitties said.

To please Jack and his family, I had agreed to have our child christened in the Anglican Church. Actually, it didn't bother the Freethinker defining me, as that church struck me as being more liberal than the majority of religious organizations. And I had learned by then something about the importance of ritual to most people. The baptism had to be postponed, however, until we were finally able to emerge from the farm over a month past Tommy's first birthday.

Our son had been happily thriving throughout all the season's tribulations. He was extremely precocious, exhibiting a linguistic and conceptual development truly remarkable for his age. This was probably furthered by the fact that I was able to devote so much time to him all winter, playing games and telling him stories. My sister Myrtle had sent a massive Christmas parcel packed with wonderful playthings and clothes formerly belonging to her little boy, Michael, as well as some new toys. So even that darkest winter of our lives, where weather was concerned, had a bright side. And, most important of all, we had survived!

My Grandfather, Charles Armitage. Taken probably in the 1870's.

Lewis Duffy & brother Tom. Late 1880's.

National Post May 31, 1904 Al (Alberta).

Patty and Jack Duffy at Acadia Valley in 1929?

At Ma's home in Oyen - about 1931.
(l-r) Myrtle, Mom with Bobby in her lap, Patty and Jack.

Oyen, Alta. 1913.

About 1936 at Lonely Trail School. Pat & Bob Duffy.
We're 4th and 5th from left.

Bobby, Pat, Jerry and Donny Duffy with mother at the
McCurdy farm near Veteran, Alberta in the summer of 1941.

Mom on top of the wood pile (Nellie Armitage Duffy Graham) 1942.

Working on farm at Cremona. Pat Duffy 1942

Bob and Don haying 1946? (Cremona Farm).

My grandmother Armitage "Ma".

May 8th, 1945 Celebration of VE Day in Oyen.

Pat Duffy on VE day in 1945. (May 8th) Taken when I made the
speech as representative of my generation at Oyen's V.E. celebration.

(younger students) Big Prairie School 1947.

Pat's Grade one One class at Big Prairie School 1947-8.

Pat in the 'dray' at Valley farm (early 1950's).

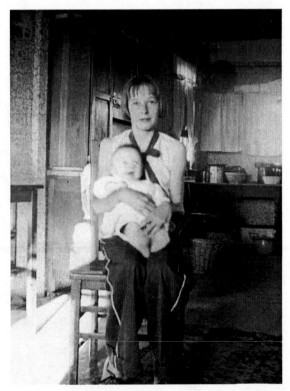

Pat Duffy and Tommy. Taken by my Aunt Annies during a visit
to us on the Valley farm (Summer of 1950).

1953 Bumper Crop. Mom on our only visit back to Armitage Lake.

1963 gradution (B. Ed) U. of Calgary.
(l. to r.) Tom, Pat, Nat Carry, Mom, Mable, Wendell Carry.

# Chapter 13

# THE VALLEY BETWEEN

For the first couple of years of my son's life, he functioned successfully as a bridge across the valley separating his father and me. My husband Jack was as close to being happy as I was ever to see him. Tommy was such a captivating and fast-developing child that it's no wonder we were both utterly engrossed in him. It was not that he was demanding, or 'spoiled' in any way. Indeed, he was always amazing me by exhibiting signs of a maturity not to be expected at his early age.

The summer of 1951, a few months after he had passed his first birthday, was a happy time for him. He was walking and playing outside on his own and had a surprisingly extensive vocabulary. I wrote in his baby book at this time that he could recite nursery rhymes and was easy to reason with, gregarious and sensitive. As usual, his Grandpa Harry came out to live with us once the snow had finally melted and the fields could be prepared for planting. But as soon as the seeding was done, Harry left to get married. It was his third try at marriage. I liked his new wife but, for her sake, had been feeling uneasy about the relationship from the beginning. My young brother-in-law, Bill Westcott, arrived for the wedding, the plan being that he would spend his entire summer holiday with us. This was to become a happy custom which continued throughout his high-school years, and until he joined the navy. Bill was a fine young teenager in spite of the fact that he had experienced very little supportive home life. His mother (Harry's former housekeeper) had given up on the marriage when Bill was a youngster, and apparently had always been forced to go out to work and leave him on his own much of the time. Tommy bonded with Bill immediately, and Bill was extraordinarily caring and supportive of his little nephew. Whenever he wasn't working he could be found playing with Tommy in the house or outdoors. He and I became very close as well. Over five decades later, at my seventy-fifth birthday party, Bill told the assembled group that I was his 'first love'.

Thankfully, Jack wasn't disturbed by the fact that his younger brother and I grew to mean a lot to one another. It was a different story, however, in the case of a youngster of similar age to Bill whom we hired to help with the chores that autumn after Bill left for school. I had become the family's official hair-cutter, following my father's footsteps. One day our 'hired hand' asked me if I would give him a badly needed haircut. Jack happened to come into the kitchen as I was doing this. He flew into a rage and fired the boy on the spot, accusing him of having an affair with me. I was learning to see the funny side of such events, so didn't allow it to upset me unduly. However, I regretted the injustice done to the innocent young boy.

In spite of such problems, the summer and autumn of Tommy's second year of life seemed to rush by like one mad race. It was hot and dry, which was a good thing as the extremity of the previous winter's snowfall had made seeding late. Our little rascal was quite adventurous, so I had to watch him closely. For the first few months of his walking I had built a small fenced-in area at the outside door, but he soon outgrew the confined space. He developed a habit which reminded me of myself as a child. He had a tendency to climb to the tops of any object within reach, then freeze there and wail for help.

However, the only really bad scare he gave me was one day when, as usual, I had taken him out with me while working in the garden. It was located beyond the yard fence, close to the bushes surrounding the farmstead. One day I became too absorbed in my weeding and suddenly realized that Tommy had disappeared. I found him about a half-mile down the trail leading to the crossing that connected us with the road from Acadia Valley. He was having a happy time exploring his surroundings. The memory of that initial surge of panic when I discovered him nowhere in sight comes back clearly even now.

Another painful memory of the time has to do with a tendency of Jack's to explode with anger if he felt thwarted in any way. I had learned to tread very carefully around him in my ongoing attempt to avoid these episodes, but one day found myself thoughtlessly moving between him and the bedroom mirror while checking my hairdo. Without warning, he swung at me, knocking me to the floor. As I struggled up, hastily apologizing, I glimpsed a little, frightened face at the window, looking in from his fenced-in play area outdoors. This glimpse, and the implications of it, were much more worrying for me than the event itself.

At the end of that year's harvest we discovered our crop had averaged from fifteen to eighteen bushels per acre, in spite of the fact that one entire field was frozen when the cold weather struck inordinately early in the autumn. Jack was so excited by the expectation of some income at last that he immediately purchased a second-hand combine for $1200, as well as a weed-sprayer and grain-loader which cost about $700. This concerned me as I was aware that we still hadn't made any payments to Harry on that section of the farm which he had sold to us. By this time we owned all of six cows, each of which was pregnant. But there would be little income from them for several years. The plan had been that our one steer, which happened to be from my cow, was to be sold and the money used for a new propane stove. However, when the time came, Jack decided that we would butcher the steer instead, and I ended up preserving the meat to help keep us eating for the year ahead. We did a lot of salting in those days, in addition to other primitive means of preserving meats, and the pickling of vegetables was a common practice as well. We must have been consuming a great deal of salt, but the hard physical labour probably helped to prevent serious effects on the body.

We had also acquired a dog by then but, like most farm pets, he was not kept in the house. It was just as well, as we couldn't trust him around children. Jack had thought we needed a ferocious fighter to keep the coyotes at bay. However, Tommy began to have nightmares soon after the dog arrived. One night when he woke screaming, "Dog bite my leg off!" I managed to convince Jack that we should get rid of that particular dog. We also owned a number of cats, for the ostensible purpose of controlling the mice. I have a shocking memory regarding them too. One day, after a female cat gave birth in the barn, I discovered that one of the males had killed all of her brood.

The winter of 1951-2 was marked by a seemingly endless series of illnesses for Tommy, which continued into the following summer. I realize now that our virtual isolation for those first few years of his life was resulting in his not having any resistance to common childhood diseases. As a result, he developed almost continuously infected tonsils, just as I had as a child. The situation became so bad that I asked Doc whether they should be removed, but he felt that Tommy would outgrow the problem.

I had my own health issues later that winter as well. I had been suffering badly from a toothache for several weeks before coming to the decision that a visit to a dentist was necessary, especially with seeding time fast approaching. I was afraid to return to Hanna to the dentist who had impressed me so negatively with his careless behaviour when I'd gone to him during my grade-twelve year at Oyen. So we made a trip east across the Saskatchewan border to Kindersley, where we got a hotel room for the night. I left Tommy there with Jack and went to the dental appointment. After informing me that all my wisdom teeth had to be removed, the dentist began his work. It turned out that the roots of each and every one of those teeth was locked around my jawbone. The experience was a nightmare, and when it finally ended I was in a ghastly state. I remember staggering back to the hotel, tears streaming down my face. After a sleepless, pain-ridden night I was scarcely able to endure the long drive back to the farm. By the time we arrived my jaw was extremely swollen and remained so for a long time. Years later I discovered that both sides of it had been broken.

Soon after Bill's arrival the following summer he took over the care of our livestock so that we could accompany two other couples and their children for a week-long break from the farm. We went to Sylvan Lake, the resort town to the north-west of us where my aunt, Laura Cutlan, lived. Unfortunately, our 'holiday' turned out be even more strenuous than daily work on the farm. We found ourselves trapped in dirty, unfinished little cabins, while the rain poured down all the time we were there. The other couples each had a child slightly older than Tommy, but he was the only one who was already 'trained'. My only pleasant memory of the week is that I had no diapers to wash, while the cabins of our friends were immersed in wet cloths hanging on indoor clotheslines. Another memory is of Tommy saying to the other children, "Why you wet your pants?"

This jibes with a memory of another friend's child—the same age as Tommy—whose mother left him in my care for a week or so after we returned home. He also was not yet trained to use the chamber pot. One day I overheard an interesting conversation between the two children. The visiting child had just had a bowel movement in his diaper, and I was momentarily too busy to see to it. Tommy was saying, accusingly, "You dirty!" The other boy would respond each time with, "I nice!" This went on for a few minutes, then Tommy changed the pattern of the conversation, "You mean you nice and dirty!" he said.

I wasn't too surprised at this play on words, as Tommy had been matching words to ideas quite fluently since late spring. I recall that the first day earlier in the spring when it was sufficiently warm for him to wear short sleeves, he surprised me by running in from outside, complaining, "Got no sleeve for wipe my nose!"

When not seeding or harvesting, Jack had the habit of sleeping most of the day every Sunday. And, when Harry wasn't on the premises, it was no easy task to rouse him on work mornings either. In response to this behaviour on the part of his dad, Tommy developed a habit of his own. He would go into the bedroom every so often, calling out, "Get up! Get up! You wazybones!" One day he came running out from one of these visits carrying the picture of my sister Myrtle's little girl Linda, which he had managed to rip out of its frame. "I got Linna!" he shouted triumphantly. His loving scribbles are on the picture still. Another of my many memories concerning Tommy's precocious command of language is associated with a dinner that year at Joyce and Tom's. During the meal Joyce began to scold her son Wayne for the way he was eating his food. This obviously upset Tommy. "Don't bodder Wayne, Auntie," he said, "cause he don't mean to be bad."

In the fall of 1952 we harvested our first really good crop. Jack immediately purchased a new ton-and-a-half truck, equipped with a hoist for loading the grain. This was most essential, as it did away with the grueling task of shoveling by hand. It cost $3,400. We also bought a cultivator to ready the land for seeding. However, these purchases meant that there was no money for clothes, or for household furnishings or appliances. I had to resort to begging Harry for enough to send an order to the Eatons catalogue for a few items of underwear and socks for Jack and Tommy. I received the usual scolding in return, for not making Jack manage our money better. It was around that time that I decided to devise ways of making a little income for household essentials, as Jack never gave me any cash whatsoever. I began to churn a lot more butter than we required, and sold it periodically to the grocer in town. He bought my extra eggs as well, and sometimes I even had a goose all prepared for him.

Where food for our own table was concerned, we lived like royalty the year round. My large garden provided all our fruit and vegetables, while the chickens, geese and other livestock produced our annual supply of meat, milk, butter and eggs. All this necessitated an enormous amount of work on my part, but that didn't count in those days, as it was what was expected of farm women. All in all, rather than being sorry for myself, I remember experiencing a blissful feeling of good fortune at being a safe distance from the dairy farm seventy miles to the south-east of Regina, where there was an outbreak of foot-and-mouth disease.

I was also thankful that, in spite of being so strapped for money, we did manage something at Christmas time that year which I had long wanted to do. Jack was relatively easy to persuade to make a trip back to what I then still referred to as 'home' in Cremona country, as he was anxious to give the new truck a test run. First, we drove to Calgary, stopping at the tiny apartment which Mom was renting temporarily in order to enable Don to attend his first year at the Calgary Institute of Technology. He had enrolled in the program of land surveying. Their move to the city had also provided Jerry with a chance to get started in high school. From Calgary we all drove out to the farm to join my stepfather Tom for the holiday dinner and celebrations.

We bought our young son a lovely little chrome table-and-chair set for Christmas that year. The choice was due to something I had observed one day just after harvest. At the time, we were having our first good visit in a long time with the Smith family. During the entire two hours of our stay Tommy never stirred from their little kindergarten set. June and Bill's older boy, Smitty, had given him a paper and pencil, and he was away! In fact, we had a hard time persuading him to return home with us. He loved playing with Smitty and Michael, and was between the two of them in age. I was always reluctant to leave the Smiths as well. June was ever the wonderful hostess. I remember particularly her outdoor corn-roasts, and the chance for the two of us to go horse-back riding, which I couldn't do on our farm.

I guess that Smitty, the older of their two boys, must have considered me a satisfactory hostess as well. One day he became unhappy because of a minor punishment doled out to him, and decided to leave home. He actually made it across the entire five-mile stretch of open prairie between our two farms. I was unutterably shocked when the little fellow arrived at our door and informed me that he was going to live with us. Needless to say, Tommy was overjoyed. Before scarcely any time had passed, however, Bill arrived, greatly relieved to find his runaway son.

Soon after that I began official negotiations to adopt a child, chiefly for Tommy's sake. Doc had warned me that I must never again become pregnant, because of the condition of my kidneys and liver. Jack didn't object, although he was definitely not enthusiastic about the prospect. However, I was hoping that he would feel different once the child became part of our family. A social worker came out from Hanna one day to assess us. After examining our home and environs, and visiting for a while with Tommy, he interviewed each of us separately. He seemed a bit uncomfortable at the end of a rather lengthy conversation with Jack out in the yard. Only a couple of weeks later, I received word that we were not considered satisfactory as prospective adoptive parents. This was devastating news for me, as I had been counting on Tommy having a brother or sister to interact with, before he got much older. Meanwhile, it wasn't long after the shock of the news that I began to suspect the social worker had discovered good reasons for his negative decision.

Throughout the following winter Tommy once again experienced almost continuous bouts of throat infections, accompanied by high fever. The situation became so worrisome that Jack finally agreed to make a temporary move into Acadia Valley for the winter of 1953-4. There had been a 'bumper' crop that year, which no doubt contributed to his decision. Mom had made a visit out to our farm just before harvest and I decided to grasp the opportunity to drive her up to Armitage Lake for one last glimpse of her old home. I watched her when, with an apparent mixture of sorrow and joy, she walked out into the shoulder-high grass then growing where the lake had once been.

Soon after that experience, we sold our pigs and managed to find a barn on the edge of town that we could rent for the poultry and cattle. By then our little herd had grown to about thirty head. Harry's home happened to be temporarily vacant because he and his new wife had moved down to Empress to live in her place. He kindly provided the house rent-free, as we were still not making expenses with our crops. Our worrisome cash problem seems to have been related to the sale of wheat at that time. We had seeded 500 acres and were able to sell only three bushels per acre, at $1.40 per bushel. That meant we took in less than $4000 all told, over $3000 of which we had to dole out for operating expenses, taxes and payments on debts.

The fact that Tommy had experienced such a minimal social life on our isolated farm was the other chief reason I had become desperate for us to spend some time in 'the Valley'—which was the way locals referred to the town of Acadia Valley. Opportunities to visit with other children his age were so few and far between that when any of them were in our home he tended to become somewhat nervous and overly protective of his toys. I wasn't surprised that it took a while, as well, for him to get accustomed to being left with Jack while I went out to visit with friends, or to community affairs. It was a relief when he began to accept this, and become accustomed as well to the give-and-take of playing with neighbouring children, and when he began to play happily with their pet dogs. I was similarly relieved when Jack managed to find something of a social life as well. He developed the habit of meeting with a group of fellow smokers to play rummy in a local café. At least this was better than sitting at home brooding.

It was during this early adjustment period in town that Tommy had a chance to see his very first movie. The experience turned out to be memorable because of the fact that it was about the death of a beloved dog. The children were all sitting together in the front row, but the moment the dog died, Tommy came rushing back down the aisle, wailing loudly. Fortunately, I had seated myself on the aisle so that I could keep an eye on him. I took him in my arms and soon managed to shush and comfort him, but he insisted on remaining close beside me after that.

While enjoying the break in town I decided to grasp the opportunity to get something done about Tommy's serious throat problems. I believe it was to Oyen that I drove him in our truck, so they must have had a small hospital by then. I was allowed to remain by his side for several days, until he was ready to come home. The tonsillectomy was an ordeal for both of us, but proved to be well worth it. It was the end of his continuous bouts of illness. It was a good thing we managed it when we did, for it was back to the farm for good as soon as spring arrived. Jack let me know that, in his opinion, the winter had been far too costly.

For several reasons, 1954 proved to be a momentous year in addition to the fact that it began during our stay in town. We finally arranged for the digging of a well which produced sufficient water for our needs as well as those of our growing herd of cattle. It cost two hundred of our precious dollars. The well was in the pasture not far from the farmyard. Also that was the year I became determined to begin my long-postponed correspondence courses from Queen's University as soon as harvest was over. So I registered for the first one, and kept at my studies from then on. This was also the year that my brother Bob was stationed to the south of us at Suffield, so we saw quite a lot of him and his wife Margaret. She was expecting their first child. I remember my new sister-in-law being rather critical of my attempts at independence, not only where the hoped-for continuation of a profession was concerned, but also my active participation in community affairs. She let me know that she saw females who did such things as "horse-faced would-be males". I enjoyed this, but was somewhat concerned as well, sensing that it revealed more about Margaret than it did about me.

Jack resented my spending the evenings studying and writing papers, but I persevered nonetheless. Prior to beginning my work at the kitchen table which served as my desk, I would always tuck Tommy into bed, then read to him for a while before saying goodnight. One night just as I had closed the book and was giving the happy little fellow his nightly hug and kiss, Jack burst into the bedroom. He was very upset, accusing me of inappropriate behaviour toward a male child.

Our momentous year closed on another dark note, with an occurrence that was to be a source of serious worry for some time to come. Just before Christmas I came down with German measles, having caught it from Tommy who, for once, had scarcely been ill at all. I, on the other hand, seemed to take forever to recover. While I was sick in bed, Joyce and Tom made a spur-of-the-moment decision to take Jack and Tommy to a Christmas party put on by the Community Club. Tommy was in a strangely worrisome condition when they returned. It seemed that Joyce had taken him to the front of the room, along with Wayne, to see Santa Claus. She had then insisted that Tommy sit on the strange-looking man's knee. I had foolishly never mentioned this myth as I hadn't wanted my son to believe in fairy tales; and in our isolated situation had neglected to prepare him for such an encounter. It was a bad mistake on my part, with potentially tragic consequences! Apparently Tommy became hysterical. This bright little boy who had attained a command of language far beyond his years was now stuttering so badly he could scarcely talk. When he and Jack arrived back home, he came crying in to where I lay ill upon my bed. He wailed that the scary looking man had threatened to sneak down our chimney in the night. That was what had frightened him the most.

"And I had n-n-n-no one to r-r-run to!" he sobbed, heartbrokenly. The tendency to stutter when under pressure was to be a burden for Tommy for years to come, although I think I was able to improve it considerably by working with him on it during the remainder of his pre-school years.

A few months later, in the winter of 1955, our situation began a turn for the better once more. Jack bought a new car, and became happily involved with driving it, so we got around more than usual. Soon after that, we arranged to trade wheat to Bill Graham—my stepfather's brother and neighbour in Cremona country—for a thousand fence posts which would allow us to enhance the size of our cow pasture. We also got sufficient lumber from him to build a large shed for the storing of all our unsold wheat. In the following summer we really began to edge our way into the civilized world when a phone line was finally built through our area. And then—wonder of wonders—our area actually got a power line! Jack had to borrow more money to get the power in (it cost $1250) but it was like the gift of life to me. I no longer had to do my ironing with flat irons heated on the stove-top. Or strain my eyes studying at night by the light of the failing gas lamps. And there was now even the prospect of some day owning an electric stove, refrigerator and electric washing machine.

Now, at last, June Smith and I could visit whenever we wanted to. The phone was a 'party line' with all calls available to all users in each small district. Our conversations were invariably lots of fun. June liked to entertain me by repeating some of what she had heard on her line. One of the most common comments, she reported, was "I've got to go now and have some tea and 'chambread'." June was puzzled about what it was that all her neighbours, mainly of Ukrainian background, were so fond of eating. I was able to enlighten her at once, having grown up among a number of Ukrainians at Lonely Trail. "It's just jam and bread!" I told her.

That summer Tommy began to learn to manage his finances. I would give him a fixed amount of my butter-and-egg-money, and he would do his own shopping. He was very careful about it, and whenever he bought something—such as a present for mailing to his cousins Michael and Linda—he would groan loudly at the cost. "That's an awful lot of money!" he exclaimed to the clerk when told the price of a pair of birthday slippers for his dad. I remember him slowly counting and doling out the pennies and nickels, looking as if he were losing his closest friends.

With the arrival of spring, I developed the habit of taking Tommy for walks around our newly fenced pasture, where we would pick a year's supply of wild mushrooms when they were in season. We always had fun observing the behaviour of the cows. For example, I noted a surprisingly 'human-like' custom on their part. Each day, a different cow was apparently assigned to care for the calves, leaving the others free to roam far and wide for their food. In addition to observing, Tommy and I did a lot of talking on our walks. He was quite ready to begin school in September, and anxious to do so. I had been asked by the superintendent at the time, a Mr. Elliot who lived in Hanna, to take over a middle-grade classroom in 'the Valley'. So I began inquiring about Tommy being accepted in for schooling in spite of being only five-and-a-half years old. When I discovered this would not be possible, I refused the teaching offer, as I had no intention of leaving my son in someone else's hands during this critical pre-school year. So I informed Mr. Elliot that I would accept a teaching job for the following year. The prospect of this began to revive my hope for the future.

Another bright note was added to my life when my brother Don arrived for a month of surveying in the vicinity. He had graduated from the Calgary Institute of Technology the previous year, and was now in the process of articling under Dave Usher in Edmonton for three years before he would write his finals and qualify as a licenced Land Surveyor in 1957. His 'rod man' stayed in a hotel in town, while Don spent most of his nights with us. I knitted him one of those giant heavy sweaters for Christmas, as he spent a lot of time working out in the cold.

In spite of such happy events, along with our gradually improving living conditions, dark shadows were forever hovering above our valley. For one thing, for several years we had all been aware of the threatening presence of polio. Several farm people that we knew of had been stricken with it. The only prospect for them after that was life in an iron lung. It was not until 1955 that the Salk vaccine came into use. We all received it as soon as possible, and were unspeakably relieved to discover that it obviously worked.

For me, personally, another threatening shadow in our valley was that of the ever-popular shotgun. There were two of them in our little attic room, to which Jack had developed the habit of retiring for hours at a time whenever he was upset. This tended to occur whenever I spoke of returning to teaching, or became absorbed in my university correspondence studies. I had a long-existing horror of shotguns, and a concern about what Jack might be thinking and doing up there by himself. Ironically, as the years passed, my fears about that particular weapon were confirmed, but in ways I could never have imagined. Two of the pupils in my first school, Empress View, killed themselves with shotguns before ever having had a chance at life. One was the younger of the two brothers with bullying proclivities, and the other was the oldest boy from the family who brought me my weekly water supply. But that wasn't the worst of the story. Years later, Tommy's cousin, Wayne Burke, used a shotgun to commit suicide in Tom and Joyce's toolshed, while still only a young man. Yes, there were shadows in that valley. And my own troubles, although seemingly insurmountable at the time, were among the least of them!

# Chapter 14

# NEW TRAILS TO CONQUER

The beginning of September in 1956 was a major turning point in Tommy's life as well as my own. School began for both of us. Many of our activities during the previous year had been building toward it. Throughout all the difficulties of the early fifties, I had held firm to two priorities. Foremost was the preparation of Tommy for his schooling. Then there was the need to focus on my own studies. In addition, the first day of that critical September was an important threshold in my life for yet another reason. It was my thirtieth birthday. All during the previous spring and summer, the approach of that particular birthday had signaled alarm bells somewhere deep within me. More and more, I was being forced to recognize a truth that, thus far, I had refused to face. I was going to have to begin working carefully on a practical plan to change the circumstances of my life before it was too late—not only for me, but for my son as well.

With each step toward the future made by either Tommy or me, Jack's mental and emotional condition had seemed to deteriorate. I guess it was inevitable that he would feel more and more excluded from the lives of both of us the more obvious our growing independence became. When I wasn't cooking meals and scrubbing the walls and ceilings in efforts to remove the dark stains from Jack's heavy indoor smoking, I was slaving in the garden and caring for the poultry and milk cow—increasingly, with Tommy's help. Every daytime moment free from these tasks was spent providing Tommy with what I considered the necessities for a smooth transfer into formal learning. Soon after I withdrew from teaching, a revolutionary change had engulfed primary-school education. The 'look-say' method of 'whole-word' memorizing had totally replaced the teaching of phonics in primary school. Because I was aware of this, and of the reading problems it was creating for children, I decided to teach Tommy all the 'sounds' of letter-combinations during his final pre-school year. Along with this, I tried to provide an environment that would also keep him open to the 'whole-word' method which he was bound to encounter in class. So I either sketched or cut out pictures of all sorts of objects and pasted them on the walls and ceiling of his room, with their names printed clearly below each of them. I made no effort to teach these to him in any formal way, counting on his being able to associate the words with the drawings on his own. I didn't want him already reading fluently, as Don had when he started school. I had learned from Don's experience that it could prove to be a handicap if he were too far ahead of the rest of his class.

I also spent as much time as possible reading to Tommy, using borrowed library books. I tried to encourage Jack to do this as well, and sometimes made an effort to introduce him to the contents of my correspondence courses from Queen's University in the evenings. But he was simply not interested in either pursuit. I was accused of either 'nagging' or 'showing off' whenever I brought up the subjects. In fact, he almost succeeded in convincing me to drop my correspondence studies after I barely survived a frightening experience on a drive to Empress, where an appropriately qualified person had been designated to officiate over the writing of my final exam in the late spring of 1956. We were experiencing a period of heavy rain, but it was only as I moved toward the bridge that I recognized the existence of a serious problem. The road was engulfed in water. At that point I should have taken note of the fact that there were no other cars in sight, but I was so desperate to get to my destination on time I merely kept on driving. I managed to navigate the flooded section of the approach, but soon realized the seriousness and potential danger of my predicament. At the other end of the bridge the water across the connecting road rose even higher. But there seemed no way for me to turn back then. Fortunately, although the engine of my partially engulfed car sputtered badly, it kept on working, and I emerged safely on the Empress side. Compared to all that, the writing of the exam was easy. However, I was forced to remain in town with friends for the night.

I received high marks for the course, and did a little bragging about it later to June and Bill Smith, on one of our visits together. They were suitably impressed. Bill took a look at the exam and said, "Geez! I couldn't even read the questions, let alone answer them!" Around that time, many of my friends were also impressed by the fact of my accidental connection with one of the greatest changes ever to occur in the large area of the countryside to the north-west of us. It involved Rod Carry, the cousin in that family who was closest to me in age. He took a gamble then which would ultimately result in his becoming a millionaire many times over, and one of the most well-known businessmen in all of southern Alberta. The company he formed provided the heavy equipment for preparing the land and hauling all the necessities for the wells being dug to access the underground gas supply then beginning to be discovered. These gas wells would one day cover the large area around Armitage Lake—the location of my mother's family homestead—and also what was known as the Benton region, where our farm and the Lonely Trail school had been. By then, this entire part of the country had become a lonely stretch of deserted prairie wasteland.

The summer of 1956 was momentous from the standpoint of formal education in the Valley area as well. A new school addition was built onto the four-roomed building in town, increasing the number of classrooms to eight. Also added were a gymnasium, kitchen, stage, and new washrooms with 'flush' toilets. Until the construction of the preceding four-room structure, the town schoolyard had been dotted with small one-room buildings, each having been built as the need increased with the gradual closure of district's country schools and their consolidation into the Acadia Valley School Subdivision. This had become a part of the new Acadia School Division, first established in 1936, with Mr. Laverty as the superintendent. Lonely Trail had been one of the first of the country schools to go. This happened in 1939, the year after we left the farm. In 1951 Empress View closed down, with its entire site selling for ten dollars! By then, all the surrounding country schools had disappeared, and a district-wide Valley bus route established. Two of the earlier small shed-like school buildings in town became available as teacherages.

Before school began that autumn, Mr. Elliott, the current school superintendent of the Acadia School Division, made arrangements for me to rent one of the teacherages. This would serve as a fall-back home for Tommy and me whenever the condition of the Valley road made commuting treacherous. I learned that I was to teach grades seven and eight, while Ellen Krempien would be handling grades nine and ten. Nick Bozak, the school principal, was responsible for grades eleven and twelve. Grades five and six were also housed together, as were grades three and four, with separate classrooms being required for grades one and two. The teachers responsible for the latter were Gert Niwa, Tommy's grade-one teacher; Janet Peers, who taught grade two; and Mary Brauss, who taught grades three and four. There was a population explosion then occurring in the surrounding community, evident in the fact that each primary grade was getting larger. A good example of the prevailing norm was one of the local farm families which had nineteen children, while the husband was still bragging about his likelihood of making the number a 'round' twenty. His wife's role in all this was ignored, but I discovered a hint of the extent of her slavery when they invited me over for tea after school one day. She served sandwiches made from a seemingly endless supply of loaves of bread fresh from the oven.

'I guess you have to bake all this bread every week," I said, in admiration. "Every single day!" was her expressionless response.

This visit occurred during a period in which Tommy and I were staying in the teacherage. Not surprisingly, we had to spend some time during each winter in what was actually a little one-room shack. It was not the most comfortable of places, as no dry-walling had ever been installed. This meant that the inside walls—even the one beside the bed—were covered with frost on cold days and nights. Nevertheless, I preferred residing there when the weather was bad to braving the narrow, winding road to the farm. Some of our trips were rather precarious. It wasn't long before Tommy began to help me change tires and resolve other problems bordering on the physical and technical. Early on, he began to remind me of my father in that respect.

On the sixth of October something occurred which was to change the entire world, but we did not realize what the consequences would be at the time. We heard on the radio that the Soviet Union had launched a satellite into space. I remember being glued to the radio whenever I could spare the time, and following the entire rather scary affair until Sputnik re-entered the earth's atmosphere in early January. Ellen Krempien and our principal, who taught the high school grades, used the event in their science classes, but neither Canada's top scientists nor political scientists ever predicted the 'Cold War' which would ensue.

Quite frequently during the school year, I was required to remain after class for teachers' meetings. I had learned that the school bus, which headed out toward the Smith's farm and dropped Smitty off, actually wound its way to the south, eventually passing the place where the exit trail from our farm joined the road back to the Valley. So I decided to try sending Tommy home by bus one day when I was detained. It turned out to be quite an experience for him: one that did not bear repeating. He had to ride for several hours, almost as far south as Empress, after which the bus traveled back north-west to the road northward past the Elliott's farm at the corner where the trail from our place met the road to the Valley, and where he was eventually dropped off. In fact, we both arrived home at about the same time. After that debacle I reached two conclusions. The first was that it was a good thing I had returned to teaching when Tommy started school, so that he wouldn't have to make that trip twice every day. Second, he would be much better off playing in the gym while I attended after-school meetings.

My Principal and colleagues sometimes insisted on evening meetings, however. If we were staying in the teacherage at these times, Tommy either remained there alone, reading or doing homework, or else he visited with his Auntie Joyce. But if the meetings occurred when the roads were passable, we would drive home after school and I would return later on my own. Jack complained loudly and often about all the gas I was wasting, even though it was my salary that provided for it, as well as paying for a large proportion of our other needs. Then he began to react to my evening absences in a much more worrisome fashion. I would arrive home to find the door locked from the inside and the house dark. I didn't dare pound on the door after the first timid knock or so, as the last thing I wanted was for Tommy to wake up and become aware of these strange behaviours on the part of his father. He already had far too many responsibilities and worries. My own greatest concern was for the safety of my son, who was all alone in the house with a man who was probably brooding up in the attic with his shotguns at hand. So I would try to make myself comfortable in the shed near the house until Jack came outside in the morning.

For some time Jack had been talking about building an addition to the house. It was to be a large front porch with a door leading in from the yard where people arrived and parked, so they wouldn't have to come around to the door at the back. He had even traded for the required lumber on one of our trips with a load of grain for Bill Graham back in Cremona country. Finally, he began the job. He got as far as putting up some corner posts and the rough boarding on a couple of the walls. But then he lost interest and left it standing there, unfinished. How I hated the sight of that ugly apparition at the front of our house—most of all because of what it communicated about my pitiful, problem-ridden husband. He couldn't seem to complete anything. More and more, I was coming to the desperate conclusion that I had married a man who was a 'border-line case'. And, to quote a remark made about her former husband by Muriel Spark, author of *The Prime of Miss Jean Brodie,* I was increasingly realizing that "I didn't like what I was finding on the other side of the border."

Tommy, on the other hand, was successful at school from the first day. A potentially serious problem was discovered early on, however. He was very short-sighted. As soon as we got him fitted for glasses, he took to reading like a duck to water. I have never forgotten his first Christmas concert. I already knew that he had a good memory, but had never fully recognized the extent of his aptitude until that night. The primary classes presented a little play on stage. Every so often one or two of them would blunder and forget their lines. With scarcely a moment's delay, Tommy stepped in each time, fluently speaking their parts.

The school term of 1956-7 seemed to fly past us. I loved being back with my friends and colleagues, and witnessing Tommy's progress in school. I was anxious to give him the opportunity to play on my grandmother's old organ, as I had done as a youngster, but there was no way I could persuade Jack to bring it out from the Oyen house which now belonged to my uncle Ed. As a result of this stalemate, one of the first things I bought when my wages began coming in was a small piano, to which Jack made no objection. I arranged for Tommy to begin lessons, and he appeared to be progressing well. However, the piano teacher made a serious mistake when she presented a concert and assigned him to play a little piece on stage. I had been worrying that her decision was far too precipitous, and should have responded to my sense of foreboding and asked her to wait on this. As I had feared, Tommy became extremely nervous, and his stuttering returned as the evening approached. In fact, he was sadly embarrassed by finding himself unable to finish his piece on-stage. Understandably, he showed no interest in going near the piano again.

Our capable little son was soon able to put that negative experience behind, however. Not long afterwards we got him a Shetland pony called Dove. She lived up to her name and was to prove exactly the right thing for him at exactly the right time. We had acquired her by a stroke of luck from Bill Graham, on one of our trips across the Province to Cremona country with a load of grain for trading. How Tommy loved riding that little horse! In fact, he was soon successfully rounding up the cattle and helping to brand the steers. Later that year he also learned how to ride a motor bike: something of which I did not approve. Jack, on the other hand, liked to brag about it. This motor-bike experience occurred one day while we were visiting the Krempiens. Doug, the older boy, had just obtained one, and was bound that he must forthwith teach his newfound skill to his younger brother Brian and Tommy, both of whom could already handle bicycles.

This was a momentous period for my brother Don as well. He had been licenced in Land Surveying by the Calgary Institute of Technology in 1954, and then articled for three years under Dave Usher in Edmonton—the owner of a large surveying business. Now, in the spring of 1957, he was graduating as a fully qualified Alberta Land Surveyor. It seemed that his life was as busy as mine.

But I was finally persuaded to go on a holiday. Immediately after the 1957 school term ended, a group of us—inspired by Ellen Krempien—decided to take our children for an adventure to the Cypress Hills country located on the south-eastern border of Alberta. We did a lot of easy hiking, and had a wonderful relaxing time camping out in the highest area, which was relatively flat. But I made one sad mistake. I was roaming around the topmost reaches of this strange hill-country wearing only sandals with no socks. Soon after returning home, I broke out in an itchy rash that had spread up almost to the tops of my thighs before I managed to get down to Empress to see 'Doc'. He told me that I had picked up a rare, ancient fungus residing only on that high ground: a fungus which had escaped being immersed in glaciers during the ice age. Fortunately, a remedy existed in the form of 'gentian violet'. The result was that I spent the entire summer with dark purple legs. Even the outdoor toilet seat was coloured purple by the time the fungus was brought under control just before I had to return to teaching.

Not that I wasn't already working! From mid-August every summer, my duties expanded into far more than overtime. How I even began to manage them I simply cannot imagine. Before school started, the entire year's supply of poultry—geese as well as chickens—had to be slaughtered and canned. Fortunately, by this time I had a new pressure cooker for the task, which helped a good deal. In addition, as much as possible of the food for harvest meals to be eaten in the field was preserved ahead of time. And there was the coming school term to prepare for as well.

In the midst of one of these mad periods, Bob and Margaret, with their daughters Emmi and Sarah, came for a farewell visit before moving to the Air Force base at Gimli, Manitoba. One day I recounted to them an incident associated with the Valley 'Community Club' for which I always did as much volunteering as possible. During the previous spring the group was preparing for their annual Grandmother's Day potluck dinner, and the United Church minister who happened to be organizing the affair that year asked me if I would provide the potatoes for it. I foolishly agreed, counting on my supply in our vegetable bin in the cellar. When the time came to cook the potatoes I discovered my remaining winter's store held only a load of tiny, left-over ones. Peeling and cooking these turned out to be a hideously tiring and time-wasting task, but what had really bothered me about the whole experience was the offhand way the minister accepted them on the evening of the event. To Bob's obvious delight, Margaret then said I had confirmed her opinion about participating in community events, and she hoped I had learned my lesson.

I think it was the following year, on the day after Bob's own birthday in late October, that Margaret gave birth to their third child, Paul. Mom traveled all the way from her Cremona farm home near the foothills of Alberta to Gimli in Manitoba to stay with them during the birth, and to care for the little girls. I remember thinking, at the time, that it was an extremely courageous and kind undertaking on her part.

In the summer of 1958 we took the trip long dreamed of by Tommy. We set off on the drive to Vancouver, where Myrtle and Mike were then settled. Ever since he was a toddler, our 'only child' had imagined his cousins as some kind of marvelous and faultless idols who would love him as he had always adored them from a distance. Linda exceeded his expectations, and he obviously enjoyed being in her company. But the behaviour of her brother toward him almost broke his heart. At the time, I wasn't aware of just what was going on as, even then, Tommy was never inclined to add to my worries by complaining. After the first couple of days I began to suspect that something was dreadfully wrong, but had no idea what it was. Tommy was withdrawing into a book whenever Michael was in the vicinity, and refusing to go out play with him. He also expressed a puzzling desire to sleep with us—something he had never done. I learned later that scary things were happening: actions on Michael's part which were no doubt intended as teasing by the older boy, but were interpreted by Tommy as bullying of a most terrifying nature. And the worst part of it all was that he couldn't escape his cousin at night. They were sharing a room with Tommy assigned to the top bunk, from which Michael threatened to dump him during his sleep.

I was able to provide my obviously worried little boy with at least one exciting and happy day, however. The two of us went up Grouse Mountain on the chairlift. It was my turn to be terrified, but Tommy loved it. Then it was time for the long drive home into the Okanagan Valley and down to Montana, and back up through the Logan Pass and Rocky Mountains to Cremona country. This journey was fascinating in the landscapes all around us, but I found it extremely tiring. Tommy continued to be uncharacteristically withdrawn during the entire trip, and Jack seemed trapped in one of his silent, strange moods. We stayed overnight at the Graham farm, then brought Mom into Calgary and dropped her off at my aunt Mabel's, where she intended to visit for a few days in order to attend a reunion of the Armitage sisters. When we finally arrived at our Valley home, I was in a state of utter exhaustion. This was not helped by the discovery that Wayne Burke, the nephew whom we had left in charge, had set the dog on the milk cow one day. We discovered her very ill, with milk fever. I think this upset Tommy as much as it did me. After recounting his unhappy story once we were safely home, Tommy never again mentioned the cousin in Vancouver whom he had for so long idolized from afar. However, it was quite a different story in the summer of 1959, when we had another visit from Bob and Margaret and family, on their way across the Province to Cremona. Their children were pleasant and friendly, and it was obvious that Tommy greatly enjoyed the company of these cousins.

By the time the end of decade approached, I had begun to visualize a crucial new pathway beckoning a little further down the road I was traveling. Once, a professor at the University of Alberta had told our summer-school class to keep in mind that each of us has only one brief life to live. And, he said, it is essential to travel that road of life—no matter how difficult it might seem at any current moment—with the expectation that the very next corner would be opening onto something wonderful. A few years previously, when I turned thirty, I had come to realize that I would round this long-hoped-for corner with its path to a rewarding future for me—and a non-destructive future for my son—only if I were able to execute a carefully laid plan by which it could be approached step by pragmatic step.

In the early spring of 1960, just after Tommy's tenth birthday, I began to to work out such a plan. Ellen Krempien was, as always, my knowledgeable and willing helper. She had succeeded in persuading her husband Howard to sell part of their farm, and in getting her family moved to Calgary the previous summer. She had immediately found a teaching job in the city's Junior College. Her brave decision inspired me to make a move as well. I was increasingly concerned about Jack's negative influence on Tommy, and the probable dead-end that lay in wait for my son if I did not change our circumstances. There was another pressing reason to act at that time. During the previous term I had learned that a few of my problem students were hounding Tommy and sometimes even brutally attacking him during recesses and noon-hours. They obviously considered bullying him as a way of getting back at me for any punishments doled out in class. He was non-violent by nature, but large for his age, so no doubt they saw him as an ideal victim. However, he always fought back, so they found him no easy prey. Ellen told me that she had learned, in the case of her boys, that this situation would only worsen over time. The fact that, unlike her boys, Tommy had never shared his problems with me, speaks a great deal about his unfailingly surprising maturity and thoughtfulness.

Whenever I had attempted to engage Jack in any reasoned discussion concerning the problems in our relationship, and the effects of the current situation on our son, I had gotten nowhere. It seemed only to trigger angry accusations and threats on Jack's part, at times accompanied by frightening behaviour. So I made a decision to take one step at a time in a direction that might eventually lead to an escape from the trap in which we existed—or would at least give me a little more control over the nature of that trap. Ellen informed me that Mr. Laverty, superintendent of Acadia School Division when I was in grade six and seven, was currently the top administrator in the Calgary school system. So I contacted him and found him most enthusiastic about hiring me for the following year. I was promptly assigned a position at a school called Colonel McLeod, to teach history and drama at the junior-high level. It was only then that I began to talk to Jack about the possibility of our selling the livestock and moving to Calgary, where he could join us for the months between harvesting and seeding time. To my great relief, the idea of escaping the lonely winters seemed to appeal to him, as did the promise of greater financial security. In my case, I was still clinging to the forlorn hope that a change in our living circumstances might bring about a change for the better in Jack.

I had almost no savings, as all my salary over the years had gone to purchasing crucial electrical kitchen appliances—once the power line had arrived—along with gas for the car, and other necessities such as clothing. However, as soon as school finished for the summer, I quietly made arrangements to sell the small herd of cattle which I owned by then: descendants of the calf originally assigned to me. I also cashed in my life insurance and borrowed five hundred dollars from Don. Then, equipped with that modest fund in the bank in my name, I set off in the car with Tommy for a brief trip to Calgary and Cremona, informing Jack rather than asking permission, and doing that only immediately prior to leaving.

While in Calgary I contacted a realtor whose daughter, Shirley Hughes, had married my cousin, Phil Carry. Mr. Hughes happened to know of a house that had just been listed for sale in his immediate vicinity. It was on the very busy Fourteenth Street near the centre of the city—between Eleventh and Twelfth avenues—and I fell in love with it immediately. Mr. Hughes, the realtor who was also to be our neighbour on the other side of the back alley, had a son Tommy's age called Butch. The two hit it off at once. The fact that Tommy would have a pal practically at our back door, and that the house was close to a school and the streetcar line, added to the desirability of the location. I thought of it then and ever afterwards as 'the pink house' as its colour was unique, to say the least. I had to go to four banks, however, before I found one willing to grant me a mortgage in my own name only. At that time, single women—even those with reasonably stable and well-paying jobs—were simply not considered trustworthy owners of property.

Once the purchase and possession date were settled, we drove out to the Cremona farm. I found Mom extremely worried about Jerry, who had dropped out of high school after a brief attempt at the daily commute to town. He was also already involved with a local girl. None of us knew it then—not even Jerry—but his girlfriend had become pregnant. As was then the custom, her mother sent her into Calgary to a home for pregnant teenagers, with the understanding that the infant would be offered for adoption. Tommy had a fun visit as he and his young uncle Jerry always got along well, but I was forced to make it brief because of all the work that had to be done in order to make our move to Calgary for the beginning of the school year. For the first time, I let Mom know something about the difficulties I had been experiencing in my marriage throughout the past twelve years. Two of her responding comments shocked me to the marrow. Why, I asked myself, had she not said these things while there had still been time for me to escape from my premature commitment? But as soon as the angry thought came I realized that I would then not have my precious son. No matter what the cost, he was more than worth it!

"You remember how Lew never said anything bad about anyone?" Mom had asked. "Well, there was one exception—Harry Westcott. He had absolutely no use for that man!" The reason this bit of information affected me so deeply was that my father's opinion on this crucial issue would have carried overwhelming weight with me, and I couldn't believe she had not been aware of it. Then, before I digested this, she came out with the second hammer blow.

"Anyway, I could never understand what you saw in Jack. I knew all I needed to know about him when he told me, that time he came out to the farm for the weekend when you were teaching here, that tuberculosis ran in his family. He actually thought his mother had inherited it. He didn't even know that TB is caused by a germ!"

Tommy and I made it into Calgary just barely on time for both of us to begin school; he in grade five at the nearby Hillhurst school and I as one of the junior-high teachers at Colonel McLeod, to which I traveled by streetcar. We had no car with us in town, and I had been able to bring little more than our personal belongings with us from the farm when Jack drove us in. Almost the only items of any size that he had been willing to pack into the truck were my small piano and bedroom suite. So life for the first month or so was difficult, to say the least. But I managed immediately to get a new bed installed for Tommy, as well as some dishes and a few other essential items. I had to buy a kitchen stove although, fortunately, some basic appliances had come with the house. There were also beautiful drapes left by the previous owner. I recall that one of the early purchases later in the year was our first television set!

School went well for both Tommy and me. I loved my work from the very first day. I taught history to grades seven, eight and nine. The students in these grades were divided into classes according to ability: the very bright ones, the regular ones and the slow learners. For my home room I was given the grade-nine students who were considered slow learners. Actually, I soon discovered that many had been classified as such because of their bad behaviour, and not necessarily because of any lack of intelligence. I found them extremely unruly and one of the greatest teaching challenges of my career thus far. The principal had warned me about them, telling me that during the previous year they had driven out several teachers. I knew from the start that I would have to be very strict, emphasizing 'law and order' above all else throughout the establishment period.

My first necessary rule was that they would never be dismissed for recess or any other break until everyone had been sitting without moving or uttering a sound for at least two minutes after the school bell had rung. I remember this particularly not only because it worked wonders, but because of an amusing incident associated with it. During one of these silent periods the door opened and a visitor walked in. I turned to discover the United Church minister from the Valley whom I remembered chiefly for my 'potato experience'. After I had dismissed the students the minister told me he was bringing greetings from some of my old friends. Then he informed me, in the superior manner for which he seemed to think his office qualified him, that I was being unduly strict with my class and it was time I learned to teach more humanely. I managed to restrain myself.

The only time I ever slapped a child occurred not long after that. The school was equipped with a sound system, allowing for the main office to make announcements. Following one of these, a particularly rude and disruptive girl burst out with abusive words about the principal, who had been speaking to us all. I felt this was so far beyond the bounds that immediate and serious consequences were called for. I walked over and slapped her in the face.

"Don't ever say anything like that again in this classroom—not about the principal or anyone else in authority!" I had no trouble with her from then on, nor were there ever any similar murmurings among her classmates.

What really resolved all current and potential problems with this previously notorious class, however, was something much more positive. I began the class in drama with them and discovered at once that, for the first time, most of them had found something at their own level that they could do well—and, in some cases, even excel in. The most troublesome student of all, a mischievous little redhead, proved to be astoundingly gifted as an actor. When I got together with the school's music teacher to plan a Christmas concert that first year, we decided to give him a leading role in a musical play which I wrote, and for which she organized the music and singing. Our drama and music classes spent most of November and early December working on it, and the students loved having such an exciting objective in view. During one of our many rehearsals before the concert, my young redhead became impatient with the music teacher who was asking him to repeat a certain line over and over.

"Jesus Christ!" he burst out, after her umpteenth request. She was a highly religious person and became so angry at this that she demanded he be removed from the lead role for committing blasphemy. I quickly interrupted, assuring her that he was merely expressing the depth of his emotions about the birth of Jesus which her choice of music for our Christmas concert was arousing in him. I'll never forget the expression of gratitude in his glance at me when she hastily apologized and reinstated him. From that moment on this former gang leader was my admiring slave.

Meanwhile, Jack had joined us for the winter. He became enthusiastic about setting up a workshop in the garage area, and spent most of his time and money buying tools and even very large unrecognizable objects which filled the space so that there remained no room for the car. Fortunately, there was a parking space outside at the garage door. The pitifully sad part of all this is that I can't recall his ever using any of this equipment. This event reminds me of the fact that one of the few drawbacks of our new home was that we had to either back in from the busy street or back out into it. I couldn't afford a car until the third year we lived there, so didn't immediately recognize the seriousness of the problem.

My life was overwhelmingly busy during our first two years in Calgary. Work continued without pause, even at the end of the school term, as I attended the summer session at what was then the Calgary branch of the University of Alberta at Edmonton. When this was completed with the approach of the 1961-62 school term, I signed up for an evening course.

One day that following winter at Colonel McLeod school, something rather puzzling happened during class. Several strange men accompanied the principal into my classroom in the midst of a history lesson, and quietly seated themselves at the back. I continued my teaching as if nothing had occurred, assuming that the principal was having me assessed for some reason. Several times during that week this behaviour was repeated—invariably when I was teaching one of the history classes. I asked some of my colleagues if they knew what was going on, but they were as puzzled as I was. However, as time passed and I was not called in to the principal's office to discuss any teaching problems, the event slipped from my mind.

Later that spring, as I was preparing both my various student classes and myself for our final exams—them in history and drama, and myself for the university evening course—one of the most wonderful surprises of my life occurred. The principal asked me to come to his office. He said he had news for me. Apparently his admiration for my teaching skills had inspired him to introduce the subject to Mr. Laverty. The two of them then decided to recommend me for one of the country's relatively few Canada Council Master Teacher Awards. And, lo and behold, I had won it! I was told that what had impressed the visiting judges most was the fact that, although I was teaching the same course content to each of the student classes monitored, I had automatically altered my teaching approach to—and presentation of—the material to suit the particular learning capacity and background of each group.

My amazement at the honour bestowed on me increased when I learned that a financial scholarship from the Alberta government was also involved: one which would allow me to return to university full-time for the following year. This was incredibly important, as I was at the point of being stalled in my studies because of the rule that I could not complete my long-sought degree without a year 'in residence'. The news came just as Jack was leaving for the farm. My success seemed to make him more unhappy than ever. Our relationship had been deteriorating at a rapid pace during the preceding winter because Jack made no attempt to contribute to the running of the household by day, and was demonstrating ever-more resentment of the life I was leading. Every time I attended night class I would arrive home to accusations of having been with a lover. The final straw for me was when he began to accuse Tommy of stealing money from him. All this forced me to conclude that I could no longer tolerate having him come in for the winter. In fact, I realized that the sooner I could remove Tommy from his dad's influence the better it would be for him as well. But as usual, whenever I tried to discuss some sort of solution to our problems Jack would not hear of it. So I began to make plans to somehow make that necessary end to our tragic marriage come about without any cooperation from him. Continuing as we were was to the benefit of no one, and was doing obvious harm to all three of us.

That summer was a hectic one for me, what with applying and being accepted into the final year of the BEd program and completing my summer course. In addition, I had to find renters for the top floor of the house and then move our belongings to the basement. I was very relieved that Tommy was able to have a wonderful trip to Disneyland with our neighbours, the Hughes, as soon as school ended. I considered it a necessary precaution to wait until he was safely back home from the farm in late August before informing Jack that he would no longer be welcome to join us for the winter. Tommy became 'Tom' soon after that, as he considered, quite rightly, that entering grade seven signaled a step away from childhood. Actually, I was forced to acknowledge that our life circumstances had stolen his childhood long before.

I could scarcely believe my good fortune when I drove over to the new university that first day of class. It was like a dream come true. I found all my courses highly interesting, but best of all was one on the Philosophy of Education, taught by a Dr. Robert Anderson. The mere thought that I could focus on my courses and not have to work at the same time seemed incredible. A moment of comedy also brightened the first couple of weeks. The university was holding some sort of opening ceremony on a weekend, and Tom thought he'd like to come along with me to check it out. We followed the crowd into a reception room and, just as we entered, I thought I glimpsed an image of myself, and muttered something about a mirror on opposite wall. Tom burst out laughing. It was a large television screen, the like of which I had never seen, and mirrored in it was the queen—whom I had mistaken for myself! I can only guess that my grandiose imaginings reflected how I felt at this wondrous moment in my life.

I should have known that the moment couldn't last. I hadn't heard a word from Jack since sending him a letter informing him about the house having been rented, and repeating the message that we could not live together any more. I was beginning to relax about it all when I came home one day in late October and found him in the act of moving into our tiny basement abode. He was unpacking in the room housing the only bed. Tommy slept on a couch in the kitchen-living area. Once more, I was utterly trapped! The only choice open to me at that point was to borrow another couch from a friend, and move it out into the porch at the back door which was shared by the family upstairs as well. It was there that I was to spend my nights throughout the winter of 1962-63. And it was there that I had to do my studying and writing of papers, as Jack would not give me any peace while we were together downstairs. I was terribly concerned about the impact of all this on Tom, but fortunately he had made some close friends with whom he spent a lot of after-school time. I also had a number of friends in the city by then, and they helped to keep me sane. One of these was a fellow teacher, Dorothy Holden. And, of course, there was always Ellen Krempien.

Ellen's boys now both owned motor bikes. Tommy began to ask for one as well and, against my wishes, Jack bought it for him almost immediately. My strongly held opinion was that combining the riding of an ordinary bicycle with lots of walking would be far better for his health. I recall Ellen musing sadly one day that the parents of our age group would be going down in history as the first to raise a generation of sedentary sons and daughters: a generation who drove everywhere.

With my own graduation pending, I had just been offered a position teaching history and language classes at Central High School. I appreciated the challenge this offered and accepted immediately, in spite of considerable regret at leaving Colonel McLeod.

I have three major memories of the first months of that autumn term: two of them happy and the other horrendous. The first memory is of a rushed trip out to Cremona to bring Mom into Calgary for my birthday, combined with a visit with her sister Mabel and her husband Joe. Mom brought an angel-food cake for my birthday dinner on the Saturday, as well as a large supply of her garden vegetables. The second is of my graduation in October as a BEd. with first-class honours. I was asked to enter the stage in third place in the long line-up of graduates. Ellen Krempien graduated that day as well, making it yet another of our many shared experiences. In addition to my son Tom, my mother and cousin Wendell Carry along with his wife Nat shared the celebration of my long-sought goal.

The third memory is a dark one. It was that terrible day in late November when I heard about the assassination of John Kennedy. I immediately put aside the lesson I was about to begin, and devoted every class for the rest of the day to a discussion of the tragic event and its possible implications for modern history. To my amazement, I learned when school was over for the day, that I was the only teacher in the school to have done so.

In late December of that year I experienced another happy occasion. My brother Don, who was then studying for an advanced degree in Town Planning at the University of Toronto, got married to a lovely, vivacious fellow-student named Donna. As Tom was spending the Christmas holiday with Jack, on a trip to the coast, I was able to arrange not only to attend the wedding, but to take our mother with me. As I had nothing whatsoever that was fit to wear for such an occasion, Ellen allowed me to choose anything I wanted from her wardrobe. She was only slightly larger than I in size, so I was able to find an all-occasion suit that worked just fine. I wore it for every outing on the trip. The entire experience was a much-needed, enjoyable break for me, and proved to be a blissful, once-in-a-lifetime treat for Mom. She loved the long train ride across the prairies and the northern lake district of Ontario. Her most memorable remark on seeing the countless miles of bush-land was "It doesn't look like very good farming country to me."

The wedding was beautiful and everything went smoothly. Bob and Margaret and family were living in Ottawa at the time, but for some reason they hadn't seen fit to accept Don and Donna's invitation to their wedding. So Mom and I decided to extend our trip and invite ourselves to the Bob Duffy home for Christmas. When the newlyweds left for their honeymoon in the Carribean, we boarded a train for Ottawa. We got there on the afternoon of Christmas Eve. They didn't seem to have anything planned for dinner that night, so I offered to prepare my usual Christmas Eve meal of seafood soup and freshly baked buns. It went over quite well. The next day Bob cooked a delicious turkey dinner. I was glad that we had intruded on them, because it gave us a chance to get re-acquainted with all three of their lovely children: Emmi, Paul and Sarah. I recall being very impressed with Paul's gift for drawing.

Jack had taken Tom on a trip to the Lower Mainland to spend Christmas with his young half-brother, Bill, who was married by then and had recently left the navy and settled in Victoria. On the way, they planned to visit Myrtle and Mike and their family. So I was utterly free for the holiday. It was fortunate for me that I was able to enjoy that pleasant interval, for once we all got back home my marital situation deteriorated rapidly. In fact, at one point things got so bad that I went to the police, asking for their help in keeping my unwanted and abusive husband away from me. I'll never forget the response.

"You just go home and learn to behave yourself!" I was told.

I think it was then that I decided to make a more radical move before Jack returned from the farm after harvest. I decided that we had to go into hiding from him, so Tom and I moved into a tiny apartment, without telling even my family where we were. Soon, however, my friend, Dorothy Holden, insisted on taking us in. She lived at Westview Drive on the northwest edge of the city, so this meant a sudden move for Tom to Vincent Massey school. Then, on Ellen's advice, I began the procedure of obtaining a legal separation, accompanied by a restraining order. The situation changed drastically almost at once. A strange thing occurred immediately the legal papers were served. Jack's training and experience in the army police had apparently left him with a respect for, and possibly a genuine fear of, the law. Whatever the cause, it soon became clear that my problems with him were over. Sadly, however, in order to accomplish this closure I did have to allow him sole access to our son for the summer holidays. In return, he would pay me the sum of $40.00 a month for child support. That autumn, when Tom returned from the farm, I discovered that he was secretly smoking. He was only twelve years old! I realized then what I had suspected for some time. Jack was so intent on making me pay for his unhappiness he was punishing me in the only way still open to him—by doing as much harm as possible to our son.

Tom completed his grade seven at the Westgate Junior High, which was fairly close to Dorothy's house. I rode the bus to the city centre for work each day. It was during this period that I decided to buy a car. I purchased a little Renault, and had some difficulty getting used to city driving. Then, by the spring of that school term I decided it was safe for us to move back into our own house. The couple who became renters of the basement area, Bob and Nobuko Gowen, proved to be most interesting companions. I had previously met Bob at the university, where he was completing a doctorate in history.

I enjoyed my high-school teaching job, but it was challenging, to put it mildly. I was teaching courses in Canadian, Ancient and European history and in English and creative writing. In addition, I was placed in charge of editing and producing the school paper. Another occasional task which I had been doing ever since coming to Calgary was serving as a member of the panel of judges for Province-wide student drama presentations. Altogether, it's difficult to see how I could have had the time to be much of a mother to Tom. In fact, he was demonstrating his typical maturity by contributing a great deal to the general housework by then, as well as succeeding in his own schoolwork.

At the same time all this was going on, another corner was approaching. One of the professors at the university had been encouraging me to return to complete a Masters degree in what was then the Department of Sociology and Anthropology. So, by the time Easter of 1964 arrived I had decided on yet another gamble. Once again, I cashed in my teacher's pension—to Ellen's utter horror at my recklessness—and applied for entrance to the graduate program in these two social sciences. My idea was to take only one year off teaching, and to complete the required two years of study in two summer sessions and the one full year of class-work and research. It sounded impossible to everyone with whom I discussed my plan, but I was determined to do it.

That year turned out to be one of the happiest and most productive of my life. Bob and Nobuko were wonderful close neighbours, and subsequently became lifelong friends, even though their lives were eventually spent mainly in North Carolina. Nobuko taught me a lot about her Japanese culture and I taught her a bit about Canadian cooking. And Bob's unfailing humour kept us all laughing whenever we were together. They tended to host us for meals much more often than I had the time to entertain them in return. One day when they had invited Tom and me downstairs for dinner, Nobuko proudly served the dessert which was an attempt to duplicate one of my recipes—saskatoon pie! The moment I tried to plunge my fork into it, I realized that she had failed to master the art of pie-crust making. As we all sat silently, attempting to eat it, she burst out," Rike a rock!"

Another memorable adventure occurred on a beautiful day in the foothills west of the city, where they and Tom and I were enjoying one of our hikes. We discovered an obviously lost springer spaniel in a pitiful condition. Tom fell in love with him at once. There was just no way that we could leave him there, starving and injured and alone. So we decided to give him a home, in spite of the fact that a pet dog was the last thing I needed at the time. Actually Tom did most of the caring for him anyway. Tom and Bob, between them, gave him the name of 'Doc'.

The four of us also tried skiing in the steeper hills further to the west. I had an experience one day, however, that made me realize skiing was no longer safe for me. I was coming down a fairly steep rise one day when, suddenly, I had the weird sensation of completely losing control of my legs. They had gone numb and were not responding normally. Somehow, I made it safely down, but it was the last time I was ever to put on skis.

I had made a number of wonderful friends at the university as well. I was happy to find that one of Professor Anderson's courses was in our Master's program, in spite of his being a philosopher of Education rather than a sociologist. Another favourite professor of mine was Dr. Donald Mills. He taught us never to rely on secondary sources, but to go directly to the original works of the masters. And there was Dr. Asghar Fathi, who made a point of requiring that we each inform him as to the thinker who had most influenced our world views. I remember identifying Bertrand Russell. Professor Fathi then told me that this choice told him a great deal about me.

One new friend who shared my world view was an extremely obese young woman from New Brunswick called Bernie Melanson. She already had a PhD in Chemistry but had become disillusioned with her chosen field after working at Suffield on chemical weaponry. She also had a Bachelor's degree in Education, and was now hoping to somehow combine all this with Sociology for a university-level teaching job in the future. Other new acquaintances who rapidly became friends were Arnold Parr, who obtained his MA two years after I did, and Phyllis Atwell, who graduated in 1969. Arnold earned his PhD some years later and subsequently had a long career as a professor of sociology in New Zealand. Phyllis was a former nurse from Trinidad who eventually moved to Vancouver and taught at Langara Junior College until retirement.

The most surprising of the friends I discovered studying in the Sociology Department, however, was a bright young former high-school student from Central High School. Although I hadn't actually taught him, we were acquainted because of his job at the Safeway store on the corner of Fourteenth Avenue and Sixteenth Street, where Tom and I did all our shopping. His name was Irving Rootman. Little could I have guessed, when I encountered him at the cash register one day, that he would play a particularly close part in my life through all the years to follow.

Tom and I were able to spend Christmas up in Prince George with Don and Donna, feasting on an enormous roast turkey. I cooked a turkey at home for New Year's Day, as my sister's daughter, Linda, and her husband, John Gyorfi, along with their two small children were planning to be with us. In 1961, Linda had met and married John when they were both students at the University of British Columbia. He was one of the 240 young forestry students from Hungary who escaped to Austria at the time of the Hungarian Revolution in 1956 and eventually found their way to Canada, where they were accepted as immigrants. UBC had established a Forestry School up at Powell River for these students and their professors who had led their exodus. This was later moved down to Vancouver. Altogether, the Hungarian refugees, whose passage to Canada was supported and financed by the Canadian government of the day, numbered about 37,000. It was one of our first large intakes of immigrants and was to prove a fortunate move for the country, as these escapees from the cruel Soviet regime of the times became extremely productive citizens.

Life was so fast-moving in those days of the winter of 1964-5 that most of what happened is a blur. I remember a professor meeting me on the stairs one day and saying, "Pat, are you always going full speed when you're not in class? I've never seen you simply walk up or down the stairs, or along the hall—don't you ever get tired of running?" I answered blithely, "When the doors of opportunity are opening to me, I've just got to dash through!"

And 'opening' they clearly were; a number of momentous ones, in fact. One day, as I was leaving class, one of my favourite professors—Don Mills—asked me to remain behind for a few minutes. "I'm interested in the fact that you appear to be a Freethinker," he said casually. "Have you ever heard of the Unitarians?" When I said I hadn't, he told me that I would probably feel at home with them. "Anyone who believes as you do," he tossed at me as we both left the classroom," should join the Unitarian Fellowship." And so I did, taking Tom with me to attend their Sunday School classes. I found them to be totally non-supernatural in those days; all scientifically inclined 'humanists' as we would say now. For the first time in my life, I had discovered a group of people with whom I could feel utterly at home.

Then came a second, almost unbelievable message. I had been awarded two Fellowships to attend top American universities: one from Stanford and the other from Yale University at New Haven. I hadn't even begun to digest this news and the choice that it would force upon me, when a third wonderful event occurred. This even surpassed the previous two as possibly the greatest surprise of my life. Professor Anderson asked me to meet with him one day in the early spring. He confirmed with me that I would be completing my thesis as planned, at the end of the coming summer, so that I could graduate a year earlier than my classmates. He proceeded to inform me that he had just been appointed to head up the Secondary Education Department of the College of Education at the Regina branch of the University of Saskatchewan—established in 1961—and that he was on the lookout for top future professors. He asked me to become a member of the faculty as a Sociologist of Education, beginning at the rank of Assistant Professor in secondary-school History Education. He added that the Department of Sociology in the Social Science Division of the relatively new Division of Arts and Science wanted me to teach a class for them as well. Then he said that he was also intending to approach Bernie, with an invitation for her to take up a position in his department. Needless to say, I was almost overwhelmed with these opportunities: three challenging pathways all opening at the same time! It only remained to choose the one that would be best for both my son and myself.

I dismissed the Stanford offer first. I just didn't think that the drug-ridden atmosphere surrounding it at that time was an appropriate or safe place for a young teenager. Then I proceeded to inquire about the possibilities of postponing the Yale fellowship. When I heard that they were willing to hold it in abeyance for up to three years, my decision was made. I would accept the teaching position at the Regina college for the coming September, and hope to become sufficiently established there to obtain a two-year study leave in the autumn of 1968. Tom seemed to be quite happy about moving to Regina just on time for high school, as he would have had to change schools then anyway. By the time this was completely settled, all that remained was the researching and writing of my Master's thesis; the selling of my house and the purchase of a new one in Regina; and then the actual move—all in time for the beginning of the 1964-65 school year. What could possibly be simpler?

Well, for one thing, my chosen pathway could have been ridden with fewer swerves and bumps. The first unexpected one was when Mom needed help in one of her sudden moves. Like me, she was grasping at what she perceived as an opportunity. The constant load of farm housework, combined with family members coming and going for visits—and the work involved in entertaining and providing for them—was beginning to wear her down. Then, not long before her sixty-fifth birthday in early May of 1964, Jerry married Dana, the girl he had been involved with off and on since his early teens. She had meanwhile married someone else, given birth to two more children, then left her husband and returned to Jerry. It was no surprise to me that Mom was not happy about this, especially given the fact that they had all moved into the farm house, preparatory to fixing up a small place of their own on an adjoining quarter section of land, which Jerry was given by Tom as reimbursement for all his years of unpaid farm work. The upside of this for Mom was that, with Jerry no longer requiring her care, she was also recognizing an opening opportunity. She perceived his marriage, combined with the receipt of her first old-age-pension cheque, as freeing her from the increasing burden of all of her longtime family responsibilities, her own unhappy marriage included. Typically, it didn't take her long to act. By the end of May she had found a tiny one-room flat in Calgary and, with my help, moved her few personal belongings in. I was amazed that she seemed to have no desire whatsoever for the furniture and other household possessions gathered so painstakingly over the years. She even left behind the antique cut-glass 'sugar bowl' left to her by my grandmother. I rescued it for myself some years later, because it carried so many memories for me. I didn't have Mom's talent for vacating the past and its relics.

She did take her old trunk along with her, however, and in searching through that I discovered something truly amazing. It was a roll of paper which, when I flattened it out, proved to be a photo of her grandmother Armitage. She said her father, in his will, had left it to her. But she'd long since forgotten all about it. I immediately proceeded to get it appropriately framed and, in the process, obtained a copy for myself. Sometime later, I had that framed as well. And that is how I happened to come into possession of the beautiful old photo gracing my wall today. And how my sister Myrtle ultimately came to possess the original.

The next bump along my path in that busy time was sadly serious in its consequences for me. On one of our Saturdays out in the foothills with

Bob and Nobuko, Tom and I and 'old Doc' were having a glorious run. At one point I took the dog's leash and we seemed to be flying along together. I've never forgotten that sensation of utter freedom—so close to the feelings aroused in me by my earlier experiences of dancing. The following day I was so revitalized by the happy outdoor experience that I tackled a task I'd been putting off for ages. I cleaned out my kitchen cupboards. But, tragically, all the reaching, along with the previous day's running, must have been too much for my over-worked body. During the night I awoke to discover that I was in extreme pain and couldn't move my legs. Tom got in touch with our good friend Bernie, and between the two of them they managed to get me to the hospital, where I spent two weeks flat on my back in traction. To placate my worries about Tom being on his own, my friends took turns staying with him, although they all agreed that he really didn't need caring for.

Fortunately, I had just completed my extensive research on the MA thesis, which turned out to be quite revolutionary in the sociology of that era in that its approach was inter-disciplinary. I had yet to put all my findings and theorizing together, however—a daunting task even for someone who was not in a badly crippled state. Sitting was impossible for some weeks, so I spent most of June and July struggling with severe pain while standing on a stool and writing on top of the fridge. By the time the thesis was formally presented and accepted, and then put into published form with a hard-cover, it comprised 160 pages. The title was "A Study of the Relationship of the Selection Process in Education to Social Change". I couldn't attend my graduation later that autumn because, long before that was to occur, I was approaching another decisive corner. After putting the Calgary house on sale and borrowing enough from my brother Don for a down-payment on a new house in Regina, I had to arrange our move. But first, it was necessary for Tom and me to make a preliminary trip by car to our new destination. We had a great time. We stayed at the Regina Inn, and Tom enjoyed walking all around the downtown area, exploring it, while I traveled about with the real-estate agent. We were fortunate enough to find the perfect house almost immediately. It was on Angus Drive, not far from the beautiful Wascana Lake and extensive park where the castle-like government legislative buildings were located. And it was priced at considerably less than I would receive for our former home. The mortgage was guaranteed by my new employer. I was confident that, as soon as the 'pink house' in Calgary sold, I would be able to repay my always helpful brother Don. There was a high school for Tom about a half-hour's walk away, and the old Regina Normal School building where the Education Faculty of the new college was still situated. It was actually within easy walking distance for me, a few miles across the park.

In spite of the concerns of my Calgary friends about the wisdom of my return to the prairies, I was finding Regina a fascinating place to live, with an equally fascinating history. I discovered that the city had been established in 1882, and named after Queen Victoria. The following year it became the capital of the Northwest Territories and then, in 1905, the capital of the newly formed Province of Saskatchewan. It was on a breathtakingly beautiful site, having been built around Wascana Lake: Wascana being the Aboriginal term for "pile of bones".

As we settled into this surprisingly attractive place I began to realize that, with Tom's unfailing support, I had made it through—even though the struggle had at times seemed insurmountable. And I assured myself that I could coast along on the flat lands now, with no more mountains to climb. From now on I would avoid all enticing corners and take time to enjoy the endless prairie skies.

# Chapter 15

# LIFE AMONG THE EDUCATORS

My career as a university lecturer started out in high gear at the beginning of the autumn term of 1965. The only downside of the move to Regina was the fact that I would miss my U. of Calgary graduation celebration at the midpoint of that term. I discovered forty years later that my MA was one of the first two graduate degrees ever awarded by the then-new Sociology Department of the fledgling University of Calgary. In fact, I was actually the first graduate to complete the entire two-year program there. This meant that attending my graduation would have been more historically momentous than I realized at the time. But, of course, I was far too immersed in getting established in my job even to consider it. However, this university where I had studied continued to have an impact on me: some of the most positive aspects of my new position as an Assistant Professor were due to my previous happy learning experience there. Thus, in many key ways, the University of Calgary remained very much a part of my professional life. Another reason for this was the fact that the initiation into my new role was made much easier than I had any right to expect by the kindness of Professor Robert Anderson. He was by then the Director of the Department of Secondary Education, and had brought me with him from Calgary to the new Regina branch of the University of Saskatchewan. In fact, he assigned me the office next to his, in the area devoted to administration—with the departmental secretary established at a desk in the open area between. The presence of one of my best friends, Bernie Melanson, who had also been hired in Calgary by Professor Anderson, was an important factor in my settling in as well—as was the fact that my son Tom seemed satisfied with his new school.

The Faculty of Education was in the process of evolution in those days, as it had replaced the former Regina Normal School for the training of teachers only a few years previously. I learned that, for the time being, my job was not only to teach the Sociology of Education as a subject, but also to prepare future teachers of high-school history—or of what was soon to be termed 'social studies'. In addition, I worked in Arts and Science, having been hired there to teach sociology as well. This straddling of the two new relatively new Faculties was to have extremely interesting consequences for me.

All my classes went reasonably well, although I found the work demanding—given my lack of experience. My new colleagues were a fascinating mix of personalities and backgrounds, both those in Education and those in Sociology. I quickly learned that I had landed in an unexpectedly revolutionary environment at a particularly revolutionary time in my country's academic history. This was the period in which a number of new universities were opening in Western Canada and the demand for instructors exploded. At the same time, and no doubt spurred by this, there was a rapid influx of qualified Americans. A large proportion of these were young men of the 'sixties generation' who held the most extreme of left-wing views; to the extent that they no longer felt comfortable—nor even welcome—in their own country. Many were avoiding service in the war in Vietnam. The Social Science Division of the Arts and Science Faculty had apparently been 'manned' (literally as well as figuratively) by such people. I later discovered that a similar situation came to prevail at the new Simon Fraser campus in British Columbia.

Immediately upon my arrival I was made surprisingly welcome by my fellow social scientists. It was only sometime later that I learned the reason for this. Apparently, a certain reputation had preceded me. I had studied under a well-known Marxist scholar while pursuing my graduate work at the University of Calgary. I chose his course not because I was a 'true believer', but because of my conclusion that, if I were to be able to assess and intelligently criticize the then-prevailing ideology within the social sciences, I had to understand it thoroughly. Although I was unaware of the fact, apparently this professor had spread the word concerning my interest in, and in-depth knowledge of, Marxism. I began to be invited by a group of these new colleagues to a number of their social gatherings. This group included the Head of the Division of Social Science, who was obviously a committed Marxist.

One day during my second year in Regina, my former Marxist professor contacted me from Calgary concerning some of his students who were traveling through Regina, on their way to the ultimate destination of China.

He asked if I could provide a night of shelter for them. I agreed, and quite enjoyed their visit. What was to be the decade-long 'Great Proletarian Cultural Revolution' had just gotten under way in the Republic of China, led by Mao Tse-Tung and his soon-to-be-notorious wife, Chiang Ching. It had followed their country's 'Great Leap Forward' of 1958-60. Because Canada had established informal diplomatic relations with China early in the sixties, it was now possible for such a trip to be made by university students—especially dedicated admirers of Mao as these young people obviously were. We had some interesting discussions during their visit that evening. As the group left the next morning, they presented me with their 'bible': *The Communist Manifesto: Marx and Engels*, which I still possess. They also promised to bring me some of Mao's 'Little Red Books' upon their return, but I never heard from any of them again. Perhaps I hadn't come across as sufficiently enthused by the Cultural Revolution to warrant such a reward. Another possibility is that they encountered evidence of the wholesale destruction of the China's ancient culture and of the new economic system that Mao was then instigating; or of the brutality occurring in his 're-education camps' which were rapidly spreading throughout the countryside. The latter, however, was extremely unlikely due to the carefully planned management of visiting academic admirers and politicians which was characteristic of the Chinese government in those days.

Not long after the departure of these left-wing students I received a letter from my brother Bob, a member of the Canadian Air Force. He had been applying for a promotion when he suddenly encountered a problem. "Your connections are causing me a lot of trouble," he wrote in a letter. "In fact, if you aren't more careful about the company you keep, it may cost me a successful future in the Air Force." Needless to say, I found his warning intriguing, while at the same time vaguely worrying in its implications.

During this hectic time I was becoming acquainted with several interesting people from fields of study other than either Sociology or Education. There was a varied group of artists at this new university, all very talented and interesting; some of whom would later become famous throughout the country. And there was a gifted musician named Bill Levant. Another intriguing person was a female political scientist who, although dedicated to the extreme left-wing ideology of her peers, was like me in that she enjoyed discussing ideas with those who thought differently. Her name was Milnor Alexander. Many of these people were quite brilliant and had resigned from some of the Ivy League universities because of American politics. The new

Regina branch of the University of Saskatchewan was extremely fortunate to have received them.

I was also discovering that I had much in common with several members of the Economics Department. Economics was then the most scientifically oriented of the social sciences. One of these economists, who was to become a lifelong friend, was the Head, Art Hillabold. Another was Jack Boan. I also remember Ishrat Naqvi, a Baha'i from India. He was a physicist who subsequently became a good friend. And there was a lecturer in the Physics Department named Don Grier, with whom I enjoyed arguing. In politics Don considered himself—rather contradictorily, I thought—a dedicated Anarchist. I also became good friends with the Head of the English Department, whose name was Les Crossman. One of my earliest memories of him was when he rose to his feet during an altercation at a meeting of our General Council to challenge the previous speaker.

"I would disagree strongly with your motion," he said, "even if the language with which you expressed it *had not* been ridden with grammatical errors!"

My new colleagues within the Education Faculty were a fascinating mix as well. Dr. Bates was the Dean at that time. Ruth Godwin taught English; Lyle Evans was our dedicated librarian; and Evelyn Jonescu was a super-intelligent biologist and fellow member of our Secondary Education Department. I also remember Don Cochrane, an intelligent young social scientist who was fond of appearing in colourful, beaded attire. A fascinating couple who were a privilege to know had arrived by way of the US as well. They were Angelita and Tony Ledesma, who were originally from the Philippines. He had left the priesthood in order to marry Angelita. They remained my friends for years, in spite of eventually returning to the Philippines, where they devoted their lives to helping the poor. And, of course, there was my pal Bernie, fellow student from the University of Calgary, who had been hired to prepare the students to teach high-school chemistry. All four were very special people. As was Don Kapour, a mathematician, and Neil Southam who was then teaching physics, but later came to specialize in business administration. Ormond McKague was also with us, as well as a married couple, Les and Agnes Groome—but I can't recall their specialties.

And then there was the intelligent young Evelina Orteza from the Philippines, who had recently graduated with a PhD in Philosophy from an American university. She had arrived just the year before. She and I were interested in many of the same ideas, and became close friends almost immediately. From the first week of my arrival, we began to spend much of our time during coffee breaks and lunch hours in the faculty lounge, engaged in deep theoretical discussions. Evelina also soon got into the habit of coming over to our house in the evenings, along with Bernie. She would play classical music on the piano, and also accompany Bernie's spirited renditions of the popular songs of the fifties and sixties, such as those of Pete Seeger. I would often become so uncustomarily relaxed listening to "Goodnight Irene" and "This Little Light of Mine" that I'd fall asleep on the sofa. Tom and I also began to see a lot of the Southams and Kapours in a social capacity, having dinner in one another's homes. I especially loved eating tandoori chicken at the Kapours. Tom was always rather amused by Don's wife, who insisted on being addressed as "Mrs Dr. Kapour".

One day we had a surprise visit from an old friend, Irving Rootman. He had taken a year off his studies at Yale for a research project at the Saskatchewan Hospital at Weyburn—pursuing comparative studies of the mentally ill in the Province's English-speaking and French-speaking communities. Irving had been a student at Central High School in Calgary when I taught there, and our paths had crossed again when we found ourselves both doing graduate work in sociology at the University of Calgary. Another of the many coincidences that were to connect our lives from then on was that we had both been awarded fellowships to Yale for doctoral studies. Unlike me, however, Irving was able to take up his upon graduation. During his brief visit in Regina, I enjoyed introducing him to some of my new acquaintances, as well as getting him together once more with our mutual friend Bernie.

Of all the interesting personalities who had been hired to form the new Regina Faculty of Education, none was quite as memorable as Bernie Melanson. She was a breath of fresh air wherever and whenever she appeared. The attention she attracted was not due to her massively overweight body but, I would guess, in spite of it. I always knew the exact moment every morning when she arrived and began to make her way down the hall. Invariably, there were merry greetings mixed with expletives echoing throughout the building. And there was the rapidly gathering group of fascinated students who would congregate in her wake, with excited questions about something they were studying. A similarly unique pattern characterized her presence at faculty meetings. She would utter a critical comment about the smoke-filled room while throwing the window open, and then sit writing notes as if oblivious of what was going on—until she suddenly rose abruptly to inform us, in no uncertain terms, of her opinions on some controversial matter.

I'll never forget the fiercely indignant phone call she made to me soon after our arrival. Just before our first Council meeting we had been told by a member of the Faculty Wives' Club that we would be counted upon to contribute sandwiches or cookies, and to help with the serving of lunch to the 'professors'. Bernie recounted how she had told the woman what she thought of the idea that, merely because she was a female, she would be expected to wait upon her male colleagues. "But we've always done it that way!" faltered the caller, obviously referring to the days of the Normal School. I was ashamed to admit to Bernie that I had thoughtlessly agreed to the request, but immediately phoned to deliver the same refusal, and for the same reasons that Bernie had. From that moment on I also decided not to allow the men to ask me to get them coffee at meetings or at our luncheon breaks in the faculty lounge, nor ever again to accept the role of secretary at our departmental meetings.

This was merely an early introduction to the sexism I was to experience within academia. I soon discovered that we were in the very early days of yet another 'cultural revolution': the feminist one which was badly needed and had been a long time coming. However, in my opinion, it took a few wrong turnings along the way. For example, this was the period during which the proposal for a program in 'Women's Studies' was first being introduced and tentatively discussed. Both Bernie and I felt strongly that such a move would amount to a self-imposed reverse discrimination, possibly increasing a perversely feminist-supported new type of sexism.

I subsequently discovered a considerable amount of sexism in a lecture series instituted by the Arts and Science Faculty. Our 'General Education' group also ran a lecture series, which was well-attended by the more theoretically inclined professors—not only among our own faculty, but by those in the Arts and Science as well. Chiefly because of the leadership of Evelina Orteza, the widespread sexism of the time was kept out of this enterprise. Not so with the Arts and Science series, however. There, the lectures were chiefly philosophical, and, as I was fascinated by ideas, I participated on a fairly regular basis. But, no doubt because I was merely a sociologist—and a female one at that—I was not expected to know anything about philosophical theories. Not surprisingly, I was sometimes made to feel rather unwelcome in these discussions. Once, as I was sitting next to a male acquaintance during a lecture, he made a murmured remark to me in criticism of the speaker's ideas. As I was whispering in agreement the speaker stopped abruptly and said, in a very condescending manner, addressing me as '*Mrs*' Westcott rather than 'professor' as he referred to others in the audience, "Are you with us?"

"She's way ahead of you!" My colleague responded before I had time to consider a reply.

Sometime during that first term I was invited to speak at the Regina Unitarian Fellowship. I suspect that Ish Naqvi suggested it, as he and his tiny local cohort of humanistically inclined Baha'i were members. My topic was the Vietnam War, to which I was strongly opposed. My talk was well received. There was an extremely attentive man in the audience who asked a number of pointed questions concerning my field of study during the wide-ranging discussion that followed. He was quite critical of the prevailing Marxist ideology within both sociology and political science at the time, and was obviously expecting me to challenge his views. I could see that he was surprised when, instead, I agreed with his intelligent and well-considered comments, and then proceeded to expand upon the subject. Later, at coffee-time, he and his wife approached me, to continue the discussion. He introduced himself as Sandy Hutcheon, a longtime farmer now currently working as an agricultural economist in the Provincial government. His wife's name was Carolyn, although she was known as 'Cardie'. Apparently they were dedicated Unitarians, in charge of the Fellowship's Sunday School program.

I met a number of other interesting people at the meeting that day as well. These included John Brockelbank, who was then Deputy Premier of Saskatchewan. "Brock', as he was called, was a pragmatic, common-sense sort of man, whom I was always proud to have known as a friend. By the time he voluntarily retired from the legislature in 1967, after having served twenty-nine years, I had come to appreciate his ethical character even more fully. Another such person was Fil Fraser, an admirable young man from Jamaica who later went on to a distinguished career as a broadcaster, television producer at Vision TV, and writer. I recall a bit of trouble he got himself into, a few years after he left Regina, by referring to "uppety women" in a media presentation—a term intended as irony, but entirely misunderstood by many feminist listeners. Yet another interesting person was Amy Dalgleish, who subsequently moved to the Lower Mainland of BC to become a well-known social activist. Others who were highly involved in leading the group were Anna and Lorne Pearce and Olina and Jim Struthers. Anna and Olina were sisters, descendants of the humanistically oriented Icelandic immigrants who had pioneered Unitarianism in the Canadian mid-west. 'Ole' was then president of the Fellowship and active in many community organizations as well. The Struthers Crescent in Regina was later named after her.

Another inspiring pair of people with whom Tom and I immediately became friends was Mac and Beth Hone and their sons. They were both gifted artists who lived and worked in their self-constructed geodesic domes in Lumsden, a village in the Qu'Appelle valley to the north of Regina which stretches across much of southern Saskatchewan. Yet another intriguing couple who became life-long friends were Marion and Bob McPherson. He was in the Arts and Science Faculty. I discovered that Jack Boan and Art Hillabold and their wives attended the Fellowship regularly as well. And that Florence and Don Grier were also Unitarians. I decided then and there to accept the enthusiastic invitations of these friendly, like-minded people and proceeded to join the organization, with my son Tom soon becoming a member of the Youth Group.

One of the many new friends we made as a result of the Unitarian connection was a young female from Jamaica, who had been encouraged to attend the Fellowship by Fil Fraser. She was in the process of immigrating, having come to the city the previous year as a 'nanny'. She was thus legally committed to working a given number of years for the employer who had sponsored her. One Sunday she unburdened herself to me, confessing that she was unhappy about her situation. I discussed her problems with Tom, and he agreed that we should offer her a home with us, while she continued to fulfil her immigration requirements by working for her sponsors during the day. So that was how the beautiful and intelligent Jamaican, Joy Graham, entered our lives! It was a decision we never regretted. In spite of her busy daytime life as a nanny, she helped us with all our household chores, including taking turns shopping for groceries on weekends and sometimes cooking our evening meal. She and Tom hit it off from the start, which was, of course a necessity in order for the arrangement to work.

The three of us had many happy times together. Whenever I brought home copies of handouts for a class, I would put the sheets in piles on the dining-room table and we would run around in circles, laughing as we picked up a page from each pile so that they could be organized consecutively. And then came the numbering, in an exciting race which inevitably ended with me in third place. And there was the joke Tom decided to play on Joy one night at meal-time. He and I had always been rather shocked at the hot spices she inevitably added to the food on her own plate. One evening I spotted Tom surreptitiously shaking pepper on to her meal whenever she turned to talk to me. We both watched anxiously each time she returned to eating. But our fun was spoiled. She seemed not to notice, no matter how much pepper was added. We often wondered how she could possibly taste the flavours in the food. She was able to repay him a few days later by having a hearty laugh at his expense when he came home from school one afternoon and began his usual greeting of "Hi, I'm home!" and halfway through, the 'home' changed to a shouted "ho-o-o-o-me!" as his heels slipped out from under him and he slid rapidly from the landing down the stairs to the basement.

Another fond memory is of one of the many sojourns Joy and I made around town with Don Grier and his wife Florence, on weekend afternoons while Tom was otherwise occupied. Their politics were much more radical than mine, and most of our walking time was spent in enthusiastic and good-natured arguing. One day Don was badly crippled with a recurring back problem and limping badly. As a couple of men passed us one of them remarked loudly, ostensibly to his companion, "That's what can happen to you when you try to take on three women!"

Our home situation was not all laughter, however. Tom's life as a teenager was not an easy one. Having separated parents made him different from the norm in those days. And being required to move to the farm to work with his dad every summer meant that he missed out on all the sports and camping activities participated in by his Regina friends. Then, just as he was getting settled back on the farm and enjoying bonding again with old Valley pals, he would once more be uprooted and sent back to the city. How he coped as well as he did was a marvel to me then, and remains so to this day. When at home with Joy and me, he assumed his share of the household responsibilities; helping to prepare supper when necessary; doing his own laundry and ironing; and keeping his bedroom and the basement sitting room with its television-watching area consistently tidy. I gave him the forty-dollar monthly-support payment provided by his father, and he used it to purchase clothes and other necessities. We had a rule that he had to be home by 11:00 at night at the latest, and I recall only once that the rule was broken. Because it had never occurred before I became desperately worried, and called the police. He had merely lost track of the time and remained overly long at the home of a friend, but the embarrassment I caused him ensured that it never happened again!

I was always concerned about the way that Tom appeared to be somewhat upset for about a month after returning from the farm. However, I think one of his saddest experiences in those high-school years was a 'first love' which went awry. The girl was of Japanese background. She was from one of the many families whose land on the coast of British Columbia had been confiscated during the war, and who had eventually become highly successful farmers in the irrigation country of southern Alberta.

During the early spring of 1968 I found myself drawn to the television set in the basement much more often than was the norm. My attention was glued to the federal Liberal Party convention. Like many of my peers I had become a victim of 'Trudeaumania'. I was convinced that in Pierre Trudeau we had the kind of star who appears very seldom on the political horizon: a person capable of fighting for social justice and keeping our country united and economically viable, while at the same time lifting it out of mediocrity, and placing us on the world stage. Of course my expectations were impossible! Another gripping story at the time was the tragic assassination of Martin Luther King in the United States. And then, scarcely two months later, came that of Robert Kennedy. I remember thinking, as I sat in my tiny basement bubble of relative security and comfort, that it was a strange, history-making time in which to be living.

On a smaller scale, we suffered our own sad event around then: an especially sad one for Tom. It was in connection with his beloved dog, 'Old Doc'. Tragically, it was all caused by a moment of carelessness on my part. Doc was an integral part of our home life. In my imagination I can still see him during the evenings when we were in the front room. He knew he was not allowed there, so would lie in the doorway between it and the kitchen and gradually edge forward on to the living-room carpet until only the toes of his back feet remained in touch with the floor behind him. He was never any trouble, as he was extremely obedient when we were home with him and seemed happy to remain in the basement during school hours. It wasn't the most desirable situation for an active dog, but we would make sure he had sufficient food and water, and always closed the door to the rest of the house.

One morning, in the midst of one of my mad rushes to get to work on time, I forgot to close the door to the basement. In one of those confluences of unfortunate circumstances that can occur in life, I was expecting a parcel in the mail that day and had left word with the mailman that the front door would be unlocked. What a sad commentary on the changed times it is that an unlocked door in those days was quite a normal thing! Doc had apparently never lost the hatred and fear of uniformed men that we had noticed when we first discovered him in a pitiful state in the Alberta foothills. A warning bell sounded for us when Tom found him outside that afternoon, growling and snarling at passers-by. I received a phone call in the early evening from the police. They informed me that Doc had been on the main floor guarding the door when the mailman entered the house, and had attacked him ferociously. I was ordered to get rid of the dog at once, or he would be put down. It was almost the end of June, so we kept Doc inside until Tom left for the summer, taking him along. Jack had agreed to care for him on the farm. I never saw my dear canine friend again, and when Tom returned to the farm the following summer, 'Old Doc' had disappeared.

Along with Tom, I too had to learn to live with fallout from the prevailing negative attitude of the times toward single mothers—especially those who had left their husbands. A surprising number of the male academics assumed that I was 'fair game' for crude sexual advances, and I was continually having to deal with these. Even a senior administrator at the college had a habit of maneuvering so that, whenever he walked down the hall with me, his arm crept around my shoulder in a suggestive way. And another colleague whom I was forced to confront politely about his actions toward me claimed that it was all my fault—that it was the sexually flirtatious manner which I consistently projected.

"For example," he said, "At meetings or conferences you're always surrounded by a group of men. Don't try to tell me, even though the subject of conversation is ostensibly ideas, that it's not basically all about sex! Or that you're not aware of it. Why those guys crowd around you like bees around a honey pot!" How on earth does one respond to such an accusation? Especially when it's made by someone with the authority to ensure that you're not ever in line for a promotion? I could see that there was simply no way I could explain to him the excited engagement spurred by a sharing of ideas, among people who were authentically interested in such matters. And that such people were almost invariably men, simply because men formed the vast majority in academic settings. So I controlled my resentment and merely laughed along with him. Even more problematic for me was the fact that, whenever I became friendly with one of my male colleagues, it was generally assumed that we were having an affair. After all, I was a woman who had run away from her husband—or, more likely, been discarded by him for unfaithfulness!

My strangest experience of that fast-moving first year at the Regina Faculty was of a different nature, however. It specifically involved relationships with the social science group—chiefly sociologists in the Faculty of Arts and Sciences and the psychologists. I was invited to attend the informal gatherings of the sociologists, which I did, assuming that we would be dwelling on the organizing of course material and other such professional matters. But I gradually began to realize that the group was focusing chiefly on political issues, and internal ones at that. Their main interest seemed to be on how to guide the university as a whole in a more radically left-wing direction. At one such meeting it became apparent that they were planning what amounted virtually to a 'take-over' of the agenda of an upcoming Council meeting. When I, in my innocence, voiced an objection to this—especially to the undercover nature of the plan, which would have us all spread about the room so that our 'group membership' would not be noticed—I suddenly became an outcast. Actually, it was worse than that. They apparently saw me as a traitor who had been planted within in order to gain the trust of the group and disrupt their plans. As I was gradually to learn, from that moment on most of my fellow sociologists viewed me as much worse than merely the moderate liberal which I was. They labeled me a 'closet conservative' pretending to be left-wing. Even my Marxist professor from Calgary went so far as to advise me, on one of his visits to Regina, that it was high time for me to "get off the fence". My response was that I preferred the view from the fence to that from any of the surrounding ideological swamps.

I also didn't help my cause within the Department of Sociology by a position I took the following year regarding one of their sociologists. He was a fellow lecturer whom I considered was being unfairly maneuvered out of his position. At the meeting of the Social Science Division where he was making an appeal I was the only person who spoke up in his favour. I was quite open in making the point that he was the sole non-Marxist with a full-time position there; and that, surely, any evolving field of study such as sociology required representation of a variety of the prevailing perspectives. My intercession failed to help him, however. By then I had lost any influence I might have had with my fellow sociologists.

I was also becoming increasingly worried about something that was apparently occurring in certain departments at the time. My concern was being fed by a growing number of students who came to my office wanting to talk about being pressured by their professors to participate in research on LSD. I soon discovered, however, that my hands were completely tied where the entire issue was concerned. These were the days when that drug was rapidly swelling in popularity, among both university students and their instructors. In fact, it had come closer to me than I had any knowledge of at the time. I only learned from Tom many years later the reason why he suddenly stopped mixing with a particular group of friends. He told me that if he had remained he would have felt forced to experiment with drugs.

Another disturbing—although also enlightening—set of experiences in those early years of academia had to do with the concept of lesbianism. I was introduced to it for the first time, in an abrupt fashion, by being propositioned by a female colleague. Due to my total ignorance about what was going on, I didn't handle it very well, with the result that I quite unnecessarily turned her into a bitter enemy. Only in the days following this debacle did I recognize that a couple of my best friends were also lesbians.

Not long after this there was another encounter in which the concept of lesbianism arose. To my great surprise I had received an inquiry from a leading Canadian publisher, who must have read my articles, concerning the possibility of my writing a textbook for them on the subject of the Sociology of Education in Canada. They sent an agent out from Toronto to meet with me to discuss the matter, and he took me out to dinner. However, the situation began to deteriorate rather quickly as he drank a good deal of wine during the meal, and I became concerned about his ability to drive home. To make matters worse, a group of my students were at a nearby table, observing it all. I attempted to cut the meeting short, with the excuse of papers to mark. Rather than call a taxi, I foolishly chanced getting into the car with him—a good example of the "publish or perish" mentality at work within me. Upon leaving the restaurant, the agent headed toward his hotel, rather than in the direction of my home. A heated argument followed before I was able to persuade him that I would not get out of the car except at my own door. Upon parking in front of our house, he began an attempt at an outright sexual advance inside the car. But I managed to fend him off—assuming, as I did so, that it probably marked the end of any chance of realizing my dream of publishing a book. As I left, he shouted, "I should have known you were a lesbian!"

A couple of days later I was pleasantly surprised to receive a call from a senior representative of the publisher, who was in town to finalize the deal. The agent was also at the signing session, busily avoiding my gaze. However, his presence failed to spoil what was to me a marvelous opportunity and challenge.

My life, in those days, was immersed in rapid change coupled with challenges on many fronts. In addition to the revolutionary atmosphere within the university, the entire Province of Saskatchewan had been, especially for the previous six years, gripped in a rising tide of radical change. When Tommy Douglas was still Premier he laid the plans for a government-sponsored universal medical-care system. By the turn of the decade, Douglas had returned to national politics, to become leader of the New Democratic Party, or NDP, which had been formed to assume the role of the CCF at the federal level. It was left to Woodrow Lloyd, my former school principal at Biggar—who had replaced Douglas as Premier—to bring the medical-care program into being. In spite of strong, wholesale opposition by the doctors' association, the program had been announced in 1959, introduced to the Provincial legislature in 1961 as the Saskatchewan Medical Care Insurance Act, and passed into law by 1962. Then, in 1966, the year after Tom and I moved to Regina, Saskatchewan's doctors went on strike. For twenty-one days in May of that year, the medical-care system would have been completely shut down if it were not for a most unique development.

Four years previous to this calamity of the strike, advertisements had begun to appear in the British medical journals for doctors who might be interested in working in a Canadian prairie Province dedicated to the introduction of universal medical care. By the time the doctors' strike actually began, there were already several community-sponsored group clinics in Saskatchewan. The first of these was The Swift Current Regional Health District, formed as a pilot project in 1945 as a result of a study by the new CCF government aimed at the establishment of a system of pre-paid hospital insurance. Local taxpayers paid premiums and the municipality provided a fee-for-service to the doctors. A clinic loosely based on this earlier plan had been established in Regina by the time Tom and I arrived. I registered us with it the following year, as I had always been philosophically opposed to union strikes by workers in secure, civil-service jobs—especially those providing essential services such as health care and education. Our new personal physician was David Road, who ran the clinic along with his partner, Peter Beaglehole. Both had immigrated from England. I found the entire project fascinating, especially because we patients took part in regular meetings concerning the clinic's operation. A problem gradually emerged after the issue was settled however. The ruling doctors' union made sure that these heroic British practitioners—who had in effect 'broken' their strike—were not allowed hospital privileges in their home cities. This situation continued for almost a decade, and was to have an effect on me of which I would not be aware until eight years into the future.

Meanwhile, back at the university, we were struggling to organize new programs in the Faculty of Education. Dr. Anderson asked if I would head up an experimental General Education Department aimed at including all members of the faculty who were not specifically involved with teaching either Elementary or Secondary-School 'methods' courses. I was happy to accept this responsibility, although I was still doing a course in secondary school history in addition to my work in sociology. There was no pay involved, but I enjoyed the opportunity for leadership in an interdisciplinary area. A change in the location of my office was required. I can't recall just why. But the position did offer me the chance to make use of the services of Dr. Anderson's secretary when I needed her help. A second pleasant surprise in the spring of 1967 was my election to the Executive of the Faculty Association for the coming term. I was also named to the committee responsible for reviewing and selecting members of the total Regina faculty for promotion and tenure. I thought then, and still do, that my being asked to join this important decision-making group was an example of reverse discrimination, in that I was there solely because it had been impressed upon the 'powers that be' that there must be at least one female on board. Regardless of this, I was pleased to have been selected, and felt that I could contribute a much-needed perspective to the decision-making.

At the same time, I was also involved in speaking engagements. In fact, during my years at Regina, I managed to average five public and/or professional presentations a year. I was battling a movement within the Province's school system which would have us follow the current of the times and move from the teaching of geography and history to a combination of the two—supposedly in addition to sociology—into a vaguely defined field called 'social studies'. In fact, my first-ever scholarly publication was "Whither Social Studies in Saskatchewan?", which appeared in the June 1966 issue of the Saskatchewan Teachers' Federation Newsletter. My concern was that high-school students would no longer receive a thorough grounding in the two disciplines which are essential to any understanding of the world in which we live. Combined with this lack of solid educational grounding was the advertised intent to include both psychology and sociology in the new study. I considered this move away from the two distinct disciplines of geography and history and into a poorly defined study of human behaviour not the step forward that was being hailed, but a regression; and that the long-term cost for the goal of solid student knowledge at the secondary-school level would be catastrophic. A further article of mine devoted specifically to the problems involved in teaching the social sciences at the high-school level was published three years later in the Saskatchewan Social Science Teacher Association Newsletter. However, I was once more struggling against the prevailing tide.

I eventually turned my attention, instead, to the resulting necessary task assigned to me by my Dean: that of developing the program for preparing secondary-school social studies teachers. My program was actually in operation for the following decade. In fact, I had been assigned membership in the Faculty's Program Development Committee, which was responsible for the task of ongoing reconstruction and evaluation of curriculum. In this capacity I developed and introduced two classes in the Sociology of Education as well. One was a comprehensive introduction to the field, and the other a graduate-level class called "Sociological Perspectives on Educational Change". Eventually, I constructed and conducted a research project for evaluating the BEd program in its entirety.

During my busy second year at the Faculty, I presented my first scholarly paper. It was called "The Sociology of Education: An Overview of Research". I had been invited to speak on the subject by The Northwest Philosophy of Education Society in Regina. I also assumed a major responsibility for developing the grade-seven Social Studies curriculum in Saskatchewan schools, and worked as a member of a two-person team on the preparation of the grade-nine curriculum. All this activity was no doubt the reason why, sometime later, I served for two years as one of two elected members-at-large of the Saskatchewan Educational Research Association.

There were far too many educational changes being carelessly considered and too-precipitously implemented during the era of the sixties in my opinion; and in the opinion of my close friend and colleague, Evelina Orteza. It's not that we weren't interested in improving what was going on. We were both dedicated to bringing about a few of what we considered constructive reforms to the teacher-training program. Dr. Anderson wanted us to consider designing a first-year course—Education 101—which would serve as a simplified introduction to the over-all processes of how children learn; the nature of knowledge; how the various required courses might vary considerably in the degree to which their content accorded to the rules of evidence; and what the process of teaching is actually about. One of my pet projects was getting the students out into the schools as early in the program as possible, for brief bouts of practice teaching, or 'practicums' as they were called. I was one of the few lecturers with experience as a successful teacher in public schools, so was in considerable demand to oversee this practice teaching, and to select appropriate teachers in the system for the task. My plan was that, eventually, we would extend the Education program to four years from three, with the final year being devoted to Educational Foundations courses. These courses would help our students make sense of what they had previously experienced as classroom teachers, and plan their future responses to the demands of teaching according to sound theory.

Both Evelina and I thought that courses comprising the theoretical foundations of Education—including our planned general introductory one—should not be restricted to the Secondary Department. Because they applied equally to all levels of teaching, we wanted them to belong to a department devoted to that particular function. We were hoping for a re-structuring of the Faculty which would involve the creation of a third department housing such courses: one which would be 'general' in its formal designation as well as its educational function.

During my first summer in Regina I taught the summer session. Tom was not at home in any case, and I needed the extra money. Then, for the summer of 1967, I accepted an invitation to teach at the University of Calgary. During the six weeks there, I became close friends with a Sociology of Education professor, Henry Zentner, and our professional connection lasted for many years thereafter. I also used the opportunity to help my mother get settled in an apartment. She had previously left her tiny rented room for a job of housekeeper for an elderly man. But he had recently died, so she was forced to make yet another move. My brother Don and I agreed to share the cost of her rent in a comfortable and well-situated place not far from the downtown area. I stayed there with her until my Calgary summer course ended. Then I made a quick trip up to Prince George to visit Don and his wife Donna, and see their new baby, Lewis Duffy. It was great to know that our father's name was going to live on in the person of this remarkable little boy.

Another source of happiness during this exciting second year at the job was my promotion to Associate Professor, with tenure. I could now hope that, when Tom graduated from high school, it might be possible for me to accept my fellowship to Yale. I would be able to apply for a two-year, unpaid study-leave. The fact that Tom was planning on a return to Calgary for his university studies also contributed to this possibility. So I gradually began the process. By the time Tom left for the farm in the summer of 1968, we had both been accepted into our respective universities for the autumn term. Joy was by then able to move on from her job as nanny, and had decided to go to Toronto, where she had friends. And I had rented our house to Don and Florence Grier.

After bidding farewell to my colleagues, I proceeded to Calgary to visit my mother and attend to a couple of critical necessities. The first was to find a boarding place for Tom and to pay the rent for the first few months. Tom's father had promised to fund his university education, so I had to trust that he would accept ongoing responsibility for this as well. Evelina, who was teaching the summer session at the University of Calgary, helped locate the room and board for Tom. She also took my mother and me out for a celebration dinner at the Sheraton Hotel, and we all attended the Calgary Stampede together as well.

My second task was a far more daunting one. I arranged to take advantage of the fact that Alberta had just introduced a new law allowing for 'no-fault divorce', in cases of long-term legal separations such as Jack's and mine. Up to then I had resisted the idea of divorce because of the difficulty of the process in those days and the emotional cost to Tom which would inevitably follow the required public accusations against his father. And because of the ugliness that would no doubt have been involved in a battle for custody while Tom was still under eighteen. So, it happened that, in late August of 1968, our divorce became the first in the Province to be considered under the new law. I found myself in court facing a stern-appearing judge, with Tom's father Jack and his lawyer off to the side—obviously ready to do battle. Following an introduction which included the history-breaking nature of the event, the judge turned to me and asked for a list of my demands regarding what I considered my rightful share of the Westcott estate. I was a bit stunned by the unexpectedness of the question, and must have been silent for a moment. "I'm asking you to specify how much you intend to ask for," he said, patiently.

"Nothing," I blurted out, "Except my freedom!"

"Are you certain you don't want anything?" he looked a bit stunned. When I again assured him of this, he turned to Jack, and his lawyer and said, "Then I really don't think we need waste a moment more of the court's time." The lawyer rose to his feet, apparently to launch an argument, but the judge raised his hand compellingly and declared, "Divorce granted." Yes, in the end, it really was that easy!

Almost before I knew it, I was on the airplane on my way to Yale University at New Haven, Connecticut. It was my very first flight, and I had been terrified at the prospect for some time. I decided to deal with all the fears crowding in on me by forcing myself to accept the fact that everything from the point of take-off was totally out of my control. In other words, "What will be, will be." It was all a matter of trust in the professionalism of the crew and the 'luck of the draw' from that moment on. Amazingly, it worked, and I became surprisingly relaxed. In fact, I discovered I had been badly in need of being, for once in my life, in a situation where nothing whatsoever in the surrounding circumstances depended upon me.

From the moment of arrival, Yale University presented me with a series of fascinating adventures. The very sight of the beautiful old vine-covered buildings seemed to be a symbol of a dream come true. All those years of sacrifice and struggle had been worthwhile after all! I was here at last, within reach of the culmination of my life-time dream! I'll never forget the feeling of complete and utter freedom from past responsibility, and of gratitude for new opportunities, which came to me with that view. It was a view of that beckoning mountain top which I had sought for so long! Everything was a surprise, as I had headed for this far-away place with little previous knowledge of it and absolutely no expectations of any kind. At the moment of my first viewing the literal 'ivy league' nature of the place, I was utterly at peace.

I was quite satisfied to discover, when I finally found it, that the box-like women's dorm consisted only of tiny single rooms, with scarcely space for a small couch, bedside table and cupboard, and with a single-toilet-and-bath down the hall. However, I must admit to a twinge of resentment concerning the relative status of females at Yale in these early days of their acceptance when, somewhat later, I was shown around the men's residence in an old building reminding me of a castle, with grandiose apartments complete with fireplaces.

However, there was one way in which being male was a disadvantage at that particular period. For the first time in American history, male graduate students were being called up for service. They were needed to fight in the Vietnam war, which was beginning to go badly for the Americans. One of the young men I came to know was an early victim of the call-up. I offered to help him settle in Canada, if he would attempt to escape. But his father was a 'big shot' at the Pentagon, he said, and there was no way he could refuse to answer the call. "But I'll never kill anyone!" he promised.

I noticed, rather quickly, that status meant everything to the attending students. The majority of them were offspring of wealthy families, and had made it to Yale—not on their own steam but because of the influence wielded by those families. And I learned that, ironically, those of us who were there because we had won fellowships for the three-year program of doctoral studies were referred to by many of these people as 'losers'. It was obvious that they thought of themselves as 'winners' and expected to come out the same, regardless of what they did or failed to do where studies were concerned.

There were two other 'losers' on my floor of the women's dorm and we soon became fast friends although they were much younger than I. In fact, as a woman of forty-two, I was almost a generation older than my fellow students. One of the girls with whom I quickly bonded was from Jamaica. The second was a black student from Tennessee. All the others who became my friends were young males, whom I met in class, except for a man about my age who was at Yale on a post-doctoral fellowship. He was a Dr. Robert Yee, who had taken a year's study leave from a California university.

Dr. Yee and I shared many interests, and would often happen upon one another in the library, where both of us spent most of our time. That library was the most marvelous I've ever known, and I still think of it with awe. Another experience which aroused a similar sensation in me was one that Dr. Yee and I also shared. We attended a lecture delivered by one of my great intellectual heroes, Hannah Arendt. The two of us had the supreme privilege of speaking with her afterwards. That was one of the high points of my time at Yale. Another was having lunch with Lee Quan Yu, the leader of Singapore at that time—in fact, sitting in the chair next to his. The professor who taught a course I was taking on South-East Asia had invited a few of his students to the luncheon. I must admit to being very favourably impressed by this great world leader.

A continuing experience lingering in my memory was the discovery that the people around me knew nothing whatsoever about Canada. There was never any mention of my country in the news—it was as if their neighbour to the north did not exist. One evening at the dorm I was called to the phone in the hall. "It's someone with the strangest name I've ever heard!" the messenger exclaimed. "She said she's 'Regina Saskatchewan.'" The name of my home Province was pronounced so weirdly that I was utterly puzzled until I picked up the phone.

One of my favourite courses at Yale was on statistics. It gave me a thorough grounding in research procedures, which was to prove extremely useful in future years. I was introduced to the computer, although the one we used filled all the walls of a large room, and involved cards rather than a keyboard. By a strange coincidence, the project I was invited to work on for the course was a study of Unitarianism in the United States: its membership and their beliefs and opinions.

I had discovered fairly soon that—due to my thorough grounding in graduate-level Sociology courses at the University of Calgary—I did not require the full two years of these as the American students did. So it was that, as the end of that first year approached, I was ready to begin the preparation for my thesis. I had been somewhat disappointed in my marks on some of the courses, however. I was not accustomed to receiving only average grades on term papers over which I had laboured long hours in the library. Interestingly, a number of these papers were later published in leading international journals. Apparently not all of the world's scholarly community were on the same wave length as the Yale professors! Or perhaps it was simply that I had learned in those subsequent years to sign my submissions with the name of 'Pat' rather than 'Patricia'.

I suspect that, during my time at Yale, I spoke up in class more than a female was supposed to do in those days. I should have kept in mind that, after all, it had only been a brief time since people of my gender were even allowed to enter those sacred halls! There had even been moments when I dared to disagree with the instructor. Once, when we were being subjected to an explanation of human behaviour that left no room whatsoever for genetic influence, I actually had the gall to object.

"But what you're saying conflicts utterly with everything we've learned about biology," I said.

"Biology has nothing whatsoever to do with human behaviour!" our professor replied condescendingly, "That only applies to animals." I then added to my original sin by claiming that, not only are we also animals, but we are not the only species capable of displaying learned social behaviours. In spite of the professor's objection, I proceeded to describe to them all how I had often watched our herd of cows organize themselves in the morning, selecting one of their group to remain with the calves while the rest roamed around the pasture, eating grass. The professor quickly changed the subject, ignoring what I had said.

When the time came for me to begin focusing on my thesis project, I learned that the person who thus far been my advisor—and whom I had met long before when he had visited the University of Calgary and become interested in my work—had been granted a study leave for the following year. Taking his place would be a professor who had not impressed me very favourably. He had always appeared to expect the female students to be silent in class, and totally ignored any of us who attempted to join a discussion. So it was with some reluctance that I went to his office for our first meeting concerning the thesis. What occurred there, in the privacy of that office, was something I could not have imagined in my wildest nightmares. How I wished, in the years to follow, that I had gone equipped with a tape recorder!

Instead of discussing my upcoming project, the conversation began to move in a direction that, at first, I found extremely puzzling. What in the world was the man hinting at? Then he made a sexually suggestive move toward me. I froze, unable to take in what was happening. But he soon let me know, in no uncertain terms, that I would be expected to sleep with him. I have no memory of what I said, or if I was able to respond at all. All that remains with me is the conclusion that struck like a hammer-blow to the stomach. There was simply no way I could remain at Yale and complete my doctoral thesis! This man was one of the most powerful on campus. No one would believe me. Compared to his, my word would count for nothing. My dream was over. I would never scale my mountain top. In fact, at the blow of that hammer, the beckoning peak had disappeared from my horizon leaving only dark clouds in its place. I left that office so stunned I could scarcely speak to anyone. I found myself unable to reveal what had happened to any of my female acquaintances, not even to a fellow Sociology student named Nancy Milio, with whom I had grown fairly close during the previous months, and who was to remain a lifelong friend.

However, two events which occurred about a week following this catastrophe—and before I boarded my flight back to Regina—helped to restore my confidence in the basic decency of most men. One had to do with Dr. Yee, the friend with whom I had shared a number of pleasant experiences and ideas. There had never been the slightest suggestion on his part that he felt anything more for me than the friendliness I had extended toward him. He left New Haven a few days before I did, dropping in to say goodbye on his way to the airport. As he was leaving he retained his usual formal manner, but gave me a warm handshake. With the extended hand had come a piece of paper, accompanied by the injunction that I was not to read it until after he'd gone. I've kept the poem on that paper all these years. It went as follows:

*One delightful snowflake*
    *Floated out of darkness*
*And danced*
    *Gaily to the moonlight.*
*Landing lightly, gently*
    *On a graceful curve,*
*He clung triumphant*
    *Listening to the beat of her heart. And then,*
    *Transformed,*
*He vanished in the warmth of his love!*

My second-last experience at Yale was a farewell get-together with the group of male students with whom I had become close friends. They had devastating news. Word had just come that our fellow student, who had answered the call of his country earlier in the year, was killed in action! After absorbing the horror and anger aroused in me by this sickening waste of a young life, I told the group about my own misfortune, which now appeared relatively minor in contrast to the previous news. When asked about what I would do, I said I was giving up any chance at a Yale doctorate and returning to Canada at once. They were obviously shocked and unhappy for me, but I got the impression that it was not a huge surprise to them. One even muttered something about this having happened before. They discussed the possibility of standing up for me as a group, and making my complaint known. But, almost immediately, this course was rejected, with each person offering the same reason, in a rather shamed fashion. Their excuse? It had been too long and difficult a struggle to get this far in their careers. There was simply no way that one could risk losing a priceless doctorate from Yale at this point.

"I hadn't expected you to," I assured them, "but I am asking for one thing, in the name of our friendship and the integrity of academic education. When this sort of event occurs in a university where you're working in the future—and occur it likely will—promise me that you won't simply turn away and let it happen." They all assured me that they would never, ever, allow such behaviour in any setting where they had the slightest influence. How many times, in the long decades since, have I wondered if they kept that promise!

# Chapter 16

# ONE HONEST MAN

My son Tom astonished me one day early in the fall of 1967 when he turned to me suddenly a moment or so after our house-mate Joy had closed the door on a guest, following a friendly goodbye. "That Sandy Hutcheon is really one honest man! Not a bit like all those university types who're always crawling out of the woodwork around here. You should marry him, Mom!"

One of the reasons the comment was so surprising was that Sandy, only recently widowed when his wife died of cancer the previous spring, had always been considered by both Joy and myself as nothing more than a good friend from the local Unitarian Fellowship—just as his wife Cardie had been. As soon as I returned to Regina from teaching the 1967 summer session at the University of Calgary, we had joined other members of our close-knit Unitarian Fellowship in providing company and support for 'a friend in need'. Not only had Sandy lost his beloved wife and the mother of his two sons, but his younger brother had died suddenly not long before. Also, he was alone where family was concerned, as both his sons were studying away from home. So it was clear to all of us at the Fellowship that Sandy Hutcheon was badly in need of close and caring friends. Another reason Tom's remark astonished me was the fact that seventeen-year-old sons of single mothers seldom even like to consider their mothers dating, much less marrying.

I had always enjoyed Sandy's company—especially his brilliant mind, combined with the frankness to which Tom was referring. I had come to know Sandy's younger son Don, an extremely pleasant twenty-year-old who was then studying at a technical institute in Moose Jaw. However, I hadn't had the chance to meet the older son Dave who, at the age of twenty-five, was then a graduate student at university. On Sandy's first visit after the loss of his wife, I served him coffee. As he left that evening he turned to me and said, "The next time I come, I'll make the coffee!" I loved that because I had always been aware that my coffee simply didn't measure up. I had long since forsaken the tedious process taught me by restaurant owner Jimmie Wong, my employer when I was taking grade twelve in Oyen.

It wasn't long before Sandy Hutcheon began to play a regular role in our social life. He loved arguing with Don Grier, our Anarchist friend, and mixing with my other close university colleagues. And we, in turn, enjoyed hearing from Sandy all about the operation of the new NDP Provincial government for which he worked as an agricultural economist. There was an important project underway in which, we learned from others, Sandy was playing a key role. It was the building of the Gardiner Dam on the North Saskatchewan River, about eighty kilometers to the south-west of Saskatoon. This eventually became the largest earth-filled dam in Canada. The resulting Diefenbaker Lake was named for the Conservative Prime Minister of the time, who happened to be a native of Saskatchewan, and was one of the chief instigators and supporters of the project.

Sandy's job was to work with the farmers of the surrounding dry-land area, persuading them to get on-side, and attempting to educate them concerning the radical changes in approaches to farming required by this new method as well as the benefits which could accrue for them in the long term. He was finding this task a considerable challenge. However, I suspect that because he could communicate with them as a fellow farmer of long experience—rather than merely a government official—he was much more successful than he considered himself to be. Many years later I was told by one of the government members in charge of the entire enterprise, that it could never have been accomplished without Sandy Hutcheon. I also learned that John Messer, the Minister of Agriculture at the time, valued him most highly. In fact the Deputy Minister, Douglas McArthur, once described him as being both diligent and productive, with a first-rate analytical ability and sharp intellect.

Sandy's main task at the time I first met him was to provide a leading role in developing and implementing Farmstart: the government land-banking program aimed at making the irrigated land available to young farmers on the basis of a secure life-time lease. This required a major government credit program for all these developing farm units. The program would lend money to farmers, through banks, with government guarantees. All this was to be accompanied by legislation both to regulate foreign and corporate ownership of farm land in Saskatchewan and to develop programs aimed at stabilizing returns for agricultural products.

Apparently one of the most difficult hurdles for the organizers was to secure the cooperation of the banks with the government's plan for financing Farmstart. There was a story concerning a key event in this persuasion process that Lyle Minogue, a young man who worked with Sandy on the project, loved to describe in the years to follow. He often told of how, one day in 1972, he and Sandy met in Regina with a group of black-suited, pompous-looking bankers. These men informed them that government employees were invariably ignorant about banking, and that Saskatchewan's bankers should be allowed to handle the matter in their own way. Sandy's response had been all-too-typical. According to Lyle, he thought for a minute and then said: "I think if we were to gather all the bankers in the Province and hang one up by his balls every twenty minutes until they had solved the problem, they'd soon come up with a way it could be done." Lyle added that, after a wave of laughter that seemed to bring them all together, the group had their solution in less than two hours!

Meanwhile, as we saw more of Sandy Hutcheon—from the summer of 1967 to that of 1968—the quality that Tom, Joy and I increasingly came to appreciate in him was this down-to-earth bluntness combined with an ironic sense of humour, along with his pragmatism and commonsense and clearly reasoned approach to problems, no matter how complex. Tom was right. Sandy couldn't have been more different from most of the people with whom I worked. During the process of getting to know him, I recognized that much of his uniqueness could well have been a result of his background.

His family were early pioneering farmers who had come to Saskatchewan from Scotland. His grandfather—the original Alexander Dalziel Hutcheon, after whom Sandy had been named—was a lawyer who had died young, leaving a wife with five children and little in the way of finances. They lived at Petter Head in Aberdeen. One of these children, Sandy's father Alex, emigrated to Canada in 1903 as a youngster of eighteen. He landed in Ontario and spent his first year working near Guelph; then moved west to Kimberley in British Columbia in 1904, for a brief stint in the Sullivan mine. After that he returned to Saskatchewan; going first to Indian Head in 1905, where he remained for one year. Alex's seventeen-year-old brother Bill joined him there the following autumn. The two boys bought a team of horses and headed for Tramping Lake by sleigh and ultimately by wagon. They ended up in North Battleford, and from there proceeded to file for homesteads in the Cleland district, not far from where the village of Rosetown later developed. Bill filed on land about five miles from Alex's. By a fascinating coincidence, this fertile farming area was the very place to which my father and his brother were then traveling up from Iowa each year with their giant steam-operated tractor to 'break the sod' for these early pioneers.

In 1909 Alex left for Scotland to marry Mary Barron, returning with her the following year. Another brother, Alfred, immigrated at that time as well, along with the boys' widowed mother and two sisters: one of whom subsequently returned to Scotland. Alex and Mary established a farmstead, and on it raised eight children. They proved to have been extremely fortunate in the quality of the land on which they settled.

Sandy was the second son in this family, but he was the one selected to be named after his father and grandfather. This may well have been why he was also expected to follow in his father's footsteps as a farmer. Even prior to adolescence he seemed to have been designated solely for farm work. He had absolutely no say in the matter. When the time came for the older children to attend high school, the father rented a house in town for their use. Sandy, however, was taken out of school after having completed grade eleven. A neighbour and fellow student once told me that Sandy Hutcheon was by far the brightest student in the class. The other three brothers—the older one, Neil, and the two younger ones, Leslie and Alan—went on to acquire doctorates. Mary, the eldest daughter (known as Dolly), married early into a local farm family. However, the remaining three girls—Winifred, Margaret and Muriel—all received higher education: something reserved for the more privileged of females in those days.

Unfortunately, Alex Hutcheon died of cancer at the age of forty nine. Sandy fulfilled family expectations by taking over the farm and marrying Carolyn or 'Cardie' Powell, the daughter of the neighbour whose family were their closest friends. Then, when he was in his late forties—and after the death of his mother, who had lived with them on the original farmstead—he decided to pursue his own goals. Sandy's ambition was to spend the remainder of his life in a situation where he might be able to influence agricultural policy rather than merely struggle with the results of bungled governmental decisions. For a long time he had been feeling that too many of these critical choices were being made by people with no practical experience in the field. So he began by completing grade twelve by correspondence. In the summer of 1962, after arranging to rent the farm to a cousin, he and Cardie moved to Saskatoon where he had been accepted into the degree program in Agriculture at the University of Saskatchewan. His plan was to follow this up with an advanced degree in Economics. It was during this period that his younger brother, Les, who was then Dean of the University of Saskatchewan's College of Agriculture, died suddenly of a massive coronary blockage. On the morning of his death

Les had taken part in a faculty meeting and, later in the day, had delivered an address to the annual conference of the Saskatchewan Field Husbandry Association in Convocation Hall, which Sandy happened to be attending. Les was also only in his late forties.

By the spring of 1965, not long before Tom and I moved to Regina, Sandy had completed his university education and obtained a job with the Provincial government. During the following autumn we met at the Unitarian Fellowship. Then, in the spring of 1967, came the tragedy of Cardie's death from cancer. She, too, had not made it to fifty. After that untimely tragedy our mutual humanist Unitarianism gradually brought Sandy and the members of our household together—initially as friends who shared many opinions and political stances.

Even when Sandy insisted on returning our hospitality with an invitation to a restaurant, Joy and Tom were always included. I never even remotely considered these outings as 'dates'. Then, in the spring of 1968, in the midst of an extremely busy period in my life, suddenly everything changed. Sandy announced the approach of his birthday. He added that he'd like to celebrate it by taking me—and only me—out to dinner. A few days later, on the way to our destination, he drove through a red light. In the midst of an embarrassed apology, he admitted to having a problem with his eyesight.

"The next time we go out," I then told him, imitating his own forthrightness, "we'll take my car, and I'll do the driving" And so it was, in all the years to follow.

That 'first date' was a dinner at one of Regina's top restaurants. Because of the way he had phrased the invitation, I sensed it heralded a subtle change in our relationship. And the ambience of the restaurant that evening furthered the feeling. Early on, the music playing softly in the background was replaced by some of the most beautiful singing I had ever heard. In response to my enquiry, the waiter told us we were listening to Anne Murray, a folk singer from Nova Scotia. An unfamiliarly warm and superbly comforting set of emotions began stirring in me that evening: all focused on Sandy. I've always associated Anne Murray's voice with the sudden change in my feelings for, and appreciation of, Sandy Hutcheon. From those wonderful moments on, we became closer in an emotional sense, as we discovered the amazing degree to which we shared an intellectual world view, along with a mutual love of arguing about ideas.

By the time I was forced to engulf myself in the preparations involved in my departure for Yale in the summer of 1968, Sandy and I were engaged—although the timing of our nuptials had to be put on hold. But not for long, as it turned out. Sandy surprised me by arriving down in New Haven in October, and we were married by a judge in the local courthouse. My young friend, Irving Rootman, was in the final process of his doctoral work at Yale at the time. He and his wife Barbara were our witnesses, and sole guests. I wore a rather plain blue dress which had long been a favourite. It was a blissful occasion, celebrated with some champagne and a gift of glasses for drinking it, from Irving and Barbara. However, I did experience strong feelings of regret that we were marking this all-important landmark in our lives—a landmark not only for the two of us but for our three sons as well—without their being present to share in the celebration. However, it had seemed extremely important to Sandy that we proceed quickly with our marriage. I discovered that he had even booked a brief honeymoon visit to New York: the one and only time either of us was ever to be there. We spent all of our time in the theatre district: another interest that we shared.

My studies were prematurely cut off due to my refusal to sleep with my thesis advisor. By the time I had returned in a state of shock to Saskatchewan, Sandy was living near the branch of the irrigation enterprise on which he was then working. This was the South Saskatchewan Region Project, covering the Outlook-Broderick area. So I left my house in the hands of my renters and friends, the Griers, and moved into Sandy's tiny apartment in the small country village of Outlook. Both my son Tom and Sandy's son Don were with us there to celebrate Easter of 1969. About a month later, my sister Myrtle and her husband Mike brought our mother out to meet Sandy, and to celebrate Mom's seventieth birthday. I recall suggesting that, as a birthday gift, all our family members share in the price of a trip for her. In planning for this, I had mentioned it in a letter to Bob, but he responded typically by telling me that he would prefer to choose his own birthday gift. It wasn't slated to happen anyway, for Mom's response revealed that she felt far too old to travel alone. In those days the seventieth birthday was considered the threshold marking a rapid and steep descent into old age.

Sandy and I lived in Outlook for only a few months. He was very busy with his work, and I spent almost all of my time writing articles for learned journals, based on the extensive research I had done at that remarkable Yale library. By this time I was identifying myself, for professional purposes, as Pat Duffy Hutcheon. I had always regretted having given up my maiden name when I married Jack Westcott, so was happy to reclaim it. I'm quite confident that my subsequent surprising success with publishers would never have occurred if the signature had revealed my gender. Admittedly, much of that success was due to Sandy. He proved to be a superb editor, supporting me in every conceivable way. He would say, concerning any of my writing that was not absolutely concise and clear, "If I don't understand it, it's a safe bet that most of your readers won't either." Whatever the determinant factors, from late 1969 to the end of 1973, a full thirteen of my articles were published, most of them in leading international journals. The one initiating the most enthusiastic responses from the English-speaking academic community was "Sociology and the Objectivity Problem" in *Sociology and Social Research*. Other highly successful ones were "Value Theory: Toward Conceptual Clarification" in *The British Journal of Sociology*, "The Classroom as a Social System" in *Perspectives*, "Academic Freedom: An Evolving Concept?" in *The Journal of Educational Thought*, and "The Urban High School" in a book called *Options: Reforms and Alternatives for Canadian Education*. I think Evelina's favourite was "Power in the Philippines: How Democratic is Asia's 'First Democracy'?" which came out in *The Journal of Asian and African Studies*.

I returned to Regina in early June of 1969, in order to teach the summer session and find us a place to live. Sandy was not comfortable with the idea of moving into my house, so I continued renting it to my friends, the Griers. During this period, I learned that Don Grier—true to form—had become the leading force in a movement against 'greedy landlords'. I told him I assumed 'landladies' were included in this attack as well, and we all had a good laugh about it. I was able to locate an apartment on Lorne Street, near where the old Regina College was located, and also within walking distance of the downtown area. It would also be handy for me to travel by road to the Education Faculty, which was in the process of being re-located to the new university campus near the edge of town. Sandy's son Don moved in with us that summer, after finding a job at a local car dealership. By then he had a wonderful young girlfriend named Vi, who happened to be a cousin of Tom's best friend in Regina.

Not long after Sandy and I got settled into our apartment, his brother Alan arrived from Lesotho, in southern Africa, where he taught chemistry. I learned at once that Alan's major passion was trying to educate the natives to live in the solar houses which he was designing, so that they would stop cutting down all their trees for firewood. He was a Quaker but strangely fundamentalist in religion—a far cry from Sandy. Then, as soon as Alan left, we drove up to Prince George to visit my brother Don and his wife Donna. Tom was studying in Calgary at the time, so was not able to accompany us. However, he did go up to Prince George for the summer of 1970 to work for Don as a land surveyor. He had by then reached the age where he no longer had to spend his holidays with his father.

Meanwhile, I was learning that there had been great change during my two years of absence from the Regina Faculty, as well as a minor rebellion in the ranks of my colleagues. At the end of the 1968-69 term, Evelina Orteza had taken up a job offer from the University of Calgary, and Bob Anderson had departed for the University of Lethbridge. Apparently, the year prior to their departure was a stormy one. Just before I left, the position of Dean became available and most of the faculty expected Bob Anderson to be offered the job. But that's not what happened. A man called Norman France was brought in from England, along with Dr. Edmonds, an expert in Business Administration, and a Dr. Smart in Educational Psychology. A majority of the faculty rapidly became dissatisfied with what they perceived as a takeover by an overly bureaucratic system of organization and governance: all of which had been imposed upon them by outsiders with no knowledge whatsoever of the Canadian educational system. A caucus of dissenters was formed after I left for Yale, led by Evelyn Jonescu. Bob Anderson did not join it. He had been placed in an embarrassing position by having been rejected as a candidate for the position of Dean.

The dissenting group raised a number of pointed questions in a faculty meeting. Upon receiving no satisfactory answers, they rose to their feet, almost in unison, and walked out. A committee was then appointed to study the situation, with the result that a more conciliatory Associate Dean was recruited in the person of Wil Toombs. The faculty then approved a new organizational structure which was established in early 1970. 'Subject Areas' had replaced the previous three 'Departments'. Immediately below the Dean and Associate Dean were now Coordinators for Program Development, Professional Development, and Student Counseling. These coordinators actually held no administrative authority. Such authority resided solely with the Dean and Associate Dean. The various subject areas elected unpaid Chairs. A new Dean, Art Kratzman, was brought in to replace Norman France, who returned to England. By the time all this was in place, Evelina and Bob had already moved to Alberta universities.

One of the new people hired that summer was Joe Malikail. He was immediately named Chair of Educational Foundations. He had arrived from India by way of a university in the United States, and was the replacement for Evelina. He proved to be a wonderful colleague and yet another 'friend for life'. He had inherited Bob Anderson's course in the History of Ideas and later developed one called The Philosophical Analysis of Educational Ideas. Dale Stewart, who had been hired when I left, was teaching History of Education, while I would once more be providing a 'methods' course in the teaching of high-school social studies as well as courses in the Sociology of Education—now to include one focusing on John Dewey. I was relieved to discover that I would no longer be required to teach sociology in the Faculty of Arts and Science as well. However, because of my public-school teaching background, I would continue to be responsible for overseeing 'practice teaching' in the school system.

I discovered that, in spite of the large number of changes, both in the organization of the Faculty and within its membership, many of my close friends had survived the turmoil. Art MacBeath was the new Coordinator of Professional Development, and there was now a John Schaller teaching social studies, Margaret Messer in art, and Fred Bessai in educational psychology, to mention a few. The two new Ed. Foundations colleagues rapidly became special friends. I found Joe Malikail to be a brilliant thinker, and a companion in the 'world of ideas' capable of taking the place of Evelina in discussions in the faculty lounge. He and I attended several conferences together, in the following years.

Joe's wife Cecilia was a gifted artist. They had two children, Stephen and Patricia. Their daughter Pat was to become like a niece to us through all the years to follow. One summer we took the entire Malikail family on a journey out to Biggar, to show them where I had once attended high school; and to Elbow and Outlook for an exploration of what had become known as the Diefenbaker Dam project. We also traveled to Rosetown and visited the Hutcheon family farm, as well as that of Sandy's sister Dolly and her husband. Our trip home included a journey through Saskatoon where we met with Sandy's late brother's family.

Another person who became a special friend—another 'friend for life', as it turned out—was a lovely young woman who was teaching classes in Music Education for students learning to teach at the elementary school level. Her married name was Danette Riddlespurger. We met for the first time in the faculty women's bathroom. I was standing at the sink when I noticed a beautiful blonde washing her hands beside me. When we began talking I was struck at once by her engaging Southern accent—something we seldom heard on the Canadian prairies. She introduced herself, explaining that she was a music educator specializing in developing the musical understanding and abilities of young children. She then added that she was from Kentucky, which explained her accent. As we rapidly became acquainted, I learned that her husband, Bill, was a professional pianist, who had not been very successful in finding full-time work in Regina. And that they had a four-year-old daughter called Beth. I don't quite know how it happened, but Sandy and I almost immediately 'adopted' them into our family.

By the beginning of 1970, we were well established in our new home and in our respective workplaces. I had become accustomed once more to prairie-winter-driving. In fact, I was followed home from work one day by a car with a couple of policemen in it. I watched in considerable discomfort as they approached me, wondering just what error I had committed during the difficult sojourn homeward. To my amazement, they presented me with a Safe Driving Award, telling me that a number of people who drove to work regularly had been randomly selected to be observed carefully for several days, and I turned out to have been the winner—the most skilled and careful in maneuvering the dangerous winter streets. That certainly brightened my day!

The entire first year back in Regina proved to be an extremely busy one for both Sandy and me. I recall particularly the day in June when I was invited to speak at an Education Conference in Winnipeg. I decided to make my topic sound as intriguingly radical as possible, so chose as a title, "The Changing Role of the High School". My major criticism was that schooling at this critical stage of young people's lives was becoming too far removed from the real world in which they would have to make a living. Its focus was on preparing them, instead, for passing entrance exams to universities which only a small proportion of them were likely ever to attend. The majority, who would inevitably find themselves in the trades and other similar occupations, were being made to feel that they were failures. By the same token, the minority of 'winners' who made it into universities would expect unwarranted rewards in terms of remuneration for themselves, balanced out by continuous low pay for the occupations of the 'losers' among them. I proposed a radical change which would require all secondary-school students to spend at least one year of organized apprenticeship in a job before returning to complete their program.

I had intended my talk to be challenging, so wasn't surprised at the strong response from the audience: a response both positive and negative. But I was quite taken aback when, in the following days, all the nation's daily newspapers carried the story. And, in spite of my awareness of the sexism of the time, I was even more shocked by the fact that the headlines referred to me as a male professor. That was probably also why my subsequent article on the subject, "Is the Urban High School Obsolete?" was readily accepted in *The Journal of Educational Thought* and read widely. For example, I recall receiving a request for it from St. Patrick's College in Dublin, Ireland.

Sometime during the spring of 1970, we received news that Sandy's son Dave was getting married at the home of his future wife, Wendy Brooks, in Halifax, Nova Scotia. They had met at the University of Alberta in Edmonton, where both were pursuing graduate studies, he in physics and she in chemistry. Now they were planning a quick wedding before heading for England for post-graduate work at Oxford. We decided to combine the long drive east to the Maritimes with a side-trip down into Iowa, for the purpose of looking up my Duffy relatives. This was something I had dreamed of doing ever since my father's death. Because of the demands of his job, Sandy's son Don planned to fly out to Halifax just in time for the wedding. Until then, he would be on his own in our apartment. So the two of us set off, all excited about our adventure into unknown territory, with me doing the driving, as usual, and Sandy being responsible for the route-planning and map-reading. I've been thankful ever since that we grasped the opportunity when it presented itself. For what an adventure it was!

I had been in touch with my father's sister-in-law for some time by then. Aunt Kate was the widow of Lew's brother Stephen. She was living alone in her house, as she was widowed and her only son had died young, apparently of a heart attack. She extended a warm invitation for us to stay with her during our time in Fairbank, Iowa, the seat of the Duffy clan. Our trip down went smoothly, except for a scare from a tornado that hovered over us briefly and then struck not very far from the road we were driving on. The other vivid impression that has remained with me is my first glimpse of seemingly endless fields of shoulder-high corn.

The few days we spent with Aunt Kate were most memorable. How we packed in so much visiting and sight-seeing I simply cannot fathom! She showed us over the entire countryside, pointing out Duffy Road, and the various Duffy homesteads; including the original one. That first house built by Patrick Duffy was still there, snug in its yard, and lived in by the cousin and current owner, Aloysius Duffy. There seemed to be Duffys everywhere. Often Aunt Kate would wave to someone walking, or riding by on a bike, and would say "There goes another distant Duffy cousin. But I don't remember his first name."

Actually, we discovered that most of my surviving first-cousins were females who had married local farmers of German ancestry, so they were not carrying on the name of Duffy. We met Lew's entire family of close relatives at a dinner party arranged by Aunt Kate with the help of Aunt Lucy—the sister who had been his favourite. Everyone seemed very interested in meeting us, and in hearing about my branch of the Duffys. We were, in effect, 'the lost ones'. What I recall most clearly about that event, however, is not the people gathered around the table. It is the startling moment when—seemingly without warning—they suddenly all leapt to their feet and made the figure of a cross in the air in front of them. And then there was the trip to see their church, which had been badly damaged in a recent hurricane. Something about all the kneeling and crossing themselves bothered me immensely. It must have shown on my face, as Sandy, quite uncharacteristically, took my hand and stood close.

Not long after that, and almost before we realized it, the long trip to our destination in Halifax was over. We checked into a hotel and then contacted Dave and Wendy at the Brooks home. The next day we had the only stressful experience connected with Dave and Wendy's wedding. It was a mix-up in Don's flight. We had forgotten to provide him with details of the Brooks' address and phone number, as we planned to meet him at the airport. But it happened that his flight was altered, due to some problem at the Halifax airport. We waited there a long time without being informed of what was happening, while he was stranded at the Dartmouth airport with no way of contacting us. We had neglected even to supply him with Wendy's family name. Finally, we were told that he and some other lost fellow-passengers had been safely delivered to a hotel in Dartmouth; so we proceeded to drive there. Worn out from stress, we all three ultimately managed to locate the Brooks family home, where the wedding was about to proceed. We hadn't messed things up too badly, as it was a very informal and small family affair, taking place in the Brooks home. The guests included one of Wendy's two sisters as well as Don and the two of us.

The day after the wedding, Sandy and I took our car onto the ferry which then traveled between Nova Scotia and Prince Edward Island. We had a dream-like adventure wandering around the island, admiring the red earth and exploring every nook and cranny of what I considered a very romantic place. Seeing Green Gables was a great thrill for me, although it meant little to Sandy who had never read the 'Anne books'.

On the way back to the prairies we had some other important stops to make. One was in Montreal, where we spent a few days with Sandy's sister-in-law, Dee Baker, and her family. Then it was on to Sandy's brother Neil in his beautiful cottage in the valley to the north of Ottawa. Next came a brief stop in Toronto, where I got together with my old friend and former house-mate, Joy Graham. I felt at the time that she had grown strangely distant, referring to me as 'Madame' when speaking to the waitress during lunch. It was as if she had been demoted from her position as my equal and pal to that of servant. I wondered what had happened to her since we'd parted. I didn't know it then, but it was to be the last time I ever saw her. I never heard from her again, nor was I ever able to find her name in the phonebook on subsequent trips to Toronto.

Then it was on to North Bay, where Bob was in charge of the radar operations in NORAD's North American Aerospace Command centre. We had a pleasant visit that evening, getting re-acquainted with his children. Paul and his two sisters, Emmi and Sara, had always impressed me with their intelligence and talents. My most vivid memory, however, was of Margaret's greeting when she opened the door. She looked past us to our car, parked on the street nearby.

"I know all I need to know about Sandy already!" she exclaimed as I made a move to introduce him. "The make and colour of his car tells me everything about the kind of person he is!" She was well-launched into a description of the details of this imaginary character by the time I managed to interrupt the flow. "That strikes me as very puzzling," I told her, "Seeing that I do all the driving in our family, and it was I who selected both the make and colour of our car!" Thus it was that our visit began as all our visits had begun and ended in the past.

This time, however, Bob treated us to a strange, once-in-a-lifetime adventure. He took us down through the underground bunker housing walls of computers and radar equipment. What a weird feeling that aroused in me! When we were safely back in their house, still injoying the excitement involved in that experience, Bob talked about the books he was reading; and Paul showed us some of his remarkable drawings. Sandy mainly watched and listened. Then, all too soon, we were into the long drive back to Regina and the world of work for both of us.

That summer I received a beautiful letter from Tom, written while he was working as a surveyor's helper up at Prince George. He had met a girl called Lana the previous year, through an old school pal from the Valley who had moved to Calgary. The friend was married to Lana's sister. In the letter he referred to his coming marriage to Lana, saying he hoped they would have a relationship as wonderful as Sandy's and mine. They were married in September of the following year, in the village of Hanna, where she had been raised. Her mother was a teacher with whom I had been acquainted a long time before. I found it of particular interest that Lana's father's mother, who attended the wedding, had originally been a Duffy. She said her family had come to Canada from somewhere in the American mid-west.

Tom's father, Jack Westcott, was also at the wedding. By that time he was living in Hanna as well, with a woman who owned a restaurant there. He had purchased some land nearby. Sadly, he had then persuaded Tom to drop out of university in order to take over the operating of his new farmstead: a plan that never did materialize. This was all-too-typical of my former husband.

I could understand why Tom felt as he did about my marriage. In comparison to his experience with his own father, there is little wonder that Sandy's forthright honesty continued to demand his admiration, as it did mine. I realize now that this new husband of mine influenced me a great deal more than I was aware of at the time, inspiring me to take certain stands within my academic environment that I might not have had the courage to do on my own. A few of these come to mind; for instance, my joining Joe Malikail in battling the ruling ideologies of the day within education.

Our Canadian educational establishment had what was to us a disturbing habit of repeating every set of ideas that had previously been popularized in the United States. The problem was that these fads would begin to be pushed in Canada at the very time that all of their flaws and the disastrous consequences for learning were in the process of being discovered by our neighbouring country. We never did seem able to learn from their mistakes. Instead, the 'powers that be' in our field appeared bent on repeating them all, in the name of 'progress'.

Joe and I identified two of what we considered the most potentially harmful of these. They had been popularized as "Humanistic' and 'Competency-based' education. I chose to point out the dangerous weaknesses of an educational policy based on a crucial misunderstanding of the term 'Humanism'. So-called 'progressive' educators were defining this as totally child-centered with little or no guidance or planning of programs on the part of teachers. Joe attacked the mis-use of the term 'competency' in the other popular approach which focused on memorizing, measuring and testing; and the utter misunderstanding of Skinnerian behaviourism on which it was supposedly based. We gave talks on the subject at one of the several educational gatherings that we attended during the busy years from 1970 to 1973, culminating in our joint presentation to the Learned Societies Conference in Kingston, Ontario in May of 1973. We spelled out our criticisms of these ideologies, and of the fact that our field of study was so prone to this sort of mindlessness. Needless to say, our presentations were not accepted very enthusiastically by the proponents of the 'latest' educational approaches. However, we were invited to submit them to *The Saskatchewan Journal Of Educational Research And Development* where they were promptly published in a piece called "Competency-based and Humanistic Alternatives to Teacher Education: Advance or Digression?".

During this period I was also doing a considerable amount of public speaking on contentious topics of the day. For example, I tackled "Vietnam: The History of the Conflict", "Sociology and Religion", "Religion and Social Change", "Education and a Radical Morality" and "Changing Sex Roles".

All of the other times when I took an unpopular position during that period were no doubt also influenced by Sandy's honesty and courage, although he would never have given me specific advice on any issue. One stand which required courage involved a student whose comments and writings concerning the disciplining of children in classrooms had begun to concern me greatly. This young man had previous experience of working in some sort of 'group home' in Manitoba, where I suspect the students—mainly Native or Metis—were routinely being ill-treated. He bragged about actions toward his charges: actions which I considered shamefully abusive. I finally went to the administration and announced I was expelling this student from my class. I also recommended strongly that he never be allowed to graduate as a teacher, regardless of the marks he might make in formal courses. I put my concerns in writing and asked that they be included in his record. Apparently this was something unheard of, and my superiors were profoundly shocked. Interestingly, a number of years later I was called back to Saskatchewan to act as a witness in a legal case involving this same student, who had been at the point of graduating when my evidence against him re-surfaced.

A similarly difficult stand was forced upon me by a situation within our department. I had been watching the development of this with considerable trepidation. A colleague who taught History of Education courses was accused of sexually abusing some of his female students. This was extremely puzzling to me, as his office was attached to mine toward the end of a one-way hall, with only a partial wall between us. There was simply no way the wild tales of weird 'goings on' in his office which the girls described could possibly have happened without my having heard or seen something suspicious, given the long hours at work required by both my teaching and my administrative duties, and our mutual lack of privacy in the workplace. I made a point of witnessing to this fact, as well as to my colleagues's character, at the formal interview concerning the matter called by the Dean. This was not the 'politically correct' thing to do at the time. The interview occurred after accusations had been publicized in all the newspapers across the country, under the headline of "An 'A' for a Lay!", with the accused professor's name loudly proclaimed. Although the administration eventually found him not guilty, this colleague was never again able to work as an educator. Thus I discovered that sexism could work both ways!

Yet another unpopular stand had to do with a seven-percent raise in salary which the tenured professors had been granted, during a year when the Provincial government reduced the over-all funding for the college. The administration had been forced to announce that, in order to grant the promised salary increase, a considerable number of the non-tenured instructors would have to be fired. I decided to attempt to resolve the stand-off by going around to all my tenured colleagues with a petition stating that we would forego our raise in pay in return for all of these instructors being allowed to remain in their positions at their current salaries.

I had fully expected my fellow left-leaning liberals to be as concerned about these lower-ranks in our midst as I was. What I actually encountered was a sad surprise and disappointment! Very few of these supposedly like-minded colleagues were willing to sign—in fact they became very angry at me for 'letting down the union'. The ones who did sign were the conservatives among the faculty, who had the vision to see that those of us who were benefiting financially would have to suffer longer hours of work and much more responsibility if we were to lose our lower-rank instructors. However, these conservative thinkers were in the minority. So all my efforts proved to be in vain. But that was not the end of the story. An uncomfortable surprise awaited me a few days after I had completed the petition and submitted it to the administration. I was called before the local branch of the Canadian Association of University Teachers, known as CAUT. They informed me in no uncertain terms that, were I ever to attempt such a subversive action again, I would be ejected from membership, and thus made ineligible to teach in any university in Canada. I was asked by one of the Board members how I could ever have even considered doing such a thing—much less actually do it. I don't recall my reply, but I should have said that, although it was my long-embedded sense of justice which had provided the motivation, I had no doubt that the source of the courage necessary for the actual move was that 'one honest man' who was now playing such an important role in my life.

# Chapter 17

# IN SICKNESS AND IN HEALTH

Sandy and I enjoyed an extremely busy, although happy and family-oriented, Christmas holiday at the end of 1972. It was a fitting ending for a similarly busy—but nevertheless enjoyable—fall university term. This had culminated in my giving a speech called "Toward a Science of Education" to the Northwest Philosophy of Education Society in Seattle. I had also been serving, for one year each, on three different university committees: those dealing with Senior Academic Programs, Academic Freedom, and Internal Operations. So I was more than ready for a break.

Sandy's second son Don, who was then living with us, didn't mind our leaving for the holiday. He was celebrating the season with his girlfriend, Vi, and her Regina relatives. Our trip began with a drive to Calgary, where we spent the night at my mother's. We then left the car at the airport and, taking Mom with us, flew to Vancouver for a brief visit with Myrtle and Mike. Upon our return to Calgary we picked up the car and then drove over to my aunt Mabel's place for a visit before settling in at my mother's for the night.

It began snowing heavily that evening, and by morning our car was almost buried in its parking place on the street. When I expressed some concern about the long drive ahead of us, Mom suddenly turned to me and said, "I never worry about you any more. You've found a wonderful husband who will always take care of you, no matter what happens." As often was the case with her remarks, I felt a degree of amusement. However, in looking back now, I'm thankful that I didn't know then the degree to which Sandy and I would soon encounter situations where her confidence in his capacity and empathy in caring for me was to be proven all too true.

256

Sandy quickly dug out the car and, after our farewell to Mom, I proceeded to drive it over to the southern outskirts of the city where we had lunch with his in-laws, Dave and Doreen Powell. His first wife's entire family had accepted me wholeheartedly from the very first, including me in all their reunions. Throughout the years to come, they would refer to me jokingly as the one 'out-law' among all the siblings and in-laws at these annual parties.

We managed to leave Calgary by 1:00 pm, driving in blizzard conditions as far as Drumheller, where the weather began to clear up considerably. We arrived safely at Tom and Lana's place in Hanna for dinner and the night. I had a little trouble recognizing my son in the handsome, slim young fellow who welcomed us at the door. Tom had been dieting and exercising and had lost about forty pounds. Although Lana now had steady work at the local post office, Tom was in the process of job-hunting. Meanwhile he was commuting to Drumheller, where he worked temporarily as an accountant for a small trucking firm. The move to Hanna in the thwarted expectation that his father would make good on the promise of setting him up on a farm he had purchased nearby had been yet another disillusioning experience for Tom.

After the visit in Hanna, we proceeded east to Rosetown country, stopping at the farm for a couple of hours, and finally arriving home in Regina by late evening of Friday. On Saturday we rushed to do our laundry and shopping in order to be prepared for Wendy and Dave, who landed Sunday morning from Winnipeg, where he had been working temporarily. Early the following day they flew on to Edmonton, where Dave had recently been hired by the University of Alberta. By then, Sandy and I were back at work: he in his government office near our apartment and I at the university. But the prairie weather wasn't through with us. By Wednesday the worst blizzard of the entire winter struck Regina, and I had a difficult struggle driving back and forth to work for the remainder of the week. I was finding good use for the system of 'plug-ins' for our engine block-heaters provided in the university parking lot. These were designed to keep the batteries of our cars working during cold winter weather.

I just barely managed the drive required to fulfil a previous commitment as keynote speaker at Saskatchewan School Trustee Seminars at both Rosetown and Swift Current. An extremely busy time was facing me for the coming year. In addition to my teaching duties and my ongoing work on the executive of the Saskatchewan Educational Research Association, I had recently been appointed to the Province of Saskatchewan Committee on Educational Evaluation.

On a lighter note, I sent a book as a Christmas gift to my brother Bob and his wife Margaret in Halifax. As usual, I greatly enjoyed Margaret's response. She informed me that she hadn't read the book, nor did she intend to. Her reason? "The author is too ugly," she explained. "His nose is like a spike and his eyes are all squinty."

It was fortunate that Margaret had provided this laugh for me because, on a Wednesday evening in mid-January soon after the letter arrived, things took a sudden downturn. I was on my way to a meeting of our community health clinic. About a block from my destination I slipped on a patch of invisible 'black ice' and suffered an extremely hard fall. Although in great pain, I proceeded to the meeting, happening to sit beside my family doctor for the duration of it. I didn't tell Dr. Road what had happened, even though the pain was worsening during the evening and had become almost unbearable by the time I made my way home. I had no choice but to remain flat on my back for the rest of the week, hoping for improvement. I did manage to drag myself to work the following Monday, however, and endured the pain while teaching for two weeks, assuming it was one of my usual 'bad back' spells. When I finally got in to Dr. Road's office for an x-ray, we discovered I had a badly fractured pelvis. He was horrified to learn that I had been working, and promptly ordered me to remain in bed for at least three weeks. My regular courses were looked after by graduate students; but for my once-weekly graduate class Sandy took time off work and hauled me over in a wheelchair. After the three weeks were up I staggered about on crutches—even fulfilling a previous commitment to be keynote speaker at a conference of the Regina Institute for Separate-School Teachers.

I think it was during this trying period that we enjoyed a welcome visit with my old friends from the Valley farm country, June and Bill Smith. They were in the city in connection with their son Smitty, who was then attending university at the time. I recall sharing a few good laughs with June in spite of having to lie flat on my back on the floor the entire time.

It was the fact that I had ignored a broken pelvis for several days that convinced Dr. Road—and he, in turn, proceeded to persuade me—of the crucial necessity for a spinal fusion. He told me that if I was suffering so much back pain on a regular basis that I had continued working with my pelvis badly fractured, something would have to be done about my condition. He had been arguing for some time that I required surgery, but I always resisted. The problem was that it would mean at least six months away from work. And, in addition, because he was not allowed hospital privileges in Regina hospitals due to having been one of those British physicians who 'broke the doctors' strike', he had to send me up to Saskatoon where both he and I would be made more welcome. I finally decided to go along with his plan to set the date for the surgery in early September, and proceeded to arrange to take sick leave for the autumn semester.

By the end of April, as soon as classes were finished, I was sufficiently recovered for us to set off with Sandy and the Riddlespurgers on a previously planned tour of the German-speaking areas of Europe. Danette Riddlespurger was a beautiful young blonde colleague from the American south. She and her husband Bill and little daughter Beth had become very close friends of ours. Beth was then six years old, and would be starting school in the fall. Bill spoke fluent German, so we had decided to rent a car and tour the countryside of Southern Germany, Eastern Switzerland and most of Austria, staying in small 'pensions' or bed-and-breakfast places rather than hotels. We had discovered a book called "Europe on Five Dollars a Day" and, because money was a crucial consideration for Danette and Bill, we planned to do our best to stay within that limit.

We landed in Zurich where, under the spire of an old church famous for its Chagall windows, we met an old school friend of Danette's. She was a career opera singer from Kentucky. Sandy and Bill quickly proceeded to select a rental car, settling on a reliable looking BMW. We then headed east through Bavaria, staying a night at a pension which—to our surprise—happened to be operated by the mother of an artist who was one of our Regina colleagues. We traveled through Freiburg to Munich, exploring a variety of splendid cathedrals and castles on the way, including the Munster Cathedral in Feiburg along with its ancient market place, the Benedictine Monastery at Benediktbeuren, the Hohenzollern Castle in Swabia and the two fairytale castles built by mad King Ludwig at Neuschwanstein. The latter includes underground caves where Ludwig had produced extravagant opera performances composed and directed by Richard Wagner. In Munich we enjoyed the famous Nymphenburg Castle.

The highlight of our trip for me was our visit to Salzburg, Austria, where we remained for several days. We had planned to go on to Vienna, but opted for spending more time in Salzburg instead. Danette took photos of us in the town centre where Julie Andrews and the children had sung "Doh, a deer, a female deer" in "The Sound of Music". We toured the Salzburg castle, which was both the birthplace and museum of Mozart; and the eleventh-century Hohensalzburg Fortress with the beautiful Mirabell Gardens in the foreground. While there, Bill lost his wallet for a stress-stricken few minutes, but we found it behind a bench where we'd been sitting. That night we stayed at a chalet located on a hill overlooking the city. My constant back pain made me exhausted by evening, so I opted for remaining in the chalet with Beth—playing games and telling stories with her prior to our early bedtimes—while the other three continued their explorations.

We had a quick visit in Dresden, where the carnage from the war was still obvious. Then it was on to Hamburg, whence we flew home. The entire experience had a happy, dreamlike quality for me, and moments from it come back clearly to this day. At the time, however, my life was so busy that I had little time to process it all. We were scarcely settled back in our little apartment on Lorne Street when I had to turn around and fly, with Joe Malikail, to Kingston, where we were both slated to speak at a conference at Queen's University.

Our European venture also came with a sad loss. Upon moving into our new apartment a few years previously, Sandy and I had both taken our furniture out of storage. I soon discovered that there was absolutely no space for the precious antique sewing machine which I had inherited from my grandmother. Our cleaning lady, on seeing my predicament, offered to keep it in a safe place for me until we moved into a house. I had recklessly accepted her offer. Soon after our return from the European trip she informed me that her house had been broken into, and my sewing machine stolen. I found it difficult to believe this was what had actually happened, but realized my foolish mistake could not then be undone. I had managed to lose both of my precious Flewelling family inheritances: the antique organ and one of the first Singer sewing machines ever made.

From the time of that disaster on, my thoughts and plans were centered on the upcoming marriage of Don to his girlfriend Vi, who was already representing, for me, the daughter I had never had. The wedding took place on August 3rd in a United Church of their choice, with a small reception following. We wanted to keep it simple, so I merely provided a large supply of Don and his dad's favourite cookies: oatmeal ones with a date-filling in the center. The major celebration was planned for the following day, in the form of a Hutcheon family-gathering. The timing was fortuitous, as we were able to include not only all the Saskatchewan-residing members, but even Sandy's brothers Neil and Alan, both of whom lived and worked a considerable distance away and seldom returned to Saskatchewan. The reunion took the form of a picnic on the beautiful Willow Island, in the center of Wascana Lake.

Then, at the end of June, I found myself at Fort Qu'Appelle giving the theme address at the Western District Unitarian Conference. I was aware that it had been well received at the time and was always somewhat surprised when people who had attended continued to refer to it through many years to follow. Then the speech turned up in an old file and, upon reading it all these years later, I find myself utterly amazed at what I was able to produce—especially given the condition of my health at the time. The title was "One World: Order or Disaster".

Near the beginning of my talk, I noted that "With the religious humanism of this century, Unitarians began at last to define our problems in terms of the concept of humanity rather than of gods: of an evolving species and culture being pushed from behind by the consequences of previous human actions and environmental reactions, rather than in terms of the ancient notion of a god pulling from ahead toward a pre-established goal somewhere beyond the realm of human experience. This is what the expression 'God is dead' really means. To the humanist it implies that at last we can begin to direct our intelligence to the identification and solution of problems created by humans throughout history, in their efforts to survive in the world. It also implies that, in forging these solutions, we have both the freedom and responsibility to seek out sources and criteria of morality more appropriate for our times than the myths and orthodoxies of past centuries." I then proceeded to discuss the various forms of tribalism currently plaguing humankind, defining them as ethnic, religious, nationalistic and sexist—or a variety of combinations of these, which could render them even more poisonous and threatening to the future of all life.

Although the conference was probably our 'peak experience' of the summer, Sandy and I completed this exceptionally busy period with another memorable event: a quick automobile trip to Vancouver, again taking Mom along. Her sister Jessie was widowed by then, and had recently moved into an apartment in Langley. Jessie decided to accompany us back to Calgary, to visit her sister Mabel and sister-in-law Annie. On the way home Jessie and Mom asked us to make a brief stop in a small town in the Kootenays, to which their sister Dot and her husband Bus had moved to a short time before. I didn't realize it then, but it was to be one of those 'last times' that occur more and more frequently as one grows older. Dot had been diagnosed with cancer and died not long after, having never even reached her sixties. At the time of our visit, the seriousness of her problem didn't fully register with me as my own life was so hectic. For example, in addition to everything else, we had scarcely arrived back home when the Dean assigned me the task of preparing a brief on behalf of our Faculty for a newly established commission on the future of teacher education in the Province. That kept me busy for the remainder of August.

It was fortunate for Sandy and me that we had such a blissful time earlier that summer, for what followed was not so pleasant. For one thing, I was missing Danette and little Beth. They had moved to Germany for a year, as Bill had taken a job there. But much more serious was the fact that my spinal fusion surgery was to occur in early September, so I had that to 'look forward to'. Actually, I didn't receive the call until the first week in October. I was to be there on a Monday. Sandy planned on taking the bus up on the evening following the surgery, and remaining with me for the long Thanksgiving weekend. For some reason which I can't fathom, I decided to take the car to Saskatoon. I must have had some sort of weird expectation of being able to drive it back home after the surgery. Or perhaps it was a subconscious desire for a means of escaping what loomed in my immediate future. I recall going for a long walk along the river bank the evening before the operation, wondering how long it would be before I could again do such a thing, and wondering even more if I were making a wise choice.

The following morning arrived all too soon. Unfortunately it marked the onset of a nightmare for me. It all began with the hideous experience of my being placed on a small, unstable stretcher and somehow my neck being accidentally twisted by the nurses so that I couldn't get any breath. I couldn't even call for help. They realized what they were doing just in time, as I was blacking out. Not a very auspicious beginning for a major operation! I don't remember anything after that until several days had passed. Upon finally regaining consciousness I found myself still in the critical care area—with no visitors allowed—and learned that I had been in severe shock and on the verge of death for some time after the operation, due to a serious drop in blood pressure.

Sandy remained at my side all of the following week, once the worst of the crisis was over. When the surgeon came in to explain just what had been involved in the operation he told me he had experimented with a new approach. The bone for the fusion was removed from my pelvis rather than from the thigh, which was the usual procedure. Upon questioning him I learned, to my horror, that it was the very side of the pelvis which had been so badly fractured only nine months previously! This was to cause me years of unnecessary suffering, returning with serious ramifications in old age. The supreme irony about his 'experiment' was that he had failed to read my recent medical record. Even worse, never once did he follow up in any way whatsoever in order to check on the consequences of what he had chosen to do. Evidence appeared to play no part in that doctor's 'scientific' research.

Wendy and Dave flew over from Edmonton to keep Sandy company for the Thanksgiving weekend. Then, I think, they must have driven him back to Regina in our car. For much of the time when Sandy couldn't be at my bedside, his sister Winnie, who lived in Saskatoon, was there. His widowed sister-in-law also visited me almost daily. After a couple of weeks, Dr. Road arranged for me to be taken home by ambulance. Not surprisingly, it proved to be a long, pain-ridden journey back to Regina, where Sandy was anxiously waiting. I was encased in a strange traction apparatus which held my body in place. For the first month back home, I had to sleep in that as well. Sandy had organized both nursing and 'home-helping' aid during the day, so I was well cared for when he had to be at work.

One of the many surprises awaiting me was a massive, hand-embroidered bedspread made by my sister-in-law Dana Duffy, the wife of my youngest brother Jerry. It must have taken her months to create it, and would have cost them an amount they could ill afford for the mailing of it. Sadly, I was never able to make use of this grand work of art, as it always remained far too heavy for my poor crippled back to handle. As luck would have it, some thirty-three years later I had an opportunity to return it to her, with the stipulation that she must pass it on to one of Jerry's two granddaughters. Both he and the only biological daughter he had known were dead by then.

Another surprise during the weeks following my return home from the hospital was an unusually lengthy letter from my brother Bob. As always, it was replete with humour, but this time the jokes were all directed at himself rather than at me. He devoted a lot of space to insinuations about how he did his best to avoid work when 'at work', and about his early retirement from the Air Force which was then on the near horizon. He even made fun of his three children, and of what they were making of their lives, but in a kindly way.

Eventually, Sandy built a little collapsible desk which allowed me to write while remaining flat on my back. Although this was very difficult at first, I was so frustrated with doing absolutely nothing productive that I persevered and gradually began to return to the task of organizing the teaching materials from my Education classes into the form of a textbook. It was to be called *A Sociology of Canadian Education* I already had a contract for it with one of the leading educational publishers in Canada at that time: Van Nostrand Reinhold, Ltd. of Toronto. The first three chapters had been written before the surgery, and I was anxious to complete the book. The fact that the Dean's secretary offered to type my first hand-written drafts spurred me to even greater effort.

Meanwhile, my sister-in-law Donna was busy planning a Duffy family reunion in Calgary for the approaching Christmas. Sandy was confident that he could fix up a wheelchair capable of accommodating me as, by then, I would have graduated to a back brace which would not be so all-intrusive. Mom felt that she could manage to have a couple of family members stay in her small apartment. Lana and Tom had recently moved into Calgary where Tom was working in a furniture store while pursuing his studies, so they offered to make room for some of the relatives. The plan was that the rest of us could stay together at a hotel. Donna was hoping that Bob and family would travel out as well.

The Christmas celebration went largely as planned, except that neither Bob nor Jerry came. So, other than Tom and Lana and Mom and Sandy and me, there were only Myrtle and Mike and their family, along with Don and Donna and their two little boys—Lewis and Bryce. We had a big Christmas meal in the hotel, but Mom later insisted on cooking a turkey dinner for Sandy and me as well. Then we left for home. Settled down once more, both of us concentrated on furthering my mending process and making a little daily progress on the book. I couldn't have accomplished either without Sandy's tireless dedication and help.

Sometime during the early part of the new year, the Regina branch of the University of Saskatchewan received its charter as a separate university, officially becoming the University of Regina. I missed out on the celebrations of its newly won independence. However, by the end of April of 1974, equally momentous personal landmarks were occurring on the road to my own independence. I was becoming able to function without the back brace, although I still required a special girdle containing metal 'bones' and laces over a second uncomfortable full-length elastic girdle. In spite of the misery of these things, they helped me eventually arrive at the point where I could navigate a short walk in the park by myself each day. Then I managed to get into the bathtub for the first time in over six months. The next step in my progress was finally to be able—although just barely—to stand in the shower without Sandy's help. We celebrated this milestone by attending a movie, "The Great Gatsby". I was proud of myself for having the fortitude to withstand the pain and see it through to the end. But perhaps the most difficult accomplishment of those gruelling days was my attendance at a full-day faculty seminar at the university, at which I had to do a considerable amount of speaking. And through it all, Sandy was still having to dress me in my panty hose etc., and to wash my feet.

It was about this time that we began to consider a major change in our lives. I had sold my house the previous year, when my old friends and tenants, the Griers, moved to Alberta. So I possessed some capital from that. Sandy had decided to sell the quarter section which housed the original farm buildings to his cousin Wally, who was renting all his land. This meant that, between us, we had adequate funds to consider a number of options for the future. He had been expressing dissatisfaction with his work at the government for some time and decided to resign after his good friend and fellow worker, Lyle Minogue, left to concentrate on farming. In mid-February, Sandy submitted a formal resignation from the Planning and Research Branch of the Department to Douglas McArthur, then the Deputy Minister of Agriculture. He felt that all the 'thinking' part of his job had been completed: the part to which he had been able to make the largest contribution. His most recent task had been the producing of a detailed map of the South Saskatchewan River Irrigation Project of which the total development, by 1989, was to comprise almost forty thousand acres. He expected to complete this by late April of 1974. What remained to be done were merely routine research tasks which he didn't consider sufficiently challenging.

In spite of many shortcomings, our lives were moving at the usual rapid pace. Dave and Wendy came for Easter. They informed us of the fact that we could expect to become grandparents sometime in November. Very soon after this, Danette and little Beth arrived from Germany on her way to Winnipeg where she was filming a TV show on the teaching of music to young children. She planned to continue to Edmonton to conduct a workshop there. On the spur of the moment, we decided to fly there with her to look after Beth and to visit with our old friends the Griers, who were then established in their own business in a nearby area called Fort Saskatchewan.

I had remained in touch with a young friend from the University of Calgary days—Arnold Parr—who, after acquiring an MA in Calgary, had earned his doctorate in Sociology in the United States and then found a job at the University of Canterbury, in Christchurch, New Zealand. One day I received a letter from him suggesting that I apply there to complete my unfinished PhD, as he was sure they would also greatly appreciate acquiring an experienced university professor such as me for part-time teaching. Sandy was very much in favour of this move. I think that his chief concern in those days was my health, and the thought of my chancing the dangers of another winter in the Regina ice and snow was simply not bearable for him. Also, he was of the opinion that we were at a stage in our lives where it was time for adventure; and the casting off of our life-long habits of hard work and no play: "If not now," he was fond of quoting, "when?"

But I was having a difficult time shedding all the concerns about security that the struggles of my past had inculcated. Leaving Regina on such an open-ended sojourn to what appeared to me as the other end of the world would involve giving up my hard-won role as a tenured university professor. Although this wasn't legally required, I felt that, in all honesty, I could not ask for a leave of absence and have the position held for me indefinitely. In an obvious attempt to soothe my concerns about our financial future, Sandy declared that, when he left the farm at the age of fifty, he had made up his mind never again to allow worries about money to dictate his choices in life. So I proceeded to apply to—and was promptly accepted by—the University of Christchurch, New Zealand. Then I handed in my resignation to the University of Regina, and Sandy did the same with his government job. It was greatly comforting to me to learn that neither employer wanted to lose us. We were both assured that we could have our positions back at any time, merely for the asking.

My most rewarding experience of that exciting period was the final completion of the textbook and having it accepted for immediate publication by my publisher. That information resulted almost in a physical sensation of the heaviest load having been removed from my long-suffering back. Sandy obviously relaxed upon hearing the news as well. Clearly, he was sharing anything stressful that affected me. Throughout all of this period in the spring and summer of 1974, I knew, deep down, that what was driving Sandy was not the issue of his own future welfare, but concern about my health problems, and what he felt was best for me. My mother had been right. I had been fortunate enough to find a loving partner dedicated to caring for me in "sickness and in health, 'til death do us part".

# Chapter 18

# AUSTRALIAN ADVENTURE

As my husband Sandy and I made our plans in the summer of 1974 for the adventure of our lives, our intention was that it would occur not in Australia, but in New Zealand. In fact, we had arranged fairly early on for our flight to Auckland in late November of that year. The plan was that we would visit my son Tom, his wife Lana and my mother in Calgary, and then Sandy's son Dave and wife Wendy in Edmonton, before proceeding to Vancouver for the long flight across the Pacific. We had timed it so that we might see our new grandchild before leaving the country. Meanwhile there was a great deal of sorting and packing to do as we divided our furniture and the majority of our other belongings among the three boys for storage. Tom drove from Calgary for a load of some of my most precious family possessions, including the piano and some china, silver and crystal pieces, as well as all his baby things. Sandy arranged for Dave to store our books and records, and we divided the old antique Hutcheon family furniture between Don and Dave. In spite of all these arrangements, however, we still ended up with three tightly packed trunks.

All through the summer, we waited for the New Zealand visa which was supposed to arrive. We were both able to meet the medical requirements, although I was shocked to learn that one of my lungs showed a scar indicative of an early—but successfully healed—encounter with tuberculosis. I assumed that someone at the Lonely Trail school must have carried the infection. Finally, only a few weeks before we were to leave, I phoned the embassy in frustration and was informed that, according to their laws, because Sandy was over fifty he was too old to qualify as an immigrant. I explained that it was I who had applied, as it was I who had the position at a university in New Zealand. I added that my husband was accompanying me in the role of spouse. The man at the other end of the phone then let me know in no uncertain terms that a mere wife was not acceptable as the official applicant. Apparently New Zealand's policy was then different from that of Australia, where all potential immigrants from a Commonwealth country were made welcome, with no questions asked.

So we found ourselves faced with a sudden, critical decision. There could be no turning back at that point, for 'all our bridges were burned'. We decided to apply for immigration to Australia and were almost immediately accepted. Our travel plans were then altered to include only a brief stopover in Auckland, and then a flight on to Sydney. With the impending publication of my book, I was reasonably confident that some sort of opportunity would be available for me in Australia. Thus began the adventure of our lives!

Our drawn-out farewell to Regina had been made more stressful by all this than it would otherwise have been. But the sorrow which I was increasingly feeling would not have been any less. For, in the months leading up to our departure, the realization gradually dawned on me that I was leaving not only our much-loved family, but the most wonderfully stimulating and supportive academic and cultural environment I had ever known or would ever likely know again. And the largest circle of loyal and caring friends. So it was with a growing sense of loss and regret that I began to face what was to come—in spite of being fully aware that, with my back problems, the prairie winter climate was no longer safe for me.

Our family farewell visits went as planned. Actually meeting our fascinating little granddaughter, Carolyn Jamie, drove home more than anything else the serious nature of the sudden choices we had made. It was too late for second thoughts, however. At least it provided fuel for a family joke. Often, in the years to follow, Carolyn would teasingly accuse us of having left the country immediately after our first sight of her. And so we did, but her arrival had made it much more difficult. However, not only did Dave have excellent career prospects, but both Don and Tom were settled in secure jobs by then, and in newly purchased houses in their chosen home cities of Regina and Calgary. So, as we planned our take-off, we were able to feel reasonably sanguine about the probability that none of the three boys would need to rely on us in the near future.

I even managed a brief meeting with my brother Jack. My brother-in-law Mike had been keeping in touch with him as he wandered the mean streets of Vancouver's downtown east-side. Mike told me that Jack had recently been given a job at the desk of a hotel for housing the homeless. So I located him there. I was shocked but not surprised at his deteriorated appearance, although happy to find him with a roof over his head for once. The most touching moment of our all-too-hurried greeting and farewell was when he refused my offer of money—something he had never done before when we touched base.

"I've got a paying job." he declared proudly. "So I won't be needing your help any more." That was the best send-off I could ever have dreamed of!

We arrived in Sydney, Australia on November 27th in the midst of driving rain, extremely sleep-deprived, and with no pre-arrangements as to location or university contacts. After the exhausting sixteen-hour journey, we had been forced to endure a fumigation process as we left our jumbo jet. A strange, but fully understandable, welcome to our new home! It was no doubt a necessary protection for Australian vegetation and livestock. We were then taken into the central part of the city by a cab driver who assured me, when I asked about the price of the toll at a gate we were approaching, "Oil pie." Not very appetizing, to say the least! After a long drive, we were deposited at the door of the beautiful Grantham Place hotel, where a room awaited us for a mere sixteen dollars a day: a special price for immigrants. However, we found our surroundings surprisingly cold and drafty, with windows covered and impossible to open and blowers on high, from some source we couldn't locate. As we were starving by then, we happily left our uncomfortable quarters and rushed downstairs to find something to eat. No one else was in the grand hotel restaurant at the time. The room literally rustled with heavy, starched linen and whispered with the decorous movements of unobtrusive, black-coated waiters. Sandy and I each ordered T-bone steak, but our meal, when it finally came, proved to be another unpleasant surprise. The steaks were the largest hunks of beef we had ever seen on plates. We soon discovered that the cooks were apparently trying to make up in quantity what was sadly lacking in quality. We refused the offer of a massive side-dish of fried potatoes, as there were already mashed potatoes with the meal along with three additional varieties of lukewarm, waterlogged, and over-cooked vegetables. The steaks were so shockingly tough that I was totally unable to chew mine. That experience proved to be the beginning of our discovery of the deficient nature of Australian cooking in those days—at least in public places.

The rain continued all afternoon, and we began to feel that we should be considering either Adelaide or Brisbane instead of Sydney, as their climates were supposedly the best in the country. However, the next morning the weather suddenly became most pleasant, and we had an enjoyable time tramping about the harbour area of the city. The Opera House and Botanic Gardens were more beautiful than anything we had ever seen. In fact, everywhere we wandered, the city had such a good 'feel' about it! The parks and downtown area all seemed to be used a lot by the people, and Sandy and I were utterly rejuvenated by the air of vitality surrounding it all. Among hordes of other fascinating objects encountered that day, I recall a beautiful old Anglican cathedral, with a large picture of someone called John Armitage at the front. Apparently he was instrumental in getting the cathedral built. According to his birthdate, I couldn't help but wonder if he had been a Remittance Man like my great-grandfather. A brother, possibly? We went on to take the Captain Cook's cruise of the Harbour, which provided a marvelous overview of the entire area; then walked back to the hotel through an older part of the city. Another wonderful experience! Everywhere the buildings were being renovated. Many of them were positively quaint—a unique style of architecture with turrets, much lacy carved wood, and elaborate, brightly painted ironwork. Nowhere was there that sense of menace and decadence that often seems to lurk in older downtown sections of large cities.

We remained in Sydney one week, during which time I contacted the university there. I was told that they would be most interested in having me—especially in light of the fact of my textbook coming out in the near future. This gave me hope that other universities would be similarly positive about my prospects, so we opted for not deciding in a hurry. I had written ahead of time to a number of leading Australian universities, and upon phoning them soon after our arrival in the country, was amazed to discover that each and every one assured me I would be greatly welcomed.

This probably had a lot to do with the fact that I had sent four highly positive recommendations, which I was not above flaunting quite shamelessly. One was from Wil Toombs, Dean of Education at Regina University. It began with an apology for the inadequacy of his brief words of appreciation for my services of the past nine years and continued with an assurance of how sorely I would be missed. He concluded by noting that I had " . . . provided considerable strength in the Educational Foundations area and the entire Faculty, and it will be very difficult to find someone able to duplicate the quality and generosity of your work."

My second recommendation was from the Deputy Minister of Continuing Education for the Province of Saskatchewan. He commended me as " . . . a scholar and researcher of stature, a sensitive and concerned teacher, and as a person who is universally respected in educational circles on this continent." His concluding paragraph was so beautifully worded I feel compelled to quote all of it. It read as follows: "I can honestly say that I have nothing but admiration for Professor Hutcheon's views and for the thoroughly honest and principled way in which she has stated them. She has, I am sure, made lasting and valuable contributions to the development of countless young Saskatchewan teachers, and I am sure educators everywhere would find her a stimulating person with views worthy of consideration."

I had also passed along a letter from Ed Tchorzewski, Minister of Culture and Youth in the Province of Saskatchewan, who expressed regret at losing me as a member of the Saskatchewan Arts Board, along with great appreciation of my contributions. And lastly, there was a letter from J.H. Archer—the Principal of what was, by then, officially recognized as the University of Regina Campus. According to him, " . . . Pat Duffy Hutcheon is a much-sought-after person in university circles for committee work and has made a notable contribution to a number which are advisory to me. She is a good organizer and a good colleague. If this sounds like a paean of praise, it is because this is a very good person."

It was the enthusiastic response of the universities I had contacted—no doubt influenced by these four letters—that made me realize we could actually have our choice of location in this wonderful country. So we began our search by taking the bus up north to Brisbane in Queensland: the sub-tropical part of Australia. We had learned by then that the hordes of flies and mosquitos attacking from all directions wherever we walked in Sydney were not to be found in similar profusion in Queensland. Also, both of us were obviously yearning for a physical and cultural context as different as possible from all that we had previously experienced. After all, what is an adventure about if not exploring the unknown?

Our bus ride was highly illuminating, and not only because of the amazingly hilly and eucalyptus-treed countryside on our left side and the beautiful gentian-blue ocean extending to the right of us. Equally amazing was our shared sensation very early on of being propelled back fifty years in time in terms of culture. One experience in particular contributed to driving this home. The bus stopped at a restaurant about halfway up the coast for us to have lunch. (We were traveling 'up' north to the subtropics.) Everyone rushed out, but we decided to wait and follow at the back of the crowd. As we arose to go we noticed an Aboriginal couple still in their seats, so we asked them to accompany us. They said they were not allowed in restaurants. We reacted to this profoundly shocking news by assuring them that we would purchase lunch for the four of us, and we would all eat together in the bus. They impressed us as being a very interesting, highly intelligent and obviously educated couple. But, whereas the sort of cultural backwardness which their treatment in the bus exemplified may well have turned off the usual foreign traveler, for us—as social scientists—it was all very intriguing.

I discovered some time later that only two years previously the federal government had established a Department of Aboriginal Affairs. And, the year after we arrived, we had the opportunity to share in celebrating the passage of Australia's very first Racial Discrimination Act. Another interesting and relevant subsequent event was to be the discovery and cremation, in 1976, of the skeleton of the last surviving native Tasmanian—Truganini—who had died a century earlier. As we gradually became more familiar with this Australian Aboriginal history—even worse than Canada's—we grew less surprised by the racist attitudes still prevailing when we arrived in Queensland.

In spite of all these cultural quirks, we fell in love with Brisbane almost at once. Even the unplanned and untidy appearance of the city was appealing in a way, as everything seemed to have been built a long time ago and never altered. I was particularly intrigued by the wooden overheads and board sidewalks in the city centre, and by all the houses built on stilts. And, even though we recognized the cockroaches and spiders populating every space both indoors and out as a possible nuisance—and even danger at times—at least they were something new. Only later was I to realize what it meant to step on cockroaches by the dozen as I walked down a city street, and to have to search my shoes carefully for spiders each time I put them on. And to sleep inside a virtual tent of netting in order to ensure that our bed was safe from insects at night. But the climate was as perfect as any climate could possibly be, so we told ourselves we shouldn't be surprised to have to share it with many other forms of life.

Our first Christmas Day was, not surprisingly, a very quiet and rather lonely one. The most memorable aspect of it was the fact that Darwin—to the north of us—was hit by a cyclone so devastating to the city that it was amazing to discover only about fifty people were killed. That day we had been exploring our closest beach at Wynnum. It had a great esplanade for walking and enjoying the view of the seaside. A few days later we ventured further afield and discovered Bribie Island, at the southernmost tip of the Sunshine Coast. A great spot for swimming, with its low tides and apparently endless stretches of white sand!

Then in no time, it seemed, I had located the district of St. Lucia and visited the university. Almost immediately I met a wonderful professor, Dr. Bassett, who was enthusiastic about taking me on as a doctoral student. While I was becoming familiar with the Education and Social Science areas, Sandy went to see the people in the Department of Primary Industry. Soon after this we had another stroke of luck. We found a 'unit' available for renting. It was located in a beautiful district called Toowong, halfway between the city centre and the university. It was actually only about three miles each way, and thus within easy walking distance of both. The unit belonged to a young medical doctor who was studying in Sydney. It was one of six in a small, three-story building with room for parking in the basement. Because it was facing the east, it benefitted from a beautiful view and exposure to the ocean breezes, which we were to learn was all-important. The rent was high according to our standards then—about ninety dollars a week in Canadian funds—but we considered it well worth the money. It was beautifully furnished and twelve-hundred square feet in size. All that it seemed to lack were screens on the windows—something we later learned was simply not the custom there. And the previous renters had left the place absolutely filthy, so we realized we would have a lot of cleaning to do. Nevertheless, we had no real concerns about it as we happily returned to Sydney to retrieve our trunks from the hotel storage. We were able to do some more sight-seeing there, while waiting a week for possession of our new quarters. Then it was back to Brisbane and to what we already felt was our adopted home.

The wisdom of that choice and our overall good fortune were soon confirmed. Not only was the climate mild the year round, but we both ultimately found work situations which intrigued and satisfied us. Dr. Bassett turned out to be all I had hoped for in a thesis advisor, and as different as possible from the one I had experienced at Yale. I was given a tiny corner desk and left largely to my own devices, except when I required advice, which Dr. Bassett was always ready to supply. I spent most of my time in the library, fascinated with pursuing my chosen subject in the manner which I was also free to choose.

The difference between the Australian system—which was still largely British—and what I had experienced at Yale was truly amazing. My dissertation proposal had to be presented not only to Dr. Bassett, as my chief advisor and overseer, but to a leading expert in my particular field of research in Great Britain as well as one in the United States. The same would apply to the acceptance or rejection process once the project had been completed. After its assessment as worthy of a PhD, it would be published in hard cover. Dr. Bassett was, like me, an Educational sociologist. I was proposing a then-revolutionary interdisciplinary thesis for research; therefore a renowned American psychologist and British anthropologist with a biological orientation were chosen to join my chief advisor both in the assessment of my proposed research project and in the final judgement of my work.

Meanwhile, Sandy had been in contact with the Agricultural Economics professors at the university and learned that a major irrigation experiment for the growing of a crop called kenaf was in the offing in the Ord River Area of northern Australia, near Darwin. We learned that kenaf was a variety of Hibiscus native to southern Asia, and could be a source of natural fiber with considerable potential for use in the twine and burlap industries as well as for newsprint. Sandy was assured that, because of his previous experience in agriculture and irrigation, his help and advice with this would be highly valued. While awaiting further development of the proposed project, he immersed himself in his own informal study of what he perceived to be the rather irrational and almost revolutionary economic and political situation in Australia. Their history and cultural evolution was much more different from ours than we had imagined, as each state was an independent crown colony before the federation which had occurred only a little over a half-century before. At the federal level, the system was an uneasy mixture of those of Britain and the United States. For example, the Senate was elected, but its elections did not necessarily coincide with those of the House of Representatives. This led to a national political process much more fraught with strife than was the Canadian one in those days. However, I was very favourably impressed with the electoral system. We quickly learned that voting in Australia was compulsory—even for new immigrants like ourselves. And that the process was a type of 'proportional representation' involving a single transferable vote. The voter was required to check the candidate of choice as well as the preferred party.

We got the impression that unions and bosses were ferociously at one another's throats, with no one apparently concerned for the welfare of the 'commons' as a whole. Farmers appeared to be in the most precarious position of all, as that industry was particularly vulnerable to the vagaries of the world market and a climate which, in many parts of the country, was extreme. It appeared that workers in the construction, manufacturing and extractive industries were fairly skilled and productive, while food, clerical and retail workers seemed most reluctant to do their jobs. For instance, I've never before nor since encountered such uniformly lazy waitresses and clerks: all of whom seemed to think that in serving the public they were granting us a huge favour.

Horse races and races involving dogs were commonplace, with betting on these among the chief occupations. News agencies were everywhere, seeming to exist chiefly for the purpose of selling tickets, just as hotels apparently existed in order to operate pubs. Domestic beer and wine were cheap, and pubs ran full blast at all hours—including Sundays. I was shocked at the sight of young people crowding the pub near us on delightfully sunny days subtly cooled by the ocean breezes, as I passed by on my walking route to and from the university. Another source of amazement was the fact that I seldom encountered any other walkers. In fact, on my first trip over to meet my advisor, I was a bit confused by the map, so was relieved when a man finally came along. But when I made my inquiry he looked at me as if I were mad. "No one walks all the way over there!" he exclaimed.

We realized we could not restrict ourselves only to walking, so we bought a second-hand car in order to see something of the countryside surrounding the city. This meant that I had to learn immediately to drive on the 'wrong' side of the street. This fact, along with the treacherous roads, wildly reckless drivers and almost total absence of signs, made our early sight-seeing trips somewhat exciting. What we managed to see on these initial adventures struck us as a fairly harsh environment for most activities—including farming. Much of the eastern coastal area of Queensland is sharply hilly, if not mountainous. It is also very rocky and was then covered, or rather dotted with, tortured-looking eucalyptus trees. Even where average rainfall was adequate, it tended to come in a three-inch downpour—then nothing for six weeks. Bush fires were a constant threat, even within city suburbs, as were flash floods. However, we were told by our neighbours that the really tough conditions were to be found in the interior.

Our early forays into our new surroundings included a visit to a large vegetable and fruit cannery, as well as one to a koala sanctuary which soon became a favourite destination for us. Here we were able to witness numerous koalas and kangaroos moving about freely, along with duck-billed platypuses. We were also fortunate enough to get a good overview of Brisbane from two high lookout points: one to the north and the other to the south of the city. All this surveying of our physical surroundings helped considerably in the difficult settling-in process.

One of the problems facing us was that, at the time we arrived, Australia was in the midst of its conversion to the metric system. This, in itself, presented an all-engulfing change in our everyday patterns of living. Becoming familiar with the mixture of working-class (or "Ocker") and upper-class English accents was yet another daily challenge. For example, we had a difficult time locating our new Grove Street rental unit for the first time, as we were told it was on 'Growv' street. At the same time, it was fascinating for me, as an educator, to learn about the role currently being played by the private-school system and the media in all this. Although it had previously been most desirable to have the upper-class manner of speaking—thus enticing even the poor to sacrifice their all in order to get their children into private schools—we were now witnessing a sort of reverse snobbery led by powerful television-and-radio broadcasters who were deliberately hiring only announcers with the most extreme of working-class accents.

We decided that it might help in assimilating all this culture shock if we had some friends who had grown up in that part of the world. One of my very early moves was to look for 'kindred spirits' with whom we could develop relationships: people who were also long-time residents. We didn't want to mix only with Canadian expatriates, nor academic colleagues—most of whom were not native Australians. Nevertheless, when I heard about a 'Newcomers Group' which met downtown, I decided to go to a meeting one evening. As luck would have it, the woman who sat next to me had also recently arrived and was attending for the first time as well. We introduced ourselves and, as we became involved in conversation, discovered many mutual interests. Like Sandy, her husband had not found the idea of a formal newcomer's meeting appealing, so she too was there on her own. Her name was May Thompson. Her husband, Les, was a land surveyor who was later to become Surveyor General of Queensland: the same position as that assigned to my brother Don back in BC almost a decade later. Also like Don when the time came, Les became involved in the process of computerizing the State system. Again, as in the future case of Don with the Province of British Columbia, this would be a pioneering venture on his part, with Queensland leading the country in establishing such a system.

Les was a high-ranking administrator in Fiji before the island's then-recent gaining of independence from Britain. May had operated as the official entertainer of visiting dignitaries, including the Queen of England. Both she and Les were actually New Zealanders. They now lived in one of the most beautiful suburbs of Brisbane, about six miles from us. We often reminisced afterwards about how we became immediate close friends, with neither ever feeling the need to return for a second meeting of the club.

Sandy and I spent our second Australian Christmas at the Thompsons', being entertained in a style to which we had never been accustomed. I found the food so different from our usual Christmas fare, and so appealing in taste and appearance, that I was overfull by the time the first two courses had been served. It was embarrassing to discover that there were five more to come. Another experience having to do with these friends concerned the snakes that we continuously encountered in their yard—and once even in a bathroom. May and I decided to do some research on the issue, and discovered that some of the most deadly poisonous snakes in the entire country were shown on the map to inhabit their district.

In our continuing attempt to find friends during that first year in our new home, we had also made an effort, soon after getting settled in early 1975, to locate some Unitarians. We learned there were none in the city, nor anywhere in Australia, although the Unitarian church had long been active in New Zealand. Nonetheless, we did discover the Humanist Association of Queensland, which was then centred in Brisbane. We found many interesting people there, and attended both meetings and social gatherings at their various homes. Early on, I experienced a few cases of embarrassment due to cultural misunderstandings. Once I was told to 'bring a plate' with us, so I brought our table settings, only to discover that it was food they meant! Another comical moment was when we responded to an invitation for supper and, after having arrived at 5:30 in the afternoon, were laughingly informed that we were not expected until near midnight.

I was once asked to speak at a Humanist Association meeting, and gave a talk that turned out to be highly controversial. I had been feeling for some time that we Freethinkers, or secular humanists, would not really gain a foothold in the general culture unless we were prepared to recognize the value of certain vitally necessary activities and roles that had thus far been assigned solely to religion. I recommended more emphasis on the teaching of individual morality, and the general ethics and social rituals both stemming from, and supporting, these. The title of my presentation was "The Failure of Humanism". I was attempting to make the point that we might possibly be too individualistic, except where political activism was concerned, and that perhaps we needed to recognize the social and cultural needs buried deep within the history of humankind. The speech was subsequently published in the local humanist journal, and provided fuel for much discussion.

Something else that I did as soon as possible after arriving was to arrange for swimming lessons at a nearby pool. I always longed to learn to swim, but had never had the opportunity. Also, I felt that it would be good for my back, which was still painful at times. I'll never forget that first and, as it turned out, only lesson. After showing me the basic moves, the swimming teacher asked if I would like to attempt a few strokes on my own. I set off immediately and swam all the way across the pool at a good clip. She exclaimed that she had never seen anyone learn so fast. From then on, I went swimming regularly, and we soon began to spend considerable time at the wonderful white-sand beach on Bribie Island. The more famous beach to the south of us, the Gold Coast, was designed more as a tourist attraction and thus not as much to our liking.

Meanwhile, Sandy and I were enjoying downtown Brisbane on a regular basis. We were especially impressed with the city hall and Civic Square, and the electric clock with its tuneful Westminster chimes. But we soon discovered that the most compellingly beautiful building in all of Brisbane was the old opera house dominating the city centre. We immediately signed up for the coming season, for both Sandy's choice of the symphony and opera and for mine, which was live theatre. Fortunately we were able to obtain Sunday-afternoon tickets. We made a habit of walking back and forth to these. One day, on our way to the symphony, I was struck by an extremely severe pain from the fused area in my spine down the length of my right leg. I persevered in spite of it. Fortunately, by the end of the program, it had eased and, with it, much of the pain and discomfort which had lingered since my spinal fusion. We assumed that some vital nerve damaged by the surgery had suddenly reconnected.

We were hearing regularly from family in Canada. Little Carolyn was thriving. Tom and Lana had made a once-in-a-lifetime trip to Hawaii. Mom had been very ill with influenza, and Tom wrote to tell me that he and Lana were the only ones who visited her. Although he phoned his uncle on the farm about it, Jerry never once managed to come in, nor did he even phone to check on her. Tom's great-aunt Mabel didn't make it over either. This experience apparently helped Mom decide to move out to Langley in the Lower Mainland of BC, where her sister Jessie already had an apartment. By then Myrtle and Mike had purchased a house in North Delta: a suburb situated between Langley and Vancouver. Jessie had informed Mom that there was an apartment in her building available for renting. So as soon as Mom recovered she made the move all on her own, even managing all her packing. I was astounded but relieved to hear the news. I suspected that what had actually spurred her on to this typically sudden decision was the need she felt not to have Jerry placed in a situation where he was facing family responsibilities to which he couldn't bear responding. I immediately sent Mom a cheque and assured her that, as usual, my brother Don and I would share the cost of her rent.

Then, early in 1975, came two extremely distressing items of news. The first was from Myrtle, telling me that our brother Jack had died suddenly of 'massive heart failure'. He was only fifty-one years old. Then came word from Regina that my dear friend Bernie Melanson had been found dead in her office. She hadn't quite made it to her thirtieth birthday. She was suffering from a severe type of diabetes, and apparently died of some sort of diabetic shock. I had a difficult time dealing with these tragedies. Somehow, my being so far away seemed to make it all worse. On the other hand, the early months of the new year also brought positive news, which helped somewhat. Word arrived from my Canadian publisher that my textbook had come out on schedule.

I received a few copies in the mail soon after. Accompanying these was the information that the Regina University was intending to use the book in the coming term; and that sixteen other universities across Canada had ordered it for the fall semester, with more orders coming all the time.

In early February of 1975—during the Australian summer—I took two weeks off work so that we could make a trip to New Zealand. Sandy's contract work on the Ord River Irrigation project had not yet begun, so the timing was good for him. We had arranged to meet Sandy's sister-in-law 'Dee' and her husband Ron Baker from Montreal. Their son, Gordon, had come to Adelaide for graduate study and then married and remained to teach school. In fact, he was ultimately hired by Flinders University and was to spend the remainder of his working life there. The Bakers were planning on going on to South Australia to visit him after our New Zealand holiday. And what a holiday it was!

Overall, New Zealand struck all four of us as a well-tended garden. The weather was much cooler than we were accustomed to by then, but we were well-prepared with sweaters, having been warned by our friends in Brisbane. We had taken the three-hour flight to Auckland, where we met Ron and Dee in a designated hotel. In the morning we hired a car and headed for the northern-most tip of the island, stopping along the ocean at Waiwera for lunch and arriving at the Bay of Islands by nightfall. This was a delightful resort area where we found a little village called Paihia where we were fortunate in locating a great boarding place. This occurred accidentally when we wandered up a narrow dirt road to a house on the very top of the cliff overlooking the entire bay. There we happened upon a retired British naval officer and his wife who were willing to take us in. After getting settled we dashed off to the beach where the tide was going out, and had great fun in the breakers. The next day we discovered a postcard-like district surrounding Waitangi and Kerikeri where the very first white (Pakeha) settlement was established in 1819. We also went on an ocean boat tour on a very stormy sea, being tossed up and down on white-caps for three hours. Our third day was spent winding along a narrow gravel road through mountains and original kauri forests. These are very high, straight trees, something like the California redwoods, which were almost totally destroyed during the early days of 'white' settlement.

In the early afternoon of the following day we sped right through Auckland and up into the beautiful, rich and rolling farmlands surrounding Hamilton. The day after that we arrived in Palmerston North, in the sheep-and-cattle ranching country with its high hills. We were constantly amazed at the way the countryside changed radically every few miles, and at all the farming activity even in the high hills. We had to stop once for a large herd of guernseys to be driven across the road in a very leisurely way; and once for about five hundred sheep which one man, his wife and two sheep dogs were trying to maneuver through a gate and across the road into another gate. We finally left the car and gave them a hand.

Many of the farmers we met on our travels appeared to be Maoris. They struck us as very capable, and a proud and handsome people. They had managed to keep their native language and culture intact, while at the same time speaking beautiful English and succeeding in a variety of occupations. In fact, the very next night after we had found a farm near Pahiatua where we were taken in as boarders, we had the privilege of meeting a Maori princess. She was the wife of a neighbour. The four of us were treated like royalty ourselves the entire time we were on that farm. We got the impression that—unlike the Australian situation—the New Zealand farmers were the most privileged group in the country. These particular families all had their children in expensive private schools and each possessed a private swimming pool and tennis court.

Finally, before taking off for home from Auckland airport, we attended a meeting of New Zealand Humanists, and met some very interesting people. All in all, it was an extremely memorable summer holiday. Ron and Dee were wonderful companions throughout, and we found we had a great deal in common. Arriving home to the news from Tom and Lana that we were to have another grandchild sometime in July put the finishing touches on that marvelous, initial summer on the 'other' side of the world. Then our first Australian autumn came and went, and we were finding the temperatures perfect. Throughout it all, ten degrees was the lowest night temperature in Brisbane, although we were running an electric heater at night. Australians didn't seem to believe in heating their houses, however, so we learned to wear our sweaters when visiting them in the evening.

In early May, Gordon Baker, the son of Dee and Ron, came up from Adelaide during a break from teaching. His wife was busy taking a course, so he was on his own. We decided to take advantage of his visit by going on a tour. We planned to make two loops: one to the southwest of the state and the other to the north-eastern coastal area. We especially wanted to visit Toowoomba, located about eighty kilometers west of Brisbane. It later became our favourite little city. While there I checked in with the Institute of Advanced Education and with the University of New England. Toowoomba is located on the edge of the Darling Downs, the richest grain-growing area in Australia. On our trip we also stopped at the University of Armidale. This leg of the tour involved a lot of mountain driving, but it was beautiful, as the trees native to the area do not shed their leaves in autumn.

The main feature of the north-coastal arm of our journey was the coral reefs. There, we took a five-hour boat trip to reach Heron Island, where we spent two nights. We then returned to Gladstone, the furthest northern point. We learned that the reef, the beauty of which we were observing, at that time stretched for fifteen hundred miles. On the way back we stopped at a place called Crocodile Adventures. We saw how Australia's crocodiles could leap upon their prey with no warning, and with almost the speed of light. It was a good lesson in the danger they posed to human beings. On our travels we also saw many miles of sugar cane, some beautiful fruit-growing districts, sunflowers and cotton fields. In between all these intensively farmed areas were large areas of sparsely located gum trees with stretches of grass and scarcely a house or any cattle to be seen.

In late May we received word that Dave and Wendy were in the process of moving to Vancouver, where Dave had been hired as a physicist at TRIUMF: Canada's new national laboratory for particle-and-nuclear physics research. This was to be located near the University of BC, and operated jointly by the Universities of Alberta and BC Those of Victoria, Simon Fraser and Carleton were to come on board some time later. Dave and Wendy rented a place in Richmond at first, but were soon fortunate enough to locate a house for sale within walking distance of his workplace, in the relatively upper-class area called Point Grey.

As we settled into our first winter in the sub-tropics we discovered that the daytime temperatures in Brisbane averaged from sixteen to nineteen degrees, with the nights only five to ten degrees lower. There were a few days of constant drizzle each month, but otherwise mostly sunshine. In contrast, Sydney suffered three weeks of rain, floods and gales during the month of June alone. We greatly enjoyed the Australian TV, which consisted chiefly of public affairs programs and repeats of various BBC series which were all new to us. As always, we were finding Australian politics utterly fascinating. As were the customs of the people we had come to know. For example, most of them expressed scorn at the very idea of eating fish or poultry. They considered only mutton and beef acceptable. We loved being introduced to new foods, many of which I found delicious. A favourite of both of us was lamb, along with all the Asian fruits plus the great variety of vegetables previously unknown to us.

We found the local Humanist organization to be quite active, meeting one evening a week. We spent an afternoon at one of their barbecues at a camp-like home of an interesting younger couple with three small children. They owned thirty acres about five miles from any shopping area, and were living in a tent while the husband, John, slowly built a more solid shelter. He was a Hungarian refugee who had fully mastered Australian language. For example, he was telling us about how they supported the new 'ripe centre' which was nearby, where women were taken after they had been 'riped'. The two of them had started out with a small plant nursery and some purebred goats. She was now in charge of these while he kept busy making furniture from logs and working full-time in a sugar refinery as well. They were typical of the humanists we came to know: reminders of our 'hippies'.

In mid-July we received a telegram from son Tom notifying us of the birth of our first grandson, Shane Westcott, in Calgary. It had been a difficult birth, but the six-and-a-half pound baby was in good health and progressing well. Just one more reason for the uncomfortable feeling of being far away from home which often engulfed us! It was a good thing that we were both so busy. I was immersed in my research project, so Sandy didn't see much of me. He took over all of the housework during that period. He had also become involved in a doing a study for the university, comparing the banking systems of Canada and Australia.

By the beginning of August my publisher informed me that the textbook had sold twelve hundred copies: a very good start in terms of the Canadian scene, they said. Only a month after that, the research for my dissertation was completed, and I was into the task of organizing the problem statement, outline, etc., in preparation for the actual writing of it. We decided to take a week off to visit Gordon and his wife in Adelaide, and to get a look at the environs in case we chose to settle there. We found a beautiful, well-planned city, and decided it would be a very satisfactory place to live, should the opportunity present itself. Sandy was particularly impressed by the wonderful wines produced in the surrounding countryside, although that countryside itself struck us as surprisingly barren and unattractive. While in Adelaide I dropped in at the university and applied for a position in the Early Childhood Education. To my surprise I received a telegram soon after my return to Brisbane, offering me a three-year contract for the position of Head. Sadly, I had to refuse it as I felt that I was not yet ready to make such a firm commitment.

By the time December of 1975 arrived, my dissertation was almost complete. Sandy had been busy working on the irrigation project, but managed to type my first rough draft. When I showed it to Professor Bassett he seemed pleased with it. That enabled me to relax and enjoy a visit with my sister Myrtle and her husband Mike Pridie, who had flown over at the beginning of December on a month-long tour. We had a bout of unseasonable rain for several weeks before they arrived, and the weather continued cloudy for some time. We thought it would be safe to spend inordinately lengthy periods at Bribie Beach, but apparently more of the sun's rays were getting through than we realized. Myrtle unfortunately suffered extreme sunburn—especially on her feet—so she was rather crippled for the first week or so. As usual, my skin didn't respond. It was strange in that I never seemed to get either tanned or sun-burned. I assumed this meant that I had no need to worry about how much time I spent in the sun. In fact, I thought Australian women were merely old-fashioned in their custom of always using umbrellas. I considered it another quirk, such as the unspoken rule that one never hung female 'undies' on the outdoor clothesline. Some years later, when I developed a form of skin cancer, I learned that my type of skin was particularly vulnerable to cancer, as it created no self-protective covering of its own.

We drove down to Sydney to show Myrtle and Mike that beautiful city and the countryside along the way; then we flew to Christchurch for our first look at the south island of New Zealand. I contacted Arnold Parr, my old friend from our student days at the University of Calgary. He laid on a delicious luncheon with a group of his fellow academics from the Sociology Department.

Myrtle and Mike went on to other parts of Australia after we returned to Brisbane, and I once more became buried in my work. By then Sandy was also busy with his irrigation study. Around this time I received two job offers: another in Adelaide and one north of Brisbane at Rockhampton. Both would have been acceptable except that I still considered it too early for me to become committed. We celebrated our third Christmas in Australia with our friends the Thompsons—this time with me cooking a turkey. Also, during the early summer season, I was called for a luncheon interview in Adelaide for the position of Head of a new teacher's college that was being established there. I remember the interview not so much for the content of the scholarly conversation between the pleasant interviewer and myself, but because of a sadly all-too-typical experience with the waitress. We both ordered rather quickly, and the woman meeting with me received her meal moderately soon. I persuaded her not to wait for my food to arrive, but to eat her own while it was hot. Time passed, filled with interesting conversation. My companion finished eating, and I still had not received any lunch. Our increasingly desperate attempts to catch the eye of the waitress, who was busy gossiping with a fellow 'worker', were to no avail. Finally, she did approach, but it was to take the dishes away and bring the bill. I seized the opportunity to mention that I had never been served my order. Rather than apologize, she stated adamantly that I must have eaten it, and was trying to avoid paying for it. I chose merely to have a good laugh about the Australian work ethic, and to eat later, but my hostess was most embarrassed.

Once this trip to Adelaide was behind me I became so immersed in the final formulation of my PhD dissertation that little else intruded on my consciousness. The title was "Socialization: Towards Interdisciplinary Consensus." By the time the writing up of my research findings and conclusions was complete, and in its final printing, it amounted to a massive document of almost four-hundred pages. I was satisfied that it accomplished what I had aimed for: an assessment of the problems within the social 'sciences' which were preventing progress from a proto-scientific condition to that of a functioning and productive science. It was no doubt not the most 'politically correct' project I could have chosen. But my advisor, Professor Bassett, wrote me a letter after he had read it, which considerably re-assured me about the wisdom of my choice of thesis topic, and the manner in which I had developed it. He ended the letter with the following paragraph.

"I must say that you have been the world's Number One model PhD student, and it was a great pleasure to be associated with you. I am sure you will have a very successful academic career."

My dissertation was an attempt to apply Thomas Kuhn's much-misunderstood concept of 'paradigm' and proceed to show how it involved four aspects: shared exemplars, values, a specific model of reality with its related heuristic devices, and generalizations derived from an analysis of evidence. My subsequent extensive research on the development and current status of the various disciplines dealing with human behaviour had then forced me to the following four conclusions regarding the standing of the social 'sciences' where these four essential aspects of science were concerned. The first was that there was little general acceptance within our field of study of specific research procedures which might serve as exemplars of how enquiry should be conducted. My second conclusion dealt with the existing confusion concerning research principles or standards of enquiry and theory building—even to the degree that the value of the scientific approach itself was still not fully accepted within sociology. I felt that the very existence of continuing philosophical debate on this issue revealed much about the level of progress here.

Concerning the final two elements of a scientific paradigm, I concluded that the situation appeared more hopeful. I had found significant evidence of acceptance, within all the social sciences, of an approach to social reality incorporating the general ideas of both evolution and systems-organization.

This was accompanied by an increasingly widespread rejection of atomistic and mechanistic models, and of uni-linear notions of causality. I noted that, although there was still much ambiguity in the use of the term 'system', this was not necessarily a serious problem. What was more significant, I thought, was a growing agreement concerning the broad notion of interrelatedness; and of the need for a developing organization of research increasing in complexity according to the principles of evolution.

I proceeded to define the fourth element of an authentically scientific paradigm as a system of generalizations or concepts. My conclusion here was that there currently existed—throughout the social sciences—considerable agreement on the nature of cognitive, affective, linguistic and moral development; although the exact aspects of that agreement were still very much subject to debate. In my opinion this continued to present a huge challenge for sociologists and their cohorts in neighbouring studies, as human developmental processes are central to that socialization/enculturation process on which all social-scientific research must be based. Therefore consensus here had to be crucial! Without that consensus, each researcher is forced to go back to first principles with every study, and repeatedly justify his or her most fundamental working assumptions. Without it there can be no shared foundation and no possibility of accumulation of research findings—thus no possibility of knowledge-building within this field of study. Accordingly, I was forced to concede that psychology, sociology, anthropology, political science and economics were still at the proto-scientific level of development. Definitely not the sort of conclusion likely to guarantee political popularity in my chosen field!

By the time the summer was over and the autumn semester well underway, this courageous (or recklessly foolhardy?) dissertation had been accepted by the examining committee of educators and sociologists at the University of Brisbane. But it was to be a considerable time before I would receive word that it had passed the entire rigorous process involving the American and British experts in the other fields of study with which my interdisciplinary project dealt. My advisor, Professor Bassett, warned of the possibility that my PhD might not be formally finalized until the convocation at the beginning of January in 1977. This was to prove all too true.

I had also learned, during this exciting but stressful period, that the selection committee for the position at Adelaide were utterly deadlocked over two candidates, myself and a male professor, and they had decided to postpone the decision for another year. So that was the end of the chance I'd been counting on, of our remaining in Australia! Because my interviewer had been so positive, I had already turned down the last job still open to me: a teaching position at the University of Brisbane which would have required me to accept a step backward in rank.

Meanwhile, I was busy contacting Canadian universities. Because my textbook had become well-known by then, and was being used across the country, I wasn't really worried about being unemployed if we returned home. So I was not too surprised when three offers arrived in rapid succession: one from Memorial University in Newfoundland, one from the University of Regina, and the other from the University of Calgary. All promised a tenured position at my current rank of Associate Professor. Sandy and I were drawn to all three locations, for different reasons. But there remained that worry about my back, and the fear of my having a serious fall in the winter conditions of Saskatchewan and Alberta. Newfoundland, although appealing to our sense of adventure, would mean that we could never hope to be an integral part of the lives of our grandchildren.

Then came a phone-call from the Educational Foundations Department at the University of British Columbia. I was offered exactly what I suspect I was most hoping for all along. It was a permanent job beginning as an Associate Professor, and accompanied by the promise of a fairly rapid promotion to Full Professor. The climate of British Columbia was all that we could possibly hope for. And we would be in the same city as one of our grandchildren, with the distance from the others a manageable one. It's not surprising that I agreed almost immediately, phoning back to clinch the deal after a brief discussion with a very enthusiastic Sandy.

By late May we were on the way back to Canada. Our wonderful Australian experience was over. We had planned for a few days in Fiji in order to provide a break from the long flight across the Pacific. It proved to be all that we were hoping for, and more. We began by flying across the island in a small airplane. Then we rented a car and made our way back along the north coast. By stopping at tourist places along the way we were able to get a tremendously varied experience of the small, newly independent country. I recall most clearly being awakened early in the morning of our last day there to the sound of the Muslim call to prayer: my first experience of this. It was as if we had entered an entirely different world. Adding to this sense of uniqueness was the fact that Sandy had forty-eight hours in which to celebrate his sixty-third birthday, as we crossed the International Dateline. Then there were three glorious days on a beach in Hawaii. All in all, we spent most of our long return voyage basking in the after-glow of what was already recognized as a highlight of our life together. What lay ahead we could not know.

# Chapter 19

# EARLY RETIREMENT

We arrived in Vancouver from Australia with our hopes high. I had been assured of a permanent position at the University of British Columbia from September of 1976 on, beginning at my current rank of Associate Professor. With this previously established—albeit not yet in the form of a written contract—we felt we could concentrate for the remainder of the summer holiday on re-connecting with family and on house-hunting. Becoming acquainted with our granddaughter was the first priority. Upon visiting Sandy's son Dave and his wife Wendy, we found little Carolyn to be everything we had hoped for—and much more! Our second priority was buying a car, in order to get all the other necessities seen to. We purchased a little Renault which made it easier for us to get out to see my sister Myrtle and her husband Mike in their beautiful new house in North Delta. And, from there, we were able to drive further southeast to Langley where my mother had rented an apartment. We found her well-settled and happy to be in the same building as her sister Jessie.

Fortunately, it didn't take us long to find a new home for ourselves which filled all our expectations. And the price was right: $90,000 for an attractive house with two bedrooms and bathrooms plus finished basement, along with a garage and spacious front-and-backyard gardens. It was located on Angus Drive, just a half-block off Marine, the main road leading westward to the university. There was a beautiful little park across the street with a children's playground. And it was merely a short block southward to the north arm of the Fraser River dividing Vancouver from Richmond. The river bank was covered with hordes of blackberry bushes where Carolyn and Jennie later came to love helping us pick the berries. My brother Bob happened to be out visiting Mom at the time and we took advantage of this to ask for his advice on the house, in addition to that of the rest of the family.

Throughout these first months of what was supposed to be summer, Sandy and I were freezing most of the time, as our bodies had become so accustomed to the sub-tropics. It was then that we understood why British Columbia's south coast was referred to by tourists as 'two-sweater country'. However, our quick trips back to Regina and to Calgary soon helped us adjust to the Canadian climate. We discovered that our son Tom—now the father of a one-year-old—had recently given up his position in the furniture store for a more promising career in real estate. We found him busy with studies as well as the new job. Little Shane was tremendously cute and bright. But what grandmother ever thinks otherwise about the children of her offspring? In Regina, our son Don was progressing in his position with the automobile company, while his wife Vi—who seemed more than ever like a daughter to me rather than a 'daughter-in-law'—was continuing with her secretarial work in a law office. They also had exciting news: the prospect of our third grandchild in the late autumn. All this confirmed for us our choice to return to Canada.

On the way back to Vancouver, we decided to make a brief stop in Oyen. I was longing for one last look at my grandmother Ma's house, as I had heard that my uncle Ed was selling it. But locating the old homestead was far from easy. I had some difficulty even in recognizing the Oyen turn-off from the highway between Hanna and Alsask. Everything seemed so different. Oyen itself had spread considerably, so I found it impossible to find the two houses which we had rented during my childhood. Even the search for Ma's old home proved to be quite a challenge. It was the fact that the school was still in the same location which eventually solved my problem; and eventually we were able to park close to the remainder of what originally had been her brother George's homestead. In fact, only the house still stood in place, and where the out-buildings and the remainder of the estate had once been there was now seemingly endless construction.

Fortunately, my uncle Ed was home. I scarcely recognized the frail old man who opened the door to us. But this was nothing to the shock awaiting me after we had entered. None of Ma's beautiful old United-Empire-Loyalist furniture was in sight! Not one item could I find as I raced despairingly from room to room! My organ had disappeared as well, and even the pictures of Ma and my grandfather Armitage were absent from their familiar place on the wall. When I demanded answers from Ed he assured me that he had kept the paper photos—only the beautiful old original frames were gone. "I'm going to give the photos to Mabel," he assured me. Although my grandmother had always intended them for me, I didn't demur, as I was confident that my aunt Mabel was aware of this as well. In fact, only a couple of years later, when Ed was dying, she made a trip to Oyen and recovered the photos for me.

"You see, I was renting the place most of the time, while I still lived on the farm," Ed now explained lamely. "That worthless old furniture gradually disappeared, and it didn't matter all that much anyhow. I just figured that, when the renters were able to afford new stuff, they'd junked the old worn-out things. I couldn't blame them." Sandy snorted, obviously not believing that the old man could be so stupid. But I actually believed him. It was not so much stupidity that my uncle Ed had always suffered from as utter ignorance; and the renters no doubt guessed that it would be easy to cheat him of his valuable inheritance. So there remained none of the antique family furniture that I had been vaguely hoping to ship out for our new Canadian home. I had always been aware that Ma was depending on me to take care of it, as her sons and daughters—including my mother—were of the generation that considered only new items to be of any value. But, once more, I had failed Ma! The remainder of the journey back to Vancouver remains a blur to me.

My shock concerning the tragedy of this loss soon receded into the background, however, as other concerns demanded attention. Once we had become settled in our new house, and had bought the minimum of articles required to furnish it, I grew anxious to get acquainted with my new workplace and academic colleagues. Immediately upon arriving in the city I had phoned the Head of the Educational Foundations Department, but was disappointed to receive surprisingly little in the way of a welcome. After a few frustrating weeks of waiting for an invitation, I decided to explore the environs of the university on my own. I wandered around the entire area for several days, mapping out the location of the various buildings, without encountering anyone who knew anything about me. With some difficulty, I was finally able to obtain appointments with both the Departmental Head and the Dean of the Faculty. When the day of these meetings arrived, I was kept waiting for some time before finally having the opportunity to introduce myself to my new boss and, eventually, to the Dean as well. The latter was most welcoming, mentioning the fact that my textbook was being used in several of their courses. This was in direct contrast to my brief meeting with the departmental administrator a half-hour earlier, when I had felt much less comfortable—especially after having been introduced to my disappointingly tiny office in a set of small, temporary-appearing shacks near the main Education building.

Throughout all this, no one made any move to present me with a formal contract or to discuss the details of my new position, or of my upcoming classes. I found myself feeling increasingly uneasy as time went on, both that first day of meeting the administrators and throughout the remaining summer. A growing suspicion of something being dreadfully wrong began to haunt me. Had I made a terrible mistake in choosing this option among all those that had been—but were no longer—available to me?

Nevertheless, I was determined not to let this strange introductory experience colour what lay ahead. In the week previous to the beginning of the autumn semester I moved into the tiny office and attempted to get to know my new faculty colleagues. Some of them were quite friendly, especially the psychologists and those in Social Studies Education. On the other hand, I was gradually to learn that my interdisciplinary writings had made me rather unpopular with a certain few of the people in my own department, who felt that I was intruding in their areas of specialization. This was brought home to me in two vastly different ways by two professional gatherings at which I was invited to speak: one that very autumn on the Philosophy of Education held down in Oregon; and the other a full decade later at an International Sociology Conference in Montreal.

At Montreal, in the then-far-off days to come, I was having lunch with a group of fellow sociologists, when a newcomer joined our table and a friend proceeded to introduce us. "Most of us spend our entire professional lives specializing in one tiny section of the large, still-relatively unorganized area of sociology." she said. "But Pat, here, attempts to cover not only our entire field in one fell swoop, but to include psychology, anthropology and biology as well!" Everyone had a good laugh at my expense, myself included.

But the UBC situation in the late seventies was very different. No laughs for me then. Not long after my arrival I discovered that my new department's entire philosophy contingent were planning on attending the Oregon conference. So I informed them that I had been invited to speak about my textbook at it, and asked if I could accompany them on the trip. At first there was only shocked silence on their part. Then I was told that I must be mistaken, given that the conference was on philosophy. When I explained that both my book and PhD dissertation included considerable social-and-educational theory, their reaction was less than enthusiastic. Consequently, when the time came, I found myself making the trip down the coast all alone. And the next day, during the lively discussion following my talk, the only negative comments were from these members of my own department, along with a few graduate students who had obviously accompanied them on the trip: all of whom were strangely scattered throughout the hall.

If it hadn't been for the wonderful response I was receiving from my undergraduate classes by this time, I would have been extremely worried about what lay ahead for me in my new position. Indeed, my experience at this conference did serve to increase my concern sufficiently that I decided to speak to the Dean. I wanted to get his opinion on the fact that, since I had come on board, there had been no regular departmental meetings nor any other chances for me to get my position clarified and contract signed. My conversation with this very honest and pleasant man was illuminating, although not at all re-assuring.

He began by asking me what I'd been told about the position for which I was hired. I was embarrassed to have to confess that, since the phone call to me in Australia which had offered a tenured position at my current rank of Associate Professor, there had been nothing but silence on the entire matter. And, thus far, my monthly pay appeared to be much lower than what I'd been led to expect. The only explanation forthcoming had been a vague comment that the promised job was not yet open, and until it was, I would be working merely as a visiting lecturer.

"I'm afraid that's not true," the Dean said. "The tenured position which you were promised was, in fact, available when you were hired. But apparently it's being held by the Department of Educational Foundations pending the availability of a well-known Marxist sociologist who is currently teaching in the United States." The Dean had assumed I was aware of this, and thus the temporary basis on which I had accepted the job. He was obviously angry and ashamed that such a game had been played on his patch, and promised to do what he could to influence the administrators in my department. But he was reluctant to interfere in any formal way.

Dean Andrews then went on to explain why he felt his hands were tied. He said that it may well have been his interference in the past which initiated the problem. Apparently, he had pressured the Head of Educational Foundations—who was below him in administrative rank—to hire me when he heard that I was returning to Canada and would be available. "Here we have a Canadian scholar rather than an American one," he had admonished the Head. "One who happens to be a successful author of the first-ever textbook on the Sociology of Canadian Education; and a female at that. And all this in the academic world of today where qualified women are still so scarce! Why would you prefer an American male with no background whatsoever in Canadian education?"

But I had lost all hope in the instant the realization struck that I had merely been used to hold a position for someone considered my superior. This forced me to reflect on the meaning of an argument which I had partially overheard the previous day. One of my new colleagues had been referring rather scornfully to the idea of taking on a "post-menopausal female"! Now realizing that I had been the person about whom the two were angrily disagreeing, I could almost hear the walls of the stairwell leading to the culmination of my university-teaching career crashing down around me. In fact, I would have lost all confidence in the entire world of academia at that moment and in the months to follow had it not been for the positive attitude of a number of my new colleagues; and especially the honourable behaviour of that wonderful Dean of Education, Dr. John Andrews. And also the support expressed by letters written on my behalf by some of the students, once they heard the news of my approaching departure later in the spring.

Among all these other concerned people at the Education Faculty was George Tomkins who headed up the Social Studies Department. As soon as Dr. Tomkins heard I might be available he offered me a tenured position at my current rank, to begin in the summer of 1977. I decided not to take the job only because I felt that my involvement in that particular area—although extremely happy and productive—had been left behind me when I began to specialize in sociology during my latter years of teaching and study. I didn't really want to reverse all this.

I realized later that I had made a serious mistake, especially after the subsequent year when my choice of doing half-time work in the Early Childhood Department failed to provide the satisfaction I had hoped for. I actually worked full-time in this position (but at half-time pay) for the 1977-78 university year. I did this because of my great interest in the area—although voluntarily and with no expectation of appropriate remuneration. Besides teaching the usual complete load of classes, I developed a new Teacher Education program for the department. Then I heard that one of the tenured males in the faculty, who had done almost no work on the project, was giving public presentations concerning it in which he claimed full authorship. This struck me as the final straw. I had become so disillusioned with the academic life by that time that I decided, virtually on the spot, to retire early and devote my time to other pursuits.

The fact of my error in failing to accept the offer of the position in the Social Studies Department came home even more when, some years later, a former colleague told me that he had once queried either Dr. Andrews or Dr. Tomkins (I can't remember who it was) about things in his professional career that he might now wish had been done differently. Surprisingly, the answer was, "I think the worst mistake we all made was to let Pat Duffy Hutcheon slip through our fingers."

At the time it did indeed feel as if I were 'slip-slipping away' from everything my working life had aimed for and revolved around. It was a good thing for my self confidence that I had finally been officially graduated as a PhD at the beginning of January of 1977. Another positive was that I not only had Sandy's support in all this, but he was very vocal in his desire for me to make a new start. So much that he had witnessed directly, as well as heard about from me, was repulsive to this honest man with whom I now shared my life. It was his dependable presence in that life which helped me survive the last day of my academic teaching career. I remember it all too clearly.

I was invited to a quiet little farewell lunch in the professor's lounge by a young Dr. Foster, an educational psychologist who had become a good friend through his interest in my book. After that I returned to my office in the building housing the Early Childhood Department, in order to take one last look and to check that all my possessions had been removed. Then—saying goodbye to no one, and with no one saying goodbye to me—I went quietly out the door, wearing the long, wool rain-cape which had become stylish in that decade.

I don't think I ever wore that cape again, although it has hung in my closet all these years. For a while I felt as if I had completely lost my hard-fought-for identity as a professional educator, and I think now that I unconsciously identified my rain cape with that precious identity. I was aware that I had to make a new life for myself: one that couldn't include the cape and all that it stood for. So I immediately set about to accomplish this.

Not that my life wasn't full as it was. Sandy had begun working on a book of his own by then, although he was also spending regular interludes of several weeks at a time doing research back in Regina at the Saskatchewan Department of Agriculture. I was happy to have time to help with some editing and advising on his book, which had been accepted for publication by Press Porcepic of Toronto. It was a perceptive and knowledgeable book, and could have contributed a great deal to the effective operation of this country's economy, if it had only been publicized to a greater extent. It came out in 1980 under the title of *Rescue: Saving the Canadian Economy*. Typically, Sandy thought the title—selected by the publisher—was a bit presumptuous, but his own choice had probably been considered too subtle. When the book was published we celebrated with our old friends Don and Florence Grier, who had sold their business and moved to Victoria by then. I remember

Sandy saying, with an air of relaxation and relief, "Now I'm totally content to retire!" But I wasn't.

During the first year in our new Vancouver home we had established what was to become a close and lasting relationship with Sandy's niece Karen, the daughter of his sister Winnie. Karen was doing social work, and had returned just before that from a year in Sweden. We had a number of pleasant visits during the ensuing years with Karen and her husband, Don Fedora. I remember one in particular. We had been struggling to get our kitchen renovated, by a man who was good at what he did, but who did it at a frustratingly leisurely pace. One day Karen and Don arrived from Regina where they had then settled. As soon as our carpenter—who just happened to have dropped in that day to work for an hour or so—learned that Don was also in the renovation business, he came into the front room and joined in the conversation until it was time for him to go. As usual, the kitchen was left in a wild mess.

But at least that renovator provided us with lots of laughter and, ultimately, left us with a classy new kitchen. So that was a good thing. It was also a good thing that the remarkable privilege of 'grandparenting' was replete with wonderfully fulfilling experiences during those years of the late seventies and early eighties. The two of us bonded with all our grandchildren from the first glimpse of each eager little face. Included in this were the sons of my brother Don and his wife Donna—Lewis and Bryce Duffy—who always seemed like grandchildren to us as well. Fortunately, we saw a lot of them, even though they lived a considerable distance to the north, at Prince George. From the Christmas of 1976 onward, they made a practice of driving down to celebrate with us. Myrtle and Mike often joined us as well and, of course, my mother. We usually shared New Years Day with Dave and Wendy and family.

The spring of 1977 had brought a sister for Carolyn. She was named Jennifer, or 'Jennie'. I was 'Nana' to them and to little six-month-old Robbie in Regina. By the summer of 1979 Shane, in Calgary, had settled for 'Grama'—his own private version of 'Grandma'. His special spelling for it emerged once he taught himself to read and write between the ages of three and four by watching Sesame Street. As luck would have it we, along with his two Vancouver cousins, were to see a great deal of Shane throughout his early years. This was due not only to the fact that his mother had chosen to work full-time soon after his birth, but also that his parents' marriage was falling apart. Because Sandy was commuting to Regina doing part-time work for the government during the late seventies and early eighties, he was able to pick up Shane in Calgary and then return him on schedule. And, of course, it helped that Lana and I remained friends.

Shane was always an independent little fellow, possibly because his family situation forced him to mature beyond his years. The very first time Sandy and I had visited them at their home in Calgary after our return from Australia, when he was a one-year-old, I presented him with a dark, navy sweater which I had knit for him. He took one look, then tossed it over his shoulder saying, "Don't yike it!" I chided myself for not realizing that small children naturally prefer bright colours.

We developed a custom of his spending the summers with us from 1978 on. Consequently, he and the girls—Carolyn and Jennie—became extremely close. Another result was that Shane routinely spent his birthdays with us, as he was born in mid-July. One day Tom overheard him telling a little friend that 'Bancoober' was where the birthday cakes were. I recall his third birthday in particular, and the little party shared with Carolyn and Jennie. The following day I served us each with a piece of left-over cake. "And now I'm four!" Shane proudly exclaimed. All through his childhood his parents made it possible for us to continue this custom of having him with us for the summers—and, consequently—for his birthdays. Almost always, it meant that the girls would be there too.

I had a drawer full of costumes and other devices that the three children could put to creative use, and they did so with great abandon. There were seldom any problems among them, but one day I was surprised to overhear a loud argument. "You are SO twins!" Shane was saying in a loud voice, and the girls were responding just as vehemently that they were not. That reminded me of when Don and Vi came out for the Christmas of 1977, when Robbie was just one year old. I cooked the dinner that year, settling into what was to be a long tradition. Tom and Shane were present as well. Robbie was trying to address Carolyn by her name. I recall her insisting—albeit in her usual quiet manner—"It's CaroYIN! Not CaroYINE!"

One of my fondest memories of the girls is of the day the three of us came upon an outdoor artist on one of our many visits to Stanley Park. I noted the impressive portraits he had done, and asked if he would paint one of Carolyn and Jennie. He set to work immediately, and produced a wonderful picture of them, which hangs on the dining-room wall of their family home to this day. Both Sandy and I realized how fortunate we were to have these sorts of opportunities when the children were young. We always wished we could see more of our Regina grandchildren as well, but distance and lack of time prevented it.

In the summer of 1979, Tom moved out of the house he and Lana had purchased in Calgary and came to live with us, bringing with him only his television set and radio along with his private belongings. He was able to make himself at home in our basement, which served as a rough sort of apartment-like area providing a degree of privacy for him. He then enrolled in courses in real-estate appraisal and law at Langara College, and obtained part-time work close by. This settling-in process was somewhat disturbed by a stroke of bad luck, however. Only a few days after his arrival we went out for dinner to celebrate my fifty-third birthday. On our return we discovered that thieves had broken into the house. They had apparently begun by cleaning out the basement, then moved upstairs. They must have just started there when something interrupted them. We later learned from our neighbours that their dog had begun barking fiercely about the time this had all happened, so we assumed that was what had saved the majority of our possessions. But not poor Tom's. All of his belongings were gone! I marveled at the way he took this succession of losses with a remarkable placidity.

Not only was the summer and autumn of 1979 extremely busy for us, but the entire year to follow continued at the same rapid pace. The result was that I really had little time to miss teaching. For one thing, soon after arriving in Vancouver Sandy and I had joined the local Unitarians. Their beautiful new building wasn't officially called a 'church' in those days. The sign at the front proclaimed it as The Unitarian Centre. There we discovered a large group of humanists like ourselves. Freethinkers were still in the majority among North American Unitarians in those days, especially those living in the mid-western and western parts of both countries. We felt very much at home among these new friends, and both of us became active almost at once within this welcoming organization of 'fellow travelers'. I realize now that joining the Unitarians played a large part in my difficult transition process away from the teaching and academic life. Without them, I suspect I may have been in danger of losing my sense of professional identity.

It just so happened that the Unitarian connection led to one of the most intriguing and important activities of our lives. It was the time when the 'boat people' who had escaped from Vietnam were being held at camps in various locations in south-east Asia. A Unitarian friend and well-known actress, Joy Coghill, had obtained information through her international connections concerning a young seven-year-old refugee and her two teen-age brothers who were desperately in need of rescue. The three of us went to the Unitarians for help, as only charitable organizations were allowed by the Canadian government to officially sponsor immigrants. The Unitarians agreed to allow us to use their name, but specified that we would have to accept responsibility for all arrangements concerning transportation, as well as the costs and personal support entailed in rescuing the family and getting them successfully settled in Canada. We agreed, and proceeded to gather a small group of members to share in the task. One of these was a young male university student who left his studies for a year so that he could contribute to the work involved. Another was a great humanist Unitarian named Joyce Griffiths. Sandy and I accepted major responsibility for helping the three youngsters get accustomed to life in their new home and begin acquiring the basic elements of Canadian culture.

We found a basement apartment for them in East Vancouver, and even had the fridge stocked with basics on the day that Sandy and I and the young student met them at the airport. Apparently their entire contingent of Vietnamese refugees had been landed first in Edmonton. We didn't know this, so were profoundly puzzled when the little group we were waiting for entered the airport in bulky winter parkas and snow boots. But among them all there was only one threesome containing a small girl. So I approached them, with the two men at my heels. Sure enough, it was the Giangs: Nguyet, Hoa and Minh. They were actually of Chinese ancestry, as their father had previously emigrated to Vietnam from China.

Getting them settled into their new home was a bit hectic, as the interpreter we had arranged for failed to appear. Only the little girl seemed to know a few words of English and, of course, we were ignorant of both Mandarin and Vietnamese. I rushed madly from door to door in the immediate neighbourhood—where a number of Chinese Canadians lived—attempting to find someone who understood Mandarin. But they all spoke Cantonese. Finally I gave up on that, and we decided that taking our little family out for a good meal was now our first priority. I tried to communicate this, but Nguyet got the wrong message. She rushed to the fridge and began reaching for some eggs and grabbing the frying pan. I soon learned that this response was all-too-typical of her. Already, at the tender age of seven, she saw her role in life as tending to the needs of others. This was how she had ended up in this situation in the first place. The parents of their large family had wanted one of the older girls to accompany the two sons, whom they were sending off in a boat as a means of escaping conscription into the Vietnamese army. But none of the girls would agree to risk the dangers, even in order to assume their typical role in that culture, where males were concerned. So, according to an essay she later wrote for school, Nguyet had spoken up.

"I will go," she said, "I want to see the world." But, as I was to learn by watching and listening to her through all the years to follow, what she had really wanted was to look after her brothers. And she did indeed spend her school years serving their needs and ultimately those of the remainder of her large family—after they had immigrated—rather than her own.

We soon found beginning jobs for the boys in the automobile industry and got Nguyet settled into school. Many of our Unitarian friends were helpful. One was our dentist, Don Marshall, who repaired their teeth for free. Others organized into small groups to rescue two additional branches of the Giang family who were also in refugee camps. Altogether, the project kept us very busy, but Sandy and I agreed that it was one of the most rewarding experiences of our lives.

Minh's first birthday in his new country was spent at Wendy and Dave's. We all wanted them to learn about how Canadians celebrated birthdays, which was not one of their customs. The three Giang youngsters seemed to enjoy the family gathering, especially the chocolate birthday cake which I had baked. Tom and Shane were with us as well. I particularly recall Shane cuddling up to his father on the sofa and saying, over and over, "Daddy's here." Shane and Nguyet had become good friends from their very first meeting. And, of course, he always loved being at Carolyn and Jennie's place. It was not only because they played so well together but also what they had available to play with. I don't think Shane had ever seen such an abundance of interesting toys. And I'm sure that Nguyet had not.

During this busy period we set up table-tennis equipment in our basement, which the youngsters loved to use when they were visiting. Actually, Sandy and I played on it sometimes as well. One day we decided to re-adjust the table and I, in my usual awkwardness with anything requiring technical 'know-how', somehow got my fingers in the wrong position. Two of them on the left hand were suddenly—and neatly—sliced off at the upper knuckle. Sandy phoned 911 and, fortunately, help arrived very quickly. The fingers were re-connected within a couple of hours. Interestingly, in all the years since, those two fingers have been stronger, and the fingernails less fragile, than is the case with any of the others.

Our lives became increasingly hectic from the beginning of 1980 on, so we were fortunate to have Tom to look after the place while we were away from home. We traveled to Regina in late January to see our new granddaughter, who had arrived on the 24th. While enjoying getting acquainted with beautiful little Tanya, we received devastating news from the west coast. A niece of Sandy's, Marion Powell, along with her husband Roger de Mong and three young children—Laura, David and Kathryn—had all been killed in a head-on collision with a truck on the Vancouver Island highway. It was only a month or so since we had visited them, which we did fairly often in those days as we had always been close. Marion had baked fresh scones especially for us.

Then, a few months later, yet another dreadful event occurred: this one out in Acadia Valley. Tom's cousin Wayne Burke had shot himself dead with a shotgun in the shed behind Tom and Joyce's house. He was the only surviving child of my former sister and brother-in-law, Joyce and Tom Burke. Tom arranged to go to the funeral in the company of his uncle Bill Westcott, who was then living in Victoria. It would have been very difficult for me to return to the Valley for such an occasion and, fortunately, I had a good reason for not attending. Sandy and I were on the point of leaving on a trip down to Chattanooga, Tennessee, to visit our friends from Regina days: Danette and Bill Riddlespurger and their daughter Beth. Danette was then teaching at the university there while Bill's work-career was, as usual, on the 'iffy' side. And we had Mom's eighty-first birthday to celebrate before we left. She was happy to have it in her apartment, and even cooked the dinner herself, with her sister Jessie there as well. Sadly, it was to be the last such celebration in her own place, as Jessie became ill only a month or so later and went into a seniors' residence. Soon after, Myrtle persuaded Mom to move from her apartment to their place on what was to be a temporary basis. We were on our trip south at the time and weren't aware of all this until our arrival back home.

The visit with Danette, Bill and their daughter was most enjoyable. Beth seemed to have become so 'grown up'. As always, it was wonderful to get re-acquainted with her. She had to be left behind while they showed us all around the countryside, however, as school was still on. Bill and Danette provided experiences for us in a part of the United States about which we knew very little. These included exploring Lookout Mountain in the Grand Canyon by the Tennessee River and even driving as far as Atlanta, Georgia and Williamsburg, Virginia.

The voyage back to Vancouver was even more adventure-filled than had been our travels with the Riddlespurgers. It happened that the return flight was on May 19, the day after the volcano on Mount St. Helens erupted. We had no inkling of the gravity of the situation until we learned, while in the air, that our airplane had to travel by way of Spokane and then circle back toward the Vancouver airport, rather than making the usual temporary landing in Seattle. It didn't help us relax to be told by our attendants that ours was the first flight allowed over that part of Washington and British Columbia since the volcanic eruption. The cabin was filled with smoke; so much so that we could scarcely see our fellow passengers. Our plane was immersed in dark cloud, and we could see nothing else until just before reaching the runway at the Vancouver airport.

We had little time to relax and sympathize with Tom over the ghastly loss of his cousin Wayne, as we were slated to attend a Hutcheon family reunion out at Rosetown in early June. It's a good thing we made it, as it turned out to be the last one ever held. In the case of Sandy's in-laws—the Powell clan—it has always been a vastly different matter as, for many decades, they continued to organize one almost every year. On the other hand, the uniqueness of this Hutcheon reunion made it an especially memorable get-together. We had the chance to visit with members of Sandy's entire extended family, and in the rural area and on the original homesteads settled by their ancestors. Dave and Wendy and the girls were there as well as Don and Vi and their two children.

That summer Tom moved back to Calgary, where he obtained a management position with the real-estate branch of Canada Trust. He and Lana had decided to give their marriage one more try. Shane came out for his usual birthday celebration with us. During this visit I launched him on the road to becoming a highly skilled swimmer as a result of lessons at our local Kerrisdale swimming pool. Dave and Wendy and the girls had moved to France for a year, where Dave was to work at that country's nuclear accelerator. It was a great loss for us, and for Shane as well. At the end of the holiday, he informed us gravely that he was starting pre-school soon, and would no longer be able to visit us as often.

"I can't be coming out here all the time," he said, "I got my own work to do now!" But we managed to see the following New Year in with him and his parents, on our way home from a Christmas spent with our other delightful grandchildren, Robbie and Tanya. My strongest memory of that happy occasion in Regina is a shopping expedition with Vi and Robbie, in which I was assigned to keep track of him in a department store. I had quite a time performing my task, as the little rascal made a game of hiding from me among the racks of women's clothing.

For the entire year of 1982 we seem to have been entirely focused on family, including our new family of the three young Giangs. By then our little group of Unitarian friends had also sponsored the youngsters' aunt and uncle and three young children, as well as an older sister and her husband and two little boys. Patience Towler, a tireless volunteer throughout the years, took on the kind of personal responsibility that Sandy and I had assumed in the case of the first two families, for integrating the third one into the Canadian culture. The extent of her success was demonstrated years later when both boys—speaking perfect English—became medical doctors. In fact all of our adopted youngsters turned out to be successful in their chosen careers.

Other family doings during that period included Shane's visit at Easter, and Sandy's brother Neil's move from Ottawa to live in a seniors' residence near us. Neil had retired a few years previously from his position as Head of the Building Engineering Branch of the National Research Council of Canada, and had come to the decision that he wanted to spend his final years close to us. His lungs were in critical condition by then from a lifetime of heavy smoking, and he had recently lost his longtime male friend who shared a summer cottage with him. We spent a lot of time together from then on. He still had all his keen intelligence and memory and, as always, I found conversation with him both illuminating and satisfying. Not long after he arrived we all enjoyed what was to be the one and only visit of their youngest sister, Muriel, from New England, along with her daughter Merry.

In June we were off to Regina to catch up with family there. On the way, we stopped over in the Okanagan at the summer cottage of my cousin Thelma Dray—the only daughter of Les and Annie Armitage. They had invested in a piece of land along one of the lakes, where they were then proceeding to build a number of cottages. She and her husband, who was already successful in Alberta's thriving oil business when they met, were then spending their winters in Texas, where they had purchased a home. They also owned a beautiful house in Calgary's upper-class district of Mount Royal.

Don and Vi and children returned in July for another visit and were there, along with Shane, for his seventh birthday. Then, on the first day of August, Dave and Wendy and the girls arrived home from France. Both girls were already surprisingly fluent in French. Apparently Jennie hadn't said a word in class for the first term at kindergarten, then suddenly began to speak French in her sleep. From that time on she had no problems communicating at school.

We celebrated Easter of 1983 by hiking in the North Shore hills with Dave and Wendy and the girls. Not long after that, Mom came to live with us. However, the plan was for it to be only temporary, while we waited to get her established in a seniors' home. Myrtle was arranging for a place in a very pleasant Danish residence in south-east Vancouver, where her meals would be supplied. Mom was not very happy about the move, and would have preferred to remain with us. However, we felt that, with Neil requiring a lot of our time and attention—and given the fact that she was still well able to care for herself—we just weren't prepared to take that on at the time.

There was an additional reason as well. We had another major travel plan in the offing.

Tom and Lana's attempt at reconciliation had failed and, in December of 1983, he married a fellow real-estate broker, Ellyn Mendham. She had two children: twelve-year-old Derek and Dana, who was ten. On our first trip out to get acquainted with our new family, we took them all to dinner. Shane, then eight years old, was a bit annoyed when the other two children began to address us as Grandma and Grandpa. "They're MY grampa and grama!" he exclaimed, sidling closer to us. But he soon became reconciled to the changed family situation and, before long, was happily following his new sister and brother around. During this period of change, the hope Tom continued to cling to was that he and Lana could agree to share in the parenting of Shane. There was little chance of a father gaining legal custody in those days, regardless of a mother's problems. Fortunately, we were able to continue having Shane visit frequently, as Tom was most cooperative in continuing to deliver him to the airport for his Grandpa to pick him up.

In March of 1984 we took off on something which we had been planning for several years: a return trip to Australia. Mom was well established in the seniors' residence by then, and we had a good visit with her on the day before our departure. Much to her surprise she was finding the close-knit little community a happy and supportive place to be. She had even made friends with a man who had a room in the same hall; and she soon also found a couple of compatible female neighbours as well. This was not customary for her, as she had possessed few close friends throughout her life. So I felt more sanguine abut her situation than I had for some time.

Our plan for the Australian trip included visits with a number of friends, along with our nephew Gordon Baker and his family. Also, we hoped to see a few areas of the country that we had missed when living there. We arranged to leave our house in the care of a male friend. That turned out to be most fortuitous as, at the moment our plane took off, I realized I'd forgotten to remove a load of washing from the machine. But with our home in reliable hands, I was free to 'wash' all such mundane concerns from my mind, and settled down into the eighteen-hour trip to Auckland. Once there, because of a lengthy wait in the airport, it was another seven hours before we landed in Melbourne. We weren't very favourably impressed with the city, largely because a lengthy walk through a 'tough' neighbourhood was required if we were to get to the downtown area. We were happy to leave, three days later, for Adelaide, where a welcome at the home of Ericka and Gordon Baker awaited us—including our first meeting with their daughters Aislin and Haydee.

The following day they left the children with a baby-sitter in order to for us to tour the city and environs. We began with a look at the 'posh' private school where Gordon was teaching, then went on to explore a couple of marvelous beaches, ending the afternoon with dinner at the Hilton hotel in the heart of the city. Here we had one of the most memorable experiences of the entire trip. We had just finished what we all considered a wonderful meal, when Gordon suddenly leapt up to head for the bathroom. He had taken only a few steps when he collapsed, unconscious, on the floor. We all three rushed over to him. The next instant, upon suddenly realizing my purse was left on the table, I turned back to retrieve it. That was the last thing I remember until my awakening some time later in a hospital emergency room. Obviously, the old low-blood pressure problem had kicked in. By then Gordon was beginning to recover, but Ericka had succumbed as well. Eventually we were all able to return to the Bakers' home, where we spent the remainder of the night with the three of us racing past one another back and forth to the bathroom. Typically, Sandy slept through it all, snoring peacefully in accompaniment to the noisy rattling and roaring of his stomach.

A few days later we were all fully recovered and off to Sydney for a great tour of our most beloved areas. While there, we visited briefly with Vivien and Alan Millar-Rosen, who were relatives of a Vancouver Unitarian friend, Marianne Millar. Marianne had been one of the last Jews to have escaped to Britain from Germany in Hitler's time. Then it was farewell to Gordon and family and on to Canberra, the capital city of Australia, which we had never seen before. We now had close friends there, as Pat Malikail, the daughter of my old friend and colleague, Joe, was working for Foreign Affairs and representing Canada in Australia. Her husband Brad Gilmour, who also worked for our Federal government, was with her. From Canberra we traveled up to Brisbane, where a warm welcome from old friends awaited us. We spent most of our time with the Thompsons, re-visiting former haunts. One major shock and disappointment was the discovery that the downtown area had been greatly altered, with the beautiful old opera house demolished and the quaint little streets with their wooden overhangs all gone to make room for the new.

Our last big Australian jaunt was a bus tour around the Townsville and Cairns areas. Then it was off to Auckland to give that city a thorough exploration—rather than, as usual, merely passing through—before departing on the flight to Fiji for a week-long stopover on our way home. We had an unexpectedly pleasant ride to the airport. Our cab driver was a handsome, intelligent and knowledgeable Maori who drove a methane-fueled car—something widely used in New Zealand, he said. Our flight to Nadi was smooth and pleasant. But, once there, we had a four-hour wait in the insufferable heat. Then we took off for Suva in a most unsubstantial-looking, small twin-propeller aircraft. It was so crowded that we couldn't even move our arms. Miraculously, it seemed at the time, we eventually became airborne and laboured over green valleys and rugged, jungle-covered mountains—struggling through increasingly unfriendly banks of smouldering clouds. After what felt like an eternity, the pilot managed to land us safely in the pitch-black night at the airport near Suva.

We were again fortunate in our choice of cab driver from among the insistent hordes surrounding us at the exit. He was an Indian Fijian by the name of Ali—not as pushy and obviously tricky as most. His car was in good shape; he drove masterfully and even tried to point our a few sights through the blackness. The sensation I experienced was a strange one. The road was dark and narrow, with people walking everywhere, drifting in and out of our vision. How our driver managed to avoid hitting them I couldn't imagine. We actually got occasional glimpses into small homes lining the driveway. Many had walls of bright blue or pink, or a rainbow mixture of all these, with white curtains on the open windows.

Our hotel was a familiar and grand oasis in a desert of strangeness. Friendly and beautifully dressed Fijians welcomed us and showed us to our rooms. This was a far cry from what we experienced next day, as we sallied forth to do some exploring. Suva struck us as far more seedy than it had been eight years before, with the street hawkers and merchants much more objectionable. Even the new artifact and trade centre was rendered most unpleasant for us by the rude pushiness of the sellers. On the day following this, an extremely heavy tropical downpour struck, and we were confined to our hotel. After that we made a three-hour journey to Naviti, where we had arranged to stay for several days. We called on our reliable cab driver, Ali, and had a pleasant trip. However, the location proved to be disappointing for me, but it may have been because I suffered from another bad bout of food poisoning for almost the entire period.

The remainder of our flight across the Pacific provided us with a further unpleasant experience—one that was thoroughly frightening as well. Our seats were in the tail of the airplane, which probably made things worse when we flew into a fierce storm over the Pacific. The plane was tossed around in such a terrifying way that, for about a half-hour, I was sure we would never survive. Of course I became ill once more. Sandy, as always, remained calm and tried to keep me so. But I kept asking myself why we had put our lives at such risk, and vowed never to make another trip back to Australia. And we never did.

Throughout these years of immersion in family matters and in travel, I was also continuing to pursue professional interests. From the moment of my departure from UBC, I had been determined to find some niche where my training and skills could be put to use. Three opportunities were already on the horizon on that final day of my teaching career, when my cloak-covered self had silently slipped away from all that I had worked toward for all those many years. An administrator in the Dean's office had suggested an available opening with the Vancouver School Board which she thought I might wish to consider. Another was the new Knowledge Network which was then still in the planning stage. After a very positive interview with the latter, I felt that I might well be considered for one of their administrative roles.

Then a third possibility entered the picture: so attractive that I opted out of competition for the other two. As I recall, this third option had come about through my connection with my longtime friend Irving Rootman, who then had a leading position in the Health Promotion Branch of the Department of Health and Welfare in Ottawa. I received a definite offer to head up a national program which was still in the planning stage: one with the objective of creating the "first smoke-free generation in Canada". I was given to understand that I could do some of the work from Vancouver, so accepted quite readily, and had signed a contract for the still-non-existing position by the autumn of 1978.

The following winter brought a stressful 'waiting game', as I kept expecting definitive word concerning the new program and my participation in it, but nothing arrived. Then came the Federal election of March of 1979, and the Liberal government was replaced by Joe Clark's Progressive Conservatives. I soon learned that this 'progressiveness' did not include what was no doubt perceived as a costly, and possibly Utopian, enterprise. So I received word that the project had been cancelled, along with my contract. I understand that, some two years later, a similar effort did get underway, under the title of "Generation of Non Smokers" and, in 1985, Health Canada launched a successor to it under the title of "Break Free". But I was out of the picture by then.

During the early 1980s I was only able to retain my hard-won professional identity through research and volunteer work of various kinds, few of which involved remuneration other than for travel expenses. Again because of my connection with Irving Rootman, I was hired by the Health Promotion Branch in Ottawa on an informal basis as a research advisor for their National Health

Promotion Survey. We conducted, and analyzed the results of, two surveys in all. Also during this period, due to the influence of another helpful friend and fellow author, Blanche Howard, I became the British Columbia director of the Ottawa-based Vanier Institute of the Family. In addition, I was then also doing research for the Vancouver Council of Women on day-care and nursery-school needs and services in the city of Vancouver. My study, "Day Care and Nursery School Needs for the City of Vancouver" was published in 1982. Soon after this I was interviewed regarding the subject of day care on a national CBC program. There were a small group of us and, as usual in those days, I was the only female. All during the program, the men were addressed as 'Professor' or 'Doctor', while the host referred to me merely as 'Mrs'. When I voiced an objection to this treatment afterward, the talk-show host couldn't seem to comprehend what my problem was.

For the summer of 1981 I taught a course on the Sociology of Education at the summer session at the University of Regina. That was a great opportunity for me to spend time with family and renew old friendships. Myrtle traveled with me as far as Calgary, and we stayed overnight with our aunt Mabel. The night was made particularly memorable by the fact that Mabel had three chiming clocks in the house, each of which rang at a slightly different time. After the sleepless night I took 'the long way round' to Regina by driving southward by way of Medicine Hat, to visit with my old friends, June and Bill Smith. A terrifying storm struck during the drive, but I managed to make it through. The Smiths had sold part of their prosperous farm to neighbours by then, and were renting the remainder of it to the purchasers. June was recovering from breast cancer. Soon afterward they moved to Victoria, where they bought a home, and began a long period of commuting to Arizona for the winters.

Also in 1982, the Vanier Institute published "The Effects of Media Violence on Human Development" which I had completed with the aid of a Unitarian friend—a psychologist and former college instructor, Al Cox. Al was a gifted folk singer as well, and later became a fellow hiker and member of the BC Humanists. During this busy period yet another highly interesting but demanding role came about through my involvement with the Unitarian church. I was selected to be the Canadian representative on their international Fellowship Committee: the body responsible for assessing graduated candidates for the ministry and recommending either their acceptance or rejection as ministers. I was also the committee's contributing sociologist, among a small group of professionals which included a philosopher and psychologist in addition to a number of leading Unitarian ministers. This role required a considerable amount of travel, as we gathered for regular meetings at least three times a year: in Boston, Chicago and San Francisco.

I enjoyed this opportunity to meet and discuss ideas—and to wrestle with important decisions carrying long-range consequences for the American and Canadian Unitarian Universalist movement—in the company of a highly intelligent and knowledgeable group of professionals. Also, the making of regular visits to those three great cities was a once-in-a-lifetime privilege. Boston was particularly special in the experiences it offered: especially Beacon Hill Park and the farmers' market in the harbour. Not so pleasant, however, was the marked change in direction within the committee which I was observing during my four years of service. It was a change opposed by the other two academics as well, but supported by an increasing number of younger ministers within the group. We seemed to be witnessing a shift away from the scientific naturalism of the Unitarianism of former times, and back toward a variety of approaches to some sort of undefinable form of supernaturalism. I even began to notice that some formerly humanist students, with whom I had become acquainted at the various universities involved in training future Unitarian ministers, were beginning to buy into the new world view. Something was obviously happening in those theology classes. After a few heated disagreements between the academic and ministerial components of the committee, I decided to leave when my first four-year term was finished, although I was asked to remain.

Around the same time, I began to consider ending my participation in all my Ottawa-based activities as well. There were a number of reasons for this. The Health Promotion branch didn't really need my research help any more. And, perhaps partly because I was one of only two female members of the Board of the Vanier Institute of the Family, I had felt for some time that I was not really being very effective there. Neither were any of the other members, for that matter, as the directors were obviously in charge of the operation. I don't think it was an issue of sexism, but I enjoyed a moment during a discussion concerning a proposal to make it mandatory that Board members be divided evenly along gender lines. I was against this kind of reverse sexism. Anyway, it wasn't necessary, as I pointed out at one of the last meetings I attended. "Why don't we try selecting members strictly according to ability?" I suggested. "Who knows—we might even end up with a few males!"

One of the major reasons why I decided to end all commitments involving travel was that my mother's health took a serious turn for the worse just after we had left for Australia. Upon our return we learned that she had rapidly deteriorated to the stage where she required full-time care. She was staying with Myrtle temporarily; but by the late autumn of 1984 was insisting on being transferred to our home. Sandy, who had cared for his own mother during the last year of her life, was more than willing for us to assume this responsibility. So, the two of us became my mother's major care-givers. Because of the seriousness of her condition I had finally found myself—in actual fact—immersed in the isolation of early retirement!

# Chapter 20

# THE GOLDEN AGE

During much of the year of 1985, the very idea that Sandy and I might experience anything even remotely resembling a 'Golden Age' would have been inconceivable had it not been for our discovery, a few years previously, of a group of active hikers in their mid-fifties and over. These remarkable people had coined the term to describe their hiking organization. We were hiking with them for several years by the time my mother became bedridden, although my attendance was usually somewhat irregular due to professional commitments. The club proved to be the major support for us throughout a very difficult time: my mother's last, cruel year of life, when Sandy and I cared for her in our home. Ever since our second year in Australia my back had been relatively pain-free: a necessary prerequisite for a full-time care-giver as well as for a pastime as a happy 'Golden Ager'. So each Thursday we hired a 'home helper' to look after Mom for the day, while we hiked with this wonderful group of friends in the surrounding mountains, sea-walls, lakes and meadows. Looking back, I can't imagine how Sandy and I could have made it through that stressful period without our weekly break. It was a day when we could be totally free from all worries and responsibilities—immersed in the wilds and wonders of the beautiful British Columbia coastal area, and in the company of like-minded companions.

The Golden Age Hiking Club was pioneered in 1978 by an amazing pair of people, John Liebe and Karla Maidstone. The initiator of the idea was John, who had previously divided all his time between solitary mountain hiking and attempting to start a Vancouver branch of the World Federalists. The advertising and most of the organizing of the hiking club was done by Karla Maidstone. Both were immigrants from central Europe, with Jewish backgrounds and fascinating histories. Another early member was Fred Fuchs, who knew the mountains surrounding Vancouver like the back of his hand, and immediately became chief hike planner and leader. And there was Julie, his wife, an established and gifted artist, who loved painting mountain scenery. Some of the other pioneers were Minnie Inglis, Thomas Wagner, Margaret Lawrence, Klara Patriasz, Ruth Liebkowsky, Dick Herzer, Hilde Godideck, Ilse Heisted, Myrtle Harrigan, and Lila Levitski.

The club first came to our attention through another of these early members: Helen Fairley, who happened to be the next-door neighbour of Dave and Wendy. It was during the year that they and the two little girls spent in France. We became acquainted with Helen because of our regular visits to the Hutcheon house, checking on the renters and responding to their needs. From the very first, Sandy and I were attracted to the varied and interesting group accompanying us on the hiking trail. By the time we joined, members included people such as Andy Mate, a Hungarian refugee who played the mouth organ as we hiked; and Joan Ostry, who was already familiar to me because she had led the Calgary branch of The Voice of Women when I was teaching there in the early sixties. Altogether, it was the comradeship and intelligent conversation with these people, and numerous others, that proved to be as 'golden' to Sandy and me as was the actual hiking.

However, the notion of the concept of the 'golden age' being applied in a more general way to the current period in our lives only began to occur to me in late autumn, following the death of my poor, long-suffering mother. My major response at the end of it all—after the first rush of irretrievable loss—was an overwhelming sense of relief, as the realization struck home that we had all been freed. For her, it was freedom from the seemingly endless months of increasing agony, as her bones began to collapse into her vital organs. All we could do through this was to take turns sitting beside her, with no effective and safe way to ease her pain, for her digestive system was unable to handle even small Aspirin tablets. In those days, family doctors were not allowed to provide morphine for patients if they chose to die at home. Therefore, when Mom's death finally came, what we experienced most was a release from the helplessness of watching her suffer. So I guess it was not surprising that, with this sad ordeal finally over, we made a long-postponed trip to Regina and Calgary to visit family and friends. Sandy had persuaded me that extending those 'days off' with the Golden Age hikers to actually getting away from it all for a while—even from our own house with its memory-laden rooms—was what we needed most at the time.

Our trip provided us with exactly that. First, there was the chance to see Tom and Shane and to become better acquainted with our beautiful and capable new daughter-in-law, Ellyn Mendham, as well as with her children, Derek and Dana. Then it was on to Regina, to spend additional quiet family time with Don and Vi and re-establish bonds with our other grandchildren, Rob and Tanya. It was a relief to find both sons happily established in their people-oriented professions: Don in the automobile sales business and Tom in real estate. This family visiting was in itself almost like a revival of sorts. As was the chance to renew close connections with old friends, such as Joe and Cecilia Malikail and Art and Jane Hillabold, and with Sandy's sister Meg and her husband Les Crossman, another former colleague and friend of mine. There were also two of Sandy's nieces who now had families and were settled in Regina. These were Kay Butler and Heather Sinclair, the daughters of Meg and Les. Most important, the experience in its entirety helped us mark and celebrate what amounted to a major turning point in our lives. I had finally made the decision to end my hectic period of profession-related travel and turn to other, less stressful, pursuits.

Meanwhile, the hiking club had been growing rapidly, and I soon became sufficiently familiar with the trails to take my turn at leading our weekly wanderings. Sandy often helped me in this, although he was not interested in assuming leadership himself. He preferred to commit his time to working on the trail in Deep Cove, the upkeep of which our club chose to assume responsibility when we joined the 'Adopt a Trail Program'. For a number of years I led the hike up Hollyburn Peak as well as a much easier one in Lighthouse Park. However, my favourite of all our great hikes was the one requiring one of the longer drives—always a key part of the day for me, as I was a designated driver. It was the trail up to Garibaldi Lake, a virtual paradise of turquoise water located just to the south of Whistler.

Most of our hikes went well, but once in a while something either scary or funny—or a combination of both—would happen, as carefully laid plans went awry. For example, I managed to lose a member of the group one day in Lighthouse Park. We had arrived at the end of the three-hour hike when I did my count and discovered we were one person short. A couple of us went to look for the missing woman, repeating the entire hike—only to discover her wandering in circles among the trees almost back at the starting point. She had stopped for a smoke and, knowing we would not approve, told no one of her intentions. Then she found herself utterly lost.

We had a different kind of pleasant diversion in the autumn of 1985, when my old friend and former renter of the basement of my Calgary house,

Bob Gowen, came for a brief visit. He was by then a history professor at the University of North Carolina, and was in the city to research the story of the Japanese settlers in the Lower Mainland—prior to their having been uprooted en mass during the Second World War, with no remuneration for their land or businesses. From the moment Bob arrived at the door I realized that his famous sense of humour was still intact. As I directed him down to the basement, where our guest room and bath were located, he replied—subtly referring to the old days when he and Nobuko had rented our basement in Calgary—"Don't worry! I know my place."

During Bob's stay with us, I treated him to as much of the fresh local fish as possible, assuming it would be a great treat. After his return flight he phoned from his home in Greenville to let us know he'd arrived safely, and to thank us for our hospitality. "Only one problem on the plane," he said. "Every time we flew over a river I was struck by an irrepressible urge to leap down into the water and swim upstream."

With all our hiking, grandparenting, traveling and entertaining during this 'golden' time, I had decided to take somewhat of a break from research and writing as well as professional traveling. However, I did enjoy the fact that a 1986 publication of the American Unitarian Universalist *World* included an article of mine which had been based on a talk presented earlier at a service for the Vancouver Unitarians. It was called "Suffer the Little Children" and dealt with the explosion of various forms of violence and pornography in Western culture: whether virtual or real. After a discussion of the possibility for a future of widespread cultural decadence and even barbarism, my article concluded with the following:

What will be the fate of our own society? Will we continue to expand the limits of tolerance for the kind of deviance that destroys human dignity—until the ratio of barbarians to sensitive, caring persons is overwhelming, and there is no safe refuge for our grandchildren? Think about where you stand on this issue. Our ancestors understood that there exist social imperatives no less firmly grounded in the nature of things than are the physical laws of gravity. One of the most fundamental of these is the requirement of a safe, protective, nurturing social environment during the relatively lengthy period of childhood: a necessity for the continuing evolution of the species. Another is the law of consequences, operating within human social groupings as the choices of individuals initiate irrevocable and relentless ripples of effects throughout the entire network of society. There is no family so educated, so affluent or so powerful that it can keep those ripples out. Once we allow our cultural stream to be polluted, there is no place to hide. The danger is no longer just to the most vulnerable ones: to the children of the poor; or to the children of those already rendered violent and dehumanized. To paraphrase the words of Arthur Miller in his play, *All My Sons*, "They are all vulnerable now, and we are all accountable for all of them. They are all our children."

This publication coincided with the beginning of one of the most 'golden' of our experiences of the period. It was the Canadian National Exposition of 1986—'Expo' as we all referred to it—which took place in Vancouver. Sandy and I felt as though we were operating a hotel throughout the entire late spring and summer. And so we were, to the extent that we had asked family and friends to plan ahead for the timing of their visits and to check with us for 'openings'. Almost all of our extended family and long-time friends came out to Vancouver during that exciting period. Sandy and I spent almost every day of every week—except for our hiking Thursdays—at the Expo grounds showing visitors around. We got off to a good start on the very first week of the show, with the arrival of Cecilia and Joe Malikail from Regina. I think it was during that wonderful summer that I fell in love with the False Creek area of Vancouver city. We spent so much happy time there with our various grandchildren, visiting every part of the fairgrounds and going on all the rides. Rob and Tanya loved experiencing Expo when their parents brought them out, and we attended countless times with Carolyn and Jennie.

Tom and Ellyn and family arrived later in the summer. It was fun for me to watch Shane enjoying the company of his new sister Dana and brother Derek. Shane had been with them that summer since school-closing in Hanna, and they had spent some time as a family at a cottage in the mountains before arriving in Vancouver. I could see that the three youngsters were bonding by then, and the Expo sojourn obviously helped. The arrival of Tom and Ellyn and family had aroused a vivid memory in me of Dana's first visit with us. It was not long after her mother had married Tom. She asked me about the pictures of my ancestors which were kept on the wall. I proceeded to tell her all about them. "And now they're my ancestors!" she then exclaimed happily.

Hiking had become such an important part of our lives by the end of that magical year of 1986 that Sandy and I began to plan on attending one of the many 'walking' tours which were then common in Britain. We selected a couple organized by the Holiday Fellowship, a non-profit organization that had owned and operated old country houses as hiking or 'rambling' centres throughout the United Kingdom for about seventy-five years. Our first tour was planned for the Cornwall coastal area, to be followed by second one to Barton-on-Sea and the Isle of Wight. We set off on our journey in the spring of 1987. It proved to be one of those great adventures that one can look back on, forever happy at having grasped the opportunity when it arose.

After a long, sleepless night we landed at Gatwick on the eighth of June, and then traveled by train to Par, Cornwall. There we discovered that a couple of hiking friends, John and Dora Fulton, had been riding the same train. The four of us shared a taxi for the four miles to Fowey Hall, fascinated by the narrow, twisting country lanes our driver had to navigate. Even more intriguing was the lovely old manor house where worn-looking, but comfortable, bedrooms awaited us. The only problem was that all during the night we were awakened by the creaking of the ancient wooden floors. The sound resembled nothing so much as a dragon bellowing and groaning. After that, I could better understand the origin of many of the ancient British myths about haunted houses.

Fortunately, we were well rested by the time the first walk was scheduled. The weather was perfect—cloudy until mid-afternoon—but warm and dry. We were shown a castle in the village of Fowey: one which had been in the hands of the same family ever since the time of William the Conqueror. Apparently this family still owned the entire village of Fowey, except for Fowey Hall. Then, a couple of miles beyond Fowey, we visited the church in which the famous author, Daphne du Maurier, was married; and we later saw the place where she had lived. The remainder of the hike that first day was along the high ridge overlooking the seaside. There were some stiff slopes to conquer, but the view of beautiful scenery, with its background of vividly green, rolling hills, was well worth it, as was the education we were receiving from our hike leader, a bouncy little gnome of a man called William. We learned that the area near Fowey was one of the two largest sources of china clay in the world. In addition to our daily history lessons, the meals he and his cohorts provided were astounding, at least in size. Every day we were supplied with four of them: a huge 'English breakfast', a bag lunch, a lavish 'elevenses' break at a tea house along the way—complete with bread and jam, cookies and two kinds of cake—and a full-course dinner back at Fowey Hall in the evening.

We had a number of exciting experiences, including the theft of several pairs of hiking boots from the cellar in which we had been told to leave them at the end of each hike. They were soon recovered, however. A group of hippies was caught attempting to sell them in the village. But, because our own boots had remained safe, I think the most momentous events for me at the time were those having to do with visiting historical sites. One of these was an old church which had been created in the tenth century. Another was the experience of lunching at Plymouth Harbour, across from the place where the Mayflower set off for America with the Pilgrim Fathers on board. On one of our rambles we were shown the harbour where pirates typically landed, as well as the bay from which ships went to and fro carrying Irish monks on their journey between Ireland and Spain. We also hiked a key section of their trail which eventually led to Wales, on a day when we were taken to the north coast of Cornwall by coach. On our last evening at Fowey they held a concert at which each of us was expected to perform in some way. I wrote a silly little poem which I read aloud. It reflects a lot of the sheer fun we experienced.

### What Tribe is This? (Or "Creepy Creatures of the Cornish Coastline")

*What tribe is this that daily wanders*
*Up and down the Cornish scene?*
*The stalwart Father William leading,*
*With Peter and the fair Eileen?*

*Every morn a hearty breakfast*
*Sends them forth from Fowey Hall*
*Urged on by friendly local canines*
*And the parrot's clarion call.*

*Many coloured are their garments*
*Bent with burdens are their backs,*
*Their gait is firm and heavy footed,*
*And stuffed with sandwiches, their packs.*

*For miles the villagers sound warning*
*E're the strange line passes by,*
*For 'tis said their din can deafen*
*And appearance shock the eye.*

*And 'tis noticed that their rituals*
*Are e'en more dreadful than their din;*
*For pubs their progress do imperil*
*And every tea house lures them in.*

*And oft they wander from the pathway,*
*And oft they straggle in the rear,*
*And oft they circle in confusion*
*'Til William calls, "I'm over here!"*

*With bursting lungs they gain the highland*
*As the holy grasp the grail.*
*Only to turn and hear their leader*
*"Chop-Chopping" down into the dale.*

*All day the grim procession struggles,*
*Their bodies bent and wracked with pain.*
*But all day William herds them eastward*
*And then he herds them west again.*

*Wild and wet their favoured weather,*
*Rough and rugged their terrain.*
*Not for them the cozy fireside,*
*Nor the shaded country lane.*

*What grievous wrongs are they atoning?*
*How savagely they must have sinned!*
*Fore're condemned to rain-drenched tresses*
*And noses flattened by the wind.*

*But Lo! The afternoon is fading*
*And William calls, "For home! Ahoy!"*
*Then slowly, like a conquered army,*
*The weary band drifts back to Fowey.*

From Fowey, Sandy and I proceeded to the second part of our hiking trip, to be launched from Barton-on-Sea and the Isle of Wight. A pleasant woman from Holland, Maria Smid, had also booked this one, so we had a companion. She was practising her English, and enjoyed Sandy's sayings. One in particular she began to imitate. Each time we gained the top of a hill, or succeeded in some other difficult struggle, she would exclaim, "So far so good!" This second hiking sojourn proved to be another extremely enlightening experience, as it took in a large area of the British south coast, including Dorset and the city of Christchurch. Here we met another interesting pair of people: two young gay men, who became long-time friends.

When it was all over, Sandy and I returned to London, where more great times awaited us. The brother of my old friend, June Smith, was an international businessman who happened to own a beautiful apartment in the relatively new Barbican district near the city's centre. He was kind enough to lend it to us for our stay. We could never have afforded a hotel room in such an upper-class area. This location made it easy for us to become familiar with the theatre district, Houses of Parliament, the London Bridge and River Thames, and the British Museum; and to have many adventures before finally departing Gatwick for the flight home to Vancouver near the end of June.

The busy summer to follow was replete with family matters, including a visit from Shane during which the three of us accompanied Dave and Wendy and the girls on a few pleasant hikes. In late July another happy trip awaited us. The town of Hanna, Alberta, where Shane then lived with his mother, was celebrating its seventy-fifth anniversary. It was a special time for Shane, as he had been selected as the only non-adult to act in the community's stage production of a play. In addition, he was taking part in various events at the community pool. Sandy and I watched proudly as he won the race for his age group, and made a good showing in the one for seventeen-and-under swimmers as well. We were sitting quite high up near the back of the attending crowd, and I couldn't avoid spotting Jack Westcott below us, also rooting for his grandson. I was torn concerning what I should do, but gave in to the emotional urge not to mention it to Sandy, nor to go down to speak to Jack at the end of the proceedings. This was a person who definitely had no place in our wondrous 'golden age'. It was the last time I was ever to see my former husband.

Not long after we returned to Vancouver, Sandy's brother Neil approached us with the idea of our taking him on what would be his one last visit to family in Saskatchewan. As his lungs were now failing badly, we felt we couldn't deny him that. He had to take his oxygen equipment along, so traveling was a bit stressful. We decided to go by way of Kindersley and on to the farm at Rosetown, as that was somewhat shorter than the southern route through Regina. After Neil had spent time with most of his family at Rosetown, we drove in to Saskatoon where he was able to visit several more of them. We also met with Don and Vi, who had come up from Regina. Sandy and I booked a room near theirs at the Travelodge, where we had a chance to share some close times with the little ones while Neil stayed with his sister Winnie and her family. The hotel had a large play-pool for children. It was wonderful for us to watch Robbie diving in and swimming, and Tanya enjoying the slide.

Neil and Sandy both particularly desired to see their sister Meg in Regina, who hadn't been able to make it up to Saskatoon because of the precarious nature of her health. So we decided to return by way of Regina. It was sad to see the usually lively Meg in her current condition, but we were grateful for the opportunity for what turned out to be a last farewell.

After all the driving we were happy to get home and become immersed in weekly hiking once again. By this time our club had increased its membership considerably. Some who had quickly become close friends were Phyllis Norris, John Wood, and Anne and Arlo Seidelman. Another remarkable couple with whom we soon became acquainted were Pam and Graham Humphreys. He was a retired engineer and she was a part-time writing instructor in Continuing Education at a junior college. We found we had a lot in common, and enjoyed many interesting conversations on the trail. And there was Graham's unfailing humour. He had a comment which he used whenever we met youthful hikers who were obviously amazed at encountering such elderly people on the mountains. He would tell them that the old folk's home had just let us out for the day. Not long after we met, the Humphreys and Sandy and I discovered that we shared a love of live theatre, so the four of us began what was to become many years of acquiring season's tickets for both the Playhouse and the Arts Club theatre. Prior to this we had attended with our old Unitarian friends, Fran and Tom Cluett, but Tom was then becoming too frail.

Sometime during 1987—with Graham's capable advice and help—we began to expand our hiking adventures beyond the North Shore mountains. We even tried a section of the famous Vancouver Island 'West Coast Trail', as well as part of the 'Skyline Divide' on Washington's Mount Baker. On my first climb on the latter, I wasn't able to make it all the way. I have a picture of Pam and me sitting at a spot where a number of us had given up and decided to relax and wait for the return of our hardier companions. Someone had written the caption "What the hell!" under the picture. Other exciting hikes were the ones to Gibsons Landing and to all the major Gulf islands—especially Mayne Island, a favourite of ours. Others were Newcastle Island, and Bowen Island, which included Crippen Park and Killarney Lake, Another favourite was a very steep climb up Elk Mountain. The latter provided views of both Cultus Lake and Harrison Lake as well as the Border Peaks, one in Canada and the other in the US.

In early November of 1987 Carolyn passed an important turning point. Our first grandchild had become a teenager. I thought it would be a good idea to mark the occasion by taking her shopping for a gift from us, with Jennie along to help her with the decision. From their thirteenth birthday on, I announced to both of them, the three of us would go to the Oakridge Mall. I would tell them the price limit, and together they would do all the necessary searching and decision-making, while I found a comfortable chair in each store and watched events unfold. This was, in fact, my favourite role where shopping was concerned. The process eventually became a twice-annual ritual to which I think we all looked forward. Around that time Carolyn had also begun music lessons on the flute, while Jennie began with the cello the following year. Sandy and I tried our best not to feel that they were growing up too fast. The previous summer I had been reminded of how quickly the time was passing by a visit from my brother Bob's daughter Emmi, who taught school in Toronto. With her were her husband Mark Krieger, and two daughters, Abigail and Alice. We had a pleasant gathering around our barbecue in the back yard, with Shane there as well, along with Carolyn and Jennie and their parents. My closest niece throughout all these 'golden years' however, continued to be Linda, Myrtle's daughter. We saw a lot of her and John on a regular basis, even after they made a move north to Kitimat, where both were to spend most of their working lives.

The year of 1988 was busy in yet another way. For a number of reasons we came to the decision to sell the house, much as we loved it. For one thing, the upkeep of the yard and buildings was getting too much for Sandy, and he wasn't one to sit idly by while a hired man did the chores. A second, and similarly compelling, reason was that we had been the victims of two further robberies since the one in which Tom lost all his possessions. This third one was particularly scary for me, as someone managed to enter through the chained front door while I was home alone and busy working in the garden at the back. Our location seemed to attract burglars, possibly because of the seldom-used park across the street, and the fact that we had a lane at the side of our lot with trees surrounding both it and our back yard. This time we did manage to get some amusement out of it all, however. The missing items included a bottle of powerful pills for diarrhea which a doctor had prescribed for me when I came down with a severe case of food poisoning from a lunch served at the Unitarian centre in Boston, during my last meeting there. We enjoyed the thought of our thief suffering endless days of severe constipation in place of the 'high' he had expected. "That'll teach him!" Sandy exclaimed.

All this took me back to another negative memory concerning our location. This event occurred when Shane was about four years old. The next-door neighbour happened to have her little grandson visiting as well, and we had developed the habit of allowing the two of them to play on their own for brief periods in the park across the road. However, there was a strict rule that they were not to leave the little children's play area for any reason. One day when I went over to check on them, they were nowhere to be found. I flew into a panic as this was in the days just before the serial killer, Clifford Olsen, had been apprehended. There were three other adults in the park and their response was obviously similar, in that they immediately rushed off to search in the surrounding area, one by car and the others on foot. Suddenly it occurred to me that the children may have returned to the neighbour's house, so I raced over there. Her little one had indeed arrived safely, but there was no sign of my grandson. Then he came running down the back lane toward us, sobbing, "I came home, but no one was there!" No moment of my life could possibly have been more 'golden' with relief than that one.

I then proceeded to have a serious talk with Shane about the dangers lurking in a big city. I began by asking him if his parents had explained about never talking to strangers. When he assured me they had, I asked him what 'strangers' were. "Oh they're those scary looking things with horns that I saw on TV." he replied. So much for our confidence that children actually receive our intended message!

Taken together, these experiences lessened our regret concerning the upcoming move to a condo. I think some of my reluctance stemmed from the fact that I had lived in this particular house longer than I had ever been in any one place in my entire life. But I knew we had to move. After considerable searching we settled for a place on the south side of False Creek. It was part of a row of small three-story condominium units, with a view out over the creek and the waters westward to the Burrard bridge and beyond. I had told Sandy, when he first suggested the move, that the only way I could be persuaded to give up my beloved house and garden was if we were to find a place near the water. Sandy was extremely happy both with the new location, and the inevitable change in life style accompanying it. One of these was his daily walk all around our side of False Creek, along with a custom which he quickly adopted. Typically, he felt compelled to make himself useful by combining a service to the community with his own enjoyment. So he always took along a pair of rubber gloves and hooked stick, which he used to pick up carelessly dropped garbage and deposit it in the bins along the route. My choice was a daily bicycle ride, east to Cambie bridge, then over it and west along the north side of False Creek to Stanley Park, and eventually south across Burrard bridge and back home.

There were two occurrences not long after we were settled which worried me, although I didn't mention them to Sandy. One was due to my finely honed sense of smell. I had considerable confidence in this trait, due to an incident sometime earlier at the Beacon Hill Unitarian building in Boston: the administrative centre of the American branch of the church. During a meeting there, I noticed an odour of gas near the entrance, although no one else could smell anything wrong. This worried me sufficiently that I reported it, in spite of advice to the contrary, and a city gas inspector came immediately. We were ordered to vacate the premises at once. He had discovered a serious problem which he told us would have worsened rapidly—possibly blowing up the entire building. Therefore, when I began to detect a faint hint of mildew in the downstairs bathroom of our new home, even though Sandy couldn't smell anything, I became suspicious, hoping of course that it was something minor. My second concern arose when Neil managed to make his one and only visit there. We should have had him pass it before making the purchase, but his lungs had been keeping him confined to an oxygen machine in his room at the intensive-care section of his seniors' residence. I watched the expression on Neil's face as he examined the place room by room. The fact that he made no comment, in itself, told me more than I wanted to know about the error we had made in our choice of new home. Neil was the former Director of Building Research at the National Research Council of Canada, and he was the chief author of the first textbook on Building Science ever published. Sandy and I were unaware of it at the time, but he was already becoming gravely concerned about deficiencies in the building code then being used in the Vancouver area.

Looking back at our busy summer and autumn of 1988, it's difficult to see how we found time for selling our house and purchasing a new home—not to mention the actual packing up and moving. So it's easy to understand how we may have made a hasty decision. We had gained over $150,000 on the house exchange because of the $300,000 increase in price since our original purchase in 1976; that may have affected our judgement. Vancouver house prices had taken an astounding upward surge during the years since we had arrived, due largely to a flood of wealthy immigrants from Hong Kong. And, as usual, we had been overly busy. Not long before the move, we had a wonderful visit from Pat Malikail and Brad Gilmore and their two small sons, on their way home from her current Foreign Affairs job in China.

Immediately after we settled into the new home, Shane arrived for his usual summer visit. Initially, he was sad about the loss of the house in which he had spent so many happy summers. But he soon came to love the False Creek area and the adventures it offered. He tried taking lessons on rowing a canoe for two people, but that resulted in a near disaster with the boat overturning and both boys ending up in the deep water. Fortunately, they were good swimmers. After that, he was satisfied to swim with Carolyn and Jennie at the Kitsilano pool, which was only a short walk from our new place, and to accompany us on boat rides with a couple of good Unitarian friends, Rae and John Smith, who had a son Shane's age. The two boys spent considerable time playing basketball in the park between our homes. We also did some hiking with the three grandchildren. Sometime during that happy period Jennie began to play ringette, a game in which she was to become quite an expert. Carolyn had followed her mother's example in taking up Scottish dancing.

While Shane was with us in August of 1988 we visited my brother Don and his family for the twenty-first birthday of his son Lewis. This included a lengthy ride on the ferry over to their cabin on Mayne Island. There we had a chance to go sailing on their small boat—an experience very rare for us, and especially thrilling for Shane. Sandy and I were in Victoria the previous June as well, for the high-school graduation of Lewis' brother Bryce. Fortunately for us, they had moved down from Prince George several years previously, when the economic situation had taken a downturn. Don had then sold his surveying and town-planning business for a job with the Provincial government where, ultimately, he gained the position of British Columbia's Surveyor General. With them being so close, it was possible for us to celebrate as a family quite often. Every other Christmas, Dave and Wendy and family would go out to the Okanagan to spend the holiday with her parents and, on those occasions, we developed the custom of going over to Victoria, or to Myrtle and Mike's place in North Delta.

The following winter whirled past us, with another visit from Pat Malikail and family—either on their way to or from China. We seemed to do a lot of entertaining in our False Creek quarters, including a ninetieth birthday party for Ursula Whitehead, a Unitarian friend who was a member of what we called our 'Neighbourhood Club'. We succeeded in maintaining this tightly knit group of special Unitarian friends throughout the years, in spite of the fact that we had all moved to different neighbourhoods at one time or other. But gradually, as time passed, our membership dwindled in size—something that all-too-often happens to groups of friends during their 'golden age'!

In the late spring Sandy and I made another of our road trips back to Saskatchewan. While in Regina, we discovered that Rob was already adept at playing hockey, with Tanya not far behind him in skating ability. After visiting Don and Vi's family, as well as those of the nieces, we drove up to

Saskatoon. On the way, we took time to have one of our great times with Sandy's sister Winnie and her husband Bernie, out at their cottage in the Blackstrap Valley. This was followed by a tour of the Outlook and Rosetown area, where we touched base with most of Sandy's cousins. Then it was back to pick up Shane for the summer. After a visit with Tom and Ellyn and family in Calgary, the three of us drove out to Cremona country to see my youngest brother Jerry. He was on his own by that time as his wife Dana had left him and taken the children. He had been forced to sell the little farm of which he had been so proud, in order to pay her half the value of it. As a result, he was now reduced to living once more on the family farm with our stepfather, Tom. I was always very attached to Jerry emotionally, which made every visit from then on most difficult. It seemed that life was closing in on him—with none of the outstanding potential of his youth having been realized. We drove back to Vancouver by way of the Rogers Pass and, in spite of Shane's lively company—which included his spontaneous creation and recitation of a poem about traveling along the riverside—I felt sad for Jerry all the way home.

At the beginning of December of 1989 we experienced one of those dreadful shocks that life too-often throws at one. The phone awakened me at two in the morning. It was the UBC hospital, informing me that Neil had just died and asking us to come at once. I immediately woke Sandy and we rushed over. Although we were fully aware of how agonizing each day had been for him for some time, it was very difficult—especially for Sandy—to face the fact that Neil was actually gone. They asked that one of us officially identify him, and I chose to do that for Sandy, who was quite untypically upset. So I went on my own into the little room where Neil's body lay. I'll never forget the sight of that terrified, grimacing face and wide-open mouth—obscuring all that Neil was and had been. He had died of suffocation—gasping for breath. I was glad that Sandy would not have this sight of his beloved and much-admired older brother to remember for the rest of his life.

Our granddaughter Carolyn had to learn of her great-uncle's death from a distance, because in late August she had gone to Germany for a year on a student exchange. It was a temporary loss for us, but a great adventure for her. Fortunately, Jennie was fully occupied with her ringette, as the winter and spring of 1990 came and went, and we were more than ever involved in our Golden Age hiking club. It was from some of the members that we learned about organized hiking opportunities for the coming summer, not only in England but also in exciting locations such as Scotland and Brittany. Now that we were no longer constrained by Neil's need for us, I suggested the idea to Sandy; but he decided that it was beyond him just then. So I asked

Wendy if she and the girls would be interested in accompanying Shane and me on such an adventure. We could plan it so that it would coincide with the trip that Wendy and Jennie were preparing to undertake to Germany at the end of the school year, in order to pick up Carolyn and get acquainted with her host family and country. Shane was all for the idea, even though it meant he would be celebrating his fifteenth birthday in a foreign country. However, when we planned to start out in early July, Jennie would have just turned thirteen, Shane would still be fourteen, and Carolyn not quite sixteen. I had such a strong feeling that it would be the last summer, ever, when the three of them would be available for a summer holiday together. My life had already taught me that such a coincidence of fortunate circumstance was unlikely ever to occur again.

After seeking advice from hiking club members and doing some research on my own, I first contacted the Holiday Fellowship, which Sandy and I had used for our previous hiking trip. Then, upon looking further, I found the Countrywide Holidays Association—again, a non-profit organization—which had been dedicated for almost a century to providing 'rambling' vacations at modest prices. Although for the most part these were organized around old guest houses in the UK, an increasing number were beginning to focus on other areas in Europe. Ultimately, I decided to make arrangements with both organizations, although Wendy and the girls could accompany Shane and me only on the first adventure: a hiking trip to the Scottish highlands on that country's upper west coast. Upon looking over our pictured choices, we settled on Loch Awe. This was largely because Jennie had fallen in love with the castle-like appearance of Loch Awe House. Then Shane and I chose Brittany for the second hiking—or 'rambling'—adventure. The central location there was a monastery which would be available for only this one summer.

Shane and I set off on the second week of July on what was for him, a first flight over the Atlantic. The plane was very crowded, with each of us crammed into a middle seat. In those days smoking was still being allowed on flights as well. We were thankful finally to land at Heathrow and walk the quarter-mile to the other terminal, where our plane for Glasgow awaited us. That fairly brief flight was smooth and fast, and almost before we realized it we were settled in the Kelvin Hotel in Glasgow. After having been served a filling breakfast by a friendly, bird-like little woman, we took the train for a three-hour journey north to Loch Awe. We both enjoyed this, as the scenery was superb. On arriving at our destination, we found Loch Awe House much as advertised, although greatly in need of upkeep and repair. It was actually a large, old country hotel dating back to Victorian times.

Wendy and the girls arrived from Germany about three hours later. We discovered that Shane and I had to share a room, and I was a bit nervous about how he would take this. But he didn't seem to mind, as there were two beds. It rained steadily during our first full day of hiking. In spite of being clothed appropriately, we all felt like drowned rats by the end of the day. The girls and I had chosen the second-level hike, while Wendy went on the third level and Shane on the fourth. Ours turned out to encompass six miles on a picturesque road beside a river, then six miles of scrambling back along the opposite side through a pathless bog. Shane's hike took him about ten miles, including up to the peak of one of the surrounding mountains. He told us afterwards that the climb through all the thick cloud that day felt as though they were moving above the earth into outer space. However, it was probably a good thing that we had that initial experience of rainy, fog-covered Scotland as, for the remainder of the week, the sun shone unceasingly.

Every day's hike turned out to be a unique experience. Usually the coach took us a considerable distance before we began walking; then it picked us up, tired and dirty, exactly at the appointed time and place at the end of the day. We spread like beetles over the countryside for miles around, some taking the high road to the rocky, jutting mountain peaks, and some the low road along well-worn trails by the shores of Loch Lomond, or down into a coastal village, or across uncharted moors.

A few, unaccustomed to hiking, developed blistered feet and aching muscles and wondered if they could possibly survive the pace. But ultimately, in the cool of the evening by the deep, dark lake, they basked in the pride of having made it through the day. This had been the case for Shane after one of his too-ambitious hikes. Others reveled during every moment in the sheer joy of the pastoral surroundings. The only accidents were amusing ones: a boot sucked off and swallowed by the bog; another boot that began to disintegrate in the mud before our eyes; and coaches too tired to make the hills unless we all disembarked and trundled up ahead. Once, while hiking on the West Coast Trail stretching seventy-five miles northward from Glasgow to Fort William, we met a foursome from Canada on only their third day out. Obviously just beginning to toughen up, the agony of those early days showed in the baleful glances directed at the leader by the other three.

"If only we had guessed on time that the woman was mad!" one of them muttered to me as she grasped her pack and staggered off after the others.

This was merely one among many examples of how, even more than the starkly beautiful surroundings, it was the people who made the entire experience unforgettable. Our sojourn happened to coincide with a Holiday

Fellowship offering of two 'special interest' trips. The first was for singles aged eighteen to thirty-five; and the second was for the 'natural history' buffs who were organized as a group to study the region's wildlife. Besides our family, there was only a smattering who belonged to neither of these categories. One of these was a female insomniac who, in defiance of the house rule, was driving her roommate crazy by chain-smoking all night long. Others were a delightful middle-aged couple from Germany; a jovial amateur botanist from Holland who argued unceasingly with the official plant book carried by our leader; two genteel ladies from Cambridge; and a mother with two uncontrollable sons apparently bent on demonstrating to all of us that they were there against their will.

The young singles spread among us, hiking at all four levels of difficulty and making us feel welcome at the evening activities. On the last two nights we joined their 'caelies': one at a nearby community centre and the other in Loch Awe House. Carolyn, Jennie and Shane courageously joined in the Scottish country dancing. They were also obviously enjoying the bagpipes and haunting vocal renditions, as well as the games. On our day off, Wendy and the girls and I chose to accompany a group which traveled by coach to Inverary for the annual Highland Games. We found a large, round field of grass, fenced off, within which was placed a sizeable platform for Scottish dancers. A great deal of spare space was taken up by throwers of large, lead balls at telephone poles—playing 'tossing the caber'—along with all manner of runners. Surrounding this circular arena were booths selling memorabilia and food and drink. Interspersed among these were small platforms on which pipers were apparently competing. There was also a parade consisting of a pipers' band in full array.

After several hours of sitting on the ground and watching all this, I became bored and took off on my own, walking about a quarter mile to Argyll castle. I had been told that a Duke of Argyll was beheaded there during the Civil War. Members of the original family were still living in the castle, but a part of it was open to the public so I went to look inside. I learned that a piper appeared on the balcony each morning to awaken the inhabitants. There were many armaments and shields, coats of arms, flags, etc.—identifying Argyll's Campbell clan—and the walls were covered with paintings and tapestries. What a lifestyle! Wendy went to see it all later. She had a special interest, as her ancestors were of that clan. Until then I hadn't realized that we were hiking in Campbell country. The history and culture of the place was emphasized on our last night when we were treated to a feed of haggis, along with the usual 'mushy peas'. I think I was the only one of the family who appreciated the haggis. But we all enjoyed the ceremony as it was being piped in.

Most important of all during this entire holiday were the leaders. These were dedicated hikers who had given up weeks of their vacation period to make the organization work. They were able administrators and kindly people who functioned as the very heart of the structure. It was they who made our holiday unforgettable. They described each hike the previous evening, so that we could make appropriate selections; got us started on time in the morning; kept us moving at the necessary pace all day; and ensured our safety at all times as they charted the course—often across unmarked territory. It was a hike leader who welcomed us upon arrival, who arranged for a birthday cake for Shane, who took us to the Highland Games at Inverary, and who saw us off at the week's end. And, as we wended our way by slow train through the now-familiar countryside back to Glasgow, it was a hike leader who pointed out the peaks of the mountains we had climbed and who shared with us a fond farewell to Scotland.

Wendy and the girls then traveled back home while Shane and I remained in London. We stayed in a hotel in the famous Bloomsbury area, where I found the literary history associated with it fully as thrilling as the sight-seeing and the chance to spend time in the British Museum. We also did considerable wandering about the theatre district. My sharpest memory is of Shane suddenly freezing with fear as we were about to enter the Underground. The pushing crowd and darkening area ahead of us was just too much for this Alberta country boy, even though he had moved into the city of Calgary the previous year in order to live with Tom and Ellyn while attending high school. He was much happier when we left London behind on our journey to Stratford-on-Avon. In fact, Stratford was in many ways the highlight of our entire trip that summer. Shane was already fascinated with Shakespeare as I had provided him, throughout his childhood years, with numerous children's books of the great man's plays, etc. At Stratford we attended the theatre, wandered the riverbank, and saw what is purported to have been Shakespeare's home. Then came a journey to Oxford, where we spent a couple of days admiring the buildings and atmosphere, before proceeding south to Kent. There we had a brief stay at the home of Dennis Hart and his partner, the pleasant gay couple whom Sandy and I had met on our hiking trip to Fowey several years earlier. They had been to see us in Vancouver previously and had invited us for a return visit with them. After that, it was off to Brittany, for the last adventure of our once-in-a-lifetime trip.

This final stage of our trip was labeled 'By Coach and Sea'. And so it was. We met our fellow travelers on the dock in Portsmouth, just prior to the rudest and roughest embarkation I was ever to experience. A storm coming in from the Atlantic was almost overwhelming the dock. We managed to board the ferry and then, with us each carrying two bags of luggage, began to fight our way to our cabins. I survived the struggle up five flights of narrow stairs, losing Shane in the process. All the way, I had to push against the upcoming hordes from the cars. Then I wandered, utterly lost and totally bereft of my limited French vocabulary, through a seemingly endless maze of narrow hallways peopled solely by non-Anglophones. By the time I finally located and crawled into my top bunk I had neither the energy nor the courage to take in the emergency instructions coming over the loudspeaker. I had by then determined to go down with the ship rather than endure a repeat performance on the dreaded stairways. Shane would have to either sink or swim, I decided. I settled down for a difficult night, confident that he was by now sufficiently travel-wise and muscular to have made his way to his own cabin. The ship continued to lurch violently all the way across the Channel and I struggled with sea-sickness all night long.

When the whistle blew in the morning to indicate our imminent arrival at St. Malo, I felt like one of the walking dead. But Shane's immediate appearance, along with his gleeful recounting of the previous evening's un-chaperoned adventures, helped my recovery. Apparently, he had become acquainted with a number of our future companions, all very friendly English folks, he said. The one problem for him was that they seemed to be middle-aged or older—and mostly women. All this came out as we were getting off the ship, which was only a shade less brutal than getting on had been. The sight of the waiting coach and its friendly, waving driver also lifted my spirits. We were soon off to our first destination—a pleasant little village in the woods where lunch and a rest awaited us.

Thus began a remarkable ten days of exploration, by foot and coach, of the coastal areas of Brittany. We were part of a group which included seventeen British people, led by a knowledgeable amateur archeologist clothed in a Breton cap and sweater, who had an engaging smile and the rolling gait of an old sea captain. We stayed at three centres in all: Plancoet, Le Tronchet, and Le Bono. Each time we were housed in a beautiful old abbey in the process of being renovated into a hotel. So it was a once-in-a-lifetime opportunity in more ways than I had realized. Our days were packed with walks along coastal or riverside trails, tours through the streets and castles of medieval towns, and swims at the white-sanded beaches. Perhaps most fascinating for me were the numerous visits to the magnificent megaliths and dolmens left in that part of France by Neolithic man. Shane, who had been working on his French during the previous spring, established a custom of sitting in the front seat of the coach with the driver. He quite rightly figured that it would be a great chance to practise the language. I had to be satisfied with attempting to speak French to the local storekeepers, etc. I was rewarded (I think) by one of them telling me that at least I didn't have that atrocious Canadian accent. I realized later that the speaker was referring to Quebec's joual dialect.

Even our lunches proved to be gourmet affairs, in spite of their being carried in the coach's refrigerator and eaten picnic style in the countryside. At day's end we gathered for leisurely dinners featuring French cooking that was outstanding in both appearance and taste. I think that Shane enjoyed the meals, although he always made a point of sitting at a table apart from mine, where the few males in the group gathered. But I was amused by the reaction of the people at my table to the food. Much of it they refused even to taste, simply because it was—happily for me—very different from British cooking. The dinner was usually followed by some form of entertainment provided by the locals, culminating, on our last evening, in a Breton dance.

Our group members made interesting travel companions. They were mainly teachers, as well as school librarians and administrators released from work for the summer. For most of us the culture shocks were few. Nevertheless, in spite of my country background, I was somewhat taken aback by the little wooden public toilets, with their massive foot supports on opposite sides of a gaping hole in the ground. Shane's most difficult moment came with the discovery that he was expected to change for swimming on the open beach in front of all his female companions. But he took it in stride quite admirably and, as the only non-adult, soon became the spoiled darling and favoured object of group teasing. The women all referred to him as their 'toy boy'.

For both of us, the days passed rapidly. In no time, it seemed, we found ourselves heading back to St. Malo and the infamous ferry. Once aboard, amid promises to keep in touch, our kindly shepherd deserted us and headed below for a much-needed rest. Suddenly the group disintegrated, as such groups do, into our various isolated privacies. Our thoughts were now all directed homeward, and we knew that our wonderful holiday was over.

The following year was another happy and busy one. In fact, I recall it as one of our best ever, as far as hiking and family were concerned. Shane came out for the Easter holidays, and we spent several days of it at Mayne Island, with Don, Donna and their boys. And, as always, we saw a lot of our foster granddaughter, Nguyet, as she and Shane had been particularly close since childhood. I recall only once that I overheard an altercation between them during their early years. Shane had been pressuring Nguyet to play a game about pirates. Not surprisingly, I discovered her frozen by the fearful memory of the little boat in which she and her brothers were making their escape from Vietnam being entered by pirates on the high seas. These attackers had stripped them of everything of any worth. "But your mother's wedding ring?" I asked when she told us the story, for I recalled that she had arrived with the ring. "How did you manage to keep that from them?"

"I put it in my mouth," she said, triumphantly. Quick thinking for a seven-year-old!

In May of 1991 we celebrated Sandy's seventy-eighth birthday and Jennie's fourteenth. Then, during the summer, there occurred an important event for me as well as for Shane. It was a French-immersion holiday which Tom and I arranged for him in Trois Rivière, Quebec. We were able to do this only because of the invaluable help of a friend, Claude Kershaw, who had once lived there. Our good friends, the Malikails, were settled in Ottawa by then, so they met Shane at that city's airport and made sure he was safely boarded on a train for the remainder of the trip. It turned out to be a high point in his teen-age years, and an important maturing experience.

During the same period, Sandy and I were enjoying an extended visit with Maria Smid from Holland. The three of us spent much of our time hiking, both with the 'Golden Agers' and on our own. One of our greatest adventures was a week up in the Coastal mountains at the Cathedral Lake Lodge on Lake Quiniscoe, near Glacier Lake, where we hiked the Diamond Trail. The lodge provided comfortable beds, lunches for our hikes, and nourishing evening dinners. Other day-long hikes in the vicinity were around Goat Lake and Ladyslipper Lake. During our trip we also spent time up at Manning Lake, with its hot springs. Maria was thrilled with our mountainous surroundings, and never tired of exploring our trails.

Somehow we managed to combine a lengthy visit to the prairies with all these adventures. This was at the request of Maria, who wanted very much to see more of Western Canada. We took the picturesque southern route and, on the way, spent a day wandering around Lake Louise in the Rockies with my cousin, Harold Armitage. He was the son of my mother's brother Les and his wife Annie, who had provided a home for Bob when he was a teenager. I had always felt particularly close to him and his sister Thelma. Then we proceeded on to Calgary, where we spent an enjoyable time with Tom and Ellyn and their children, and saw their new house. Our route then led to Regina for a happy get-together with son Don and daughter-in-law Vi, and

Robbie and Tanya—and with all the rest of Sandy's family who were living there. Next came Saskatoon, with pleasant visits with his sister Winnie and husband Bernie as well as their daughter Karen Fedora and her husband and girls. Finally, it was homeward by way of the Hutcheon farm at Rosetown, where we spent time with Sandy's sister Dolly and several of his cousins. Maria especially appreciated a tour of the Hutterite colony near the farm. Altogether, it was a happy, fulfilling trip, one that caused our friend from Holland to express a degree of envy of our extended family.

Maria remained with us for my sixty-fifth birthday that summer. Then, just before she left for Holland, we had a little dinner party at our place to celebrate the birthday of a longtime friend, Conrad Hadland. We invited Theo and Marjan Meijer, a Dutch-Canadian couple who were close friends of his, and whom we liked very much as well. Sandy and I thought it would be a pleasant send-off for Maria to meet some folks who could speak her language. And we were confident that she would be greatly entertained by the friendly arguing in which Theo and Conrad loved to indulge. In fact, they almost outdid themselves that afternoon. Theo began it all by giving a toast to Conrad, referring to him as a 'heartless landlord' who had evicted tenants just before Christmas the previous year. Conrad owned a house up in Prince Rupert for which there was no sale in those days; he had discovered that his renters were wrecking the place. I think that Maria must have wondered if her English was failing her, especially as we continued to laugh uproariously as the insulting remarks escalated between the two. I have often found, throughout the years, that humour is the most difficult aspect of culture to communicate.

In 1992 we had another year of happy hiking: from the fishing village of Steveston in the south-west by way of the Richmond dikes to Garibaldi Lake in the north and the coastal mountains to the east. I was the president of the club at the time, as well as on the Board of the British Columbia Humanist Association. Both organizations provided us with many like-minded friends, with whom we were increasingly spending our free time. By then there were two couples among our many companions in the hiking group who had connections with my brother-in-law Neil Hutcheon. Gordon and Teresa Sauder lived next door to Walter Ball, who had worked with Neil in Ottawa. The second couple, Adah and Carl Crawford, had come out to Vancouver from Ottawa, where he had also worked for the government under Neil, and joined both the Golden Agers and the Unitarians. Another friend I made during this period was Fran Hodgkinson, who joined our Humanist Association after hearing me speak on the subject of a humanist perspective on spirituality at the Vancouver Unitarian church. She also became a fellow hiker, and consequently, a member of each of our three groups of close friends.

It was also another enjoyable year of family gatherings, including a visit from Sandy's youngest brother Alan. He had then been settled for a number of years in Lesoto—formerly the British colony of Basutoland—as a professor of chemistry in the university there. Alan's beliefs were very different from ours, and disagreements over these provided endless fuel for friendly arguments whenever we were together. He was also as different as possible from Neil whom I had found, from our very first introduction, to be a 'kindred spirit': another Freethinker. The only commonality shared by these two brothers of Sandy's was the fact that neither had ever married. Alan was very fundamentalist for a Quaker, and was devoting his life to an idealistic—and I often thought, Utopian—attempt at improving the lives of the African people in an environmentally friendly way. Unfortunately, he had been undergoing many years of constant disappointment and personal financial loss.

Sometime during that summer Sandy and I arrived at an important decision. On days when the weather permitted and I was free to do so, I had been continuing to do my 'circle cycle' over the Cambie bridge, along the seawall around Stanley Park, and back home over the Burrard bridge. As time went on, I found myself paying increasing attention to a particular high-rise in what appeared to be a community of surrounding buildings. It was located immediately east of the Burrard bridge, and encompassed the area from Beach Avenue down to the seawall. I was noting the careful construction of the high-rise in the centre of the development, which was being built on what appeared to be solid rock. More and more, I began to think that this would be an ideal place to live, as well as a very safe investment for the future. I discussed it with Sandy and he thought we should talk to Tom, who was in the real-estate business, before making any decisions. Tom advised us to make a list of ten of our most important housing priorities before going any further, then apply these to each abode considered. He was obviously impressed by the location of the high-rise, especially the fact that no one could ever build in front of us to spoil the view, and that it was on the north side of False Creek and within easy walking distance of the heart of the city. He suggested that, if we decided to pursue the idea further, we should select an apartment at the middle height of the high-rise, possibly one of the first levels at which we could get a good view over the bridge out to English Bay and the ocean and mountains beyond. His reason? At the beginning of such a project, the builders are in the process of learning, and often make a number of errors. And, the higher the building goes, the more their bosses begin to put pressure on them to hurry, with the result that they tend to become careless. Thus mistakes are increasingly likely to occur. All so obvious, but how many buyers think of such things? Some time after we had made our move, in the following autumn, I asked our next-door neighbour, who was a Baha'i, his reason for choosing the ninth floor. He replied that, according to his faith, it was a lucky number. So both families had ended up with the same choice, but by entirely different routes!

Sandy and I were shown around the high-rise one evening by a realtor recommended by Tom. Almost immediately, we both fell in love with the ninth-floor apartment in the building which had initially appealed to us. The most memorable moment of the evening was our entrance to the front room, when we looked out over False Creek and saw a virtual fairyland of sparkling water and coloured lights. We were again fortunate in selling the other place for well over $100,000 more than we paid for the new apartment, and were able to make our move in late November of 1992. Sadly for the people who had purchased our property, less than a decade later it was discovered to be one of Vancouver's many 'leaky condos'. But for us, the decision to move had been timely for another reason as well. In fact, we had left it almost too long, as Sandy's health was beginning to fail, making the packing and unpacking very difficult for us. But we managed, and within a couple of weeks were fairly well established in a comfortable home in what is unarguably one of the best locations in all of the Lower Mainland. No more stairs to climb; greatly improved security; the seawall immediately below us, with False Creek to gaze across; within a five-minute ferry ride of Granville Island on the other side of the creek with its farmers market and profusion of other attractions combined with easy walking to the downtown area—and all this enriched by a view over the bridge to the ocean and the mountains of Bowen Island and beyond. What more could one ask for in the golden years of life?

Speaking of which, almost our very first guests were fellow members of the Executive of the Golden Age Hiking club, who came over for a meeting one evening. I remember the concierge at the desk of our lobby introducing me to our condo manager the following day, with the comment: "Not only is she a mountain hiker, but I discovered last evening that she's the leader of the pack!" For Sandy and me, our amusement at this—and appreciation of the wonderful staff in our new place—added to the pleasure of the settling-in process. Our comfort in this lovely setting was such that we were even somewhat reluctant to leave for a couple of days to celebrate Christmas with the Duffys in Victoria. But of course, as always, Donna's food and the pleasure of being with the four of them more than compensated for any temporary absence from our wonderful new surroundings.

Looking back on it all now, I guess we shouldn't have been surprised that such a blissful period of outdoor activity with family and friends couldn't last forever. But the suddenness with which it all ended was shocking in the extreme. Our Golden Age club had just completed the annual New Years hike in Stanley Park on the first Thursday of 1993, and Sandy and I were on the short bus trip home. We were standing in the crowded aisle—packs on our backs and hiking sticks in hand—as the driver slowly approached the bus stop. Then, virtually at our destination, the bus lurched forward with such a surge of power that a number of us were thrown off our feet. Unfortunately, I crashed into the edge of a seat-back on the way down. I knew immediately that something was dreadfully wrong with my back and left side, but managed to navigate the remaining block to our home with Sandy's help. My dark premonition was to prove correct. That was my one last hike! But, almost at once, my sense of horror and foreboding was superseded by a quite different realization: one that was as comforting as the first had been alarming. For both Sandy and me, the Golden Age that had defined our lives for so long consisted of something wonderful in addition to hiking. It was the unparalleled privilege of grandparenting. And that fulfilling and life-expanding experience, no accident could ever take away!

# Chapter 21

# FALLEN LEAVES

In the spring of 1945, when I was a grade-twelve student at Oyen, I wrote the following poem in the school publication which our teacher, Mr. Freehill, had called FALLEN LEAVES:

## SUNSET

*The afternoon is drawn and tired, its brilliant colours spent*
*All living things bow wearily with care and sorrow bent*
*Sudden as if a shade were drawn by some almighty hand*
*The harsh light fades and from the west a glow spreads o'er the land*
*A rosy glow, it touches all, transforms the dull and plain*
*Fills weary hearts with hope anew, like sunshine after rain*
*But, as it came, the magic moment passes fast away*
*Sombre shadows rise around us, all the earth is grey*
*Our world has crossed the bridge between the evening and the day.*

Strange how those words express so well what I felt when my 'Golden Age' of hiking came to its abrupt end more than a half-century later! I realize now that, no doubt because of my personal loss of loved ones at such an early age, I had gained a somewhat premature comprehension of death as a normal part of life. Just as trees grow from seeds and green leaves develop in the spring and gradually wither and fall as the seasons change, so too must human life—and the morning, day-time and evening within that life—have a beginning and an end.

Sometimes life's endings come too suddenly and far too soon, as happened in the case of my father and all the young men such as my friend Max who never returned from war. In other instances, the leaves wither on the vine in a dry and wrinkled state for much too long, imposing on all concerned a seemingly endless period of suffering and loss. And there is, as well, the normal extended and sorrowful experience of becoming, oneself, a slowly withering leaf—while, at the same time, watching or hearing of family members and friends gradually dropping and rejoining the dust from whence they came. Most of us, until we experience it ourselves, are not fully aware of this particular aspect of the life cycle. The fact that it is an integral part of family ties and social networking was driven home to me rather powerfully as a consequence of the close connections with Sandy's family and former in-laws as well as some of my own; with members of our hiking club, our Canadian and BC Humanist Associations and the Unitarian movement; with neighbours; and with my 'virtual world' community of like-minded professional colleagues. Increasingly, as I traverse the evening of my years, I learn to live with these all-too-natural losses and the gradual diminishing of personal community which necessarily results.

## MY BROTHER JACK

It was the gradual loss of my brother Jack which began the earliest experience of loss for me and extended over the longest time. Or perhaps I should describe it as the experience of watching from the sidelines—unable to help in any fruitful sense—as my brother, equally helpless, allowed the chances of life to slip away. As long as we were attending school together, I tried my best to guide and protect this dysfunctional older brother from the bullying actions of others, including teachers; although often the problems were consequences of his own behaviour. But nothing seemed to do any good in the long run. And then there were the numerous catastrophes that struck him: the first three while he was still a youngster. These were the severe ear problem which left him partially deaf, his being deliberately run over by horses ridden by schoolmates at Lonely Trail school, and his robbing of the post office at Oyen after we moved there. Following all this was the disastrous war experience during the invasion of Europe which served to compound the cumulative results of what had occurred in his early life. Then, having returned from the front with severe mental and emotional problems, he stole our stepfather's car and dropped from the horizon of the entire family for many years. All those events appear to have been the major signposts on his tragic 'road of no return': that journey which ended several decades later on what was then called 'Skid Road' in Vancouver's Downtown East Side. This particular district's name was a fitting description of what was happening to Jack, as it was a reference made by the loggers in the early days of settlement to the task of skidding logs along a corduroy road especially made for this purpose. There was a particular hotel in the city, The Grand Hotel, whose manager would hold the monthly pay for these forest workers when they came to town, and dole it out carefully for them during their days off, in order to prevent their spending it all on drinking, and thus 'hitting the skid' and being unable to return to their jobs.

All through the years, my brother Don and I tried our best to help Jack. I sent him money whenever he contacted me, always hoping to rescue him and, at times, even keep him out of jail—if I had any to spare, that is, and could hide the knowledge of what I was doing from my husband, Jack Westcott. And Don once gave him a job in his Prince George business. But Jack could never be relied on to show up for work. He admitted this to me, ruefully, the last time I saw him. "I was a hard worker whenever I was on the job," he said, "but sometimes I just couldn't manage to get up in the morning. And my bosses never liked that. Finally, even Don couldn't put up with it."

Myrtle's husband Mike had been kind enough to maintain contact with Jack as he skidded downwards after moving to Vancouver, and was able to tell me where to find him when Sandy and I were setting off as immigrants to Australia. During our brief farewell, Jack, for the first time in his life, refused to take any money from me. Proudly, he let me know that he was no longer drinking, and had been given a steady job at the desk of a shabby old hotel established for Vancouver's homeless. "My only worry now," he said, "is that the 'druggies' are taking over our neighbourhood." Less than a year later my no-longer-lost brother Jack died of a heart attack. He was not yet fifty. Mom's chief response, in a letter to me, seemed to be mainly one of relief. "I won't have him to worry about any more," she wrote. She had never seen him since she moved to the Lower Mainland. I think he was too ashamed of what he had made of his life to face her. Or, possibly she was too fearful of forcing this on him to attempt the contact.

## *LOSS OF A MOTHER*

Two other deaths of beloved family members were preceded by similarly lengthy periods of deterioration—both of body and of selfhood. My mother's was particularly difficult in that her lifetime of maintaining a contradictory world view became increasingly a problem for her. Just after moving in with us in the late autumn of 1984, she had spent some time in hospital, where she had been subjected to two instances of cruel treatment. One of these was being told by a doctor that her previously undiagnosed and untreated condition of osteoporosis was all her own fault. He accused her of never having eaten the right food. The second involved frequent visits by a minister who was attempting to "save her soul" before it was too late. This experience had apparently been uniquely terrifying for her. The result of it all was that, by the time she came to us, she had developed a horror of hospitals and begged me never to send her back to one.

I was touched by Sandy's kindness to Mom during those last eight months of her life. He sat by her bedside for many hours each day, engaging her in simple conversation in attempts to take her mind off the endless pain. During one of these times, when we were both with her, she mentioned that Don was the only member of the family who had never caused her a moment's worry. This was one of her few positive memories, as she continuously agonized about the way she had lived her life. As her condition worsened, she became ever more convinced that the God of her childhood was punishing her for all her bad behaviour. No matter how many times I assured her that the world doesn't work that way, I failed to succeed in comforting her.

We had found a new doctor—one who specialized in geriatrics—and he came to the house quite frequently. But he was frustrated by the fact that he could do so little to ease her pain. He informed us that her skeleton was beginning to collapse into her vital organs, and there was no way to prevent it worsening day by day. Combined with this was the fact that the law at that time did not allow a doctor to administer morphine to a patient who had chosen to die at home. Mom's digestive system was already so bad by then that even one Aspirin resulted in vomiting. The doctor told me he would risk treating her with morphine to ease her pain only if I could guarantee that none of her family would cause trouble for him about it. I realized that there was simply no way I could do this, given the vagaries of my siblings, so the opportunity was lost to us. Meanwhile, Mom continued to refuse to go into the hospital, stiffening with terror and almost screaming when anyone suggested it.

Through it all, she maintained her ability to think clearly. She requested that I help her write a will and asked, tentatively, if I would mind if she left the total of her banked savings to Jerry. I assured her that none of the rest of us were in need of her money, and that I fully agreed with her decision. Only then did I learn that she had retained intact what seemed to her the large sum of seven hundred dollars, which Tom had given her for what he considered to be her share of the farm. She also told me that she did not want a memorial service; nor did she want her body placed in a coffin and buried. What she wished for was a cremation, "with no fuss of any kind." I wondered, at that moment if she, too, had been haunted all these years by the memory of my father's funeral. I also suspected that she was seeking to avoid placing Jerry and Bob in a situation where they would feel required to come out to Vancouver to attend a formal ceremony. As always, her chief concern was in preventing possible embarrassment for her two absent—but much loved—sons. After hearing all this, I arranged for a will to be drawn up, signed and witnessed, while she was still able to wield a pen.

She had also retained her capacity to make courageous decisions. She began to talk about her mother's death in the hospital in Calgary, and how her sister Mabel told her afterwards that Ma had refused to drink or eat after arriving there in a horrific condition. Then, one day, she decided to do the same, stubbornly turning away when I attempted to force a little nourishment, or even liquid, into her mouth. One night about a week after this I was awakened by Mom's faint voice calling for me from her bedroom. I found her on the floor, moaning in pain, with blood dribbling from her lips. I could see that she had been vomiting blood. We phoned the doctor and he told us that we had no choice but to call Emergency. I accompanied her to the hospital and remained at her bedside except for a few hours off once when Mike took over so that I could go out for a walk and lunch. Mom died the following night. Myrtle sat in the car throughout their several hours' visit to the hospital, obviously unable to cope with what was occurring. But by then there was actually nothing unpleasant to witness, as Mom had been given morphine upon our initial arrival and was at peace during that last twenty-four hours of her life. At one point I even noticed a smile on her face, and asked if she was feeling any pain.

"No pain," she responded, "Just sleep." And then she was gone. Not long after I completed all the necessary arrangements following her death, I wrote a poem in her memory.

## NO MORE

You wouldn't let a dog suffer for months like this!"
Her brown eyes accusing me, from that hopeless bed of pain.
No, only a mother, I wanted to say.
Only a mother who had devoted her life to easing the pain of her children.
Too many children from too many bone-destroying pregnancies,
Too little food for the children's mouths—never a surplus for nourishing a mother
Who, in her last stay at a hospital, was told by a misogynous doctor,
"It's all your own fault, you know. You just never ate the proper foods."
"Suffering," intoned an uninvited visiting pastor, "Is required of us by God.
You must trust that He will not assign you more than you bear."
No more," she begged me after that, "No more hospitals."

Torture is sanctioned for mothers—encouraged by our traditions.
Skeleton collapsing on her vital organs, little by little.
Morphine disallowed, "if patient insists on remaining at home."
But she had lived her life at home, struggling against endless drought to grow a
         garden and feed her poultry—
Those precious lifelines of "proper foods" for her offspring.
Sending older children at night to our grandmother's house for bags of coal,
"Dufflebags", we were called by classmates, when being scorned for the brother
Who robbed the post office to buy candy for the little ones.
Selling one piece of furniture at a time,
Waiting for funds from my father in a neighboring Province,
Desperately seeking paying jobs somewhere.
A fighting Irish father, dying too soon from too much hard work and far too
         much despair,
Succumbing at last in the grease beneath a crippled car,
Tools of his proud trade in hand.

"No more," my mother said, at last, and closed her lips.
She had found a way—a cruel way for none but the very brave and strong.
I took the water from the room and could only hope the path ahead would not
         be long.
Then a tortuous and tortured week that only mothers could endure
A dreadful crisis in the night, an ambulance and finally
The blessed morphine shot, the blissful rest so long denied.
"Are you feeling any pain?" I asked, beside her bed that afternoon.

*"Just sleep," she smiled, at peace at last. "No pain. No more."*
*No more.*
*This must not happen. Not to mothers. Not again to anyone.*
*No more.*

Soon after Mom died I received a strange letter from Bob. When I opened it I expected to find some comments about our shared loss, and possibly even an expression of appreciation for what Sandy and I had managed to do for our mother. But, instead, there were only a few words of reprimand concerning her cremation. He objected strongly to it, and appeared to suggest that I had done it against her will. He said nothing about his failure to come out to say goodbye to her. His last visit had been in September of 1984, when Mom was living with Myrtle and Mike. He had then also taken the time to visit Sandy and me in our house. During our few hours together we engaged in a cursory conversation, chiefly about what we had been reading. I recall being surprised by the fact that we were interested in exactly the same books. Bob then concluded his visit to BC by going up to Prince George for a one-day stop, during which time he played baseball with Lewis and Bryce. When Don told me about it later he said, with a wry grin, "He never once played ball with me when I was young."

## MY BROTHER JERRY

The story of Jerry—like Jack, a red-headed brother—is equally sad, but in a very different way. As the male 'baby' of the family, he was adored by our mother, but never provided with any discipline or motivation to do anything well. All-too-often I witnessed her blind reinforcement of the very worst of his egocentric behaviours. This was a tragedy of monumental proportions, given that learning was so easy for him because of his extremely high intelligence. I was very fond of him and tried my best to overcome Mom's blissfully well-meaning, but developmentally devastating, socialization. Jerry seemed always to be aware of my concern in some vague way, for he showed an uncharacteristic fondness for me until the very end. That fondness was expressed only in letters, however, and never when we were in direct contact. Except for the last time I was ever to see him, as I said goodbye at the farmhouse doorway, I noticed his face convulse and his eyes fill with tears. Then he muttered—almost as if talking to himself—the most heart-wrenching words I've ever heard from anyone. "I now realize," he said, "that every decision I ever made in life has been the wrong one."

I wanted to hug him closely to comfort him but, in our family, that was just not done. So both of us reached out and touched awkwardly, then turned away.

Throughout the years, I had always sent him one or two Christmas packages of edible treats and basic clothes: and then similar gifts for his birthday in June. I would inevitably receive a late Christmas card in response, and almost always a card for my birthday. This note on one of the former was typical:

"Just a quick line to let you know that your last two parcels arrived safely and everything was great. I have a letter started and will try to finish it this week. Knowing me, I would not bet on it if I were you, but I will try." The letter never arrived.

A letter from him dated August 25 of 1991, which he did actually mail on time for my sixty-fifth birthday, reveals a great deal about how he was functioning during the decade or more after his wife had left him and taken the children. One of those children was his biological daughter, Susan: the only one that he then knew about, that is. However, I was told that just before he died, the long-lost one who had been adopted out when born—without his having been told at the time about the pregnancy—did manage to contact him! I'll quote from some of that birthday letter.

"Since you didn't phone from Calgary, I guess I must have hurt your feelings by saying I was too busy for company. That was not my intention. I just did not want you to feel obligated to 'do your duty' by paying me a visit. Things have not gone well here for the past year or so and I was really trying to avoid embarrassment for any of us. Tom has lost it mentally and I am drinking far too much and have a rather nasty disposition these days. We have virtually no visitors anymore. I'm sorry I have not written for so long, or thanked you for the things you sent me for Christmas and my birthday (I really liked the Balkan Trilogy) but I feel like I'm on a treadmill. One day off in six years can get to you after awhile. Anyway, thanks for everything, and most of all, your letters. They are one of the few things that I have to look forward to in this miserable life."

Not long after this, our stepfather, Tom Graham, was placed in an institution by his sister, and Jerry was left with the task of operating the farm with no funds and no legal authority to do anything. I sent him a sizeable cheque to carry him through until matters could be settled. Tom died not too long after this. Fortunately, he had made out a will which left all the land and livestock to this favourite stepson but, unfortunately, not a cent of his money. I immediately lent Jerry sufficient funds to see him through this crisis as well. In response to my attempts at helping him he wrote, "Even if I never do the right thing, I appreciate all the time, money and effort you have put in over the years. You always made me feel as though I was not completely alone." Eventually, he paid back all of the money I had sent.

Jerry had written a letter on the thirteenth of May,1992, which informed me of the loss of the only father he had really known. It began with the usual apology for not having written, then continued with: "Tom died in April and I'm still having a problem accepting the reality of his death. After over fifty years, I find it hard to believe that he won't be coming home any more. He was one of the few people in my life that I knew I could always rely on to be absolutely consistent from one year to the next. I did try to phone you for three nights following his death, but I guess you were away on one of your trips. After the funeral I had some busy days going over papers with his relatives, and with the reading of the will. No one said anything one way or the other, but they didn't seem overjoyed about the fact that he had left the farm to me. Please keep the copy of the will that I'm enclosing, in case something happens to me before the estate is settled."

Never, in any of his communication to me—before he lost Tom or after—did he mention either his former wife Dana, his two stepchildren, or even his biological daughter Susan, other than to hint that she, like him, was experiencing an unhappy life. The last actual letter I received from Jerry was written at the end of July, 1995. It is all-too-indicative of the depression that had apparently worsened steadily after Tom's death. In it he, quite uncharacteristically, mentioned other members of our family. For example: "I wonder if Don can handle his retirement. You no doubt know that we have never been close in any way, but I hope you encourage him to do a lot of writing. He was very good at it when he was young." On the following page, he said that Myrtle had phoned a few days before. "I guess they were doing an Alberta tour. She asked if I would like them to drop by for a brief visit and, luckily for me, I was able to dissuade her. I probably hurt her feelings, but I have this terrible habit of telling the truth, and I'm just not in the mood for visitors these days. I don't like people very much, and I really don't see why I should pretend that I do. I try never to intrude on other people's lives and can't see why I'm not given the same consideration. Anyway, I'm sure you've got my point that if you give me a miss on your holiday I will not feel slighted. It's nothing personal. It's just that now I'm down on the whole human race."

A couple of years after this, on our last road trip to the prairies, we did make a brief stop at the farm on our way home, without letting my reclusive brother know we were coming. Sandy waited in the car while I went in to check on Jerry, as I hadn't heard from him for some time. I was appalled by the appearance of the yard. Where there had once been a thriving garden there was now only a bed of weeds. And, not far from the house, were the rusted remains of two cars—both of which we had given to him over the years, when we had purchased new ones. Not a sign of life stirred anywhere. After I had pounded for some time, Jerry did finally answer the door and reluctantly allow me to enter. The inside of the house was an even worse shambles than the surrounding yard. Jerry was so obviously uncomfortable with my presence that I stayed only a few minutes. That was the occasion of our final farewell at the door.

In December of 1999, on what turned out to be his last Christmas, he sent his card early in order to tell me not to go to the bother of shopping and mailing off a parcel to him. He was aware of how difficult my life had become due to Sandy's failing health, having gone through it all with Tom. By the time his birthday arrived I was so overcome with the stress of daily commitments and my own worsening health problems that, for the first time in my life, I utterly forgot it. So I failed even to make the usual annual phone call. The last message I was ever to receive from him was on a card that arrived some time after. "I was going to write a letter," he wrote. "However, since I live such an uninteresting life I could think of nothing worth saying."

A few weeks later, Myrtle phoned, with the devastating news that Jerry had fallen from a ladder inside the house and been discovered by his neighbour, who apparently made a habit of looking in on him each day. The neighbour had phoned Myrtle, with the information that—as it was clear that Jerry's hip was broken—they had rushed him to Emergency in the Red Deer hospital. Unfortunately, because that region had just been struck by a cyclone and suffered a number of casualties, he was left to wait on a Gurney in the hallway for hours. He died there of a 'massive heart attack'. In a subsequent phone call the neighbour told me they had found well-worn copies of three of my books on his kitchen table. Apparently, this kind man was the only person who had remained in contact with Jerry. He was the husband of the couple who had purchased Jerry and Dana's former home next door to Tom's. He and his wife were living in the little house built by Jerry himself soon after he was married, in the quarter section lost to him by the divorce.

## LOSS OF A HUSBAND

Sandy's gradual debilitation and death—and the care-giving required for it—was even more demanding for me than my mother's had been. There was, however, a significant difference between the two, something which gave me considerable comfort. Sandy had lived a productive and fulfilling life, and I think it was the satisfaction with this life that made it possible for him to accept its difficult and drawn-out ending quite placidly. This acceptance on his part was the source of a degree of peace for me as well, as was the support of the family. Speaking of which, I have a wonderful memory of the Christmas of 1997—the last one during which Sandy was close to being himself. It was also the last time I decorated our home for the holiday. My friends, the Humphreys, had lent me a small artificial Christmas tree. Don and Vi came out from Regina for the occasion, bringing Rob with them. Everything was done with as little stress as possible for all concerned. We even went so far as to order the meal ready-cooked from a nearby hotel. Just before their arrival, I had purchased my last car—the mauve-coloured Toyota Camry which I'm still driving. Don got some good practice breaking it in, as Vancouver suffered a rare extreme snowfall during their visit.

Another reason for our lack of stress during the holiday was that the previous spring I persuaded Sandy to consider selling his remaining interest in the family farm at Rosetown. I had been noticing that he could no longer manage the book-keeping and financial management required for the renting of it. On Tom's advice, we arranged for the entire matter of the sale to be looked after by a lawyer in Rosetown, the son of an old friend of Sandy's. We met with the lawyer on what we both surmised would be our last trip together to the prairies. We had flown to Calgary and rented a car there for the remainder of our trip. The sale was finalized by late summer. I could see that all this had contributed a great deal to Sandy's peace of mind during what none of us then knew would be the last Christmas holiday of which he was fully aware.

Soon after this, Sandy was diagnosed with Parkinson's disease, along with severe heart and circulatory problems. I managed to locate a good walker for him so that he could continue navigating as much as possible on his own. As long as his mind was still functioning adequately he was insistent on maintaining his independence. He continued to go for solitary walks along the seawall until, one day, he didn't return at the usual time. I called our extremely caring concierge, John, and told him what had happened. We both rushed off to look for him—taking different paths—he, driven by the kindness of his heart and I, by panic. We found Sandy wandering aimlessly in the park, some distance from the seawall and struggling pathetically to push his walker through the grass. It was not long after this that I was having a brief rest one afternoon when I heard a thud in the hall. Sandy was unconscious on the floor.

Thus began what was to be a long series of rushed trips to the local hospital Emergency. I discovered that he had suffered a stroke. Sandy hated the hospital, so I always tried to bring him home as soon as possible after every attack. But each time, one more element of the self that was Sandy appeared to have been left behind somewhere. As time wore on, our doctor discovered that he had developed prostate cancer as well; but that, in itself, was scarcely a tragedy at the time. Dr. Bluman attempted to re-assure us by telling Sandy that he would die 'with' cancer, but not 'of' it.

That first stroke had occurred in mid-December of 1999. On the day that Sandy was allowed to return home Dave came to visit him. Shane had just arrived from Calgary for Christmas. As he walked into the hospital room I noticed Sandy's face light up. "There's my old pal!" he exclaimed, with a sign of clear recognition. Shane and Dave then helped me bring him home so that he could be with us all for Christmas dinner. During the following year his condition steadily worsened, until the point came where he began to mistake me for a nurse. By then I was getting a couple of hours of 'home help' each weekday, and I assumed he was referring to these helpers. But he maintained his sense of humour and of responsibility throughout, as well as his desire to be productive. He had intended to write his life story, but had postponed it for too long. All through his last two difficult years, he would sit on the sofa and murmur comments about the course of that life which I could never quite make out. I was grateful that he didn't appear to realize the futility of his self-appointed task. All-too-soon, the time came when the only thing he could accomplish as far as housework went was to untangle the wire on the phone. This he did studiously several times every day. In one of his periods of lucidity he once moaned sadly, "I can't even earn my keep!" I assured him he had much more than 'earned his keep' throughout his entire life. Another time his typical humour re-surfaced as he asked me, "Who's on 'bum patrol' today?'

Whenever one of the home helpers arrived to provide me with a brief break, I made a practice of leaving our apartment and taking the little ferry over to the market on Granville Island. There I would simply sit at a table, treating myself to coffee and a snack, and talking to anyone who happened to come over to share the table with me. I think now that it was this brief break each day—in a cheerfully social atmosphere where I was responsible for nothing whatsoever—that allowed me to survive those terrible years.

Because of those wonderful grandchildren who were closest to him—Jennie, a student at UBC at the time, Shane who flew out from Calgary, and Carolyn who came up from her job in Seattle—Sandy's last Christmas was a happy one. Not only did all three spend the day with us, but they insisted on being in charge of the entire meal. Actually, the girls took over the organizing and cooking, while Shane went to the market on the little ferry to purchase the turkey and fresh vegetables. However, during the entire preparation and cooking process, Shane pretended to be the chief chef with the girls merely doing his bidding. The only task actually assigned to him was peeling the potatoes and then mashing them. The three of them had an uproarious time in the kitchen, and the entire apartment reverberated with their laughter all afternoon and evening. It brought back memories of the old days when they were little children, marching in circles around the house, each trying to outdo the others in some sort of imaginary theatrical performance. Grandpa sat in his special chair throughout, smiling happily. Later that evening, after the splendid meal was over and I was preparing him for bed, he murmured, "That was the best Christmas of my whole life!"

By the end of September in 2001 my health had also become severely impaired, but I was determined to keep struggling in order to do for Sandy what he had always done for others—and would have done for me if the situation were reversed. In August I had undergone a life-saving operation for an abdominal-aortic aneurysm which was at the point of bursting. This involved the implanting of a 'stent' from my heart down to the bottom of my intestinal tract. Our daughter-in-law Vi came out from Regina to be with me, and we placed Sandy in a Respite Home for a month. When he returned, I managed to continue caring for him, albeit with considerably increased home-care assistance.

I had saved my own life by diagnosing my problem from some internet research undertaken as a result of two other family tragedies which occurred during the previous two years. I was spurred on by a gradually dawning realization of the meaning of those 'massive heart attacks' which had plagued our Duffy relatives. Apparently, the tendency to develop aneurysms is inherited, but the actual attacks are precipitated by stress. One of these tragedies was, of course, that of Jerry's sudden death in the Emergency waiting room in the summer of 2000. Another happened the following year, in the spring of 2001. Once again, Myrtle was contacted—this time by Margaret, Bob's wife in Halifax. Bob had been found dead on his bed by his granddaughter Catherine, the only child of his son Paul, who lived with them. For the first time in the long series of such deaths in the Duffy family, a coroner's examination of cause of death had been made, and it was discovered that this cause was a burst aneurysm in the brain. Bob, with his ironic Irish sense of humour, would have been greatly amused by the fact that he had saved my life—not by reaching out to me while living, but by dying far too young. Another leaf dropped prematurely!

Tom and Ellyn were with us for a brief visit on Sandy's last Thanksgiving. Then in early November, Dave and Wendy and the girls came over to celebrate Carolyn's birthday. I ordered in pizzas, and managed to make a salad, which was about my limit just then where entertaining was concerned. Wendy provided the cake. A few weeks after this, a couple of good friends from our Humanist community, Hylton and Belle Smith, came over. They had brought a little chocolate cake from our Granville Island market. By this time I was having to feed Sandy mashed or liquid foods by the spoon. Belle took over the task for me—the first visitor ever to have thought to do so—and I was able to relax utterly as she gave him all the rich chocolate he wanted. I had been limiting his diet, but suddenly realized that, at this stage, he should be allowed to eat anything he desired. A few days after that pleasant interlude, Sandy had another stroke. During one of his lucid periods prior to it he had let me know that I was not to send him to Emergency ever again. So I called on John, the concierge, to get him into bed, as I was no longer able to do any lifting. Then I phoned the community health nurse, who came at once.

By the time she arrived, Sandy had become conscious and, surprisingly, was more aware of his surroundings than had been the case for a very long time. After the nurse had done some checking of his condition—and some questioning of us both—she turned to him and said, "Sandy, you're going to have to go to St. Paul's Hospice as soon as we can find you a bed."

"I don't *have* to go anywhere!" came Sandy's firm response. I had promised long before to care for him at home, until the end, whatever it required. And that's what happened. What made this possible was that I received valuable, but not generally known, information from both a doctor friend in the United States and my sister-in-law Donna in Victoria. I was told that Hospice nurses were now available to come to private homes in order to take over and provide the care-giver with help in such situations. So I asked the community nurse, who seemed unaware of this, to arrange the service for us.

Not only did these wonderful, caring young men and women take turns tending to Sandy at night, so that I could get a break, but they also provided morphine to keep him free from pain. And they taught me how to administer it. All this was done with the help and advice of our wonderful doctor, Robert Bluman, who made regular home visits. On the last of these he bent over Sandy's bed and said, "It's been a privilege to know you, Sandy. You're the only patient I've ever had who was always more concerned with what he was costing the health system than with his own needs."

Dr. Bluman supplied me with sleeping pills as well so that, for Sandy's last two weeks of life, I was able to relax at night, and to care for him on my own during the day. Then, five days before he died, our son Don arrived from Regina, to provide additional help. Dave came over to sit by his father's bed when his work hours would allow it. Also, Carolyn traveled up from her workplace in Seattle whenever she could; and Jennie was with us during all her free time.

On what was to be Sandy's last day of being able to swallow any food or drink, he whispered to me that he wanted some sherry. Amazed, I brought him a small amount of it, along with a straw, but he turned his head away, muttering, "Not like that!" After a stunned moment I realized that he wanted a proper sherry glass. I found one and then, just before managing to take a couple of swallows through the straw that I was holding for him, he said, quite clearly "To our grandchildren." That was his final drink, and those were the last words he ever uttered. What could have been more typical of all that Sandy had ever been!

Because the majority of our extended family would not all be available until mid-January, we planned the memorial service at the Vancouver Unitarian church for that time, to be arranged by our long-time friend, Conrad Hadland, a Humanist chaplain. But, as Carolyn, Jennie, Shane and Nguyet all insisted on coming to be with me for Christmas, the Humphreys and I decided to take advantage of that and have our own private 'celebration of life' for our dear departed friend, husband and grandfather. Graham and Pam led us along a short path, manageable even for me in my feeble physical condition. This path intersected the Deep Cove hiking trail, for the upkeep of which our hiking club had long been responsible. We came to a little bridge over a stream: the very bridge that Sandy and Graham had often worked together at repairing. The four grandchildren then took turns spreading their Grandpa's ashes over the stream. That experience will always remain a comforting memory for me.

At the formal service in January, a poem of mine was read. It is one that has been used—in appropriately altered form—at other farewell ceremonies as well.

## IMMORTALITY

*He who in life sought neither power*
*nor yet the wider world's acclaim,*
*may seem to leave no trace beyond*
*the fading echo of his name.*
*No trace upon the unmarked ground*
*on which his forthright steps have passed.*
*No well-paved trail to stay the growth*
*of spring's regenerating grass.*

*But time dissolves all monuments*
*to selfish fame that can accrue.*
*Relentlessly the pen moves on,*
*selecting what endures as true;*
*and marks upon posterity*
*the actions we cannot disown.*
*Our passage through this world is cast*
*More tellingly than any stone.*

*As Sandy touched the lives of those*
*his living presence gladly knew,*
*so he bequeathed a heritage—*
*an awareness of the good and true.*
*For all his actions will endure,*
*are added to the culture's store;*
*like ripples on a mountain stream,*
*his passage felt for evermore.*

*His life was marked by courage*
*and a singular integrity.*
*From such as he stems all that we*
*can know of human dignity.*
*Our world became a better place*
*for he altered everyone he knew.*
*And we are all the richer now*
*because of his brief passing through.*

## LOSS OF OTHER DEAR ONES

Although the night I went to bed on the tenth of December, 2001, had been the last time I would ever say goodnight to Sandy, it was not as hurtful as it would have been in different circumstances. As Dr. Bluman said on our phone when he was reporting to officials from our home early the following morning, it had been 'an expected death'. Similarly, it is to be expected that, during the closing decades of our lives, 'last times' multiply as we lose old friends and family members at an increasingly rapid rate. We can't really know what this means, however, until it happens to us. Many of those closest to me have dropped from the tree of life, making my own particular forest gradually more barren.

A far-too-early death occurred in the early 1980s in the case of my long-time friend, Ellen Krempien. She had been suffering from a liver infection picked up a few years earlier during a visit to Africa where her younger son, Brian, was working prior to his sudden death soon after she left. She visited us in Vancouver while attending a conference. This brief interlude in her busy life had followed her husband Howard's slow deterioration and dying process. I recall her gentle scolding of me for having been so reckless in failing to retain a secure job and pension in preparation for retirement. She, on the other hand, had even invested in a second house in Calgary. Only a few months after that visit she wrote that she had been struck down by severe liver failure. It was her last letter. She, who had worried so about security in her old age, had not even made it to sixty!

Another unexpected death was that of my youngest Hutcheon brother-in-law, Alan. He had actually died a few months before Sandy. Alan's last visit from Lesoto in southern Africa was in the early 90s. I remember the moment we said goodbye, as he was boarding the ferry for Vancouver Island to visit his brother-in-law, and my old friend and colleague, Les Crossman, who was then living out his last days in Victoria. After our farewell, Alan began to walk away. Then, suddenly, he turned and looked at us both as we all three stood, stock still—seemingly suspended in time. I realized at that instant that Alan did not intend ever again to return from Africa. It was one of those rare moments in life when I have been keenly aware that this was, indeed, one of those 'last times'.

Without previous warning, my brother-in-law, Bill Westcott died of a heart attack in 2006 when he was only in his sixties. When I heard the news

I was doubly grateful that he and his wife Rose had been able to make it over from Victoria for my seventy-fifth birthday party, which Wendy had arranged in 2001—just three months before Sandy's death. Bill had taken a turn at speaking after the meal. His words meant a great deal to me, as he told the collection of family and friends that I was 'the first love of his life'. He was referring to his early summers with us on the farm in the Valley.

Another sudden disappearance occurred in the case of my old friends, Bob and Nobuko Gowen, who had lived in North Carolina for most of his professional life as a university professor of history. This particular 'last time' is still entirely unexplained. Always, at Christmas time, he and I exchanged lengthy letters. Then, in 2005, nothing arrived from him. I attempted by every means possible to contact their home, but to no avail. Not telling me that something bad was happening was so unlike him, and made his loss as a lifetime friend doubly tragic for me. Still, when I began to muse about his last letter, it came to me that there had been a strange sentence near the end of it which may have carried a message. "At least, I'm not drooling", he had written.

There have been other times when I have been fortunate enough to have one last, good visit, as in the case of my dear friend Ross Woodward: a Humanist leader from Spokane, a longtime radio broadcaster from Lethbridge Alberta, and a former Mormon. We were almost exactly the same age and had a great deal in common. After he had been diagnosed with a terminal illness he and his wife Jan came to see me. His thoughtfulness bequeathed me a comforting memory of what was to be our last walk on the seawall: one that I can relive each time I traverse the same path. It was during that pleasant walk that he told me he had hung my picture on his wall next to that of Bertrand Russell.

Another dear friend, a fellow Unitarian named Claude Kershaw, also managed a final farewell—although I didn't recognize it as such at the time. She phoned me to re-visit our shared experiences throughout our nineteen years of friendship, then closed the conversation with a rather prolonged goodbye, in spite of the fact that she was obviously having a difficult time breathing. She had been suffering for some time from ALS. The very next day her husband Bryan phoned to let me know she was gone. He said she'd been aware of death's immediate approach, as her doctor always promised to allow her to go naturally once her disease shut down the lungs. I gave the eulogy for her at the church, closing with a quotation from Montagne, her favourite philosopher.

"We seek other conditions because we know not how to enjoy our own; and go outside ourselves for want of knowing what it is like inside us. But it is no use raising ourselves on stilts, for even on stilts we have to walk on our own legs. And, sitting on the loftiest throne in the world, we are still only sitting on our own behinds." I ended by saying that I could imagine hearing her joyous laughter as she marveled—along with Montagne—at the fads and foibles of humankind.

The deaths of Florence and Don Grier—our good friends from early days in Regina—occurred, in each case, not long after I had the opportunity to say goodbye. Our last happy time together was when both had come over from Victoria, where they had moved from Fort Saskatchewan after Don had sold his business there. They were attending Sandy's eightieth birthday party in the Unitarian Fireside Room. Don recited the poem beginning with "You are old, Father William." Then, a few years after Sandy's death, came the farewell for Florence, to which I traveled with Myrtle and Mike. At the table where the small group gathered I sat next to Don. As I got up to leave we held one another closely, each probably guessing that it would be the last time. And it was. Don did not survive long after that.

Another 'last time' of which I was aware as it was happening was a brief visit to my old home town of Oyen, on our way back to Calgary from Rosetown in our rented car, following the arrangement with a lawyer for the sale of the remainder of original farm still owned by Sandy. On the spur of the moment, upon reaching the point on the main highway where the side road led to Oyen, I turned down it with the intention of spending only a half-hour walking around on the town's old main street. I knew that the chance would never come again. The only building I recognized was the old hotel. Just outside of it, there appeared two men who looked puzzlingly familiar. I took a chance and approached them, asking if they had ever known Lew Duffy. "You're Pat!" one of them shouted. Then recognition dawned for me. "And you're the Burke brothers!" I exclaimed. We had a wonderful ten minutes of conversation, recalling happy times together. The sad part, however, was that we had no time to visit Joyce, the sister-in-law of all three of us, who was by then widowed and living in a seniors' residence in town. Sandy and I had to rush off to Calgary to catch our flight home. But at least I was able to send her a message through family members, rather than merely by mail and telephone. She, like so many others who had once been close, became a 'fallen leaf' not long after.

What happened in the case of two of our small groups of close friends within the Unitarian community is another example of the gradual fall of leaves. One of these groups, which began as a neighbourhood gathering of about a dozen, met every month for many years at one another's homes. In addition, we celebrated our birthdays and other special days together, for at least two decades. The last two of these were ninetieth birthdays: first of Ursula Whitehead, and then of Tom Cluett. Both parties were at our place. Of all the former members, now only two of us remain—Fran Cluett and myself, and we connect mainly by phone. In a somewhat similar fashion, Sandy and I were part of a set of three couples who developed the custom of having dinner in one another's homes. The other two were Blanche and Bruce Howard and Marilyn Flitton and her partner Norm Hoye. I had one of my 'last time' forebodings shortly before Bruce died, when we all met downtown in a restaurant. Before long, both Marilyn and Sandy were also dead and Norm had moved away. Now there are only Blanche and myself.

Even a number of close friends who were hardy members of the Golden Age Hiking Club have succumbed over the years. One of the first of these to go was our original leader, John Liebe. I visited him in his seniors' home in Abbotsford after his physical health began to deteriorate badly, and was amazed to find him as fervently engaged in the study of astronomy as he had previously been in hiking. After that visit I wrote a poem to honour him.

### TO AN OLD HIKER TURNED ASTRONOMER

*You who in nature's ways have trailed,*
*are now to scholarship confined.*
*But time and aging limbs have failed*
*to limit an inquiring mind.*

*For now a broader range you seek;*
*horizons new to understand.*
*You who have climbed earth's mountain peaks*
*now hold the world within your hand.*

*You who have probed life's history,*
*and mapped the contours of our land,*
*discover now infinity;*
*a universe to understand.*

*For you have found a peace sublime,*
*who knows that life can only be*
*a moment in the stream of time*
*borrowed from eternity.*

*No more a prisoner of place;*
*you reach for Jupiter and Mars.*
*For you have scaled the peaks of space,*
*and roam at will among the stars.*

Another hiking companion who, along with his wife Julie, had become a good friend of ours, was Fred Fuchs. I attempted, in the poem I wrote in his memory after his death, to express the essence of what he had always meant to me.

## TO A FALLEN COMRADE

*We miss your presence on the trail;*
*Your grasp of the terrain;*
*We miss your cheery countenance*
*Through wind and snow and rain.*
*The arguments that made the mountains echo in reply,*
*The sheer dependability of hand and foot and eye.*

*We miss the helping hand outstretched*
*In brotherhood and love,*
*The firmness of the arm extended*
*From the rock above,*
*We cherish most the leadership that helped us all to learn;*
*And we weep for all who venture forth on the path of no return.*

And there was Andy Mate, an extremely intellectually able Hungarian refugee who had escaped during the revolution, at about the same time as had the young Forestry student, John Gyorfi, who married my niece Linda. Sandy and I enjoyed numerous interesting conversations with Andy, on our many years of shared hikes. Then came the day when we were hiking over on Gibson's Landing, and he asked me to take a picture of him. I remember thinking it was rather uncharacteristic of him. A few weeks later, he and Sandy were tramping along together on the pathway up Mount Hollyburn when Andy suddenly fell. It was his last hike. We learned that he had terminal leukemia, probably as a result of his years of working in the home renovation industry as a painter.

There was a sufficiently long period of dying for him to tell me, on our last visit, the story of his escape from Hungary. I later sent the tape to his sons. Andy also used his final period of life to plan an informal goodbye for his friends. He arranged for a bench in one of Vancouver's central parks to be named for him, and had us gather around it for a final farewell. It was a sad but beautiful occasion, and so typical of him!

### ODE TO ANDY

*For years he offered firm support,*
*Our group evolved its culture and its form from such as he.*
*Although his thread is broken off*
*His strength remains within the cloth,*
*For Andy lives in memory within each heart and head,*
*A treasured chapter in our club's long hiking history.*

*I see him poised in silhouette,*
*Mouth organ raised and music floating on the noonday breeze—*
*Pied piper in a hiker's guise*
*Both innocent and worldly wise,*
*He brought his love for Canada to every hike he trod,*
*And celebrated freedom in her mountains and her trees.*

*Most of all it is the memory*
*Of his warmth and joy of living and his friendship that remains—*
*Though he is dead we feel it still,*
*And always, just beyond some hill,*
*We'll sense his presence on the trail ahead*
*And hear his laughter lilting back upon the summer rains.*

Andy's farewell and eventual death—and Sandy's as well—exemplify the inherent beauty of those colourful leaves fertilizing the ground for the coming spring. Much more tragic, however, have been instances in my life when the death of a family member came all-too-soon, just as some fierce storm or human-caused mishap results in green leaves being thrust to the ground before the approach of autumn. Possibly the most shocking of all such events was when my cousin Rita, the youngest of the Carry family, was found murdered in her home in Los Angeles before she had even reached middle age. There were no signs of a break-in and, to my knowledge, the crime was never solved. And then there was the case of my aunt Dot, concerning whose illness—which proved to be a rapidly advancing fatal cancer—I had been unpardonably nonchalant during our last visit.

Two nieces who, for various reasons, were very special to me, met sudden deaths. In each case it happened just after I had, for some minor reason, turned away from a chance for a good visit with them. Jerry's daughter Susan died at the beginning of 2002, with no previous warning, of a massive heart attack. Her three young daughters were with her at the time. Just a week before, she had phoned and asked when they could come over, as she was in the city for Christmas, visiting her mother Dana. I felt too overwhelmed by Sandy's death at the time, and put her off. Then, at the end of October in 2006, the niece who was always closest to me was killed in a car accident. It happened when Linda, Myrtle's only daughter, was traveling with her husband John on the road from Kitimat to Prince George. They were intending to celebrate their fortieth wedding anniversary. She had phoned only a few days previously. After informing me of their plans to come down to the Lower Mainland in the very near future, she began to discuss the details of her four children's lives, as she loved to do at considerable length. At the time, because my neck and back were very painful, I interrupted and suggested that we get caught up, instead, when they came to visit. So I had actually cut her off, on my last chance for a meaningful conversation!

### LAST TIMES

*If I had known that it would be*
*The one last time*
*When I would ever hear my father's voice,*
*I would not have turned away so recklessly*
*And climbed aboard the train with no farewell,*
*I would not have made that egocentric choice*
*If I had only known.*

*If I had known it was to be*
*The one last time*
*That I would glide in bliss around a dance-hall floor,*
*Afloat upon the music and my partner's skillful arms,*
*Forgetting all my problems in that momentary bliss*
*Before I sensed the closing of a door.*
*If I had only known*

*If I had known that it would be*
*The one last time*
*When I would ever run so wild and free*
*In that 'Foothill country' Western paradise*
*Behind our racing dog—so painlessly*
*When all the world seemed waiting there for me.*
*If I had only known.*

*If I had known that it would be*
*The one last time*
*I'd drift suspended in that interlude of time*
*Descending downward on my gliding skis*
*Before I lost all feeling in my legs as numbness struck*
*And terror claimed that moment so sublime.*
*If I had only known.*

*If I had known that it would be*
*The one last time*
*My 'baby' brother would be here to celebrate his birth*
*I would not have failed to send his gift and make my special call*
*Regardless of my husband's illness and the endless care required*
*I would have realized that birthday's worth.*
*If I had only known.*

*If I had known that it would be*
*The one last time*
*For a chance to bring that brother's daughter close to me,*
*After many years of missing as she passed me in the dark,*
*I would not have left the message that, as Sandy had just died,*
*She was simply one of many I was too upset to see.*
*But soon I heard that she was dead as well.*
*A 'massive heart attack', they said, her children looking on—*
*If I had only known.*

*If I had only known that it would be*
*The one last time*
*I would ever hear my dearest niece's voice.*
*In lively conversation from her home in Kitimat*
*That happy voice conveying all the news of family,*
*I would not have cut her off by reckless choice.*
*Because they planned to visit soon.*
*But a mere few days went by until her daughter's sobbing call—*
*"An accident! Their car has crashed! And only Dad survived!"*
*If I had only known.*
*If I had known?*

# Chapter 22

## SOWING SEEDS

I recall quite vividly when the metaphor first came to me. I was attending the funeral of Bruce, the husband of a close friend and fellow writer, Blanche Howard. After the ceremony, I noticed Blanche's friend—the famous novelist, Carol Shields—sitting quietly in a corner. I was aware that she had been suffering from terminal cancer for some time, and the tense positioning of her body confirmed the severity of her illness. At first I wasn't sure if I should go over to speak to her. Then, on the spur of the moment I chose to do so, and my words of greeting were utterly unplanned.

"Carol," I burst out, "there's something I'd like to say to you. I want to thank you for your beautifully expressed and thought-provoking novels. And I hope you realize that what you've been doing is planting fruitful seeds in the culture of humankind."

She turned to me, her face suddenly relaxed and smiling. "That's one of the most wonderful things anyone's ever suggested about my writing!" she said. Then her daughter approached, and they moved into the adjoining room to join the others.

I sat there thinking about the words I had just uttered so spontaneously. Not only had they obviously surprised and pleased Carol, but they had, in some strange way, shocked me to the core. But of course! That's what we writers and educators try to do! My entire lifetime of teaching, public speaking and writing had been aimed at that one goal: to leave in my wake seeds of enlightenment and reason that might someday—as they come to fruition in the minds and actions of students, listeners and readers—contribute to a more enlightened and less destructive culture of the future.

Just how successful my contributions have been I shall never know. But I do know that I have enjoyed the effort. Looking back now at my hectic life during the closing decade of the twntieth century and the first of the new millennium, I find myself deriving great pleasure and satisfaction from what I can only hope to have accomplished in some small part. This feeling is accentuated by the beautiful ocean view of Burrard Inlet and Howe Sound, and the snow-capped Coast Mountains across on the North Shore, which I see as I sit at my computer. How could I possibly have been so fortunate as to end my productive years in this marvelous Vancouver location, given those early days at that Lonely Trail School on the dusty, flat Alberta prairies! I have had such a wonderful life, in spite of episodes of loss and pain: a life filled with such remarkable people—family, teachers and friends—who planted potentially fruitful seeds in me throughout my formative years.

Many of the opportunities to communicate the ideas sprung from those seeds came from my association with the Canadian Unitarian movement, which I first discovered during my university years in Calgary. A favourite professor had remarked, "Anyone who thinks as you do should join the Unitarians." So I acted upon his suggestion, and for the first time in my life discovered a group of like-minded people. Many years later, following my so-called retirement, I received numerous invitations to speak at their services throughout the Lower Mainland and Vancouver Island. I usually accepted and enjoyed them all. My chief goal was to explain humanism in terms that might be attractive to the agnostic sceptics (or Freethinkers) still remaining in the organization, for I was concerned about the gradual diminishing of this crucially important current of thought within Unitarianism. Most of my services dealt with a humanist perspective on spirituality, non-supernaturally based moral education, and the roots of Unitarianism in the era of the Humanist Renaissance. During the same period I designed "On the Shoulders of Giants": a two-year curriculum on moral education at the youth level. This Sunday School program was subsequently used not only as part of the Vancouver church's religious education, but by a number of Unitarian Universalist churches in the American Pacific Northwest.

Another involvement which was to prove fruitful for the seeds I was hoping to sow was my connection with the Canadian and the British Columbian Humanist organizations. Most memorable was the initial contact with the journal *Humanist in Canada*. I had submitted an article called "Michel de Montaigne's Goslings" in which I quoted this great sixteenth century thinker's famous comment that man could not make a mite, but he makes gods by the dozen. "For every creature there is nothing dearer or more estimable than its own being . . . and each relates the qualities of other things to its own qualities . . . . Beyond this relation and principle our minds cannot go. For why should a gosling not say thus: 'All parts of the universe have *me* in view: the earth serves for *me* to walk on, the sun to give *me* light, the stars to breathe their influence into *me*.' Now, by this same reasoning we human beings are the end and goal of which the universality of things arises." I received an enthusiastic response from the editor, along with an invitation to send them more of my work.

*Humanist in Canada* published my article on "The Legacy of Isaac Azimov" not long after this. I had learned a great deal through the years by reading Asimov's writings: both his science fiction—which, unlike most of that of today, was invariably based on sound science—and his comprehensive essays. Before submitting the article I had sent it to Azimov for a check 'from the horse's mouth'. He immediately returned a warmly appreciative card. But before my piece was published I heard that he had died. A later publication of a version of that first article provided an opportunity for me to pay homage to this remarkable sower of seeds. The introduction to the chapter on him in my book, *The Road to Reason* (2001; 2003), goes as follows:

"Azimov was a great humanist who vastly enriched the culture of our time with his entertaining and informative books. Indeed, his influence was so pervasive that much of what he was and believed and valued will live as long as there are people to read and think and wonder. Perhaps even more important was his contribution to the struggle against one of the greatest dangers facing humankind in this century: the growth of scientific illiteracy in the population at large, and the resulting cultural dominance of pre-scientific world views."

One of the experiences I particularly enjoyed where this humanist magazine was concerned was the time the editor, Joe Piercy, and his wife and leading staff member, Blodwen, asked me to respond to a controversial piece they were publishing which attacked the then-relatively new subject of sociobiology. The author had referred to sociobiology as a 'dangerous doctrine' because it attempted to apply evolutionary principles to humans. I was happy to write a critical response with the title "Fear Ignorance—Not Sociobiology!". Soon after the two articles came out the mail brought a delightful letter of appreciation from that great American pioneer of sociobology, E.O. Wilson. This marked the beginning of an interesting and fruitful professional relationship, at least for me.

Over the many years of my contributing to *Humanist in Canada* I had the pleasure of being informed by various international editors that my articles were being re-published in Ireland, Australia and Britain. One popular piece on multiculturalism was even translated for journals in Norway, Belgium and the Netherlands. The subject of multiculturalism had been growing increasingly problematic to me as I watched what I viewed as its misrepresentation and faulty application in Canada. The idea had initially been formulated as a formal concept by sociologists who considered it—not a separation into 'Us versus Them' religious-ethnic groupings—but as a river of customs and ideals being continuously altered by innovation from tributaries flowing into it, with a gradual integration of the most successfully functioning contributions of all the immigrating cultures into that of a welcoming nation such as Canada. It was expected that this evolving process would result in an ongoing enrichment and reform of the nature of the 'commons' shared by immigrants and natives alike. In other words, the concept was intended as 'inter-culturalism'—not as the new and increasingly dangerous form of tribalism that it is now threatening to become. I had a chance to explain this in detail some years later when my former University of Regina colleague, Evelina Orteza, asked me to write a scholarly article on the subject for *The Canadian and International Journal of Education*. I called it "Multiculturalism: Good Intentions and a Clouded Vision?"

In March of 1997 I had the satisfaction of returning to UBC as the keynote speaker at their Interdisciplinary Graduate Conference. My topic was "Social Science at the Crossroads" and, during that session in the Education Tower and the follow-up discussions, I greatly enjoyed discussing the conclusions of my doctoral thesis. It was a rare opportunity to apply those findings and ideas to the current concerns and desires of my audience to move in an interdisciplinary direction.

Also, in early 1997, I was invited by the *Vancouver Sun* newspaper to submit a column in answer to one they had received from a leader of the Chinese immigrant community who was pushing for the intact retention, within Vancouver, of the culture of her homeland. My response was given the title of "Does Multiculturalism Unite Canada?". It dealt with four beliefs which the original writer had denigrated as myths. These were: (1) that 'hyphenated' Canadians might pose a threat to Canadian unity; (2) that multiculturalism, as currently practised, tends to divide; (3) that multiculturalism provides special privileges for some groups while denying them to others; and (4) that multiculturalism accentuates *differences* among ethnic groups, rather than *similarities*. I tried to show how all four of these possibilities are, in fact, becoming increasingly the case, in spite of the good intentions of everyone. In my summing-up paragraph I emphasized the overriding importance of consequences where behaviour is concerned, regardless of intentions.

"In the real world where nations either evolve a common cultural core or fragment into warring factions," I wrote, "Consequences are all! And the consequences of continuing confusion and contradiction in fundamental cultural policy could be suicidal for our fragile country."

I also once spoke on "A Humanist Perspective on Spirituality" at a joint conference in Toronto organized by the American Center for Inquiry and the Humanist Association of Canada. As the term 'spirituality' has so many supernatural connotations, I made a point of referring to its ancient meaning as 'the breath of life', rather than belief in gods, or 'spiritualism'. I defined spirituality, instead, as the sense of awe and wonder aroused in humans by the marvels of nature—coupled with, and coloured by, our imagination and values. After having suggested the possibility of mining all the ancient world religions and philosophies for possible contributions to a new world view to be pioneered by Canada—one capable of uniting rather than dividing human beings—I ended my talk with the following suggestion:

"How about the Golden Rule of Confucius; the Right Way of the Buddha; the tolerance for pluralism typical of ancient Hinduism; the Classical Greek concern for freedom and democracy; a non-supernatural rendering of the Ten Commandments of the Jews; the Taoist focus upon unity and interdependence within nature; teachings credited to Jesus of Nazareth on simple human kindness and love for one's neighbours; Mohammed's emphasis on honesty and social obligation; the work ethic of Saint Benedict; Guru Nanak's devotion to equality and fellowship; Albert Schweitzer's reverence for life and his concept of human responsibility for the survival of that stream of life? All this could then be coupled with the unfettered intellectual curiosity and sceptical inquiry method of the scientific humanist."

I was asked to write many reviews for journals in those days, and complied with the requests from editors whenever the book concerned had aroused my interest. Sometimes this led to embarrassing situations—notably when my review was critical. I recall particularly two books by John Ralston Saul. One was called *Voltaire's Bastards: The Dictatorship of Reason in the West*, which came out in 1993. The second, *The Unconscious Civilization*, was published in 1996. I discussed what I considered their weaknesses and strengths, including the possibility that the author was attacking the crucial concept of reason in Western civilization. I felt that such a negative approach to reason was the very last thing needed in the context of the times, and that it was utterly unsupported by the evidence provided. The second of my rather critical reviews of his work was published in the *Brock Review* under the title of "How About the Unreasoning Civilization?" Not long after this I found myself seated at the head table of a conference in Toronto next to John Ralston Saul! Needless to say, our conversation was extremely limited. Oh the perils of being asked to write book reviews!

Most of my reviews were positive, however. I think the book about which I waxed most enthusiastic was *The Beak of the Finch: The Story of Evolution in our Time*, authored by Jonathon Weiner in 1995. I still believe that Weiner's book should be used in all university biology classes as the most concise and clearly communicated explanation of evolution available. That same year I received an invitation to contribute a chapter to a book on the subject of 'love', and took great pleasure in doing this—especially enjoying the lively interaction with the editors and other writers which was necessarily involved. My choice of subject was "Through a Glass Darkly: Freud's Concept of Love" which became part of David Goicoechia's 1995 book *The Nature and Pursuit of Love: The Philosophy of Irving Singer*, published by Prometheus Books in the US.

In spite of all this activity during the early 1990s, my major efforts were directed toward the completion of my own second book. It came out in 1996, under the title of *Leaving the Cave: Evolutionary Naturalism in Social Scientific Thought*, published by the Wilfrid Laurier University Press in Canada. This book represented the culmination of a lifetime of research and thinking on my part—sparked by that wonderful year of teacher training at the Calgary Normal School. It was a long story of the development of this critically important current of thought from the time of the ancient Greeks to modern sociobiology. As always, I had gone directly to the original works of the great thinkers—studying them in depth until I had achieved full comprehension—and then dealing with their major ideas as concisely as possible.

I began the book with a chapter called "Distant Echoes of a Road Not Taken: Undercurrents of Naturalism in the Classical World". I then proceeded, in the following twenty-five chapters, to sum up the contributions of numerous great thinkers to the now clearly-emerging world view of what I had chosen to call evolutionary naturalism. The list included Erasmus, Montaigne, Hobbes, Hume, Rousseau, Martineau, Darwin, Spencer, Freud,

Pavlov, Dewey, Bergson, Husserl, Durkheim, Weber, Mead, Santayana, Russell, Huxley, Arendt, Fromm, Piaget, Popper, Skinner, Dawkins, Gould and Kuhn. I considered their weaknesses as well as strengths. My introduction contained the following defining paragraph:

"I discovered that the focus of social theory in every generation kept returning to the following issues, and it was the stand taken on these that identified the incipient evolutionary naturalists:

(1) a recognition of the universality of cause and effect;

(2) confirmation of the premise of order underlying the nature of all things;

(3) a recognition of the critical function of language in the process of human knowing;

(4) a spelling-out of the conditional nature of scientific knowledge;

(5) an attempt at a resolution of the 'free will' problem which recognizes the significance of the issue for morality;

(6) the possibility of a response to the question of how humans can determine 'the good' that dispenses with premises of dualism;

(7) an emphasis upon the continuity of means and ends, and thus of the inevitable contribution of human choices to the course of history;

(8) an identification of both the biological and experiential sources of moral development;

(9) a focus on the social origins of power and structures of authority, and on the enduring conflict between democratic and totalitarian approaches to politics;

(10) a recognition of the interactive nature of individual innovation and culture, and of the consequent necessary relationships among science, art, politics and morality;

(11) a concern with the nature of biological evolution, and its implications for our understanding of individual and social behaviours as complex products of an inextricably intertwined genetic-social co-evolution; and

(12) a corresponding concern with the nature of cultural evolution, and with the role of science in the process."

No doubt because of my love of poetry, this five-hundred-page summing up of my lifetime of research began with a poem by Lucretius and ended with one of my own. The beginning was from "De Rerum Natura":

*Nothing at all is ever made from nothing*
*By the gods' will. Ah but men's eyes are frightened*
*Because they see on earth and in the heavens,*
*Many events whose causes are to them*
*Impossible to fix; so they suppose*
*That god's will is the reason. As for us,*
*Once we have seen that nothing comes from nothing,*
*We shall perceive with greater clarity*
*What we are looking for, whence each thing comes,*
*How things are caused, and no 'god's will' about it.*

The last stanza of my own concluding poem—"Evolutionary Spiral"—went as follows:

*But many now recoil in terror at the thought that in our might*
*We hold potentially the power of heaven's throne.*
*So too must hominids in dim-lit caves have shuddered at the sight*
*Of fire new-captured and employed as tool—*
*Til' then the instrument of gods alone.*
*For power gives us choice and choice demands responsibility,*
*And we are ill-prepared by our beliefs in godly wrath*
*And godly grace;*
*So it may be that humankind rejects the opportunity*
*For evolutionary spiral far above the current habits of our race;*
*The violent depredations of our past—*
*And by rejecting science may prefer to pave the way that none can stay,*
*In unremitting spiral down and down,*
*And into 'hell' at last!*

The publication of this book was a defining moment for me. It was only slightly tainted by the fact that there had been a problem with the editing process, and several seemingly small errors—which I had caught and pointed out—had gone uncorrected by the editor, who came down with the flu at an inopportune time. Sadly, these errors caused the two sentences in which they occurred to express factual mistakes. There had been an unfortunate rush to publish because of an International Sociological Conference in Amsterdam at which I was slated to speak, and the publisher wanted this event to provide the formal launch of the book.

In spite of this minor problem, which has probably been noted only by me, the conference was one of the peak experiences of my professional life. My speech was on Harriet Martineau, one of the two female intellectual heroes in my book. The only other female was Hannah Arendt. I had worried about the fact that I was able to include only two women, among all the great thinkers throughout history, but was forced to concede that the social situations in those times had made it virtually impossible for women to succeed in the world of ideas. My talk was extremely well received, and during the enthusiastic discussions in the following days I met many interesting fellow sociologists from around the world. Two of these with whom I was later to work on a book about Harriet Martineau were Michael Hill from Illinois and Susan Hoecker-Drysdale of Montreal.

After the conference was over my friend Maria Smidt picked me up at the hotel and we then proceeded to tour Holland, from one end to the other. She even took me to visit the only Humanist University in existence. I had another opportunity of a lifetime when we went to The Hague and spent several days in the art gallery there. Maria lived in Haarlem, so we began and ended our adventure in that city. It was all a world removed from anything I had ever known. So many features of her country were fascinating to me. Among these were the world-famous dikes, wooden sidewalks, and the orderly progression of both bicycles and pedestrians. One of the most amazing experiences was my reception everywhere, whenever Maria mentioned where I was from. You would think that I, myself, had been one of the Canadian war heroes who had liberated the Netherlands from the Nazis.

Not long after this exciting trip I was contacted by an agent for an American publisher, informing me that they had been very impressed by *Leaving the Cave*, and asking if they could bring out my next book. I responded at once as I was, in fact, already deep into the writing of another one. This became *Building Character and Culture*, and was published by Praeger Press, a branch of Greenwood Publishers, in 1996. In a way, this book represented the logical consequence of all of the conclusions in that doctoral thesis written at the University of Queensland two decades before. For example, I recognize many echoes of my earlier research and theorizing in the concept of the 'triple helix'—an original term coined by my husband Sandy. I used 'triple helix' in the book to explain the three-way interaction among biological mutations in our species and selective feedback not only from the physical environment, but also from the social-cultural surroundings of human beings. I focused on the need to recognize that human distinctiveness resides in our propensities to build both character and culture, and in the key process of socialization connecting the two. This means that we can never resolve our rapidly worsening problems until we face up to our unique capacity for learning: to the fact that humans learn both from the socialization/enculturation process upon which we are so dependent for the content of our beliefs, values and ways of behaving, and also from the physical environment confronting and challenging us at every turn. And both of these are affected by genetic inheritance. I emphasized that it is our immersion in this three-way interactive feedback process of maturational and developmental change that defines the learning human as the most complex of all the dynamic adaptive systems generated by evolution.

Chapter One is devoted to the power of culture; Chapter Two deals with what it means to be human; Chapter Three with the major agents of socialization, and Chapter Four with how children learn. Chapter Five addresses the question of where character actually comes from; and Chapter Six is on the controversial issue of the culture of violence with which we are faced today—whether we admit it or not—and the way in which television, 'killing' games and movies contribute to it. Chapter Seven is about socialization in later life. Chapter Eight is called "A Tale of Two Cultures: The Culture of Affluence and the Culture of Poverty". Chapter Nine asks if we want a culture of pluralism or one of tribalism, and the final chapter is "The Culture of Fantasy: Gullible Victims and the Spinners of Delusion".

The book concludes with two appendices. The first provides specific guideline for moral education, beginning with a list of desired learning outcomes. I chose the following: (1) compassion, (2) honesty, (3) nonviolence, (4) perseverance, (5) responsibility, (6) a sense of justice, (7) courage, (8) respect for the rule of law, (9) respect for life, and (10) respect for human dignity. I then suggested specific means of teaching these to children in each of six stages of intellectual development, beginning with early childhood and ending with teenaged youth. The other appendix contains an annotated bibliography of research on the adverse effects on human development of media portrayals of gratuitous violence and pornography.

At the time *Building Character and Culture* was published my grandson, Rob Hutcheon, was attending the University of Regina Education program. One of his professors brought the book to show to the class, and used the chapter on "How Children Learn" as the basis of his lesson. He told them that no one should go out to teach without having read this book, and mentioned something about the author. I was told that Rob sprang to his feet and blurted out, "That's my Nana!"

A few years after this, I was contacted by Douglas Todd, the *Vancouver Sun* writer who does a regular column on religion and ethics. He had also read my latest book. By this time my husband Sandy's health was deteriorating badly, and I had to settle on being interviewed by phone. Mr. Todd wrote a glowing column on me and my work, referring to me as a 'classy' humanist. In the column he told of how a Tennessee inner-city school had built its program for moral education around *Building Character and Culture*—even labeling hallways by the names of the ten values listed in it. All this provided yet another high point in my lifetime desire to 'sow seeds' which might have a positive nourishing effect on others.

In 2001, Canadian Humanist Publications published my fourth book, *The Road to Reason*. It was reprinted in 2003. It was aimed at intelligent general readers, and was a collection of previously published articles on the great thinkers whose ideas have shed light along that road, beginning with the Buddha and concluding with a chapter on the nature and sources of free will. I explained humanism in terms of its necessary premise of evolutionary naturalism—in contrast to spiritualism, transcendentalism and any other form of dualism. I noted three additional premises implied by this major defining premise of humankind's common origin with other animals, all three stemming from the distinctiveness of the human species within that common nature. These are: (1) an emphasis on the process of human knowing, and on the priority and universality of the scientific approach as a means of building verifiable knowledge; (2) an appreciation of the products of the human imagination and technical skill; and (3) an overriding focus on morality—with universally applicable humanitarian principles in the role of guideposts—as the unique responsibility of humankind. The epilogue was a poem set to a tune I loved; although the original words of the song, and dishonest source of those words, I had always found revolting. The tune was that of "Amazing Grace", the author of which had, in fact, remained a slave trader for years after writing it. Some years later, my song came out on a CD of that name produced by the singer, Dan Mayo.

### *AMAZING LIFE*

*Amazing life, how great the code*
*that carves a course through me,*
*to futures yet uncharted from*
*some long-forgotten sea.*

*No master hand defined my fate.*
*No gods created me.*
*Star dust and ocean current sparked*
*the genes that led to me.*

*O'er eons of uncounted time,*
*like shifting dunes of sand;*
*from grasping paw on groping limb,*
*evolved the human hand.*

*Amazing hand, how great the tools*
*that humankind could wield.*
*How wide the world that hitherto*
*from animals was sealed.*

*But symbols were the crucial key*
*that opened culture's gate;*
*for language carried consciousness,*
*and knowledge in its wake.*

*Amazing power of human thought*
*that carves a course through me;*
*to futures yet uncharted from*
*some long-forgotten sea.*

I was surprised and pleased when a Unitarian who had heard me speak in Victoria offered to act as my agent in introducing *The Road to Reason* to the Asian market. He was a retired McGill professor originally from Korea, whose name was Wan-Yong Chon. He was aided in the translating task by Kimiko Hymans, a young woman originally from Japan. The book was subsequently translated and published in 2004 in both South Korea and Japan.

My next writing project was a novel, in which the central character and story-teller was a female scholar who personified all that I had never wanted to be: an accomplished compromiser! The story shows how, in her willingness to achieve success in academia at any price, she gradually lost her morality. I used imaginary contexts and altered examples of events which had actually occurred in my own academic experience, as well as some of which I had been told by others. The book was called *Something Lost* and was published in 2004. Not surprisingly, it did not become a best-seller!

I have very fond memories of most of the conferences to which I was invited as a speaker during those difficult years. Often my granddaughter Jennie would fill in for me, becoming a temporary care-giver for her beloved Grandpa Sandy. Fortunately for us, she was then pursuing her studies in Nutrition at UBC. Sometimes I was forced to place Sandy in a Respite Home for a few days. I learned that the 'respite' is actually intended to refer to the care-giver.

In 1998 I attended what I then realized would probably be my last International Sociology Association conference. It was in Montreal. The opportunity to walk all around the central area of the city—exploring to my heart's content—meant a great deal to me at that stressful time in my home life. The conference itself was like a dream come true. I was invited to join a group of sociologists who had formed the Harriet Martineau Club. We had a pleasant meeting at which we worked out a plan for a book on our hero's life and work. My contribution was a chapter called 'The Unitarian Connection". Our project was titled *Harriet Martineau: Theoretical and Methodological Perspectives*, edited by Michael Hill and Susan Hoecker-Drysdale and published by Routledge in 2001.

Another happy experience during those few precious days in Montreal occurred when I first entered the main hall of the building where the conference was being held. I approached a woman who was standing by herself, and asked for directions. She looked at my name-card and exclaimed, "Pat Duffy Hutcheon! Why you were the person who hired me for my very first summer job! It was in the Foundations Department of the University of Regina." Talk about coincidence! It brought to mind a similar event which happened sometime before at a conference down in Dallas, Texas. I had asked one of the speakers a question about some issue, and he identified me at once as the author of *The Sociology of Canadian Education*. He introduced himself as Robert Novak, who taught at York University.

During that same busy period I attended two conferences which were held by the Foundation for the Future in Seattle. The first invitation came in 1999, and was inspired by the organizer's interest in my two latest books. It was a round-table discussion with six speakers in all, along with intriguing discussions among members of the group after each speech. We were all presenting slightly different perspectives on evolution. In fact, one woman was a proponent of Intelligent Design. Fortunately, there was an excellent chairman—Sesh Velamour—who managed to keep us all in line.

My presentation was on what I called "The Complexities of Cultural Evolution". I began by discussing common sources of confusion about the subject: the most prevalent being the notions of culture as meaning simply either 'the arts', or 'race memory', or something that is 'genetically determined', or as necessarily progressive. I identified other recurring problems as being the idea that the tribal group is the key entity of biological evolution—rather than the individual at one level and the species at the other. This misunderstanding is usually accompanied by a failure to understand the feedback and hierarchical nature of the process, and the way in which genetic and cultural evolution are continuously interacting.

In an attempt to clarify all this, I referred once more to the concept of the 'triple helix' for describing the concept of intertwined and interdependent feedback systems at the levels of human biological, psychological and sociocultural development, with all three of these levels operating in an ever-changing context of challenges from the physical and social environment. I explained that we need to think of the developing child as a feedback system born with certain biological propensities, but whose values, beliefs and behaviours are continuously being shaped by the reinforcing influences of other people and objects in the surroundings. I then pointed out that a social organization is similarly a 'triple helix' in action, with society's—often unrecognized—incentive systems operating in a feedback or selective capacity within the limits set by whatever cultural function the organization is required to serve in a particular physical setting. Finally, I tried to lead them all to the conclusion that culture itself evolves in an analogous fashion, with systems of knowledge, theologies, ideologies, ideals and mores being formed, transmitted and maintained across the generations—all this in response to the pressures of geography and climate as well as biologically inherited drives and needs.

I'm not sure that I convinced anybody, but was pleased to discover, on the last evening of the event, that I was seated at the banquet table between Walter Kistler, the head of the organization and the chairman, Sesh Velamour, who had impressed me so favourably. It was a fun-filled evening for me, during which I actually downed two glasses of wine. This was something I had scarcely ever done in my life. Fortunately, one of the group had been allocated the hotel room next door to that of myself and daughter-in-law Wendy, so I didn't get lost afterwards, although I was floating down the hall alongside of him. Wendy had grasped the chance to accompany me on the trip in order to visit her daughter Carolyn who worked in Seattle. She teased me afterwards about my arriving back at the room so inebriated that I fell asleep as soon as my head hit the pillow—something else I have scarcely ever done.

The memory of relaxation provided by this break from care-giving—during which Jennie had remained with Sandy back home—aroused a good feeling in me for the difficult months to come.

The following year I attended another Foundation for the Future conference in Seattle. This time I had to pay my own way as I was not one of the speakers. I had come because E.O. Wilson was being honoured. During the informal pre-banquet period I saw him in the coffee room and approached, hoping for a chance to express my appreciation of his comments on the first draft of my chapter about his work in *Leaving the Cave*. Only then did I realize that he was being interviewed by a journalist. Just as I began a hasty retreat, Wilson noticed my name card and greeted me warmly. Then he murmured something to the journalist and said to me, "Let's grab a cup of coffee and find a little table in a corner somewhere, so we can have a good talk." What a wonderful human being this great scholar proved to be—a quality as remarkably evident in person as in all his published works! I had earlier discovered Richard Dawkins to be a similarly fine person, in that he, like E.O. Wilson, had helped me considerably with my chapter on him, editing it and correcting minor errors. Two other great lights of the sociobiological academic world—Paul Gross and Robin Fox—have been similarly helpful to me.

It was a good thing that the conference provided this high point because, not long after, I had quite the opposite type of experience. During another lull in the proceedings, I happened to glance over to the far side of the room and saw the very person who personified, for me, the dark side of academia. It was the Yale professor whose sexist behaviour had caused me to leave that Ivy League college with my hard-fought-for PhD thesis unfinished. I realized immediately that I should confront him, but I just couldn't bear to go anywhere near the man. It reminded me of the similarly uncomfortable moment of choice when I had avoided approaching my former husband, Jack Westcott, the last time I saw him. Whether fortunately or otherwise, something about the personality formed by my childhood experiences has always prevented me from confronting people who have done me grievous harm or, as in the case of Jack, someone in great need whom I had failed to help.

The highlight of all these public-speaking experiences for me was the Conference of the Humanist Association of Canada at Winnipeg where I was named Canadian Humanist of the Year 2000. I considered this a very great honour, and the occasion was further highlighted for me in the course of the many informal interludes—especially by the humour of a longtime Vancouver friend, Glenn Hardie. Glenn is a retired college instructor and writer. At one point in a casual get-together, I was having a conversation with another fellow author, Earl Doherty. Earl is a bible scholar and had recently published an intriguing book called *The Jesus Puzzle*, which raises profound questions about the actual existence of Jesus. Earl and I were so deeply involved in our talk that, without realizing it, we had stopped in the middle of a crowded doorway. Glenn then approached us with the remark, "I guess this is what they call a writer's block!"

The subject of my conference speech was the continuing danger posed by a misguided approach to multiculturalism. The title was "Us Versus Them: Can Humanism Stem the Rising Tide of Tribalism?" I ended with a paragraph on the need for a global village of the new millennium, and on the possibility of humanism providing the pathway forward. "Apart from its emphasis on reason and scientific inquiry," I asked, "what is it about humanism that makes it uniquely capable of combating tribalism? First and foremost, its world view offers an inspiring and workable foundation for meaningful living and life-sustaining support of that village. There appears to be no competing frame of reference that can, as adequately, provide the guiding principles capable of promoting peaceful relations among the varieties of human cultures that now must interact and work together. The speed of technological advance has forced the world's myriad competing tribes into a co-existence for which their religions and ethnic traditions have left them dangerously ill-prepared. The world cannot afford to wait for these outmoded belief systems to alter and advance from within. Only humanism has a planetary perspective already in place. We must persuade the more open-minded members of the world community to join us in rejecting tribalism before it's too late."

My last conference was when the American Humanist Association honoured me with the Humanist Distinguished Service Award for the year 2001. It was set in Los Angeles, providing me with my first and only visit to that city. The conference proved to be an exciting experience in many ways—both good and bad. I was slated to make the banquet presentation on the Saturday evening, and the two other award winners, one of whom was the famous Stephen Jay Gould, were on for Friday. When the time came for my speech, I was happy to find that some good friends—Jan and Ross Woodward from Spokane and Alan Levine and his wife from Illinois—were seated at one of the tables in the large hall. Al was an American sociologist who had kindly set up a website for me after having read my book, *Leaving the Cave*. I spoke for about twenty minutes on the subject of "Beyond the Quest for Certainty". I tried to make the point that a strong need for beliefs in all-powerful supernatural gods was no doubt necessary for survival in the seemingly unknowable, life-threatening surroundings of our cave-dwelling ancestors. And that we need to recognize this if we are to move beyond it. Then the peak experience of the affair arrived, as Bette Chambers, the Assistant to the President of the American Humanist Association, approached the podium and presented me with my award. I felt doubly honoured upon learning that a previous recipient had been the famous scientist Francis Crick.

Sometime after that, I was told by the organizers that they had set up a debate for the following morning, between Stephen Jay Gould and me. This news shocked me to the core, as I was already aware of strong feelings of anger radiating toward me from Gould, whenever we happened to be in the same vicinity. I guessed that he had read *Leaving the Cave* and hadn't appreciated the criticism contained in it concerning his book, *Wonderful Life*. I had disagreed with his conclusion that the discovery of the Burgess Shale proved Darwinian evolutionary theory inadequate, in that Darwin's approach left no room for huge differences in the speed of biological change in certain eras of pre-history. What was needed to correct this error, according to Gould, was his own new 'punctuated equilibrium' theory. The claim appeared highly questionable to me—as Gould should have realized had he thoroughly studied Darwin's theory and its origin in that great man's observance of the pace of change among the finches of Galapagos Island. In the opinion of most scientists there is nothing whatsoever in Darwin's theory of evolution that requires a consistent pace of change!

The discomfiting news about what was ahead of me on Sunday morning was followed by a lengthy period of mixing and nibbling on appetizers, as we circulated. Later, we sat down to a dinner with fish as the main course. I left rather early for my room as I was beginning to feel unwell. Then came one of those disastrous strokes of misfortune to which my body has always been prone. I was deathly ill from food poisoning throughout the entire night.

By morning I managed to get to the debate on time, but was not at all sure if I could navigate what threatened to be a terrifying ordeal. I approached the front table which was arranged to face the crowded auditorium, and sat in the chair alongside Stephen Jay Gould. When there was no acknowledgment from him, I introduced myself and commented, quite truthfully, that my husband and I always bought his books as soon as they came out, and enjoyed reading them. He half-turned toward me and replied, in a condescending manner, "Well, you couldn't have understood them!" Thus the morning confrontation began!

Gould spoke first, attacking some weird, manufactured notion of what I stood for. All in all, he came through as strangely antagonistic toward any suggestion that the concept of evolution might be applied to human psychological, social and cultural development. I replied as well as I was able and, as I continued speaking, began to feel a strong sensation that the crowd was with me. However, I can't remember a word of what I said. As I ended the rebuttal of Gould's accusations, my table of friends stood up to applaud, and then something like an ocean current of standing, clapping and shouting began to move through the crowd. I have never experienced anything like it, in all my years of public speaking. The morning ended in a book-signing by both of us, with the waiting lines at my table much longer than those at Gould's. I have had mixed feelings about the entire morning ever since, as Stephen Jay Gould died of a heart attack not long after.

I survived the trip home, in spite of being struck mid-flight by insufferable pain in both legs. Before leaving I had arranged for Sandy to remain at the Respite Home until the day after my return, in the expectation that I might be very tired. Little did I expect anything remotely like my current condition! I staggered from the taxi into our apartment, intending to sink into bed for an undisturbed rest. But, just after my jacket was removed and the suitcase readied for unpacking, I heard a knock—followed by the door opening. There were Dave and his dad, complete with walker and luggage! Apparently Sandy had been very upset with his lodging place, and anxious to get home. I was struck first by a wave of dismay, because of my illness and exhaustion; and then a wave of guilt. How could I not be happy at this early arrival of my beloved husband; and the immediate prospect of twenty-four hours of daily attendance which it seemed no other person could adequately provide? But it was not the 'self' that had been Sandy who stood there now, so demanding of my care-giving. It was his shadow, who actually thought I was a hired nurse. And this sad remnant of his former self suddenly reminded me of how—in previous, happier days when Sandy waited eagerly for my report on the event—my arrival home from conferences had been one of the best aspects of the entire experience.

Fortunately, there have been good times since then as well as bad, in this process of the years gradually closing in. One of these was the satisfying end to my teaching career provided by the experience of contributing to 'Continuing Education' courses on Humanism in a local Junior College, as well as to one on 'A History of Free Thought' at Simon Fraser University. A further reward was knowing that they were using *The Road to Reason* as a textbook the following year. Another was my 'one last hurrah' in a high-school classroom, when I was invited to speak to a class about what it was like to have lived on a drought-stricken Alberta prairie farm during the 'Dirty Thirties'. And yet another highlight of these years was the opportunity, in 2003, to serve as the sole Canadian on the editing committee for Humanist Manifesto III. The first such manifesto came out in 1933, and one of the famous people who designed that one was my great intellectual hero, John Dewey.

Yet another great source of satisfaction for me has been Richard Dawkins' courageous decision to make his world view of evolutionary naturalism accessible to the general population. Following this is the recent publication of quotes from the now-famous letter written by Albert Einstein but never disclosed until recently, when it went up for auction. I had always been disappointed by the fact that this great scientific thinker had failed to be unequivocal when asked about his views on the supernatural. This letter makes his position very clear. "The word God is for me nothing more than the expression and product of human weaknesses," he wrote, "the Bible a collection of honourable, but still primitive legends which are nevertheless pretty childish. No interpretation no matter how subtle can (for me) change this." Would that the majority of today's scientists find the courage to follow the example of these great thinkers!

Finally, on a more personal note, the pleasure of witnessing the success of grandchildren in their chosen professions has been an unparalleled experience for me. In addition, their happy partnerships—enriched for all concerned by my marvelous great-grandchildren—have provided me with life experiences the quality of which I could never have imagined. In one of those fascinating coincidences that occur in life, I now have a granddaughter—Tanya Hutcheon—with an important position in the University of Regina's Department of Kinesiology; while grandson Shane Westcott is a manager in the Computer Science area of the Calgary Board of Education. Both organizations were my former employers

Then, as if my life's journey required an even greater culmination, there came—in mid-July of 2007—the birth of the great-granddaughter named Patricia Kathleen. Yes, another Patricia Westcott, in that same city of Calgary where I, as an earlier Patricia Westcott, taught school and was given the once-in-a lifetime opportunity for both a Bachelor of Education and Master's Degree in Sociology! And where, in 2003, I was officially honoured by the University of Calgary, when they celebrated their forty-year anniversary, as a pioneering graduate of the Master's program in their Department of Sociology. Nevertheless, as much as I have appreciated this and the various other recognitions received in this wonderful life, they cannot be even remotely compared to the honour of having a great-grandchild named for me! The event has caused me to register anew the literal interpretation of my metaphor; and has brought home the biological-evolutionary aspect of this life process of 'sowing seeds'. If it had not been made possible for that precious 'pulse of life' which became my son Tom to survive against all odds—during those far-off, difficult days in the Valley—there would have been no grandson Shane; and this young Patricia Westcott would not be here today. No matter what happiness and sense of achievement comes to me in my remaining time, nothing could compare with my delight at the birth of Patricia, my great-granddaughter and namesake. With that event this eighty-two-year old sower of seeds—this evolutionary naturalist, scientific humanist and Freethinker . . . has reached the joyful peak of her life journey. It's been a wonderful life!